# CANNABIS

# CANNABIS

## A HISTORY

# MARTIN BOOTH

Thomas Dunne Books
St. Martin's Press ∭ New York

THOMAS DUNNE BOOKS.
An imprint of St. Martin's Press.

www.stmartins.com

Library of Congress Cataloging-in-Publication Data

Booth, Martin.
Cannabis : a history / Martin Booth.—1st ed.
p. cm.
Includes bibliographical references (p. 334) and index (p. 339).
ISBN 0-312-32220-8
EAN 978-0312-32220-5
1. Cannabis—History. 2. Marijuana—History.
3. Cannabis—Law and legislation.
I. Title.

HV5822.C3B66  2004
362.29'5'09—dc22                          2004045058

First published in Great Britain by Doubleday, a division of Transworld Publishers

First U.S. Edition: June 2004

10  9  8  7  6  5  4  3  2  1

For Alex and Emma,
who would have enjoyed the Sixties

# CONTENTS

# ACKNOWLEDGEMENTS

I am indebted to the following individuals, organizations and institutions for their assistance, without which the writing of this book would have been considerably harder: John Keep, Dr James Roy/University of Nottingham, Asa Hutchinson/US Department of Justice, Anne Chippindale/*Antiquity* Publications, Dr Jonathan King/North America Curator in the Department of Ethnography at the British Museum, William Breeze, Gerald Laishley, Free Rob Cannabis, Chris Hinett of Henry & Company/Solicitors, Devon County Library, Drug Enforcement Administration/Washington DC, Federal Bureau of Investigation, Central Intelligence Agency, HM Customs and Excise, the Historic Dockyard: Chatham, the Metropolitan Police/London, the Ashmolean Museum, the Bodleian Library, the British Medical Association, the State University of New York Upstate Medical University Health Sciences Library, the Kappa Alpha Fraternity, the Library of the House of Lords, GW Pharmaceuticals Ltd, Princeton University Library, Hemcore Ltd, Penn State University, National Museum of Health and Medicine/Washington DC, United Nations Office for Drug Control and Crime Prevention/Vienna, the Body Shop International, NORML and, finally, my wife, Helen, whose research skills are quite immeasurable.

# PREFACE

As a student in the mid-1960s, I lived for a while in two attic rooms in a Victorian terraced mansion in Muswell Hill, North London. It was the heady, hippy era of free love, universal peace, rock music and pot. Wherever one went in London, marijuana was there for the asking, if one knew who to ask. No one questioned if it was dangerous and everyone regarded it as *risqué* and romantic, a harmless kick against the authority of men in grey suits or policemen's uniforms, both of whom drove black Jaguar saloon cars. Harder drugs – heroin, cocaine – were unheard of and the only really dangerous substance was LSD, which I assiduously avoided.

The rooms below mine were occupied by a window dresser from one of London's big department stores. His name was Richard but he called himself Ric. Thin and lean, he wore hipster corduroy jeans and flowered shirts with flounced sleeves, and broad kipper ties. In his tiny kitchen, he kept half a kilo of marijuana in a plastic tea dispenser screwed onto the wall. When he pressed the button, he was delivered a sizeable joint's-worth of grass which dropped into his Rizla cigarette-paper machine ready for forming between two small rollers. He obtained his supply from

*Author's note*: Where financial statistics are given – for example, *Albania exported marijuana worth forty million dollars* – the sum quoted is the street value of the drug to the end user, not the wholesale price or income earned by the producer.

a friend, a student at the Royal College of Art. From time to time, the scent of his joints seeped up into my rooms, vaguely thrilling and exotic.

In common with most, I knew little about marijuana or hashish. It derived from the cannabis or hemp plant, came from Morocco or India, was illegal, made you high and cost more than I could regularly afford. As for personal experience of it, Ric's second-hand smoke aside, I had eaten it on a few occasions at parties, baked in cookies, but never really undergone the full extent of its euphoric powers.

It was not until my return to the Far East in the summer of 1967, where I had previously lived, that I came upon marijuana in any significant amount. In Vietnam, practically every American soldier and most non-commissioned officers had a personal stash in a pouch, draw-bag, polished brass cartridge case or cigarette box. They seemed never to be without a joint between their lips, except when mustered on parade, and not to show the courtesy of sharing what they offered was tantamount to a personal slight. Those I met on R & R in Hong Kong smoked it in the girlie bars of Wan Chai or on the cross-harbour Star Ferry. Few people recognized the perfume of it and the few police officers who did ignored it. That summer, the Royal Hong Kong Police Force was too busy combating Communist-inspired anti-Imperialist riots and the random nail-bombing of bus and tram stops to be bothered with a few battle-weary US soldiers or sailors.

Back in London in late September, re-entering the impoverished world of the student and facing my last year of higher education, I assumed marijuana would be a passing fad, like flared trousers or boots with Cuban heels, that once we all grew up, graduated from university and moved out into the world, we would look back on the occasional joint or hash cookie with nostalgia.

I was wrong.

MARTIN BOOTH
*Devon, England, 2003*

# CANNABIS

# THE FRAGRANT CANE

ONCE UPON A TIME, ACCORDING TO A STORY RECOUNTED BY THE
Islamic chronicler al-Maqrizi (1364–1442) in AD 1155, the founder of
the Persian Sufi Hyderi sect, Haydar, left his cell in a monastery in the
mountains near Neyshaur, in the Khorasan region of north-eastern Iran,
and went out for a walk. Discovering a plant standing unwithered by the
blazing sun, he grew curious and wondered how it withstood the
desiccating heat, so he cut a few leaves and chewed on them as he went
on his way. Usually a taciturn man, he returned in a fickle frame of mind,
with a smile on his face. Swearing his fellow monks to secrecy, he told
them what he had discovered. Thereafter, it is said, he remained in a
capricious mood until his death sixty-six years later. What he had
purportedly discovered was a drug from a common plant. The plant was
cannabis.

Cannabis is the generic name for hemp, an adaptive and highly
successful annual found growing throughout the temperate and tropical
zones of the world. Its classification was, for a long while, a botanical
enigma. First considered a relative of the nettle (*Urticaceae*), it was then
thought to be a member of the *Moraceae* which includes the fig but, today,
it is regarded as an herbaceous plant with its own specific botanical group,
the *Cannabaceae*, in which only cannabis and *Humulus lupulus*, the hop, are
included. The plant received its full botanical nomenclature from Carolus
Linnaeus, the Swedish 'father of botany', who named it *Cannabis sativa* in

1753. The latter specific name derived from the Latin meaning 'cultivated'.

Linnaeus' chosen generic name was not plucked from the air. He based it upon the word *kannabis*, the classical Greek word for hemp which, in turn, derived from the Sanskrit *cana*. Other languages had used similar names: Assyrian *qunubu* (or *qunnapu*), Slav *konopla*, Hebrew *qanneb*, Arabic *qannob*, Persian *quonnab*, Celtic *quannab* and Spanish *cañamo*. It has been suggested the name may have come from the Assyrian *qunnabu*, meaning 'noise': it was thought the Assyrians used cannabis as an incense in religious ceremonies and were quite vocal after inhaling it. On the other hand, *kan*, which was common to many ancient languages and referred to both hemp and cane, might be a more apt derivation. That said, the third syllable *bis* more than likely comes from the Hebrew *bosm* or the Aramaic *busma*, meaning 'aromatic'. Cannabis, it seems, is the fragrant cane.

There has been much controversy about whether there exists one species of cannabis with different varieties (described as monotypic) or several distinct species (polytypic). In 1783, the famous French naturalist Jean-Baptiste Lamarck suggested that the hemp plant found in Europe was sufficiently different from that growing in India for them to be separate species. He reclassified them, retaining Linnaeus' *Cannabis sativa* for the European plant and naming the Indian *Cannabis indica* after its country of origin. Then, in 1924, a Russian botanist called Janischewski, studying wild cannabis growing in the Volga River system of western Siberia and central Asia, recognized this as a third species which he named *Cannabis ruderalis*. Consequently, the polytypic side of the argument has mainly come to be accepted although, even now, there still linger doubts because the cannabis plant, being very ready to botanically adapt to its environment, has been found capable of botanically 'adjusting' itself. It has been discovered that seeds taken from, say, a European *Cannabis sativa* plant and cultivated in India come to display some of the characteristics of the *Cannabis indica* plant in just a few generations – and vice versa.

Of the three species, *Cannabis sativa* is the most widespread. A gangling, open-branched plant, it can grow to 6 metres in height, whereas *Cannabis indica* grows only to about 1 metre and is conical in shape with dense branching. *Cannabis ruderalis* reaches only three-quarters of a metre at best with few if any branches.

Where cannabis originated is unknown. Most studies imply, with justification, that it probably evolved in the temperate zones of central Asia, possibly near the Irtysh River which flows from Mongolia into the western Siberian lowlands, along the edge of the Gobi desert south of

Lake Baikal or the Takla Makan desert in China's Xinjiang province, north of Tibet, where it still occurs wild wherever the earth has been disturbed, by erosion or flood. On the other hand, it is also found in abundance across central Asia from the Altai Mountains to the Caucasus, in the Yangtze and Yellow River systems in China, throughout the southern foothills of the Himalayas and in the Hindu Kush.

The fringe regions of such topographical locations as the Gobi and Takla Makan deserts have for thousands of years provided the perfect climate for the evolution of annuals that rely upon wind as a vehicle for pollination. If cannabis did originate here, the prevailing winds would certainly have aided its distribution to the surrounding regions. The picture is further confused, however, by the fact that cannabis was one of the first plants to be cultivated by mankind and present-day areas of wild growth may have resulted from plants escaping from prehistoric cultivation.

To say cannabis is versatile is to understate its resourcefulness and adaptability. It can grow at altitudes of up to 8000 feet, has a life cycle of only three to five months and germinates within six days: in a fortnight, it is well established as a seedling and can grow at a rate of 15 centimetres a day, although between 2 and 5 centimetres is the norm. Requiring very little water except during germination and early growth, it will easily grow in poor, sandy soils; to realize its maximum potential, it prefers loamy earth. As it is heliotropic, preferring direct sunlight, it does not thrive in shade but prefers open ground and is less tolerant to low temperatures. It is, furthermore, dioecious, which means that the plants are individually male or female, the former producing pollen and the latter seeds: hermaphroditic plants are not unknown but are rare. In many cannabis-producing areas, male plants were traditionally destroyed as it was thought that if the female plants were fertilized, they would produce an inferior intoxicant.

The plant stalk is angular, hollow, branched and covered in fine, matted hairs: it can reach 5 centimetres in diameter. The leaves are distinctively palmate and serrated. The male plant is the taller and usually comes into flower approximately a month ahead of the female plant. The male flowers are small and pale green, yellow, or purplish-red or -brown in colour. They appear in dense pendulous bunches and release thick clouds of wind-dispersed pollen after which the plant withers and dies. The female flowers, which grow tightly together to form clusters, consist of a pair of white stigmas approximately 1 centimetre long in an erect V, joining an ovule at the base which contains a small green pod formed of modified leaves called bracts and bracteoles. The flowering period usually lasts between four and eight weeks, the seed taking from ten to thirty-five days to mature, depending upon growing conditions. Once the female flowers have been fertilized, the plant concentrates much of its strength into seed development and tends to lose many of its leaves. The fruit is a slightly flattened oval achene, which by definition is small, dry and contains only one seed: it does not open to liberate the seed, which is brownish in colour and hard.

Both male and female plants produce an amber-coloured resin, although the latter produces a far greater amount. Smelling vaguely like peppermint and found throughout the plant with the exception of the roots and seeds, it is predominantly secreted by tiny, pluricellular glandular hairs on the anthers of male stamens and the perianths of the female flowers and the leaves closest to them. It may be so prevalent as to make it appear as if the plant is covered with dew. Production of this resin continues to increase until the female plant reaches maturity when, the seeds near to ripening, it ceases abruptly.

The primary function of the resin is unknown. It has been postulated that it aids in preventing the seeds from suffering high water loss due to transpiration for, the higher the ambient temperature, the more resin is produced. Indeed, in very hot climates, the cuticle can split to allow the resin to ooze down the stems. When caked on the plant, it hardens to an impermeable, water-insoluble varnish. Other theories suggest it is to protect the seeds from ultra-violet radiation or to trap pollen. The resin has another property, however. It contains a powerful intoxicant drug which has led some observers to believe its function is to discourage birds and insect pests. This does not seem likely for cannabis can be infected by whitefly, spider mites, cucumber beetles and thrips.

For many centuries, cannabis has been the source of a versatile natural fibre, an oil-rich seed and, most famously, a drug with the power to affect human consciousness. Cultivated in prehistory, it may well have been amongst the first plants to be farmed or, at least, utilized. As with the opium poppy, it is reasonable to believe its psycho-active, mind-bending properties were discovered very early in man's agricultural development.

The fibre, made from the stalks and one of the strongest and most enduring in nature, is commonly known as hemp, the name deriving from the Old English *henep* or *haenep* and the Old Saxon *hanap*. Most commonly, it was – and still is – used in rope-making but it was also used in the manufacture of coarse cloth, hessian, twine and paper.

The method of fibre extraction begins with a process called retting.

The stems are soaked in water until they partially decompose or break down through osmosis, the non-fibrous tissue falling or being stripped away. This complete, the stems are bent to separate the fibres which can then be spun as thread or twisted into rope. Today, the word hemp is generally used as meaning cannabis grown for its fibres. However, there are other sources of 'hemp' including Manila hemp or *abaca* from the Philippines, derived from a plant in the banana genus, sisal hemp from the sisal cactus, New Zealand hemp from the harakeke plant, Deccan hemp from a species of hibiscus and jute (also, confusingly, known as Indian hemp) from the jute shrub. The real thing, however, comes from cannabis.

The cannabis seed contains a greenish-yellow oil, rich in unsaturated fatty acids, which in the past was used as a lamp fuel and in the manu-facture of soap. Supplanted by hydrocarbons, it was then used in the making of high-quality varnish, as an emulsion in the pharmaceutical industry and as a substitute for linseed oil in artists' oil paints. The oil content aside, it is also a foodstuff, containing substantial quantities of sugars and albumen. Birds eat it in the wild, where it seems to act as a tonic for them, as do rabbits, hares and other mammals. Where humans are concerned, crushed cannabis seed has been used as a food source during famines and shortages, such as in China during Mao Zedong's disastrous 'Great Leap Forward' of the early 1960s and in Europe during the Second World War. In India, it is a staple of the poor who make *bosa* and *mura* with it, the former consisting of cannabis seed mixed with goose grass seed, the latter a mixture with amaranth or rice and parched wheat. Cannabis seed is also used to flavour alcoholic drinks and, on occasion, chutney. In parts of sub-Saharan Africa, ground cannabis seed is some-times used as a baby food.

Yet cannabis is most famous throughout the world as a source of a drug and it is as a psycho-active agent that it is most used. Indeed, it is arguably more widely taken than any other drug save tobacco, alcohol and aspirin.

Plants which contain psycho-active compounds are divided into two groups. One category produces psychotropic drugs which affect the central nervous system whilst the other provides psychotomimetic drugs (sometimes known as hallucinogenic or psychedelic drugs) which affect the mind, altering perception. Cannabis is of the latter category, but it differs from others in the group in that most hallucinogenic plant chemicals are alkaloids, but the active ingredients of cannabis are non-nitrogenous substances called cannabinoids and unique to it.

Of the approximately 460 known chemical constituents of cannabis, more than sixty have the molecular structure of a cannabinoid, but the most important of these, present by up to 5 per cent by weight, is $\Delta^9$-tetrahydrocannabinol, more commonly known just as tetrahydrocannabinol or THC for short. It is this, perhaps in collaboration with other cannabinoids, that is the psycho-active element.

In addition to THC, there occur cannabidiol (CBD) and cannabinol (CBN) which appear as the resin ages. CBD has no psycho-active capability but CBN is a mildly psycho-active chemical. Tetrahydrocannabivarin (THCV) and cannabichromene (CBC) are also important cannabinoids with others, such as cannabicyclol (CBL), being formed not by the plant itself but by the chemical decomposition or degradation of THC or other cannabinoids. Apart from the cannabinoids, cannabis also contains six essential oils, at least eight alkaloids, flavonoids and sugars. As well as being a euphoric intoxicant, THC also works as an analgesic, muscle-relaxing, anti-depressant and anti-emetic agent, it can reduce epileptic fits, stimulate appetite and dilate bronchial tissue. Why the plant produces THC is unknown but what is certain is that cannabis grown in temperate climates contains less THC than cannabis raised in hot ones, but a higher percentage of CBD.

The study of cannabinoids goes back over a century. CBN, at first thought to be the principal psycho-active agent, was identified in the 1890s, then, in the 1930s, CBD was isolated. However, it was not until 1964, with the post-war advances in organic chemistry, that two Israeli chemists, Gaoni and Mechoulam, isolated and identified THC. Since then, studies have discovered a long list of other cannabinoids, many of which have yet to be fully investigated.

Three tests exist to determine the presence of cannabis by identifying the presence of CBD. The Duquenois Test, which has been modified a number of times since its development in the 1940s, uses vanillin, acetaldehyde or metaldehyde, methanol and hydrochloric acid, producing a violet colour if added to CBD. It is not, however, specific and shows similar results with coffee, citronella, myrrh and orris. The Furfural Test, developed in the early 1940s by an American chemist, Charles C. Fulton, also identifies the presence of CBD, but additionally shows the presence of, amongst others, cinnamon, ergot, nutmeg and tea. Only one test, the Beam Test, developed about a hundred years ago, is specific. The plant resin is extracted with petroleum ether which is evaporated off to leave a residue which is then mixed with ether, alcohol, hydrochloric acid and potassium hydroxide. The presence of CBD is indicated by a red, violet or purple coloration.

Most of the THC (and other cannabinoids) in a cannabis plant is synthesized in the resin-producing glands and concentrated in the resin itself, the female containing more than the male, the highest strength being found in unfertilized flowers.

The psycho-active products of cannabis are hashish, marijuana and, rarely, hashish oil. The THC content of these is 5–10 per cent in marijuana, up to 20 per cent in hashish and as high as 85 per cent in hashish oil.

Hashish is usually made from just the resin or resin glands of the female plant. The name, which has in the past been spelt 'hasheesh' or 'haschisch', most likely comes from the Arabic word for dry fodder or herbage. For a while, it applied to any cannabis preparation, most of them involving drying and powdering either the whole plant or the flower heads. However, hashish today is made by isolating and concentrating only the resin and resin glands.

Two collection methods are used. The traditional time-consuming and labour-intensive technique, found in the Indian sub-continent and South East Asia, involves rubbing the living flowers with the hands or a leather apron or cloth. The resin sticks to the skin or surface and is then removed either by robustly rubbing the hands together or by using a strigil or similar blunt blade. The process has given rise to one of the many romantic stories to append themselves to cannabis. In the nineteenth century, it was said the resin was collected by people running naked through the cannabis plantations, their bodies becoming caked with it: the story was false, told to gullible Europeans by whom any exotic story was believed. Once collected, the resin is compressed by hand or simple press into malleable blocks which quickly blacken as they are exposed to air.

The alternative process is sieving. In this, the resin is collected from harvested and dried plants, sieves used to separate plant tissue from powdered resin which is then compressed and gently heated. The resin melts and, whilst elastic, is pressed into blocks and sealed with cloth or cellophane. Sieving is less labour-intensive than rubbing, less material is lost in the process and a higher purity and quality control is possible. Up to 25 grams of resin can be collected per day per person by rubbing but sieving can produce a kilogram in two hours and is, therefore, more likely to be used for commercial produce. Furthermore, hand-rubbed hashish only retains its potency for a few months whilst sieved hashish, being of higher purity, can last three years if stored at a low temperature, wrapped to exclude air and maintained away from bright light.

Regardless of how it is made, hashish varies widely in colour, form and consistency depending on its origins. The resin may be shaped into blocks, round cakes (like ice hockey pucks), sticks or bars. It may be soft and pliable or hard and dry, powdery or brittle and can vary in colour from a light golden yellow (like rich honey) to dark brown, red-brown or black. In its purest form, hashish consists of only the resin glands and the resin but, in practice, impurities are rarely absent.

Less psycho-actively potent than hashish, but nevertheless very effective as a drug, are the dried cannabis leaves and flowers, commonly known as marijuana (sometimes spelt marihuana or, rarely, mariguano). The whole plant, except the root, is simply dried, and crushed or crumbled then either stored loose, compressed into bricks or, in bulk, bound into bales. Marijuana without a flower content is less powerful. However, marijuana made only with the flowering tops of the plant is considered of top quality as a drug and is called sinsemilla. In the production of sinsemilla – the word comes from the Spanish *sin semillas*, meaning 'seedless' – which is centuries old, all the male plants in a crop are destroyed as soon as they appear, thus preventing fertilization and the production of seeds. The female plants then continue to produce resin and flowers in large quantities for up to nine months. The flower heads become huge and cone-shaped, often leaning over under their own weight when they are referred to as *colas* (tails). Judicious and expert pruning increases the number of *colas* forming. A watch is kept for any hermaphroditic plants and the male flowers quickly pricked out. If, by chance, a sinsemilla plant does become fertilized, its seeds are carefully conserved for planting the following season.

To achieve a psycho-active response from hashish or marijuana, THC must enter the bloodstream and pass through it to the brain. Once in the blood system, it is chemically changed by human metabolism into a compound known as 11-hydroxy-THC, which is absorbed by fatty tissue and, after about half an hour, is released back into the blood and taken to the brain. A dosage of 4–8 milligrams of THC will result in a three-hour-long intoxication. Excessive use of cannabis can cause large amounts of 11-hydroxy-THC to become stored in the liver.

The two ways of imbibing THC are by smoking or by ingestion, the former preferred because inhaled THC is absorbed rapidly through the lungs. The resulting effect is comparatively light and cerebral, lasts only a relatively short while and has fewer physical side effects. When eaten, THC can take up to an hour to become absorbed into the bloodstream; the psycho-active effect, however, lasts longer and induces far more intense reactions. It follows, therefore, that smokers are in more immediate control than eaters. If the effects are adverse, smokers can quickly halt them whilst eaters cannot. This can be quite serious when one considers that hashish is up to three times more potent when eaten than smoked. The cause for this lies in the fact that, although at 200°C cannabidiol (CBD) is converted into at least five different types of THC not found in the actual plant, between 50 and 90 per cent of the active ingredient is decomposed or oxidized by being burnt.

When smoked, the effects of the THC take longer to be felt with marijuana than the more concentrated hashish. The maximum effect is experienced in about an hour. The brain does not attain such a high level of THC as other organs such as the liver, kidneys, lungs and spleen. At least half of the THC is excreted from the body within twenty-four hours but traces may remain for some days.

Despite the potential effects of eating THC, hashish and marijuana have been incorporated into the cuisine of many countries, in some cases for centuries. As cannabinoids are insoluble in water, they are usually dissolved into fat, clarified butter (*ghee*) or vegetable oil being commonly used in confectionery, most often associated with Middle Eastern and Oriental cuisine. The commonest sweetmeat is *majoon* which consists of small pellets of hashish, honey and assorted spices. Another, *manzul*, is made of hashish mixed with spices, cocoa butter, sesame oil and chocolate, whilst in north Africa, hashish is occasionally added to Turkish delight and stuffed dates. When marijuana is used in recipes, it is usually as the basis for a tea-like drink called *bhang* or added to home-made sweets, biscuits and cakes. In Cambodia, dried cannabis plants are often sold as an essential ingredient in the traditional spicy soups whilst in Thailand, cannabis is frequently added to curried dishes.

Cannabis products are smoked either through a pipe or in the form of a cigarette. The pipes come in a vast array of sizes and forms but often have long stems or incorporate a hookah-type water filtration system (in which case they are often known as a *bong*) to reduce the harshness and temperature of the smoke which can scald the throat. Cigarettes are by far the more common, convenient and popular method. Hashish or marijuana is crumbled into self-rolled cigarettes or added to tobacco which gives it a ready burn: hashish or marijuana on its own does not readily stay alight but commercial tobacco, which contains persistent combustion additives such as saltpetre, overcomes this problem. As the cigarette is smoked, the THC vaporizes and tends to become increasingly distilled down its length: the butt end therefore may come to contain a concentration of THC. In fact, THC vaporizes at a lower temperature than it burns, so there is no reason why cannabis cannot be smoked in vapour form, being brought to vaporization temperature without being combusted. Indeed, a vaporization method does exist using an apparatus that passes very hot air or steam over it. The vapours are not only purer and less toxic than smoke but also cooler and more highly psycho-active because none of the THC content has been burned off.

As with most drugs, cannabis has given birth to its own jargon spoken by those who use it. The colloquial names given to cannabis, hashish and, especially, marijuana are legion. In English, they were or are variously known as grass, hash, weed, pot, dope, skank, skunk, wacky baccy, cake, dank (or diggity dank if the quality is high), muggles, gage, buddah, king bud, Mary Jane, cheeba, stuff, smoke, spinach, Mr Alexander (or Mr A.) and tea. Some names, such as *ganja* (Jamaican but derived from the Hindi) and *kif* (Arabic) have moved over into more general usage. A hand-rolled marijuana cigarette is known as a joint, reefer, spliff, doobie, blunt (which uses cigar leaf), bomber, jay, hooter and jive. To score is to purchase marijuana or hashish; a toke is a single puff of smoke whilst to hit is to inhale; a roach is a joint butt; a high, a trip or a buzz is the psycho-active effect of the drug on the brain and to be stoned is to be under the influence (throwed, wasted or lambasted means to be very stoned); a dope- or pot-head is a regular user; a head shop is a store that sells cannabis users' equipment; a stash is a personal supply; a narc (or pot cop) is a drug law-enforcement officer. Much of the slang originated in America, some (such as muggles and jive) dating back to the jazz era of the Roaring 1920s.

Arguably the most common name in use is pot, applied specifically to marijuana and in use since at least as far back as 1938. It is said to derive either from the Mexican Indian/Spanish word *potiguaya* which is itself a slang word for marijuana, or from an association with the Arabic *kif*. Literally meaning 'pleasure', *kif* is a colloquialism used in north-west Africa for cannabis preparations, more specifically a finely chopped stimulant mixture of dark tobacco and powdered cannabis. One observer, John Rosevear, in his book *Pot: A Handbook of Marihuana*, suggests that elderly Moroccan men who sat about all day smoking their pipes kept their *kif* in small jars or pots, giving rise to the expression, 'Let him have his pipe and pot' – hence the name. The name weed arose because, in many places, cannabis is just that, a weed that grows wild on any vacant ground. Dope was first used derogatorily by teachers and anti-drug activists, but it gained common parlance in the 1960s' hippy years and, after being at first used satirically, became a standard name.

Today, marijuana and hashish are the commonly seen and used forms of cannabis but there exists another, hashish or cannabis oil. It is a liquid concentrate chemically extracted from cannabis resin with solvents such as acetone or petrol. With an exceptionally high THC content and known as smash, it first appeared in the USA in the late 1960s having been, it was thought, produced in Vietnam by US soldiers. It was smoked using a glass pipe in which it was vaporized over a low flame, or smeared on cigarette rolling paper or impregnated into tobacco. Today, even in countries such as the Netherlands where a permissive attitude towards cannabis prevails, hashish oil is illegal and classed as a dangerous drug. This is not dependent so much upon the THC content but on the by-products of the solvent extraction process which can be very harmful.

Considered pharmacologically, cannabis is a mild hallucinogen which, in low doses, produces a sense of euphoria but with high dosage gives a more powerful reaction in which ordinary perception is reconfigured. THC affects specific areas of the brain. It acts upon the cerebellum which co-ordinates movement and balance, the hippocampus in which linear thinking and memory occur and the rostral ventromedial medulla where pain response is modulated. In 1992, it was discovered that, just as the brain produces opiate-like substances called endorphins so does it also manufacture a cannabinoid-like chemical called anandamide – also found in cocoa beans and red wine – which is thought to play a part in controlling pain and sleep patterns and to be a neurotransmitter for pleasurable sensation. Research has shown that THC 'locks on' to the same cell receptor – a protein found predominantly on cells in the hippocampus and cerebral cortex – as does anandamide and that a lack or reduction of it causes neurological disorders and possibly illnesses such as multiple sclerosis.

There are researchers who use the fact that the human brain contains specific cannabis receptors to contend that, clearly, nature intended humans to use the plant. Those who disagree are of a mind that cannabis somehow hijacks the human brain and that when THC 'locks on' to the receptors it is doing so much as a magpie might grab a shiny piece of jewellery left in a window, not because it either wants it or needs it or can gain value from possessing it, but merely because it is there. Going free, so to speak. Neither argument is as yet proven or disproven, there needing to be much research to discover the truth.

The effects of marijuana depend not only upon the individual user's body chemistry but also upon their mood, expectations, situation and personality: some do not enjoy it whilst others remain unaffected by it.

Hashish, on the other hand, being much stronger, invariably exerts an influence. Dosage is crucial although, with no standard quality control existing, the ideal dose can rarely be determined by the user.

Primary psycho-active effects are pleasurable feelings of elation and well-being, a loss of inhibition and an altered sense of time often indicated by feelings of *déjà vu*. Imagination increases but levels of concentration are known to be reduced. Behaviour may become compulsive but very rarely indeed is it violent or aggressive. Visual sensitivity increases, patterns may appear with enhanced peripheral vision and raised visual imagery. Touch, taste, smell and hearing are augmented whilst some users report receiving the 'paranormal phenomena' of telepathy and empathy. However, it must be stressed that the drug only affects the imagination. It does not create visions but merely extrapolates these from existing stimuli. Just as Thomas De Quincey, the first writer to substantially chronicle the effects of drugs, stated of opiates, it does not create anything new but embellishes what already exists, heightening the awareness of latent thoughts and imagination. As De Quincey put it, a man who spent his life talking about oxen would dream of oxen under the influence.

Psycho-activity apart, cannabis exerts other effects. Heart and metabolic rates increase and blood pressure may rise, putting those with vascular problems at risk. Skin temperature rises but core body temperature does not. The eyes redden and tear ducts and the mouth dry up. Appetite increases and, with marijuana, sweat glands can exude a faint, burning-grass-like odour. The long-held belief that cannabis is an aphrodisiac has been discounted. Any romantic inclination felt whilst intoxicated is due to the temporary suspension of an individual's natural reticence rather than a chemical effect upon hormones or whatever else might control libido.

The effects of taking hashish are more intense than for marijuana. The French pharmacologist Pascal Brotteaux, in his book *Hachich: Herbe de folie et de rêve*, published in 1934, noted four stages of intoxication: nervous excitement, hallucination and loss of mental stability, ecstasy and profound tranquillity and, finally, deep sleep. Hashish users taking high dosages can also undergo alarming bouts of paranoia, schizophrenia, marked mood changes, panic attacks, extra-corporeal experiences, disorientation, delirium and loss of psychomotor control. None of these, however, is permanent and they disappear with abstinence. There is, furthermore, some reason to believe both marijuana and hashish can affect short-term memory.

For all this, cannabis is not toxic. No deaths have been recorded from overdosing. Indeed, it has been suggested that it would take 800 joints to kill, death coming from carbon monoxide rather than cannabinoid poisoning. By comparison, 300 millilitres of vodka or 60 milligrams of nicotine would be lethal. The main reason for the non-toxicity is that there are very few cannabinoid chemical receptors in the cells of the brain that control the body's reflex life-support functions.

Where cannabis smoking is dangerous – as opposed to taking it orally in food or liquids – is that the smoke itself, as with tobacco smoke, can injure the lungs and exacerbate or aggravate respiratory diseases. Cannabis smoke contains many of the harmful chemical constituents of tobacco including carcinogenic tar, cyanide and carbon monoxide.

Tolerance, by which increasing amounts of the drug are required to achieve the same level of psycho-activity, can occur and, certainly, it is possible for regular users to build up a tolerance to both the psycho-active and physiological effects. Some users claim a reverse tolerance, that the effects increase with use, but scientific investigation lends this idea little credence. With some drugs, such as heroin, tolerance leads on to a physical, chemical dependency, evidenced by withdrawal symptoms if dosage is reduced or abstinence enforced. In the case of marijuana and hashish, this seems not to be the case. Cannabis is considered not habit-forming and a halt in usage does not bring about the agonies of withdrawal such as a heroin addict might suffer. However, it has been dis-covered that about 8 per cent of cannabis users can become heavy imbibers who may, in some cases, form a physiological or psychological dependence to it. An equivalent level of addiction might be that experi-enced by heavy coffee drinkers to caffeine. Those displaying the symptoms of psychological dependence – based upon their perceived need to keep on experiencing the drug's pleasure – may, upon no longer taking it, exhibit an irritability, nervousness and restlessness which can cause insomnia. This type of reaction, however, is not at all common and only applies to very heavy users.

Because the cannabis plant has different uses, different varieties are grown according to what is required of them. Some of these varieties are naturally occurring whilst others are the result of careful husbandry. The disparities can be quite marked.

In Italy, where hemp growing provides for a textile and paper industry, coarse fibre varieties are grown that reach heights of 9 or 10 metres in one season whilst other forms are not 2 metres high, with straight, thin stems providing fine fibres. In Thailand and Burma, plants grown for their

THC content, and harvested for hashish, are barely a metre high but thickly leafed and rich in resin: others, 5 metres high, yield half a kilo of marijuana per plant.

Plants raised for their fibre tend to be sown close together, reducing the amount of sunlight thus forcing the plants upwards, whilst resin-producing crops are planted farther apart so that they receive substantial sunlight which prompts them to produce more resin. Although growing conditions such as soil nutrient levels, altitude and climate greatly affect the fibre quality or potency of the resin, the genetic content of the seed is of paramount importance and farmers are careful to harvest the seed of selected varieties. Such is the skill of cannabis husbandry that farmers licensed to grow hemp for fibre in countries where controls are strict are provided with seed from which the ability to produce THC has been all but bred out.

Just as different varieties have been bred to produce specific qualities and types of fibre, so too have they been propagated for their THC, with different varieties providing different kinds of psycho-active or physical reaction. There seems to be a distinct relationship between altitude and the quality and type of the psycho-active high. Ironically, the higher up the mountain the cannabis plant is grown, the higher the high. Marijuana and hashish farmers, rather like viticulturists, develop strains for the different qualities of the resultant drug.

The best marijuana has a smooth flavour and a musky aroma: some varieties sharpen acuity whilst others dim it, some develop their high slowly and others give an instant hit. It is an imprecise science but the experts, whether they grow their plants on Himalayan mountainsides or illicitly in suburban attics ringed with solar lamps, know their stuff.

There are a great many varieties of marijuana and hashish, often named after their places of origin. Amongst the best known to connoisseurs are Lebanese Gold, Colombian Gold, Hawaiian Blue, Jamaican Blue Mountain, Nigerian Black, Mexican Green and Orange Bud. One variety developed in California, Juicy Fruit, is preferred by cancer and motor neurone disease patients using marijuana to alleviate their symptoms.

There is probably not a country in the world, save those with very cold climates, where cannabis is not to be found growing either wild or in cultivation. It exists from Manchuria and the steppes of Mongolia to the rural shires of southern Britain, from the Ganges plain in India to the prairies of the American Mid-West and Hokkaido in Japan. Under culti-vation, it is to be found throughout the Indian sub-continent, South-East Asia, the Caribbean, Central and South America, most of sub-Saharan and parts of north Africa, and southern Europe – and that is just in the open, not under glass. It is, without doubt, the most widely distributed hallucinogenic plant on the planet.

Since prehistory, it has been in partnership with mankind, to become one of the most varied of cultivated crops, its dispersal not only reliant upon the natural forces of wind and water, bird and animal, but also those of men. The lines of its global dissemination follow those of human trade and cultural history. And yet, unlike many other cultivated plants, it has never become dependent on man, has always been ready to escape his control and, as pot-heads would say, go off to do its own thing.

# OUT OF THE LAND OF MULBERRY
# AND HEMP

THE EARLY HISTORY OF CANNABIS IS UNDERSTANDABLY SOMEWHAT murky and there are almost as many theories on it as there are theorists. To make matters worse, modern pro-cannabis apologists cloud the issue by making every effort to affirm that cannabis has been socially acceptable since the dawn of time.

The story probably begins with the first agriculturalists who were likely to have unconsciously encouraged cannabis to grow. Its love of nitrogenous soils would make it an eager colonist of tilled soil and the middens around newly permanent settlements. It would only be a matter of time before the first farmers investigated it. Once aware of its potential, it was cultivated and, in due course, became one of the most widespread cultivars.

The first likely use of cannabis was for its fibre, although it may also have been grown for its seed. Prehistoric farmers, who were beginning to grow seed crops, were almost certainly aware of the nutritional value of cannabis seed. At what stage the psycho-active properties were discovered is unknown but it could have been very early on. The resin could easily have been accidentally or even purposefully eaten. It takes no great leap of the imagination to visualize the impact this would have had upon superstitious, primitive man. Cannabis would have quickly become a magical plant and an adjunct to religious practices. This, in turn, would have led to a knowledge of the medicinal properties.

The most likely indication is that cannabis was first cultivated in central Asia, from which its use spread by trade and invasion, its range accelerating in the third millennium BC by the taming of horses and other beasts of burden, which permitted travel over greater distances and considerably aided military expansion and conquest. Quite possibly, the first cannabis farming occurred in far western China or Chinese Turkestan. The oldest existing historical records and subsequent archaeological evidence, though not extensive, seem to support the theory that cannabis was being grown at the dawn of Chinese civilization. Indeed, China was sometimes referred to in classical times as 'The Land of Mulberry and Hemp'.

One of the earliest recorded instances of cannabis use comes from a prehistoric site excavated at Yangmingshan, near Taipei, on the island of Taiwan. Dating to between 10,000 and 3000 BC, pottery shards of the Tapenkeng culture were discovered, into the clay of which had been impressed pieces of hempen cord as decoration. Mid-Neolithic excavations in the Yellow River basin, of sites dating to around 5000 BC and occupied by the Yang-Shao and Ta-Wen-Kou cultures, indicate that cloth and netting were made with hemp fibres. The Yang-Shao also used rope decoration on pottery as did the Lung-Shan people in Hunan province between 1170 and 230 BC. A Neolithic site in Zhejiang province produced both hemp and silk textiles, whilst a Shang dynasty (1700–1027 BC) hemp weaving site has been found at Taixi in Hebei province. A third-century BC dynastic tomb discovered near Xi'an in Shanxi province in 1957 contained hemp, whilst a Western Han dynasty (260 BC–AD 24) tomb found in Gansu province in 1974 yielded up hemp shrouds covering silk grave clothes, all of them bound together with hemp cord.

Cannabis growing was of major economic importance in China well back into antiquity. Edicts promulgated the advantages of hemp cultivation. The oldest Chinese treatise on agriculture, the *Xia Xiao Zheng*, written around the sixteenth century BC, named hemp as a main crop. In *The Book of Songs* and *The Annals*, written during the Warring States period (475–221 BC), mention is made of the six crops commonly planted: cannabis is one of them. Several other tracts mention hemp farming, going into detail about aspects of cultivation such as ploughing and sowing depths, ideal planting times, fertilization, irrigation, pest control, harvesting times, fibre quality control through selective eradication of seedlings and fibre extraction techniques. The first Chinese dictionary, the *Er Ya*, names both male and female hemp plants as *xi ma* and *ju ma* respectively. *Ma* meant hemp.

Before the discovery of silk, garments made of hemp cloth were commonplace but, once silk was being woven, hemp became the cloth of the ordinary man, silk that of the nobility and the rich. In the *Li Qi* (*The Record of Rites*), written in the second century BC, after the invention of silk, it was said that the bereaved should wear simple (undyed) hemp cloth out of respect for their ancestors, being humble in their presence. The practice lingers on in the wearing of plain white by the principal mourners at traditional Chinese funerals.

Inevitably, with hemp having a prime economic value, it became the subject of conflict. Local warlords zealously guarded their crops. Plates of body armour were sewn together using hemp twine and hemp replaced bamboo fibre as the ideal material for bow strings. In some places, hemp was used to pay both taxes and tributes. Yet its use went far beyond bow strings and coarse cloth.

During the Han dynastic periods (207 BC–AD 220), hemp pounded with the bark of mulberry trees made a cheap but durable paper. According to the *Hou-Han Shu*, the fifth-century history of the period, the discovery was made in AD 105 by a eunuch called Cai Lun serving in the court of the Emperor, He Di, but hemp paper predating him by at least a century has been discovered in graves in Shensi province. Being flexible, strong and waterproof, it was used for official documents, imperial books and the work of scholars.

Paper aside, hemp was also used in the manufacture of one of China's most exquisite artistic achievements, lacquer ware. The lacquer was made from the sap of a tree, *Rhus verniciferas*, which was strained through hemp cloth so that the fibres became saturated in it. It was then thickened by simmering, shaped over a mould and left to harden. It was very durable: grave goods including lacquer cups have been excavated from a Han dynasty tomb in Jiangxi province.

Cannabis was also cultivated as a grain crop along with soya bean, millet, rice and barley. The seeds were either roasted or ground into flour and cooked as a thick gruel. The cultivation for food, however, died out in the sixth century in preference for other, better cereals. A large seed-producing variety of cannabis still found growing in northern China is thought to be a descendant of plants bred for their grain. The extraction of hemp seed oil was developed much later, the seeds being milled and hot-pressed.

The medicinal use of cannabis was begun by shamans, magicians-cum-medicine men who sought to drive out the demons which it was believed caused illness. Using talismans, invocations and incense, and beating the walls and bed of the sick with cannabis stems, the shaman could supposedly exorcize the evil spirits. Real scientific investigation, however, is credited to the legendary Emperor Shen Nung who lived in the third millennium BC. Concerned at the frequent failure of shamanism, he set about studying Chinese flora, often testing the plants on himself: it is said he turned green and died of self-administered poisoning. His knowledge was said to have been collected in the *Pen Ts'ao Ching*, a Chinese pharmacopoeia of which the earliest known version dates only to the first century AD. It became, however, the standard reference work for Chinese medicine, leading to Shen Nung being known as the father of Chinese medicine and his deification. (His idol is traditionally green.) Shen Nung advised the use of 'hemp elixir' – probably a tea made of cannabis leaves and flowers – to treat a wide range of ailments from gout to malaria. He also accepted hemp as a payment of tribute.

That the Chinese were familiar with cannabis being dioecious is proven by the *Er Ya* and, later, in the Eastern Han dynasty by another dictionary, the *Shuo-wen chieh-tzu*, in which four variations for *ma* are given. Shen Nung noted the female plant's enhanced medicinal value whilst, in the Qi dynasty (AD 479–502), the pricking out of male plants was a major public ceremony.

By the second century AD, Chinese medicine was the most advanced in the world and it was then that a famous physician, Hua Tuo, is said to have discovered that cannabis resin mixed with wine was an effective analgesic. It was called *ma yo*. He also invented another anaesthetic, *ma-fei-san*, a mixture of cannabis and aconite, and is said to have been able to conduct major invasive surgery by using it.

With such interest in and widespread use of cannabis, it was inevitable that the Chinese should be the first people to record any psycho-active effects but these were viewed with contempt. From about 600 BC, with the rise of Taoism, intoxication was seen as antisocial. In the fifth century BC, a Taoist priest dismissively recorded that cannabis was used by shamans to predict the future through time-altering dreams. By the first century BC, with Taoists becoming increasingly interested in alchemy and magic, cannabis is thought to have been employed as a vision-inducing incense. Indeed, the written character *ma* took on the meaning 'chaotic' implying madness or inanity.

The use of cannabis, however, never really became more than a passing phase. Chinese culture, being based upon social order, family values and the reverence of ancestors and the elderly, looked down upon drugs. Besides, the use of alcohol and opium was prevalent and already causing a problem. Society did not need, nor did it demand, yet another vice.

The knowledge of cannabis reached Japan from China, brought by sailors and fishermen. Known as *asa*, it was used as a fibre and by Shinto priests. A ritual staff, a *gohei*, with a tassel of raw hemp fibres on one end, was waved above a sick person's head to expel evil spirits, an obvious extension of the shamanistic practices found in China. The idea was that purity and impurity could not co-exist and, as hemp was a pure natural fibre of great strength, it could counteract demons.

From China, the knowledge of cannabis – and no doubt the plant or its seeds – also moved west to the Indian sub-continent, carried by traders or invaders, or both. Around 2000 BC, nomadic tribes started to spread out from central Asia. The first were the Aryans from whom it is thought the Indians acquired the name *bhang* (or *bhanga*) for cannabis.

The Aryans' religion was animistic and cannabis played an important role in their rituals. According to the *Vedas*, the four seminal books of the Hindu faith written in Vedic (early Sanskrit) about 1100 BC, the god Shiva brought cannabis down from the Himalayas for the pleasure of mankind. According to legend, cannabis was created when the gods stirred the heavenly oceans with the peak of Mount Mandara, possibly Mount Everest. A drop of celestial nectar, *amrita*, fell to earth and a hemp plant sprouted from the spot. It became the favourite drink of Indra, the Lord of Kings, and was subsequently consecrated to Shiva. When evil demons tried to acquire it, they were defeated, hence cannabis being also called *vijaya* meaning 'victory'. Another myth has it that Shiva went into the fields and lay under a cannabis plant for shade: then, being hungry, he ate some of it and decided it was his favourite food. He is, consequently, sometimes known as the Lord of Bhang as well as by his more common title, Lord of the Dance. The *Atharva Veda*, the fourth book, says one communes with Shiva through the use of cannabis, calls it one of the five sacred plants and contains a prayer asking it to deliver mankind from disaster, disease and demons. Through its use, mankind is cleansed of sin. The *Venidad*, one of the volumes of the Zend-Avesta, the ancient Persian religious text written around the seventh century BC purportedly by Zoroaster (or Zarathustra), the founder of Zoroastrianism, and heavily influenced by the *Vedas*, mentions *bhang* and lists cannabis as the most important of 10,000 medicinal plants.

For a long while, cannabis was identified as the magical plant *soma*, mentioned several hundred times in hymns and chants in the ninth section of the first book of the *Vedas*, the *Rg Veda*. However, no proof exists that *soma* was cannabis and it is now thought to have been *Ephedra sinica*, which contains an adrenalin-like nerve stimulant alkaloid.

Interestingly, it too originates in China where it is called *ma huang* or yellow hemp.

At first in India, cannabis and its resin were the preserve of Brahmin priests and holy men who believed it took them closer to enlightenment and the gods, helping them to overcome hunger, thirst and pain. Men walking on hot embers or lying on sharpened blades or stakes were said to use it. Only at important religious festivals were the public given access to it. Orthodox Hindus, for whom alcohol is forbidden, would drink cannabis tea while the drink was often taken on the festival of Deshera, celebrating a victory of the Hindu god Rama over another deity. Although today forbidden all intoxicants, Sikhs used also to drink cannabis tea on the *gurpurb* (festival) which is held to celebrate the birth of Guru Nanak Dev Ji, the founder of their religion, in October 1469.

Cannabis was also revered by Buddhists. According to a Mahayana Buddhist legend, Prince Siddhartha, who became Buddha, is supposed to have existed for six years on an exclusive diet of hemp seed, whilst seeking enlightenment. Apparently, he ate just one seed a day. In the Tantric religious movement that affected both Buddhism and Hinduism from the second century AD, cannabis played a central role. As with other beliefs, Tantrism was based upon a fear of, and a need to quell, demons. Spells and mantras were chanted as cannabis was burnt to drive off devils and it was used in the rituals of meditation and Tantric sexual yoga, consecrated to the goddess Kali.

Although not an aphrodisiac, the ability of cannabis to lift one onto another plane of consciousness can enhance sexual physicality and create a sense of sexual union. The aim of Tantrism was to create a feeling of oneness in spirit and body, not to concentrate upon the orgasm or pleasure of copulation.

When not being used to prolong sex or meditation, cannabis was used to calm the nerves of soldiers going into battle, encouraging them to feats of bravery. It also fought off fatigue. To this day, Bhutanese and Nepalese porters, the beasts of burden in the Himalayan foothills, use cannabis as a stimulant. It was also a common medicine used in the treatment of dysentery, insomnia and fever.

In due course, *bhang* took on a social role. It was drunk at weddings, presented as a cup of hospitality, and used to oil the wheels of social intercourse. This, not surprisingly, led to what might now be termed recreational use.

Unlike alcohol that had to be distilled, or opium that had to be processed, cannabis was literally there for the picking. What was not cultivated could be found growing wild. In a country rife with poverty, famine and disease, cannabis provided temporary respite from the miseries of existence.

With widespread usage, cannabis came to be graded into three types of preparations: *bhang*, *ganga* (pronounced 'ganja') and *charas*.

The cheapest and least psycho-actively potent of these is *bhang*, the Indian equivalent of marijuana in the West. It was by this name that early European travellers to India often described all the forms of cannabis they came across. Consisting simply of desiccated, crushed leaves, with or without added seeds or flowers, *bhang* is smoked, used as a food additive or made into a sort of boiled tea containing cannabis leaves, milk, sugar and assorted herbs and spices. In modern India, its usage is, as it has been for centuries, extensive.

*Ganga* is the second grade, made from the dried flower clusters of female plants. If cultivated, the plants are raised with care in the absence of male plants. The resulting *ganga* is a mass of cannabis resin and tightly compressed flowers. It is generally smoked and is two to three times more potent than *bhang*.

The third grade is *charas*, a high-quality hashish obtained from plants grown at altitudes ranging from 4000 to 7000 feet. Traditionally, the resin was collected by hand and purified in warmed copper pans. It was then crafted into small sticks, blocks or cakes containing up to 40 per cent pure resin. As is the case today, it was stronger than most hashish found outside India. The very best *charas* is an even, mid-brown colour. Slightly lower quality *charas* appears as green-brown cakes often flattened in leather pouches called *turbahs*. Usually smoked in hookah-type water pipes, it can also be crumbled into cigarettes with tobacco. In addition, it can be used in *majoon* or as a sweet semi-alcoholic variously scented beverage.

Aryan expansion was not restricted to the Indian sub-continent. By 1500 BC, their diaspora had reached and settled in Persia, Asia Minor, Greece, the Balkans, Germany and eastern France. And where they went, cannabis went with them.

Aryan influence had impinged upon the Assyrians by 900 BC, who used cannabis for religious purposes, calling it *qunubu*, meaning 'the drug for sadness'. Cuneiform clay tablets dating to around 650 BC, almost certainly copied from older texts, were found in the excavation of the library of the Assyrian king Ashurbanipal at Nineveh on the River Tigris in northern Iraq. The Phrygians, who overran the Hittites around 1000 BC, also used hemp for its fibre. Archaeologists recovered eighth-century-BC hemp fabrics from the Phrygian city of Gordion, near Ankara in Turkey.

Much effort has been expended, especially by those who would wish to lend cannabis an added credibility by giving it biblical connotations, in trying to prove that the ancient Hebrews used cannabis. Certainly, the Israelites were in constant contact with cannabis-using cultures but, at one stage, it appeared as if there was no direct mention of the drug in the Old Testament.

In 1936, however, Sula Benet (writing as Sara Benetowa), an etymologist working at the Institute of Anthropological Sciences in Warsaw, claimed that the original Old Testament text made positive reference to cannabis both as an incense and a psycho-active drug. Her evidence came from Exodus 30, verses 22–33, in which it states God instructed Moses to produce a holy anointing oil with myrrh, cinnamon, kassia and *kaneh bosm*. The latter, she claimed, containing the root word *kan* (meaning both 'hemp' and 'reed') linked to the adjective *bosm* ('aromatic'), referred to cannabis. Previous biblical scholars had translated this as being calamus, a fragrant water plant known as Sweet Flag, their error compounded from the oldest known Greek translation of the Bible. Yet the ancient Hebrews used a holy oil to put themselves into a trance during which the voice of God spoke to them. It must also be remembered that the word *Messiah* means 'the anointed one', through whom the word of God was given. Subsequent research has supported Benet's hypothesis and, more recently, it has been suggested that cannabis was widely used in Hebrew temples in antiquity, up until the reign of King Josiah in 621 BC, during which it was suppressed, although some scholars believe Christ may have used cannabis-based oils in his healing ministry, to treat eye or skin ailments.

With the ancient Egyptians, the evidence is not conclusive. Hemp seems to have been used for rope. Fragments of hemp were found in the grave of the pharaoh Akhenaton (Amenhotep IV), and hemp pollen has been detected on the mummy of Ramses II, suggesting to some – without any real basis of fact – that hemp played a part in funerary ritual in the second millennium BC. The ancient Egyptian word *šmšmt* has been said to refer to hemp, with stone inscriptions and texts written on papyri supporting its medicinal use as a poultice, enema, sedative and as a cure for glaucoma. Claims have been made for the presence of cannabinoids in Egyptian mummies but this may be erroneous for apparently traces were also found of cocaine, which was definitely not present in Egypt. That the ancient Egyptians had an extensive knowledge of natural drugs and medicinal plants is irrefutable but nowhere is there a mention of cannabis, or anything that could be specifically identified as cannabis, and, surprisingly, no hempen mummy windings have yet been discovered. It would therefore appear that, whilst the Egyptians knew of hemp, it did not play an important part in their lives, save perhaps as a rope fibre, and they were either unaware or dismissive of its psycho-active capabilities.

Around 800 BC, another migration of Aryans occurred. Known as the Scythians, they came from the region of the Altai mountains in southern Siberia although they had been trading as far west as Greece before their exodus commenced. They were also trading partners with the Semites in the Middle East, who referred to them as the Ashkenaz, a war-mongering race who, in the seventh century BC, invaded the area now covered by Israel, Jordan and southern Syria. They brought cannabis with them and it is through contact with them that Europeans first came to know of it.

Herodotus of Halicarnassus, the Greek historian living in the fifth century BC, was the first European to write about cannabis. An inveterate traveller – he journeyed as far afield as Egypt and the Crimea – he was fascinated by the minutiae of different cultures and societies, and recorded a detailed account of Scythian funeral customs. Visiting a Scythian settlement in north-eastern Macedonia, he noted how, after the funeral of a high-status person, the Scythians purged themselves in a pit covered with woollen mats and containing heated stones, much as one might find in a sauna. Once in the pit, they *took the seeds of hemp and cast them upon the red-hot stones where they smouldered and gave off more steam than a Greek steam bath: transported by the fumes, they shouted in their joy.* As the seeds of cannabis contain no psycho-active chemicals, it is believed the Scythians were actually casting cannabis flowers onto the stones but no positive proof exists.

In 1929, the archaeological excavation by a Russian archaeologist called Rudenko of a fourth-century-BC high-status burial site at Pazyryk in western Mongolia produced censers that had been fashioned for inhaling smoke, perhaps as part of the burial ritual. These consisted of small cauldrons filled with stones and covered by awnings of leather or felt. In with the stones were discovered cannabis seeds. In addition, clothing made from hemp fibre was found. More recently, in 1993, the Russian archaeologist Natalya Polosmak conducted an excavation of the tomb of a Scythian woman of position in which were found personal possessions including a pot containing cannabis. Both graves fitted the description of Scythian burial rites given by Herodotus.

Not only the Scythians came under Herodotus' scrutiny. Whilst with the Thracians in the eastern Balkans, he noted they were expert at working hemp fibre so finely that it resembled linen. A Thracian tribe in Dacia (now Romania), the Getae, maintained a cult called the *Kapnobatai*, thought to mean 'those who walk in smoke', cannabis being a contender for the source of the smoke because of the universal word *kan* appearing in the name, despite the intrusive *p*. Democritus, a contemporary of Herodotus, knew of a plant he called *potamasgis* or *potamaugis* which, when mixed with wine and myrrh, caused delirium. Theophrastus, a Greek botanist (371–287 BC), failed to include cannabis among the native plants of Greece, although he may have been referring to it when he mentioned a plant called *dendromalache*; nor is there specific reference to cannabis as a drug in the Greek myths, although datura and mandragora were listed as psycho-active plants used in shrines and by oracles. Three centuries later, Plutarch (46–127 BC), the Greek essayist and biographer, noted that the Thracians often burnt the tops of a plant resembling oregano, inhaling the fumes, becoming intoxicated and eventually falling asleep. Yet cannabis was not proven to be involved in any of these instances. Once again, speculation is rife.

Another cannabis controversy centres upon the drug *nepenthe*. Mentioned in Homer's *Odyssey*, written in the eighth century BC, it was correctly known as *pharmakon nepenthes* and of Egyptian origin. Variously identified as opium, belladonna, henbane, mandragora and cannabis, it was said to banish sorrow. Indeed the name consists of the noun *penthos*, meaning 'anxiety', with a negative prefix. Diodorus Siculus, a Greek historian from Agyrium in Sicily, recorded it was used by women in Thebes.

In the *Odyssey* Helen, daughter of Zeus, visited one Polydamna in Egypt who supplied her with a drug. Many years later, at a banquet in Sparta given by her husband, Menelaus, thoughts turned to his old friend Odysseus, of whom no word had been received for a long while. The guests grew depressed with sorrow. Helen, remembering the drug, fetched it and spiked the wine with it. Everyone drank of it and cheered up. Scant though the details are, there has been speculation that the drug was cannabis. This seems hardly likely. Cannabis does not retain its potency over a length of time. On the other hand, opium – a common Egyptian drug and often taken with wine – does.

The probable truth is that the Greeks knew of cannabis, and its effects as a drug, but this knowledge either did not enter the public ambit or was ignored by most, remaining of interest only to priests or scholars. Certainly, Greek doctors in the employ of the Romans possessed a knowledge of cannabis.

Pedanius Dioscorides (*circa* AD 40–90), a Greek physician who was a

Roman army doctor and travelled widely on campaigns throughout the Roman empire, studied many plants, gathering his knowledge into a book he titled *De Materia Medica* (*On Medical Matters*). Published about AD 70, it became the most important medical tome of the next 1500 years. Irrefutably included in it was cannabis, both *kannabis emeros* and *kannabis agria*, the male and female respectively. Dioscorides stated bluntly that the plant which was used in the making of rope also produced a juice that was used to treat earache and suppress sexual longing. He did not mention its psycho-active potential: that was left to another Greek.

Claudius Galen (*circa* AD 129–99) was born to Greek parents in Pergamum, a Roman city in what is now Turkey. After studying medicine at the behest of his wealthy father, he became a doctor attending gladiators. Their wounds often being horrific, he learnt much about anatomy and physiology, publishing his findings and thereby elevating his importance to that of Dioscorides. In about AD 160, Galen wrote that hemp cakes, if eaten in moderation, produced a feeling of well-being but, taken to excess, they led to intoxication, dehydration and impotence.

Both the Greeks and the Romans traded in hemp for its fibre. At first, the latter raised virtually no domestic hemp crop at all, importing it from the far-flung corners of their empire which reached as far east as the Caspian Sea, well into the heartland of cannabis. But by the first century BC, the rapid expansion of the Roman navy placed such a demand for hemp fibre for the making of rope and sails that Roman settlements in the region of the Volga started growing hemp along with those in Palestine and Mesopotamia.

It was only a matter of time before the Romans decided to begin cultivating their own hemp supply. The Greek historian Pausanias stated that hemp was being grown around Elis, in the west of the Peloponnese in southern Greece, in the second century BC. The Roman satirist Lucilius wrote of it in 120 BC. In his thirty-seven-volume *Historia Naturalis* published soon after his death in AD 79, Gaius Plinius Secundus (Pliny the Elder) noted that hemp made exceptionally strong rope and went into detail about how it was prepared and graded.

Hemp as a source of quality fibre had well and truly arrived in western Europe.

# A FIBRE FOR ALL SEASONS

*CANNABIS SATIVA* ALMOST CERTAINLY GREW IN WESTERN EUROPE BEFORE the Scythian invasion, although it is unknown how widespread it was and not much is understood about its use by primitive man.

Hemp seeds have been discovered in a number of Neolithic sites across western Europe, from Eisenberg, fifty miles south-west of Leipzig in Germany to Frumusita in the Danube River valley system on the Romanian-Ukrainian border. This would place hemp use in Europe as being contemporary with its first discovery in China, but this is supposition and, whereas the Chinese were cultivating it, there is no proof that Europeans were doing likewise. Furthermore, these discoveries have prompted the speculation that early Europeans were using hemp for shamanistic purposes – that is, as a drug. Yet the chance of cannabis plants so far north producing sufficient quantities of resin, even assuming a major climate shift, make this theory exceedingly slim indeed.

The first solid evidence of the presence of hemp use comes from a fifth-century-BC funerary urn discovered at Wilmersdorf in 1896 by the German archaeologist Hermann Busse, since when a number of other finds have been made. Whether the hemp was locally grown or imported by the Scythians cannot be verified, nor can the purpose of its use, although being associated with burial suggests a religious connotation.

It was with the expansion of the Roman Empire that hemp and its cultivation became commonplace. Probably the earliest piece of many

Roman hemp rope fragments found in Britain was discovered as far north as the Roman fort on the Antonine Wall at Bar Hill, between Glasgow and Edinburgh. Built around AD 80, the fort was initially occupied by the First Cohort of Baetasians, formed of men from the Baetasii tribe from the area of Germany between the rivers Meuse and Rhine. Being Roman infantry, and from the centre of Europe, they more than likely brought their rope with them. What this shows, however, was that hemp stretched to the very edges of the empire for, except for the occasional military incursion into Scotland, the Romans did not venture beyond the Antonine Wall.

As the Roman Empire began to fade, and after its fall, the need for domestic supplies of hemp in the former countries of Roman occupation arose to replace the imports the occupiers had brought in. At the same time the Franks, a western Germanic people thought to have originated from Pomerania on the Baltic Sea coast, began to spread across Roman Europe. They were eventually to settle most of the Roman province of Gaul, roughly the area of modern France and Belgium, as well as conquering much of Germany and moving into Italy. Agriculturally more advanced than the Romans, they invented the three-field crop-rotation system. One of their crops was hemp, grown for its fibre. When tombs in the crypt of the Cathedral of St Denis in northern Paris were opened in the early 1960s, the body of the Frankish Queen Arnegunde, consort and second wife of Clothar I who died in the mid-sixth century, was discovered. Adorned in jewellery and attired in silk and linen, her corpse was protected by a blanket of hemp cloth.

About AD 400, the cultivation of hemp reached Britain. The first recorded growing of hemp – with flax – was at Old Buckenham, fifteen miles south-west of Norwich. By 600, with the arrival of the Saxons, hemp growing was well established. At about the same time, the Vikings extensively used hemp, samples of hempen rope, fishing line and sail cloth having been found in Britain and Iceland, prompting the theory that the Vikings, who purportedly discovered North America, may have introduced the plant to the New World.

By the ninth century, ocean-going Arab dhows were trading as far east as Indochina and it was inevitable that they would, sooner or later, discover what the Chinese had been doing with hemp for centuries – making paper. When the Arabs extended their conquests to the western Mediterranean, occupying southern Spain, they took the technology of paper-making with them.

The first paper factory in Europe began producing about 1150 in

Játiva, fifty miles north of Alicante, using locally grown hemp. Other paper mills followed in Valencia and Toledo. The Arabs kept a tight monopoly on the manufacturing process but, as Arab influence in Spain began to decline in the fourteenth century, the knowledge of paper-making escaped and spread across western Europe. Hemp, until then predominantly used as a fibre for cloth and rope, went through a minor revival. At about the same time as paper started to become more widely available, movable type printing was invented. Johan Gutenberg first printed the Bible on hempen rag paper in Mainz around 1456, the paper made with the same process as the Chinese had been using for a thousand years: his printing was based upon the Chinese use of woodblocks.

Although a number of varieties of hemp were known in Europe, they were not extensively cultivated. Crops tended to be grown only for the immediate domestic market and there was little trade in the fibres. This changed in the Middle Ages in Italy, where cultivation on a grand scale commenced, accelerated by the Renaissance. There was a sound reason for this: the need for ships' cordage.

The city states of Italy survived on maritime trade, the most powerful of them being Venice. Famed for its merchants and shipbuilders, it had risen to prominence using imported hemp. This left it vulnerable to supply: a competitor or enemy had only to cut off supply or, worse, raise the price, to bring the Venetian merchant fleet to a standstill. Consequently, the Venetians founded their own hemp industry operated through a state-owned factory called the Tana. Situated in the Arsenale, the hemp was retted there, the fibres twisted by cord-winders into rope or woven by sail makers. A guild of hemp workers was established and statutes insisted on all vessels using Venetian rope. Quality control in the Tana was very strict, fines being imposed for sub-standard work. The result was that Venetian rope was considered amongst the best in the world for three centuries, the Venetian merchant fleet controlled Mediterranean trade and its warships were the most feared throughout the region until the city finally fell to Napoleon in 1797. After the demise of Venice, however, the growing of Italian hemp continued apace. Within fifty years, Italy was exporting hemp to England, Portugal, Germany, Spain and Switzerland. Techniques in fibre processing had so advanced that hemp was being spun into yarn almost as fine as silk but stronger than cotton, which was much in demand for expensive fabrics.

Outside the sphere of the Mediterranean, four other nations vied for maritime power, the English, the Spanish, the Portuguese and the Dutch. A need to trade with the Far East and the African seaboard without going overland, not to mention exploration to the west in order to find a route to the Indies, meant building sturdy sea-going vessels. As ship design improved, sail technology developed, one of the most important of the innovations being the adoption in the early fifteenth century of the jib and lateen, triangular sails first invented in the ninth century and used by the Arabs in their ocean-going dhows, which permitted ships to sail to windward. Long-distance sea travel, in which the Venetians had not indulged, now became a real possibility. One problem of this kind of sail, however, was its need to be very durable and tear resistant, for it was subjected to considerable strain. Hemp gave it the necessary qualities.

It was the Dutch who spearheaded the development of hemp. Using the power of windmills (which were driven by hemp sails), they were able to streamline the labour-intensive fibre extraction process to such an extent their production outstripped domestic hemp supplies. The country simply was not big enough to grow the hemp required. Consequently, the Dutch were forced to import from Scandinavia, the Baltic states, Russia and even Italy, which they were trying to oust as a maritime nation.

Seeing the Dutch in ascendancy, the English followed suit, building a merchant fleet and a navy for its defence. Yet they, too, faced the same supply problems as the Dutch: England being an island meant its resources were finite and both ship-building timber and hemp had to be imported.

It has been estimated that it took 80 tons of hemp to rig a Tudor man-of-war: at the time, an acre of hemp could produce on average 18 pounds of dressed fibre. The fleet that drove off the Spanish Armada in 1588, consisting of 34 ships of the line and 163 smaller vessels, had therefore required the output of about 10,000 acres of hemp. King Henry VIII, the founder of the English navy, realizing the strategic importance of hemp, issued a Royal proclamation in 1533 which levied a fine of 3s. 4d. on any farmer who refused to put a portion of his arable land under hemp or flax. The rate of cultivation commanded was a quarter of an acre for every 60 acres. The farmers were not pleased. Hemp did not return a good price and it was believed the plant impoverished the soil by sucking out the nutrients. The labour required to ret the fibres – not to mention the smell as the plant rotted which was, as were most foul odours at the time, considered a source of disease – only fuelled their determination to resist. Thirty years later, Elizabeth I increased the fine to 5s. but without effect, the decree being repealed in 1593.

The defeat of the Spanish Armada established England as the primary

European maritime power. Consequently, the need for hemp increased further and, even had the English farmers been willing, they would have been hard-pressed to meet the demand. Importation was essential with English vessels visiting Danzig, Riga and St Petersburg for their cargoes. At the time, Russia was the world's major hemp producer, and by 1633 Russian hemp merchants were providing well over 90 per cent of England's raw hemp requirement.

Such reliance upon a foreign producer not only all but killed off the English hemp trade but, as the Venetians had discovered, it also left the country vulnerable. There was only one answer to the problem: Britain had to turn to its fledgling colonies in the New World for supply.

Britain was not the first nation to look across the Atlantic to feed the demand for hemp. Since the middle of the sixteenth century, the Spanish had been attempting to grow hemp in their settlements in Mexico, Peru, Colombia and Chile.

It is thought hemp was brought to Mexico by Pedro Cuadrado, a conquistador serving with Cortés. The plant was successfully introduced but, in 1550, the Spanish governor reduced production. Native labourers had discovered that hemp, growing in the tropics where the temperatures were high and the days long, contained a drug and he was fearful that this might lead to rebellion or a degradation of the workforce. Only in Chile was hemp a viable commercial success. As early as 1545, it was being farmed near Santiago, almost exclusively for rope-making. Presumably the Chilean natives, unlike those in Mexico, had no need of hemp as a drug because they already used coca leaves.

A quandary exists over when hemp reached North America. The Vikings may have introduced it centuries before Columbus discovered the continent. Alternatively, it could have been spread to the west coast by Chinese explorers who are said to have sailed round the northern Pacific; it could also have been carried across the Bering Strait by birds or even by animals when Asia and America were joined by a land bridge.

Evidence for there being hemp in North America prior to the arrival of the white man is said to come from clay pipes wrapped in hemp cloth and containing cannabis residue, excavated from the famous Death Mask Mound just outside Chillicothe, Ohio. This, however, is highly suspect. Those citing this as proof date the mound to 400 BC, but the Mound Builder or Late Woodland culture is dated to around AD 1300. What is more, doubt exists about the pipes having been wrapped in cloth in the first place, not to mention containing cannabis residues. Giovanni da Verrazzano, the Florentine adventurer who discovered New York harbour and was a member of a French expedition to Virginia in 1542, reported seeing natives dressed in a clothing of leaves sewn with hemp. The French explorer Jacques Cartier also wrote of seeing wild hemp growing in Canada between 1535 and 1541, whilst George Croghan, travelling down the Ohio River by canoe in May 1785, wrote in his journal, *18th and 19th: we traveled through a prodigious large meadow called the Pyankeshas hunting ground . . . overgrown with wild Hemp*, adding three days later, *wild Hemp grows here in Abundance*.

What they assumed was *Cannabis sativa*, however, was more likely to have been *Acnida cannabinum*, the American water hemp, or *Apocynum cannabinum*, also known as Indian hemp, both of which produced fibres and were used by the indigenous people medicinally and for fibre. The first known, experimental, planting of *Cannabis sativa* was in 1606 in Nova Scotia. It was carried out by Louis Hébert, apothecary to Samuel de Champlain, the French explorer and founder of Quebec.

The early French and British colonists in the New World wanted to cultivate food crops. Not only did they need these for their survival but they were loath to plant hemp for the same reasons as farmers back in Europe. However, their masters back home demanded they produce hemp. In Quebec, Jean Talon, King Louis XIV's personal representative, had to resort to desperate measures to get the Quebecois to toe the line. In November 1666, he reported back to his superior in France, *I have found that to encourage the inhabitants to grow a great deal of hemp it was necessary to induce in them a want of thread. To this end I seized all* [the thread] *I could find here and I will only distribute it to those who agree to return a stated quantity of hemp.*

In the English colonies, hemp and flax cultivation was mandatory from 1611, by order of King James I. Settlers at Jamestown preferred to grow more lucrative tobacco but cultivated hemp under a contract signed with the Virginia Company in 1607, just prior to the founding of the colony. In fact, hemp was to save many of them from bankruptcy. When the tobacco market slumped, as it did periodically, hemp kept the farmers' cash flow going. However, to ensure the steady production of hemp, the Virginia Company issued an order in 1619 that every colonist had to raise one hundred hemp plants: the governor personally agreed to raise 5000. Later the same year, a budget of ten guineas per man was set aside to encourage hemp dressers from Scandinavia and Poland to emigrate to Virginia. To further promote hemp growing, colonial legal tender laws were enacted making taxes payable in flax, tar and hemp. In 1682, Virginia made hemp legal tender in the paying off of up to a quarter of a farmer's debts.

Subsequently, hemp production rose in Maryland and Virginia but little of the harvest reached Britain. New England merchants purchased most of it as hemp was scarce on the north-eastern seaboard, especially since shipbuilding was beginning to become a major industry. American hemp was of high quality, making good twine and rope, and by 1630 clothed half the population every winter and most of it in the summer. To meet demand and reduce imports, the General Assembly of Connecticut, sitting in Hartford in 1637, ordered all families to plant one teaspoonful of hemp seed: Massachusetts followed this example two years later.

It was in Salem, Massachusetts in 1635 that the first rope-walk was erected in America. A rope-walk was a long, narrow building up to 1300 feet in length in which ropes were made. Boston soon entered in competition, bringing a rope maker called John Harrison over from England in 1642, presenting him with a guaranteed life monopoly in the city. Thereafter, rope-walks were built up and down the length of eastern America.

The colonial authorities continued to encourage hemp cultivation. Some states, such as Connecticut, put a premium on hemp in 1722 whilst Virginia used legislation to force farmers into compliance. South Carolina took another tack and, in 1733, employed one Richard Hall for three years, to promote the cause of hemp: he was in effect cannabis' first public relations officer. Two years later, a Boston bookseller, Daniel Henchman, published *Instructions for the Cultivating and Raising of Flax and Hemp* by Lionel Slator. The same year, the state of Massachusetts accepted hemp as tender for taxes at a rate of four shillings a pound.

One of the grudges the American colonists had against Britain was the fact that they were expected to produce raw materials which had by law to be sent back to Britain for manufacture. They were then obliged to buy back the finished goods. Spinning and weaving, other than domestically in the home, were forbidden. Nevertheless, a spinning industry started up, using hemp. The British tried to restrict this activity and, under pressure from British mill owners, Parliament passed the Wool Act in 1699, depriving the colonists of the right to import wool. The strategy backfired, the colonists increasing their use of hemp and flax. In 1718, a number of professional Irish spinners and weavers, suffering from an economic downturn in Britain, arrived in Boston. Over the next twenty years, hundreds of others followed them to the American colonies, bringing the latest skills and techniques with them and giving birth to the American textile industry. With the Parliamentary ratification of the Stamp Act of 1765, which imposed a tariff on imports landed in America, there was a virtual boycott of British goods which led to an acceleration in home spinning and weaving, as well as an increase in commercial mill output. By the outbreak of the War of Independence, the colonies were more or less self-sufficient in cloth – and hemp. Any surplus that arose was exported – mostly to the French, Britain's main mercantile competitor and enemy of long standing – with the proceeds used to purchase munitions.

In the decades following the end of the war, hemp became more than a commodity: it became a currency. The various states had had their own monetary systems but, with the foundation of the Union, a federal currency was introduced that undermined them: one thousand dollars of Virginia's currency was worth only one US silver dollar. Because of the lack of confidence in local currencies and paper money, which was readily counterfeited, hemp became a currency in itself. Hemp's more or less constant quality and the permanent demand for it made it ideal for barter.

It had not been universally used for paper, however, which was primarily by then made from flax, cotton and rags. Indeed, some paper makers on both sides of the Atlantic decried the move from hemp. In 1765, an English paper maker called Christian Shaffer thought of using hemp once again. His sentiments were echoed in 1777 by Robert Bell, an American printer, who suggested hemp paper be made as, the country now being an independent nation, there was a need to reduce reliance upon flax and cotton, a substantial amount of which was imported. The first drafts of the Declaration of Independence in 1776 had been penned on Dutch hemp paper. Bell need not have worried. Hemp now being plentiful, paper mills turned to it.

Both George Washington and Thomas Jefferson, who were landowning farmers, cultivated hemp as an important cash crop on their own farms. Jefferson, who preferred growing hemp to tobacco, produced his own cloth from hemp grown on his estate, Monticello: by 1815, his slaves were producing 2000 yards per annum, although some of this was made with wool and cotton. Soon after, however, he stopped hemp cultivation, writing in his journal that . . . *the breaking and beating* [of] *it, which has always been done by hand, is so slow, so laborious, and so much complained of by our laborers, that I have given it up.*

Where Washington is concerned, there has been much speculation about whether he not only used hemp for its fibre but also for its resin. In his diary for 1765, he regretted not having separated the male from the female plants prior to fertilization. This has been taken to imply he was, in today's terminology, growing his own stash. However, this is inconclusive. He may just as well have been separating them as part of good hemp husbandry. Towards the end of the eighteenth century, Washington started raising what he termed Indian hemp but which was, in fact, *Cannabis indica*, the seeds imported from India. This fact has also been used to suggest he used cannabis as a psycho-active substance. So too, it is claimed, did other early presidents. It has been alleged that Washington preferred hemp leaves to alcohol, that James Madison was inspired towards democracy by smoking hemp, that James Monroe discovered the pleasures of hashish whilst US ambassador to France, that Andrew Jackson, Zachary Taylor and Franklin Pierce also imbibed. The 42nd US President, Bill Clinton, whose middle name is coincidentally Jefferson, and who famously admitted to smoking pot but not inhaling the fumes, may conceivably have had some quite prestigious antecedents.

Thomas Jefferson's appreciation of the rigours of hemp farming was not lost on others. Land set aside for hemp had to be ploughed and tilled until the soil was friable. It was not unusual to require two or three sowings for the seed, which had to be fresh and sometimes failed to germinate. Once ready for harvesting, the farmer had to face either pulling the plants up by the roots or scything them down, stacking them in bundles like withies to dry in the wind. Once dry, they had to be retted. Ideally, this meant immersing the hemp in water, but many farmers carried out what was called dew retting. Instead of soaking the newly cut hemp, they let it lie on the ground overnight then, when it was soaked in dew, they tied it into damp bundles to rot out. Winter retting involved leaving the plants on the ground to rot under cold winter conditions. Once retted, the crop had to be dried again then broken, either by being threshed by hand or with the use of hand breaks, two vertical planks hinged together, the hemp being placed between them and the top plank swung down with sufficient force to crush the stems but not fracture the fibres. It was this work about which Jefferson's slaves complained. To address this, Jefferson modified a horse-drawn threshing machine but, like many hemp cutting and retting machines that were to follow, it was only partially successful.

After cotton, hemp soon became the most important agricultural crop in the southern states, where slavery provided the necessary manpower. It was primarily grown in the blue grass regions of Tennessee and Kentucky where, by 1810, hemp was the staple crop of the latter state which, by 1889, produced hemp valued at $468,000 from 23,468 acres under cultivation. The success of Kentucky hemp was aided by the soil being unsuitable for cereal crops, a 1792 Act of Congress that put an import tax of twenty dollars per ton on foreign hemp which rose to sixty dollars by 1828, and the increase in the number of slaves bought by plantation owners.

It was assessed that it took three slaves to manage every 50 acres of hemp. Despite the hard work, the slaves preferred hemp growing to other tasks. They were usually set a daily target which meant they had time off if they reached it early. Furthermore, some plantation owners paid 'wages' to encourage production. At harvest time, some slaves were given one cent per pound of fibre broken in a day, over a minimum of 100 pounds. With much sweating, a sturdy young male slave could earn up to two dollars a day. Some earned enough over a few seasons to buy their liberty.

Without slavery (or machinery), the hemp industry could not have operated. Indeed, in Kentucky, hemp was so associated with slaves and, after emancipation, black tenant farmers, that it was known as a 'nigger crop'. Slaves who understood the cultivation and preparation of hemp, or worked in rope-walks, were amongst the most sought after and therefore expensive.

The 1830s saw a rapid increase in the invention of hemp machinery, especially for the making of rope and hessian. In 1838, David Myerle of Philadelphia built a steam-driven factory at Louisville, Kentucky, based upon an invention by one Robert Graves of Boston, from whom he bought the patent. Then, in 1841, Andrew Caldwell of Lexington, Virginia invented a mechanized system in which raw hemp fibre was separated, spun into yarn and sewn into hessian sacking. Suddenly, there was an alternative to slave- and horse-power although it was several decades before the machinery really took over, after the US Civil War and the ending of slavery.

The hemp growers of Kentucky did not, however, have it all their own way. Despite the import levy and the United States Navy declaring cordage produced by the Graves machinery to be stronger than other rope, and an 1842 Congressional order demanding domestic product be used by the military at every opportunity, manufacturers using hemp in the New England states were reluctant to purchase American hemp, preferring to buy their fibre from Russia, passing the tax burden on to consumers.

At the root of this reluctance lay the most commonly used retting process. American hemp growers' fibres were not as good as the water-retted hemp imported from Russia because dew retting reduced the quality. It was adequate for cheap twine or sacking but not good enough for ships' cordage.

As Americans started to cross the Mississippi and push west, hemp was invaluable to them. Apart from the harness ropes and canvas awnings of the 'prairie schooner' covered wagons, it was an ideal pioneer crop providing both a basic fuel and fibre. Blankets, tents, cord and tough work clothing were all made out of it although not, as many believe, jeans which were made out of duck, a heavy cotton fabric. It was not long before the word hemp entered the western vernacular: a hemp collar (or necktie) was the hangman's rope, a hemp committee was a lynch mob and someone who was on his way to the gallows was said to be sowing hemp.

The Union forces looked into the possibility of growing hemp during the Civil War, to replace the cotton they were no longer receiving from the Confederate states, but the plan did not materialize although, inevitably, the war increased the need for hemp and the price rose accordingly. The rebel states produced less hemp during the war: what was not destroyed by the scorched-earth tactics of the Union troops was replaced by cotton that could be sold overseas for much-needed foreign currency with which to bolster the war chests. After the surrender, cotton came to dominate, imported jute replacing hemp. At the same time, paper became increasingly made of wood pulp. Regardless of a brief revival in the 1870s and '80s, when it was cultivated in Illinois, Nebraska and California, hemp production declined steadily, many farmers turning to cereals. The demand for marine rope tailed off, too. Increasingly, steel-hulled steamships were replacing sailing vessels. Sailcloth was becoming redundant. Rigging was made of high-tensile steel cable and, with the American occupation of the Philippine Islands, Manila hemp could be imported from there. Some factories continued but cultivation was much reduced: in 1909, Kentucky, the 'hemp state', had only 6800 acres put to hemp, and this was 76 per cent of the entire national hemp acreage. Tennessee had none.

Hemp, it seemed, had had its day. At least, as a source of fibre . . .

# THE SHRUB OF EMOTION, THE MORSEL OF THOUGHT

THE ARABIC WORLD DEVELOPED ITS OWN CANNABIS CULTURE AND, although not universally popular within Muslim societies, hashish in particular has played an important historical role.

In early Arabic texts, the term *hashish* referred not only to cannabis resin but also to the dried leaves or flower heads and sweetmeats made with them. It was at the time eaten, not smoked.

When cannabis was first used as an intoxicant in the Arabic or Islamic world is open to conjecture. One legend states that an Indian pilgrim introduced it into Persia during the reign of the Sasanian emperor Khosrow I (531–79). Other sources claim it was acquired from itinerant Chinese merchants or mendicants in the seventh century: one suggestion is that Huan Tsang, a famous Chinese Buddhist scholar who visited the Punjab in or around 641, was one of them. Another hypothesis has the knowledge of cannabis gained during one of the many military incursions made into the Indian sub-continent by the all-conquering Ghaznavid King Mahmud, the Muslim ruler of Afghanistan from 998 to 1030.

The truth is likely to be less romantic. Cannabis was used medicinally across the Arabic world in Roman times, applied to a wide variety of ailments (from migraines to syphilis) and as an analgesic and anaesthetic. The great ninth-century Islamic physician Rhazès, also known more properly as Abou Bakr Mohammed ibn Zakariya Ar Razi, prescribed it widely; a contemporary, the Arab physician Ibn Wahshiyah, warned of the potential effects of hashish which he wrote was a lethal poison. What was more, the writings of Galen, Hippocrates and Dioscorides had long been translated into Arabic and were widely available to scholars.

Cannabis use, aside from the medicinal, spread across the Middle East with the expansion of the Islamic faith in the late seventh century. In part, it was passively promoted by the religion for, in the Koran, the faithful are specifically forbidden alcohol but no prohibition is made of cannabis or its products. That its psycho-active properties were well known is indicated by the metaphors by which it was referred to in early Arabic texts: the 'bush of understanding', the 'shrub of emotion', the 'blissful branches' and the 'morsel of thought'.

It is generally accepted that the use of hashish, for what would nowadays be termed recreational purposes, was well established in Arabic society by the eleventh century and the subject of controversy amongst Islamic priests and scholars. Ibn Taymiyah (1263–1328), one of Islam's most important traditionalist theologians who was opposed to hashish use, damningly associated it with the accursed Mongols, who had destroyed Baghdad in 1258. The main thrust of the argument lay in what Mohammed intended by prohibiting alcohol.

The Koran (2: 219) specifically prohibits *intoxicants, gambling, the altars of idols and games of chance.* The word used for intoxicants, *khamr*, is open to interpretation. The root word from which this comes is the verb *khamara* meaning 'to cover'. The implication, therefore, is that any substance that 'covers' the mind is sinful. The teaching adds that this prohibition includes the use of intoxicants in medicine. The morality of hashish imbibing in Islam is, therefore, somewhat ambiguous.

Permissive Muslims argued – and still argue, centuries later – that, in forbidding wine, the Prophet was intending to stop the faithful from resorting to a substance that promoted violence, as can alcohol. Hashish, they maintained, induced pacificality and did not truly intoxicate and was, therefore, outside the Prophet's restriction. Furthermore, doctors declared it was a valuable analgesic, much less dangerous than the other narcotic commonly used, opium. To comply with the Prophet's wishes, Muslim doctors attempted to establish a dose of hashish that killed pain but did not intoxicate.

The dice were loaded against hashish. The *imams* justifiably dreaded the thought that prayers might be offered to Allah while the supplicant was intoxicated. The upper classes supported the ban not only on the grounds that it was sinful but also because it threatened to undermine the labour force. Arabic civil laws questioned whether a divorce pronouncement was deemed legal if issued whilst the husband was under the influence of hashish, while it was also forbidden to feed cannabis plants to animals unless to fatten them up.

There was an exception. The mystical Sufi Muslims believed spiritual enlightenment was attainable through a state of ecstasy or altered consciousness and used hashish specifically for that purpose. To them, hashish was sacramental, a portal through which to commune directly with Allah and therefore not a substance to be regarded lightly. Haydar, its supposed discoverer, had warned his disciples to keep it from the ignorant for fear they would abuse it. Yet the secret was not kept. It is said, as he was dying, Haydar requested cannabis be planted round his grave and, through this, pilgrims learnt of it, spreading the knowledge. Additionally, the Sufi poets whose mystical didactic verse is central to Islamic literature referred to cannabis infusions as the 'cup of Haydar'. It is hardly surprising, with such publicity, the secret leaked out.

Sufis were not looked upon kindly by mainstream Islam. As the Albigensians were to Christianity, so were the Sufis to other Muslims. Their form of worship, Sufism, was regarded as a deviant religious movement. Their members were existentialists who lived an ascetic communal life of self-denial, dressed differently from other Muslims and used hashish. They were seen as dissidents and subversives, challenging orthodox theology and claiming a direct communication with Allah. For this they were, and in some places still are, reviled within Islam, every Sufi considered by orthodox Islam as being of lower moral standards and classed as a *mulhida*, or heretic.

There was more to this proscription than theological dislike. Sufis were usually from the lower, working-class strata of society. A religion that catered specifically for them was sure to be denounced. That the poor used hashish, and that their religion used it for heretical purposes, only further drove them into cultural isolation and religious persecution.

Hashish was considered the vehicle of their fall from the grace of Allah. It was seen to weaken their resolve, both physically and spiritually. They were regarded as lazy misfits who failed to play their part in a conservative society that was based on conformity. Amongst Sufi society, initiates were referred to as *hashishiyya* ('users of hashish'): it was to become a derogatory term of abuse in the rest of Islam. Thought of almost as outlaws and certainly often as common criminals, Sufis nevertheless contributed much to Islamic learning. Sa'd od-Din Mahmud Shabestari was one of Islam's greatest poets, whilst 'Abd al-Qadir al-Jilani was a great evangelist who regarded Sufism as a personal *jihad* (holy struggle) against the inner will. Al-Ghazzali, a Sufi theologian who did much towards making Sufism acceptable to orthodox Muslims, was a close friend of Ibn Sina (known in the West as Avicenna), the most famous physician and scientist in early Islam. Nevertheless, orthodox Islam wanted hashish banned.

Sufism, or, to give it its correct name, *tasawwuf* (meaning 'to wear wool'), first began to arise in the late seventh century. As it developed, it increasingly came under attack from orthodox Islam and increasingly disseminated itself over the Arabic world, taking with it its use of hashish.

By the mid-thirteenth century, there was a substantial Sufi population in Cairo. The community centred itself upon the gardens overlooking the Khalig which had been built by Abu al-Misk Kafur, an Ethiopian slave and advisor to the Ikhshidid dynasty who was the *de facto* ruler of tenth-century Egypt. Here they conversed, conducted their religious services, took hashish and grew cannabis. In 1253, the authorities, considering the Sufis a threat to public order, raided the gardens, uprooted all the cannabis plants and burned them on a pyre, the smoke visible for miles. Thereafter, the Sufis raised their crop out in the Nile valley, local farmers only too pleased to oblige them for a fee. This *status quo* lasted until 1324 when the authorities organized a purge throughout the countryside, troops destroying all the cannabis plants they discovered. For a while there was a hashish shortage: then business picked up again as the next crop came to maturity. Now wise to the risks, the farmers in turn bribed local officials to turn a blind eye.

Fifty-four years later, in 1378, the Ottoman emir in Egypt, Soudoun Sheikhouni, determined to stamp out hashish use, instigated martial law. Crops were burned to the ground: so were farms and villages. Farmers were imprisoned or executed and those found guilty of consuming hashish were said to have had their teeth pulled. Five years on, it was as if nothing had happened.

Hashish had become an integral part of Arab life and would not be suppressed. It was sold and consumed openly. Officials, many of whom used it themselves, accepted bribes to ignore law enforcement not only because this was a source of additional income, as well as intoxication, but also because they were tacitly in favour of it. When the authorities did from time to time clamp down, it was with severe measures, but this did nothing to reduce the drug's popularity.

It was not only in the souks, bazaars and coffee shops that hashish was prevalent. It was widely mentioned in the Arabic literature of the time. In his book *The Herb: Hashish versus Medieval Muslim Society*, published in 1971, the Arabic scholar Franz Rosenthal remarked that he thought there could hardly have been an Arabic poet writing between the thirteenth and sixteenth centuries who did not refer to it. To the ordinary reader in the non-Arabic world, one of the most famous pieces of Arab literature is the collection of stories written between 1000 and 1700 and entitled *The Thousand and One Nights*. Hashish features particularly in the stories 'The Tale of the Second Captain of Police', 'The Tale of the Two Hashish Eaters' and 'The Tale of the Hashish Eater'. In the latter, a beggar stands on a nail and cuts his foot. To wash it clean, he enters a *hamman* or Turkish bath. As he tends his foot, a fellow bather offers him some hashish which he eats. Immediately, he is filled with hilarity then collapses into a deep sleep. He dreams he is attended by masseurs before being taken to his bride. In a separate chamber, a young boy leads in a girl little more than a child into whose hand he places his penis. At this moment, he feels terribly cold and wakes to find himself surrounded by laughing bathers, some of them emptying jugs of cold water over him. He is holding his penis and it is made clear he has been masturbating, much to the amusement of those present who ask him why he is not ashamed to have been 'fornicating with the air' whilst under the influence of hashish. Such an image of the drug debasing its user was a common theme, except in mystical Sufi literature.

By the end of the sixteenth century, with the arrival of tobacco from the New World, the craze for smoking swept through Europe and on into the Middle East. Hashish, until then eaten, started to be smoked instead.

Tobacco smoking, which was soon recognized to be addictive, introduced the concept of burning dried vegetable material as a means of acquiring the drug content, and, as tobacco smoking quickly spread across Europe and North Africa, and into the Middle East and Asia, the smoking of cannabis followed.

The conscious inhalation of burning cannabis smoke had been practised for some time amongst various cultures in the Old World, and an awareness of the euphoric possibilities of passively breathing it in from a censer or incense pot was fairly widespread. The fumes may even have on occasion been taken through a hollow reed or straw, but the active smoking of cannabis in a specific form of pipe was unknown prior to the advent of tobacco.

The pipe required some adaptations before it could be used for cannabis but these were soon invented, allowing hashish to become even more widespread than before. With smoking, users found the effects were quickly experienced (in a matter of minutes as opposed to hours) and readily controlled. The effects of a pipeful of tobacco/cannabis mix did not last more than an hour at best: a spoonful of hashish could last twelve hours or more. Smoking, therefore, became socially more acceptable, a pastime rather than an indulgence, a cocktail in a non-alcoholic society.

Two sorts of pipe evolved, one delivering the smoke directly, the other indirectly. The former, made of clay, was similar to an ordinary tobacco pipe but with a pebble halfway along the stem to prevent the ignited ash from being inhaled. To cool the smoke, which is hotter and coarser than that of tobacco, a filter consisting of a damp cloth was sometimes held over the mouthpiece. In India, the pipe was known as a *chillim* (sometimes spelt *chillum* or *chillam*) which derived from the Hindi *chilam*, meaning a chalice. Cannabis pipes today are sometimes known as chillums and have given rise to the colloquialism 'chill out', meaning to take it easy and relax.

In indirect pipes, the smoke was passed through water before it reached the smoker. The smoke was cooled and made much smoother by being filtered through water, but some potency was lost. Iranian potters are credited with inventing the water pipe, variously known as a *hookah*, *shishah* or *narghile* or, in the West, as a hubble-bubble, the name being an onomatopoeic interpretation of the sound of the smoke bubbles passing through the water.

Under Arabic influence, cannabis use spread across North Africa and south into sub-Saharan eastern Africa, although even an approximate date for this expansion outside the Islamic sphere is uncertain. It has also thrown up a controversial question about smoking.

Ethiopia was trading with the Arabs since at least the second century: known to the Arabs as the Land of Incense, it became a Christian nation from the fourth century. A Monophysite form of Christianity, the Ethiopian Coptic faith has used cannabis in its rituals for centuries – Ethiopia is famous for producing a very potent hashish – but a question lingers as to whether they inhaled it as an incense or actually smoked it. Archaeological proof has been promulgated to suggest that the smoking of cannabis may have predated the spread of tobacco. In 1971, two clay water-pipe bowls excavated at a site near Lake Tana in northern Ethiopia were found to contain residues of THC which were said to be carbon dated to about 1360. However, the carbon-dating method used had a wide margin of error which could have placed the residues as recently as 1550 and, as the collecting method is unknown, the sample may have been subject to environmental contamination.

Wherever Arab traders went in Africa, cannabis was introduced. From about the third century onwards, they were a frequent presence along the East African coast where, by the twelfth century, there were Muslim settlements on the islands of Zanzibar, Pemba and Kilwa, with mainland Arab centres at Lamu, Gede and Sofala, south of Beira in Mozambique, to name but a few. They also travelled up navigable rivers, such as the Zambesi, searching for slaves. In this quest, they reached at least as far as eastern Zambia, their campsites recognized to this day by the presence of tamarind trees grown from Arab slavers' discarded seeds. This is not the only remnant of Arab influence: the Swahili word for cannabis is *bangi*, derived from the Hindu *bhang*. There is even a suggestion that cannabis might have reached East Africa carried by the Chinese: Chinese traders were certainly visiting the coastal areas of Kenya as early as the late thirteenth century.

Arab incursion into central Africa took cannabis westwards whilst Africans themselves extended its range southwards to the Hottentots, Bushmen and 'kaffir' tribes of South Africa such as the Xhosa and Zulu peoples. In southern Africa it became known as *dagga* whilst in western Africa it was called *diamba*: today, *dagga* is widely used across Africa, the name sometimes applied to any psycho-active plant material.

By the time Europeans started to reach eastern Africa, cannabis use was well established, both as a recreational drug and in a religious context. *Dagga* achieved cult status in some places in central and southern Africa, cannabis being regarded as a magical plant capable of rendering its user omnipotent and as a symbol of fraternity. It also became a valuable trading commodity.

One of the earliest European books on Africa, *Ethiopia Oriental*, which appeared in 1609 written by the Portuguese Dominican missionary João dos Santos, recorded cannabis being grown in the region of the Cape of Good Hope. Dos Santos wrote of the natives eating the leaves and becoming drunk as if on a surfeit of wine. Jan Anthoniszoon van Riebeeck, the founder and first governor of the Dutch colony at Cape Town in 1652, wrote in his journal of the Hottentots' use of cannabis which he noted acted like opium on them.

Cannabis smoking in southern Africa, if it had been introduced by the Arabs, seems to have died out but, with the arrival of the Dutch, it was taken up again. The Europeans smoked tobacco from pipes and the natives soon learnt the method although some had been inhaling cannabis smoke in ritual ceremonies, such as in the ancient civilization of Zimbabwe.

The African tribes who took to smoking soon developed their own pipes made out of anything from wood and stone to carved bone. Some, in particular the technologically advanced Zulus who traded slaves with the Arabs, made water pipes out of pottery, reeds and horn. As cannabis smoking developed into a communal social activity, earth pipes were constructed, a sort of hybrid between hand-held pipes and primitive incense burners. A small hole was dug in the ground and filled with a mixture of dried herbivore dung and *dagga*. Once this was alight, the smokers cupped their hands over the hole and inhaled through a gap between their thumbs. This method of smoking was common amongst bush tribes until the advent of the cigarette.

Probably under Arab influence, cannabis came to be regarded in Africa as a medicinal plant. It was used to fight malaria and blackwater fever, as an anaesthetic during childbirth and as a cure for asthma, respiratory disease, dysentery and even anthrax. Its efficacy, needless to say, was not always a foregone conclusion.

As Europeans increasingly colonized or explored Africa, so did their attitudes towards cannabis alter. By the eighteenth century in South Africa, some Dutch settlers actually grew cannabis for their native workers, partly to ensure their continued presence. Not all the tribes, however, encouraged the smoking of *dagga* or, when it was introduced, tobacco, which many Africans found too mild for their liking. There were also Europeans who frowned upon the use of *dagga*, albeit for other motives.

The American explorer Henry M. Stanley, who considered Africans to be a sub-species of humanity, said cannabis weakened them to the point that they were useless as expedition porters. Others noted how Zulu impis took *dagga* before going into battle, the intoxication giving them the ability, as A.T. Bryant wrote in his book *The Zulu People*, published in 1967, *under the exciting stimulation of the drug* [to be] *capable of accomplishing hazardous feats*. At the battles of Isandhlwana and Rourke's Drift in 1879, between the British and the Zulus, it is widely believed Zulu warriors were under the influence of cannabis: they routed the British at the former and were unlucky not to win the latter encounter. However, *dagga* taking had not always paid off. At the Battle of Blood River in Natal in 1838, between Boer *voortrekkers* and the Zulu army under the famous chief Dingane, four white *voortrekkers* were injured in the fight but 3000 impis were slain.

Whilst the Zulu impis almost certainly did take *dagga*, it must be remembered that cannabis tends to calm rather than excite and they can hardly have used it as a battle stimulant. What is more likely is that they also took another drug, either on its own or in association with cannabis acting as an hallucinogen. Drugs that excite are not uncommon amongst East and Central African tribes. The Masai, for example, use a drug called *olkiloriti*, an excitant which also aids digestion and is obtained from a preparation of the bark and roots of the acacia tree. Warriors take *olkiloriti* before battle to fend off fear and fatigue: it can send them into a state of frenzy. Zulu traditional medicine contains a number of similar tonics.

David Livingstone, the greatest of all white African explorers and missionaries, noted that the Bakota tribe – more commonly known as the Sotho or Basuto people – also took *dagga* to build up their courage. In his *Missionary Travels and Researches in South Africa* (1858), he wrote, *The Bakota of these parts are very degraded in their appearance, and are not likely to improve, either physically or mentally, while so much addicted to smoking the mutokwane* (Cannabis sativa). *They like its narcotic effects, though the violent fit of coughing which follows a couple of puffs of smoke appears distressing, and causes a feeling of disgust in the spectator. This is not diminished on seeing the usual practice of taking a mouthful of water, and squirting it out together with the smoke, then uttering a string of half-incoherent sentences, usually in self-praise. This pernicious weed is extensively used in all the tribes of the interior. It causes a species of phrensy, and Sebituane's soldiers, on coming in sight of their enemies, sat down and smoked it, in order that they might make an effective onslaught. I was unable to prevail on Sekeletu and the young Makololo to forgo its use, although they can not point to an old man in the tribe who has not been addicted to this indulgence. I believe it was the proximate cause of Sebituane's last illness, for it sometimes occasions pneumonia. Never having tried it, I can not describe the pleasurable effects it is said to produce, but the hashish in use among the Turks is simply an extract of the same plant, and that, like opium, produces different effects on different individuals. Some view every thing as if looking in through the wide end of a telescope, and others, in passing over a straw, lift up their feet as if about to cross the trunk of a tree. The Portuguese in Angola have such a belief in its deleterious effects that the use of it by a slave is considered a crime.*

Cannabis did not have an entirely deleterious effect upon all African tribes.

The German explorer and soldier Herman von Wissman, who suppressed the Abushiri in 1890 and was a governor of German East Africa (now Tanzania), observed the Bashilange tribe during his expedition of 1881, which he described in his volume *My Second Journey through Equatorial Africa*. Also known as the Baluba or the Barua, the Bashilange lived in what is today the eastern region of the Democratic Republic of the Congo, bordering on the western shores of Lake Tanganyika. They had a well-earned reputation as belligerent war-mongers and slave dealers until, around 1850, they discovered cannabis. A religious cult sprang up around the plant which they called *riamba*, the adherents to the cult calling themselves the Ben-Riamba, or Sons of Cannabis. The cult grew and, under its influence, the people became placid and enacted a system of laws, which they had previously been without. *Riamba* became a metaphor for peace. This utopia did not last. As the Bashilange mellowed, inferior tribes in their area, which they had previously forced to pay tribute, now regarded them as weak and refused to comply. Dissident factions of Bashilange suppressed the cult in the 1870s and the tribe returned to its old ways although it retained cannabis for recreational purposes.

For a brief time, cannabis showed that it could work for the common good but, in general, wherever it was used it gained a bad reputation. Sometimes, this was justified. Often, it was not.

# MYTHS AND MURDERERS

AROUND 1271 OR 1272, MARCO POLO, THE RENOWNED VENETIAN merchant adventurer, was on his way through Persia *en route* for Cathay when he came upon a story told by travellers in that region. Twenty-five years later he recounted it in his book *Il Milione*, better known today as *The Travels of Marco Polo*.

The story concerned a remote area ruled by one they called the Old Man of the Mountains, whose followers were notorious for their ruthlessness. According to Marco Polo, they had been in existence since the middle of the eleventh century and there was not an Arab leader who did not go in mortal dread of them. The disciples of this leader were kept loyal to their master by the promise that, were they to die whilst in his service, they would assuredly go to Paradise. To strengthen their resolve, the Old Man of the Mountains gave initiates to his following a preview of what it would be like in Paradise by maintaining a fabulous garden within his mountain stronghold. In this pleasure ground, exquisitely beautiful houris wandered ready to fulfil any desire, the fountains ran with milk and honey and the flowers were beyond compare. However, it was said, to enter this fabled place the would-be acolyte was first given a powerful drug and, only when unconscious, allowed in: before leaving, he was again drugged. After their induction, the initiates were given a solid Islamic education but were also taught the arts of murder, killing anyone whom their master commanded be put to death. Before going into battle, they apparently partook of the same drug to increase their courage. The drug was hashish.

The veracity of Marco Polo's writings has long been suspect, yet the story has stuck, enhanced and exaggerated as the centuries have passed. The legend of the Old Man of the Mountains has become nothing short of unassailable fact and his followers, notorious as much for their merciless cruelty as their gargantuan appetites for hashish, have become a byword for brutality. Even the name by which they came to be known derived from the drug it was alleged they took: they were called the Hashshashin. They are now known as the Assassins.

The truth is somewhat different.

Within a century of the foundation of Islam by Mohammed in 622, the religion had divided into two branches, the Sunni and the Shiite, each containing a number of sects, often at theological or ideological loggerheads with each other. One such sect, a schism of the Shiite branch of Islam, was known as the Nizari Ismaili. It was founded around 1090 by Hasan ibn-Sabah, a famous Islamic dissident who was born in 1050 in the city of Qom, south of Tehran, and educated in the orthodox thinking of Islam, tradition has it sharing the same teacher as the famous Islamic writer Omar Khayyam. His father was a Shiite Muslim from Kufah, a city on the Hindiyah tributary of the Euphrates in southern Iraq. The family claimed to be of Yemeni extraction and descended from the Himyarite monarchs of Southern Arabia.

With his sect, Hasan ibn-Sabah intended to politically promote the Ismaili cause across the Arabic world, which meant giving support to the Ismaili Fatimid rulers of North Africa. They took their dynastic name from Fatimah, the Prophet Mohammed's daughter, from whom they believed they were descended. Through this bloodline, they believed they were consequently the guardians of the true faith.

His politico-religious stand put Hasan ibn-Sabah at odds with the rest of Islam. He was vilified and regarded as a dangerous renegade, cunning, ambitious, determined and exceedingly zealous: he allegedly had two of his own sons put to death, one for drinking wine and one for an alleged murder. Yet even his adversaries allowed that he was a highly intelligent and learned Islamic philosopher and theological scholar whose every action was reasoned. His philosophy was known as the New Propaganda, through which he asserted that Islam had become decadent and needed to return to the true path. Only through unquestioning faith and obedience could salvation be found. A charismatic preacher, he soon acquired a dedicated following.

With his sect established, Hasan ibn-Sabah required a base from which to operate. He chose the castle of Alamut in the remote, inaccessible Elburz Mountains in northern Persia, about 45 kilometres north-west of the town of Qazvin. Perched on a narrow, 400-metre-long ridge, it commanded a cultivated valley, about 50 kilometres long and 5 wide, several hundred feet below. Access to the castle was by a precipitous and convoluted path.

Once ensconced in the castle, Hasan ibn-Sabah set about improving it. The fortifications were extended and strengthened, trapment canals built for water and an irrigation system constructed for nearby fields. According to Edward Burman, the author of a definitive study of the Assassins who visited Alamut in the 1970s, it is likely that some sort of gardens were also laid out for they played an important part in Persian noble life. These gardens were not, however, the grandiose Paradise of Marco Polo's dubious chronicle. A 1950s British expedition to Alamut and several other nearby Assassin strongholds found no area in the ruins large enough to hold even a small garden, but the castle had been substantially damaged by earthquakes in 1485, 1639 and 1808 so it is not inconceivable that land may have been lost in these or covered by rubble.

The occupants of the castle lived an ascetic existence but, despite the hardships of life in the mountains, Hasan ibn-Sabah continued to gather followers and acquire more castles across Persia, mostly to the north and east of the Dasht-e Kavīr, or the Great Salt Desert. With the expansion of his power base, Hasan ibn-Sabah started to meet increased territorial opposition. Anyone who was not sympathetic to the Nizari Ismaili cause faced death for, in Hasan ibn-Sabah's eyes, this made them false prophets of which Islam should be cleansed.

One means of ridding society of this blight was secret assassination. Such judicious (or religious, judicial) murder was commonplace in the Islamic world, homicide being a well-tried political *modus operandi*. Hasan ibn-Sabah, however, developed this into a method of killing that chilled the blood in his enemies' veins. Knowing his preaching alone could not make more than a dent in the armour of orthodox Islam, he devised a system by which a small and dedicated unit of men could effectively strike at, and overwhelm, a superior enemy. In effect, he instituted a sort of Islamic élite commando force. Many considered it a terrorist organization.

The first step was to organize his disciples into ranks. With himself as grand master, he structured those beneath him in six grades, the last being the *fida'i*. Meaning 'the devoted ones', the *fida'i* were the foot soldiers who, without consideration to their own personal safety or life, would unswervingly carry out their orders. If necessary, they would bide their time for months until the moment was ripe, studying their victims' lives in intricate detail. To die in the pursuit of their duty was considered a privilege and would ensure entry into Paradise. This dedication to the task and fanatical lack of fear for death made the *fida'i* feared throughout Islam.

Their first victim was Abu Ali Hasan ibn-Ali, or Nizam-al-Mulk, the vizier of the Saljuq sultanate, who was killed on 14 October 1092 by a *fida'i* dressed as a Sufi. He was followed by a long line of prominent Islamic rulers, advisers, officials and even priests who had attacked Nizari Ismaili teachings or sought to repress the sect. With every killing, the *fida'i* – the term came to mean killer in Nizari Ismaili circles – saw themselves as religious soldiers earning their place in Heaven. Their enemies regarded them as fanatical criminals.

As the reign of terror escalated, the Nizari Ismaili extended their activities into Syria where their main opponents, the Saljuq, were gaining influence. Hasan ibn-Sabah sent missionaries into this new enemy territory to spread his doctrine. Perhaps to his surprise, many came over to his side, not merely because they agreed with his teachings but because they saw in the Nizari Ismaili a force that could rid them of Saljuq rule and help them combat another, potentially more dangerous foe that was threatening Islam – the Christian Crusaders.

Hasan ibn-Sabah died in 1124 but his sect continued under new leadership, consolidating its power base in Syria and launching a new wave of assassinations.

The greatest of the Nizari Ismaili leaders in Syria was Rashid ad-Din as-Sinan, who ruled over their affairs from his castle at Masyaf from the early 1160s until his death in 1192. Rashid ad-Din as-Sinan referred to himself as *shaykh al-jabal* – the Mountain Chief – and it was from this that the moniker the Old Man of the Mountains arose, cemented in time into the popular consciousness by the use of the title by other and subsequent leaders.

It was whilst under the leadership of Rashid ad-Din as-Sinan that the Nizari Ismaili came into contact with the newest enemies of Islam, the Crusaders. Indeed, it was the Crusaders who gave wide currency to the nickname the Old Man of the Mountains. It was also they who spread the term from which the name Assassins derived. This they gleaned from Muslims opposed to the Nizari Ismaili, who used various derogatory terms for them, such as Hashishiyya or Hashshashin.

From their first encounters, the Crusaders learnt to respect and fear the

Hashshashin. It was under Rashid ad–Din as–Sinan's orders that the German contender for the crown of the kingdom of Jerusalem, Conrad of Montiferrat, was murdered in Tyre in 1192, the *fida'i* who carried out the commission spending months disguised as Christian monks and living with the Crusaders until such a time as they saw their opportunity. Although the French, German and British Crusaders were in a permanent state of mutual political upheaval – the English king, Richard Coeur de Lion, was unjustly accused of having been involved in the killing – the death of Conrad unnerved them and served to considerably bolster the reputation of the Hashshashin. Chroniclers of the Crusade wrote at length of the Islamic sect with its dissident views, ruthless terror tactics and strange, mythical leader. The legend of the Assassins was born and a new verb, to assassinate, entered the dictionaries of Europe.

Yet even with their efficient killing apparatus, the Assassins' days were numbered. In 1256, the Mongol invader Hülegü, a grandson of Genghis Khan, conquered Persia, over-running the castle at Alamut as well as several other neighbouring Assassin strongholds and establishing his own Il-Khanid dynasty. At the same time as the Mongols were sweeping through Persia, Al-Malik as-Salih Ayyub, the Mamluk ruler of Egypt and successor to the Kurdish general Saladin, was attacking the Crusaders and taking control of Syria. Between these two invaders, the power of the Assassins was broken. The Nizari Ismaili deteriorated into a minor heretical sect, split in the fourteenth century by a schism from which it never recovered.

The Assassins' library, which had been founded by Hasan ibn–Sabah and kept at Alamut, was destroyed, losing to both history and Islamic scholarship most of the truths about his sect. Consequently, whatever is known about the Assassins has been sourced primarily from records compiled by their opponents, particularly medieval Sunni scholars hostile to Shiite philosophy in general, which they considered heretical, and that of the Nizari Ismaili in particular, the term Hashishiyya being first applied to the Nizari Ismaili in a pamphlet denouncing them in Cairo in 1123.

That said, several other derivations for the word 'assassin' have been proposed. One suggests it comes from the Arabic verb *hassass* ('to kill'), another that it derives from Hasan ibn–Sabah's name, but these are now generally believed false.

It is not unfair to say that the Assassins were highly motivated, skilled and trained merciless political killers. Yet there is one fundamental puzzle about them that has never been satisfactorily answered and is of considerable importance to the history of cannabis. Despite their name, it is by no means certain if they ever used hashish at all.

There have yet to be found any contemporary Islamic texts that state the Nizari Ismaili categorically used hashish. They may have done so: as Burman suggests, hashish was an important part of Persian mysticism, in which it was used as a soporific which intensified the religious experience. They were also influenced by Sufi theology, so may well have adopted the Sufi use of hashish as a means towards attaining visionary experience. Yet this is no conclusive proof, even of an unpartisan nature: furthermore, they were ascetics and likely to shun such vices.

Even if they did use hashish, it cannot – as was believed in their time and as has been perpetuated ever since – have been in order to raise their courage and excite their battle rage. Hashish does not produce any mental state that would incite either violence or brutal murder. There is simply no historical basis for the assumption that the assassins were driven to assassinate by being in a hashish-induced state of mind. Quite the reverse. Any Nizari Ismaili who was under the influence of hashish would have been a distinct liability to a military operation. As J. Mandel wrote in an article entitled 'Hashish, Assassins and the Love of God' in the journal *Criminology* in 1966, *Religion leads to assassinations, not hashish. The supposed hashish-induced 'visions of paradise' are as responsible for assassinations as the religiously fortifying drinking of wine and eating of wafers are responsible for the bloody crusades.*

The truth is, the Assassins have been given a reputation they did not really deserve and, through them, so has hashish.

Whatever misinformation was promulgated by Sunni propagandists was embellished by Western chroniclers who seem not to have appreciated the fact that the Assassins' name was abusive; nor did they understand the position of the Nizari Ismaili sect in the political structure of Islam. Being largely ignorant of the Muslim religion, and always eager to tell a good tale, they came to present a grossly inaccurate picture.

The Crusaders found it hard to understand how the *fida'i* could be so fanatically devoted. To try to rationalize this, they assumed the devotion was drug-induced. The storytellers, Marco Polo amongst them, picked this up. The drug, because it was prevalent in society, was assumed to be hashish.

Furthermore, the *fida'i* daring made a great impression upon the Crusaders who admired their valour and dedication, even if it was drug-inspired, and it was this and their loyalty that was first reported back in Europe where the word 'assassin' became a metaphor for loyalty unto death and not an act of bloody murder.

Well before the Crusades were over, the legend of the Assassins was gathering pace. It was said that the *fida'i* were so loyal that they would commit suicide if ordered by their master. The French nobleman Henry of Champagne, whilst on a visit to Syria in 1194, was said to have witnessed two *fida'i* throwing themselves off a tower on the command of their leader. His report only made the Assassins seem all the more exotic back in Europe.

That hashish is not specifically mentioned by Marco Polo but only by subsequent chroniclers, that whatever drug was used was given for entry into the 'garden of paradise' and not fed to operatives on active service, and that it was a soporific, not a stimulant, has been conveniently over-looked. The fact, had anyone stopped to think about it, that the drug induced stupor and produced visions of Paradise suggests it was far more likely to have been an opiate, widely known to have such effects. Yet this did not make a good, intriguing tale. 'Unknown' hashish did.

As if this is not sufficient to cast doubt upon the story, it must also be remembered that Marco Polo did not actually write his tale down him-self. He dictated his book to a prisoner called Rusticiano with whom he was sharing a cell in Genoa, after the ship he was sailing with was captured by the Genoese in 1298. Over the preceding years, Polo had often recounted his tales and, Chinese whispers-like, may well have ornamented it: those coming after him certainly did. The 1818 translation by William Marsden, considered to be the most accurate, actually mentioned opium as the drug involved.

It is not improbable that Marco Polo also borrowed facts from other writers to spice up his own narrative for he was not the first to mention the Assassins – variously known also as the Haisasins, Heyssessini, Axasin, Assacis, Accini and Assassini.

One of the earliest – possibly the first – accounts of the Assassins (referred to as the Heyssessini) is found in a document sent by one of Frederick Barbarossa's envoys to Egypt and Syria in 1175. The envoy stated they were based in the region between Damascus and Aleppo, liv-ing in mountain strongholds. He then continued by mentioning their obedience, ruthless activities, the fact that their master maintained a fab-ulous garden and that he showed this to his followers after having drugged them. This story was the basis for many to come.

Eight years later William, Archbishop of Tyre, mentioned the Assassini in his *History of Matters Done in Foreign Parts*, one of the first chronicles of the Crusades. James de Vitry, Bishop of Acre in the early thirteenth century, studied secret societies and referred to the Nizari Ismaili in Syria as Assassini. Several decades later, Willem van Ruysbroeck, a French Franciscan friar who travelled to China, applied the terms Hacsasins and Axasins to the Nizari Ismaili in Persia.

By the time Marco Polo told his possibly spurious story, knowledge of the Assassins was widespread in Europe – and the meaning of the name was metamorphosed. By 1300, it no longer referred to a Muslim sect or even generically to a blindly loyal disciple. It now meant a pitiless and brutal murderer.

Dante Alighieri (1265–1321), the most famous writer of the Renaissance, was well aware of this process of linguistic evolution. In *Inferno*, one of the books of his *Divina Commedia*, Canto 19, line 50, he wrote, *la mia posizione era simile a quella del frate che confessa il perfido assassino, condannato alla propagginazione* – *my position was like that of the friar who confesses to being a perfidious murderer, condemned to death by being buried alive* – one of the most horrendous methods of medieval execution applied only to the most heinous of crimes. When Philip VI of France was considering mounting a Crusade the year after Dante's death, he commissioned an advisory report before deciding to act. The advisor, a priest called Brocardus, highlighted the danger of the Assassins whom he described as nothing short of contract killers, not mentioning their religious or political background. Where he was concerned, they were just mercenaries.

So it was that, gradually, by association with the Assassins, about whom little was really known and who had been inaccurately tarred with a barbarous brush by their enemies, hashish came to be considered a drug capable of generating bedlam, undermining society, creating chaos and turning otherwise merciful men into merciless murderers. And this grossly erroneous myth has been perpetuated ever since, right up to the modern day, by those who would proscribe or prohibit anything to do with cannabis.

# 6

# THE HERB PANTAGRUELION

THE CRUSADERS MAY HAVE HEARD OF HASHISH BUT IT IS UNLIKELY THEY associated it with hemp which was to them, being Europeans, a source of fibre and folk remedies.

The place of hemp in European folklore was well established by the eleventh century. In Baltic countries where the dead were said to return on Christmas Eve, a hemp seed soup called *semieniatka* was brewed for their spirits' succour, whilst Ukrainians traditionally made a similar hemp dish for what they call Three Kings Day, that on which the Magi were said to have borne their gifts to the infant Christ. In some places, these traditions are still extant. Even now, hemp seed is used in Poland to divine romantic attachments, thrown at weddings in place of rice or confetti and the subject of a dance by married women on Shrove Tuesday. In southern Russia, on Saint John's Eve, farmers used to feed hemp flowers to live-stock to ward off evil and illness whilst young women still put hemp seed in their pockets as they whisper charms to bring them romance: the same practice used to be carried out in the British Isles. Across Europe, festivals were once held where hemp was burnt, the smoke supposed to possess magical properties that cleansed and protected against disease.

Superstition in many parts of Europe also imbued hemp with semi-sympathetic magical properties. Farmers would plant their hemp seed on the saints' days of particularly tall saints, to encourage its growth. In the Ardennes it was believed the hemp crop would flourish if, on the first

Sunday in Lent, the farmers' wives got drunk whilst, in the mountains of the Vosges, rural families danced on their house roofs on the day of the Epiphany and in Swabia, young men and women jumped over a bonfire to achieve the same end.

Partly because of its psycho-active potential, hemp was widely used throughout Europe as a folk medicine, just as it was in many other parts of the world. Much of this was as a result of the reliance both physicians and folk doctors placed upon Dioscorides' *Materia medica*, considered a central medical text until well into the seventeenth century. The ailments treated with cannabis were many: it was used as an analgesic or anaesthetic to combat earache, toothache (it was believed it drugged or put to sleep the worms that caused the pain), rheumatism, arthritis, menstrual and labour pains, headaches and migraines and a large number of similar discomforts. It was also prescribed for epilepsy, inflammation, coughs, convulsions, fever and jaundice. A paste of cannabis flowers, olive oil and wax or animal fat was used as an ointment for open wounds. Sometimes the smoke of burning hemp (on occasion with henbane) was inhaled, at others the leaf was chewed or made into a potion in hot water. What was good for humans was also deemed of value to animals, hemp being a vital veterinary herb for centuries.

During the Middle Ages, hemp was central to any herbalist's medicine cabinet. William Turner, the naturalist considered the first English botanist, praised it in his *New Herball*, published in 1538. It was the first English herbal to contain original material derived from Turner's own researches and studies while a student at Pembroke Hall, Cambridge. Pietro Andrea Gregorio Mattioli, the noted Italian botanist who translated and wrote a detailed commentary on Dioscorides' work in 1544, identified the male and female hemp plants and promoted it as a therapeutic herb. John Gerard, the author of *The Herball, or generall historie of plantes* (1597), which, being an index of over 1000 plant species, was in part based upon the work of the Flemish botanist Rembertus Dodoens and the Italian Jacob Theodorus Tabernaemontanus, also sang its praises. The English cleric Robert Burton, one-time incumbent of St Thomas' Church, Oxford, advocated cannabis as a treatment for depression in his *The Anatomy of Melancholy*, published in 1621.

Yet it was the herbalist Nicholas Culpeper who was to draw all the previous information together succinctly in his *A Physicall Directory*, published in 1649. Sometimes referred to as Culpeper's *The Complete Herbal*, it brought together all the astrological, alchemical and scientific information available in a herbalist's pharmacopoeia. In it, he wrote of hemp, *The seed expels wind. Boiled in milk, and taken, it helps those that have a hot or dry cough. An emulsion made from the seed is good for jaundice, particularly if there be an ague accompanying it, for it opens obstructions of the gall and causes digestion of choler. The emulsion or decoction of the seed stays the lax and continual fluxes, eases the colic, and allays the troublesome humours of the bowels. It also stays bleeding at the mouth, nose and other places. It kills worms in man or beast and if the juice is dropped into the ears, it will kill worms in them and draw forth earwigs or other living creatures. The decoction of the root allays inflammations of the head, or any other parts. The herb or distilled water of it does the same. A decoction of the root eases gouty pains, hard knots in the joints, and pain in the sinews and hips. The fresh root mixed with a little oil and butter is good for burns.* Culpeper did not, of course, comment upon cannabis' psycho-active potential for the plant he would have known, growing in a temperate clime, would have produced very little THC.

Not only physicians and herbalists used cannabis; sorcerers did too. Consequently, it was not long before the Christian church moved against it. In 1231, Pope Gregory IX initiated the Holy Inquisition, its aim to root out and destroy the heresies of the previous two centuries. Hemp, being regarded as sorcerous, was outlawed as heretical. Those who used it, whether for medical purposes or divination, were branded as witches who, in turn, were considered heretics.

The persecution of witches across Europe commenced in earnest in 1484, with the publication of a papal bull issued by Pope Innocent VIII entitled *Summis Desiderantes.* This was to appear as a preface to the *Malleus Maleficarum* which appeared two years later. A detailed handbook on witchcraft, it was written by two Dominicans, Johann Sprenger and Heinrich Kraemer, who was himself Inquisitor for the Tirol in Austria. With a clever theological argument, it linked sorcery with Satan and heresy, misogynistically placing the blame upon women. Witches were predominantly female. At the same time, in order to prevent the celebration of the Black or Satanic Mass, Innocent VIII banned the use of hemp in ritual.

With the Inquisition came the next demonization of cannabis which was said to be a vital ingredient of witches' brews. Used to formulate the 'black sacrament' with opium, hemlock, belladonna and other magical or poisonous plants, it supposedly aided in driving the satanists into an ecstatic frenzy, making them hungry and acting as an aphrodisiac to ready them for their orgies. When not employed ritually, hemp seed oil was purportedly a major constituent of 'flying ointment', that which witches used to 'ride their broomsticks'.

The Inquisition may have been efficient in instilling the fear of God in people but it could not suppress cannabis which, in a manner of speaking, went underground: the continued use of it, as a medicine and for magical purposes, was common knowledge, but few ever spoke about it openly for fear their words might reach the Inquisitor's ear.

One who did was a French Benedictine monk and doctor, better remembered for being a satirist than as a priest. François Rabelais (1483–1553) famously lampooned the Church and State in the four volumes of his satirical masterpiece, *Gargantua and Pantagruel*, the first of which appeared in 1532 under the pseudonym Alcofribas Nasier, an anagram of his own name. Whilst comical, the books have a serious intention, addressing many of the social ills of the day and supporting humanist idealism. In the third volume, Rabelais wrote of the *herb pantagruelion*. It is quite plainly hemp and Rabelais was obviously very familiar with it. This is hardly surprising when one considers his father had farmed hemp at Cinais, three miles south-west of Chinon, on the River Vienne.

As an intoxicant, cannabis remained largely undiscovered by Europeans, except those few who dabbled in the occult, or scholars, or Crusaders who had travelled to the East and become aware of hashish. For most, wine and beer were their drugs. An exception was southern Spain where Arabs had introduced hashish certainly by the early fourteenth century when Muslim authors were writing about it. Hashish was in common use in Granada in the 1360s. Yet, as Muslim influence waned and then ceased under the pressure of Christianity, so too did the use and, eventually, its memory.

The sixteenth century saw a rapid increase in travel, exploration, adventure, colonization and trade. European merchants and sea-farers returning from the Orient brought with them many new discoveries – spices, fruits, precious metals, porcelain, rare timbers and drugs, primarily opium and hashish.

Amongst the first to bring back hashish were the Portuguese who established trading posts in the Orient at Goa, which they took after an attack by Afonso de Albuquerque in March 1510, Malacca on the western coast of Malaysia, taken in 1511, Liampo (now Ning-po) and Macau in China in 1557. The first Portuguese book to be published in the East detailed the use and effect of cannabis. Written by Garcia Da Orta, a botanist-cum-doctor who went to Goa in 1534 as physician to the Portuguese viceroy of the Indies, it appeared in 1563 and was entitled *Colloquies on the Simples and Drugs and Medicinal Matters of India and of a Few Fruits*.

In his book, Da Orta recorded of *bhang* (which he spelt *bangue*): *the Indians get no usefulness from this, unless it is in the fact that they become ravished by ecstasy, and delivered from all worries and cares, and laugh at the least little thing. After all, it is said that it was they who first found the use of it, when their generals and men of war, exhausted by constant watches, having drunk a little bhang with wine or opium, became as if drunk, and slept as if delivered from all cares.* That he also wrote somewhat sensationally of the psycho-active effects of cannabis only enhanced interest in it and it was not long before physicians across Europe started to regard hemp in a different light.

The medical profession was, in fact, very fortunate in having the book in its possession. Not long after his death, Da Orta's work was banned in Portugal and all copies of his books burnt. This had nothing to do with what they contained. The anti-Semitic Inquisition and the Portuguese Catholic Church had discovered that Da Orta had been a Jew who kept his religion secret. But, by chance, Rembertus Dodoens rescued a copy of the book and had it translated into English, French, Italian and Latin.

Fifteen years after the publication of Da Orta's book, another Portuguese, Cristobal Acosta, published *A Tract about the Drugs and Medicines of the East Indies* . . . He added to Da Orta's knowledge by out-lining what substances were added to *bhang* and for what purpose: it was he who gave a formula for a psycho-active drink containing hashish, cloves, mace, nutmeg and camphor. In 1596, the famous Dutch explorer of the Arctic Sea, Jan Huyghen van Linschoten, who had been clerk to the Archbishop of Goa and had read Da Orta's book, published a chronicle of his time in India. Much of his information about *bhang* – which he also spelt *bangue* – was lifted from Da Orta's book and journal-istically enhanced or distorted. In the process, he gave the impression that hashish and opium produced similar hallucinogenic effects, a mis-conception that was to linger in the literature of drugs for a long time. However, not only the Portuguese and Dutch wrote inaccurately of cannabis. John Freyer, a British East India Company physician, stated in his book *A New Account of East India and Persia Being Nine Years' Travel: 1672–1681*, published in 1698, that opium was actually made from a mixture of *bhang* and belladonna. Freyer and a Frenchman called Bernier also recorded how this potion was used as a means of execution in India.

Not all the European students of cannabis restricted their work to observation. Some tried it for themselves. A French traveller, Laurent D'Arvieux, who journeyed extensively through the Middle East and Persia in the middle of the seventeenth century, was served hashish, although he was under the impression that it was opium. Thomas Bowrey, the captain of a British merchantman who frequently sailed in Indian waters between 1669 and 1679 and published an account of his voyages called *A Geographical Account of Countries Round the Bay of Bengal*, recounted what effects *bhang* had on another English seaman.

Into the eighteenth century, exploration continued apace but not without mishap. An expedition sent by King Frederick V of Denmark to the Arabian peninsula in 1759 met with disaster, only one of the five explorers, a German mathematician named Carsten Niebuhr, surviving. When his memoirs were published they contained an account of hashish taking by Sufis.

Few governments either saw or decided to investigate the mercantile possibilities of cannabis but one did. Perhaps inevitably, it was the British.

By 1770, the finances of the East India Company — more formally known at the time as The Governor And Company Of Merchants Of London Trading Into The East Indies — were in a shambles due to a famine in Bengal. The board was forced to approach Parliament for a one-million-pound loan to prevent its collapse. The loan was forthcoming with the proviso that the Company surrender its operations to Parliamentary control, which was duly put in motion by the Regulating Act of 1773 and The India Act of 1784. In order to see a return on the loan, the British government started to impose taxes in India. In 1790, one of the commodities they taxed was cannabis. This was followed three years later by a regulation licensing the production and sale of *bhang, ganja* and *charas*, the British always referring to the different forms of cannabis collectively as Indian hemp drugs. The level of taxation was based upon the potency of the drug. As with so many taxes, it was claimed the imposition was to control consumption: at the same time, alcohol and tobacco were also taxed, supposedly for the same reason. In truth it was really aimed at raising revenue. Parliament had little genuine interest in the welfare of the native Indian population.

There was some debate as to whether or not to prohibit cannabis. The Indian ruling class blamed social unrest upon it but this argument was somewhat spurious. *Bhang* was too weak to cause much unrest whilst *charas* was too expensive for all but the very wealthy who were maintaining the *status quo* in any case. *Ganja* was cheap and used by the masses, so it came to be a scapegoat for any social problem, its suppression being called for. Even the British Governor-General wanted all drugs banned. The British declined. Cannabis was too good a source of tax income.

Up to a point, cannabis did raise some revenue but much of it escaped the taxation system. The British could hardly control the tax of a plant that grew as a common weed throughout the sub-continent. When, in 1838, the Colonial Office mooted an outright ban, Parliament devised a new means of taxation, based upon weight rather than hallucinogenic efficacy. It failed. Various states and cities tried different types of management. In Bengal, the authorities applied a quota to the sale of cannabis. In Bombay, dealers had to purchase operating licences, whilst in Lucknow places of sale had to be officially approved and certificated. Revenues trickled in but the whole system of control was a mish-mash of largely unsuccessful initiatives. What the British did not do was to trade actively in cannabis and establish an international market for it as they did with opium. Nor did they take it back home with them to Europe on any large scale. That responsibility was left to the other great trading nation of the time – France.

In order to illustrate his imperialistic and military superiority, Napoleon Bonaparte decided in 1798 to invade Egypt, his intention being to destroy British trade in the Middle East and, to some extent, the Orient. The invasion was only a partial success. Politically, it established French influence in Egypt and Syria, which then stretched from Turkey to the Red Sea, but militarily it was a catastrophe for the British destroyed the French fleet on 1 August at Abu Qir (now Aboukir), in what was later termed the Battle of the Nile. Without their navy, Napoleon's troops were marooned in Egypt.

It being an Islamic country, alcohol was unavailable. The French troops, without a supply of wine, acquired a penchant for hashish. So many started using it that in October 1800 a blanket ban was issued on all drinks containing hashish and any smoking of it. The troops largely ignored the order. Hashish drinks were then outlawed, with cafés that sold them being boarded up and their proprietors incarcerated. All hashish imports were impounded and burned. This had little effect as most of the hashish came into Egypt over land by caravan across the desert, well beyond excise control. When, finally, the British blockade was lifted and the French troops could return home, they took their knowledge and liking of hashish – and their supply – with them.

The properties of hashish were soon known in France. Not only returning troops told of its wonders but so did scholars who had either been attached to Napoleon's army or sent samples back to colleagues for analysis and experimentation. Already, by 1803, substances had been extracted from hashish in the laboratory by a Dr Virey, a French pharmacologist.

The scientific interest in hashish coincided with a renewed fascination with the Assassins, partly engendered by the French passion for conspiracy and partly by the increase in contact with the Muslim world brought about by the Egyptian/Syrian occupation. At the forefront of this revival was France's most important Arabic scholar, Antoine-Isaac, Baron Sylvestre de Sacy. Delving into the Arabic manuscript collection at the Bibliothèque Nationale, he unearthed previously unknown eleventh- and twelfth-century chronicles during his study of which he identified the word 'assassin' with hashish and the Hashshashin. He announced his findings in a paper read to the Institute of France on 19 May 1809 entitled *Memoirs on the Dynasty of the Assassins and the Origin of their Name*. Whilst he was correct in his etymology, de Sacy did not, however, appreciate the fact that this was a derogatory word and did not mean the Assassins were actual hashish users. Nevertheless, he consolidated – and brought into modern times – the belief that the Assassins had used hashish and lent them a further salaciousness by declaring that hashish caused not only ecstasy but also insanity leading to death.

Others were quick to jump on the Assassin bandwagon. *The Thousand and One Nights* was translated into all the major European languages: it quickly gained a licentious reputation and was in print for most of the nineteenth century. The Austrian orientalist Joseph von Hammer-Purgstall published his *History of the Assassins* in 1818. It warned of the pernicious corruption of secret societies and likened the Assassins to Jesuits, Freemasons and Knights Templar.

For those outside the realms of academia, the opportunity to see what all the fuss was about was never far away. Travellers freely brought hashish back from the Levant or Egypt: there were no restrictions on importation into any European country, not even excise duty. For those who could not journey abroad, there were domestic supplies. Just as pharmacists had stocked tincture of opium for several centuries so, by the 1840s, were they carrying hashish, usually suspended in an oil or heavy wine such as port or sherry.

At first, hashish taking was restricted to a small coterie of former French colonial troops and scholars but, gradually, it entered intellectual circles when it was thought it might enrich creative power.

# *A LA MODE DU HACHISCH*

BY 1820, INTEREST IN THE EXOTIC ORIENT WAS WIDESPREAD. CHINESE porcelain, silks and brocades were the height of fashion, Persian carpets adorned the floors and Indian tapestries the walls of the great houses of Europe, whilst Chinese and Japanese craftsmen were manufacturing items specifically for Western markets. All these tastes came together in what is arguably the most bizarre and tasteless building in Britain, the Royal Pavilion in Brighton, built in the 'South Hindoo' tradition with onion-shaped domes and Chinese wall paintings. With such fascination in foreign climes and cultures, it is hardly surprising there were those whose interest extended to cannabis.

The first British painter to sketch the monuments of ancient Egypt was David Roberts, a self-taught artist from Edinburgh, who went to Cairo in 1838 to paint and draw but became fascinated by the street scenes and life of the people. Of one picture, *The Coffee Shop*, he noted, *The visitors generally bring their own pipes and tobacco, but an intoxicating preparation of hemp is often smoked, and can be obtained in the low coffee-shops. When even taciturn Turks and Arabs become excited and boisterous in these coffee-shops it is due chiefly to the intoxicating fumes of this preparation of hemp.* Yet it was not artists who brought a focus to bear on cannabis, but writers.

At the turn of the eighteenth century, many writers turned to opium to boost their creative imagination. Some discovered it, and became addicted to it, through its medicinal use, but there were others who, not needing its pain-killing properties, took it to bend sensation and give themselves a new literary vision. The drug was to have a considerable effect upon European literature. Known as the Romantics and writing mostly between 1775 and 1835, these authors rejected previous literary convention and concentrated upon the importance of the imagination. Some of the greatest writers in European literature fell under opium's spell – Wordsworth, Pushkin, Coleridge, Shelley, Goethe, Keats, Byron and Scott, to name but a few. Some were to pay the heavy price of opiate addiction and come to wonder if there might not be another drug which was not so cruelly habit-forming.

At the forefront of the drug-taking writers was Samuel Taylor Coleridge. Addicted to opium when still a young man, he was not averse to experimenting with other drugs, partly in the vain hope that he might substitute one for opium. Amongst his circle of addicted friends was Dr Thomas Lovell Beddoes, a physician for whom drugs were of hedonistic as well as professional interest. Based in Bristol, where he ran the Pneumatic Institution in the fashionable area of Clifton, a clinic for respiratory and other illnesses in which patients inhaled various gases as a cure, Beddoes gathered about him others who shared his interest. Apart from Coleridge, these included the young Humphry Davy, later the discoverer of sodium, Thomas Wedgwood, son of Josiah Wedgwood the famous potter and inventor of silver nitrate photographic paper who financed the Institution, and Thomas De Quincey. Whilst employed by Beddoes, Davy discovered 'laughing gas' (nitrous oxide), which the doctor used to treat melancholia. Beddoes and his friends took nitrous oxide as an entertainment.

Wedgwood, a sick man who died at the age of thirty-four and who took drugs not only for pleasure but also in an eternal search for improved health, became curious about *bhang*. He approached Coleridge who, on 17 February 1803, wrote to him: *Last night I received a four ounce parcel letter by post . . . On opening it, it contained . . . a parcel, a small one, of Bang from Purkis . . . We will have a fair trial of Bang – Do bring down some of the Hyosycamine Pills – & I will give a fair Trial of opium, Henbane & Nepenthe. Bye the bye, I always considered Homer's account of the Nepenthe as a Banging lie.*

This interest in cannabis and other drugs might have remained within Beddoes' circle were it not for Thomas De Quincey, the prodigal son of a wealthy Manchester mercantile family who ran away from home, lived in poverty in London with a prostitute then, accepted back by his family, went up to Worcester College, Oxford with the intention of becoming, as he would have it, *the intellectual benefactor of mankind.* Whilst a student, he was prescribed laudanum (opium dissolved in fortified wine) for a bout of neuralgia and became addicted. In 1822, at the age of thirty-six, De Quincey published his autobiographical *Confessions of an English Opium Eater* which had appeared serialized in the *London Magazine* the year before. The book immediately drew considerable attention, going into detail about the effects of opium on the imagination and the considerable – and terrible – consequences of addiction. For the first time, the effects and dangers of narcotics were broadcast widely, to become a major matter for discussion at every level of society.

When De Quincey was sixty, still addicted to opium, he was given a sample of *bhang.* It was almost certainly not his first encounter with cannabis. Beddoes had investigated it decades earlier, having obtained some hashish from a contact overseas, at a time when De Quincey was involved with him in Bristol. The elderly De Quincey now decided to conduct his own experiments on cannabis with the intention of writing another controversial book, but his plan never came to fruition.

However, across the English Channel in France, there was an élite of writers who were using hashish. Like their British counterparts, they were seeking not only to stimulate the imagination but also to find the subconscious source of emotion which they were convinced was only viewed in dreams. The key to this inner world, they believed, was psychoactive drugs and, when they wrote about their experiences, they did so in great and intricate detail. That said, there must be a caveat attached to their writing about cannabis, for it was not uncommon for it to be taken in a drug cocktail. Additionally, it has to be borne in mind that these were writers in revolt against the mores of their time and intent on talking up the effects of what they considered was a new and wondrous way to arouse the creative mind. Nevertheless, their reports served a purpose for they were the first true cannabis experimenters who looked both subjectively and objectively at it, their opinions forming those still prevalent one-and-a-half centuries later.

The French writers referred to themselves as Le Club des Hachichins – The Hashish-Eaters' Club.

Experiments with cannabis in France centred upon a psychologist, Dr Jacques-Joseph Moreau, sometimes known as Moreau de Tours. A student of Jean Esquirol, one of the early founders of psychiatry, Moreau was fascinated by mental illness and hallucination, having had a nervous breakdown himself. He thought that if the cause of hallucination could be identified then mental illness could be treated, but this could only be done if he could experience what his patients underwent. To this end, he took hashish which he obtained during a journey to the Middle East and North Africa in the 1830s. In 1841, he commenced treating mental patients with hashish at L'Hôpital de Bicêtre on the southern outskirts of Paris, a former prison by now an asylum-cum-hospital which has the dubious reputation of being the place where the guillotine was invented. Four years later, he published his findings in a book entitled *Of Hashish and Mental Derangement*, stating that hashish calmed his subjects, helped them to sleep, suppressed their headaches and increased their appetites. From this, he deduced that mental illness was caused not by brain damage but malfunction, a concept that flew in the face of contemporary perceived medical thought.

Of eating hashish himself, Moreau wrote that it produced a great sense of true happiness, a euphoria akin to receiving joyful tidings. Yet he needed to be objective in his observations so, in the pursuit of scientific progress, he became hashish supplier to the members of Paris literary and artistic circles who were willing to try it, having heard of his experiments. The first writer he contacted was a friend, Théophile Gautier.

Pierre Jules Théophile Gautier was born at Tarbes in 1811. By the age of twenty-five he was both famous and infamous, his notoriety stemming from his novel *Mademoiselle de Maupin*. It told the story of a transvestite but it was the preface that established Gautier's reputation. In it, he praised those who sought new pleasures, who were willing to take risks in the chase for enjoyment; and he declared the manifesto for the French Romantics, which has echoed down the centuries: *Art for Art's sake*.

With Moreau, Gautier passed the word about hashish throughout bohemian Paris and Le Club des Hachichins came into being. The date of its foundation is uncertain but it was around 1843.

The club members met every month in an apartment rented by one of their number, the painter Fernand Boissard de Boisdenier, at the Hôtel Pimodan on the Île Saint-Louis. Originally built in 1657 by Antonin-Nompar de Caumont, the Comte de Lauzun, it had been a grand mansion at the centre of the early eighteenth-century Parisian social whirl but had, by this time, been sub-divided into apartments. Gautier occupied part of the attic. For a while, the poet Charles Baudelaire rented an apartment adjacent to de Boisdenier's, into which one could gain access through a secret staircase. The room in which the club convened had a door hung with a velvet curtain, the walls panelled and covered in discoloured gold leaf, the decorated ceilings domed, while the Pyrenean, red-and-white-flecked marble mantelpiece bore a clock in the shape of an elephant with a castellated howdah on its back. The furniture was dated and covered with faded tapestries. The hashish was served in Oriental porcelain dishes, handed out by Moreau from a crystal glass vase container. In every respect, the setting had an air of genteel decadence.

In addition to Gautier and de Boisdenier, the membership included at various times the writers Gérard de Nerval, Charles Baudelaire, Victor Hugo and Honoré de Balzac, and the painter, Honoré-Victorin Daumier. It is thought that the artist Eugène Delacroix and Alexandre Dumas, the author of *The Three Musketeers* and *The Count of Monte Cristo*, may also have been occasional visitors.

An informal association, members drifted in and out. Some remained regular attenders; others stayed only a short while. Gautier himself was a member for only a year or so, withdrawing because, he believed, a genuine writer did not require artificial stimuli to fire his imagination. Not all the members imbibed hashish. Gautier wrote of Baudelaire that he tried hashish a few times as a physiological experiment, but made no regular use of it, finding it repellent that one could buy one's happiness from a pharmacist. Baudelaire himself declared he only attended as an observer, although he was later to write of his hashish experiences. Similarly, Balzac preferred to observe but, in time, he succumbed to his curiosity, writing in a letter to his lover, Éveline Hanska, on 23 December 1845, that he had at last eaten some hashish and heard divine voices as well as seen heavenly visions.

The members ate hashish as *dawamesk*. Green in colour, it was a spread or jam which Moreau obtained from North Africa, made of hashish, almond paste, pistachio nuts, sugar, orange or tamarind peel, cloves and other spices: on occasion, cantharidin (powdered and desiccated blister beetles, *Lytta vesicatoria*, more commonly known as Spanish fly) was added as a sexual stimulant. It was usually taken with a meal, straight from a spoon or smeared on biscuits or bread. Once consumed and the main courses of the meal over, the members lay back on cushions and waited for the drug to take effect. Afterwards, they discussed their experiences, comparing them to those of other drugs such as opiates and considering how their imaginations had been affected. As with many drug users, there was a bond of camaraderie between them, but this was further joined by their political, social and artistic ideals which were to considerably impact upon French nineteenth-century thinking.

Yet their contribution to society extends beyond their art. They were the first to objectively and often dispassionately record the effects of hashish. Through their writing – especially that of Gautier and Baudelaire

– they brought a great awareness of cannabis to Europe. This was not done with any altruistic intent. Gautier knew the public were fascinated by the East and drugs and, by writing about them, he would gain a larger readership.

Surprisingly, the snowball of interest was set rolling not by a member of the club, but by an outsider. In 1843, a book entitled *Le Hachych* (*Hashish*) was published anonymously. It was a commercial success, being reissued five years later as *Révolutions Politiques et Sociales de 1848*, under the author's name: Claude-François Lallemand. A neuropathologist, he was the first person to study the functions of the frontal lobes of the brain, linking them to the power of speech. The book, a curious volume since described as a utopian anarchic narrative, proposed a new social and intellectual order. Supposedly translated from an Arabic manuscript the author found in his cabin when sailing to Marseilles, it starts with a dinner party at which a doctor, returning from Egypt and Ethiopia, passes hashish round to his fellow guests who then fall to talking about a political utopia. The basis of the argument is that hashish can give a sort of prophetic intimation of what the future might hold.

It may be that Gautier was influenced to write about hashish by reading Lallemand. His first piece on the drug was published on 10 July 1843 in a newspaper for which he was the theatre critic. It was a brief article which described the effects of hashish, outlining the hallucinatory effects and discussing what is now referred to as synaesthesia, the admixture of senses: Gautier wrote of seeing sounds and hearing colour.

Encouraged by the response of his readership and, no doubt, the success of Lallemand's book, Gautier wrote further on the subject. In 1845, he wrote an addendum for Moreau's *Of Hashish and Mental Derangement*, expanding it later that year into a longer story, the now famous *Le Club des Hachichins*, published in *La Revue des Deux Mondes* in February 1846.

It was in this story that Gautier was to write of the wonders of hashish. *I was experiencing*, he reported, *a complete transposition of taste. The water I was drinking seemed to have the savour of the most exquisite wine, the meat turned to raspberries in my mouth, and vice versa. I could not have told a cutlet from a peach.* He was later to add, *After several minutes, a general lack of sensation spread through me! My body seemed to be dissolved and transparent. Within my chest, I clearly saw the hashish I had eaten, like an emerald giving off millions of tiny sparks. My eyelashes grew ever longer without stopping and, like gold thread, rolled up on small ivory spinning wheels revolving completely alone with stunning speed. All around me flowed and rolled multi-coloured precious stones. In space, flower patterns divided ceaselessly as if in a kaleidoscope. At certain moments, I saw my comrades again, but distorted; they seemed as half men, half plants, with the pensive air of an ibis, standing on an ostrich's foot, beating their wings. So strange was this I was convulsed with laughter . . . I began to toss my pillows into the air, catching them, throwing them round and round with the alacrity of an Indian juggler.*

For all his elation, however, Gautier also issued a warning. Before eating hashish, he opined, it was *most important to be in a good disposition – both in body and mind – to be in luxurious and well appointed rooms . . . In such conditions it is probable, almost certain, the naturally agreeable surroundings will change into bliss, rapture, ecstasy, indescribable delight . . . but, without these precautions, ecstasy may readily turn into nightmare.*

Gautier's writing style was deliberately journalistic. That of his fellow hashish chronicler, Charles-Pierre Baudelaire, was – if still tending towards the literary – more to the point.

Born in Paris in 1821, Baudelaire had an unsettling childhood. His mother was a fervent Christian with the conviction of original sin and divine retribution. His father dying when he was six, he resented his stepfather, a soldier and strict disciplinarian. When he kicked against the traces and entered the world of bohemian Paris, Baudelaire's parents packed him off to India. It is possible he dabbled in cannabis and opium whilst abroad but, on his return in 1842, he moved into the Hôtel Pimodan where, within two years, he was a member of the Hashish-Eaters' Club. Intense, pensive and serious, he was in many respects a tragic figure, as was to show in his poetry, but he was also intrigued by the possibilities of altering states of consciousness, by imaginative or chemical means.

It was in 1851 that Baudelaire published an essay on wine and hashish in which he was critical of the latter, stating that wine exalted a man's will whilst hashish destroyed it, wine bringing joy but hashish isolation. Wine he regarded as part of French culture, whilst hashish was alien and he considered Moreau to be little better than an evil pusher, nothing more than a pimp for cannabis. In summary, Baudelaire believed wine to be the better stimulant to creativity. Seven years later, his literary reputation made with the publication of his collection of verse *Les Fleurs du mal* (*The Flowers of Evil*), Baudelaire published a lengthy article in *La Revue Contemporaire* which was later reissued as *Les Paradis Artificiels*. It was a powerful diatribe against intoxication as a means for seeking heightened states of consciousness, condemning those who used drugs for vicarious, as opposed to analgesic, reasons and reducing them to little more than vagrant drunks in the gutter. He was writing from first-hand experience.

An alcoholic, Baudelaire was enslaved to opium which he had first taken to address a stomach complaint. Certainly, his attitude towards drugs was biased by his own negative view of his personal addiction and the depression he frequently felt as a result of it, but he was nevertheless disparaging of those who felt they had to rely upon artificial means to get in touch with their true selves, emotions or imagination.

Baudelaire's description of the effects of hashish was impartial and accurate. At first, *hilarity, ridiculous and irresistible, seizes you. This seizure of groundless gaiety, of which you are almost ashamed, occurs over and over, cutting through intervals of stupor when you vainly try to recollect yourself . . . After a short time of quietude comes a cool sensation in the extremities* which could be so cold as to turn one into *a thinking piece of ice.* Next came lassitude and a weakness in one's limbs, one's hands would not move, the mind becoming filled with anxiety. Soon after this, the senses became more acute and hallucination followed in which shapes of surrounding objects distorted and *sounds put on colours, and colours contain music . . . It sometime happens that personality disappears and objectivity, the property of pantheist poets, develops so abnormally in you that your contemplation of exterior objects makes you forget your own existence, and soon you confuse yourself with them.* The imagination became turbulent. Finally, the eater grew resigned and in some cases slept. The following day, the body was gripped by fatigue to such an extent that Baudelaire recommended one did not attempt to take hashish unless one had nothing pressing to do. As Gautier had remarked (and as De Quincey did when writing about opium), Baudelaire noted that the effect of hashish depended upon the individual's psychological state. It did not present anything new but enhanced whatever already existed, good or bad. Comparing opium to hashish, he said the former was *a peaceful seducer,* the latter *a chaotic devil.*

Of Baudelaire's writing on hashish, Gautier was to remark after his death in 1867 how accurate his descriptions had been, reinforcing the understanding that hashish did not create ideas but merely reworked those which already existed in the mind.

Yet there is some doubt about what Baudelaire was actually taking. In his 1851 essay, he was to record that *haschish is made from a decoction of Indian Hemp, butter, and a small amount of opium.* It has also been mooted that Baudelaire was perhaps not as experienced a hashish eater as he would have his readers believe. There is reason to think that he read a doctoral thesis on hashish, *Hashish: an historical, chemical and physiological study,* written in 1848 by Edmond de Courtive, borrowing facts from it. He also used notes taken whilst talking to other hashish users, the work of Baron Silvestre de Sacy and a pharmacopoeia from which he copied extracts word for word.

Despite these reservations, Baudelaire's hashish writing is considered a vitally important addition to the literature of drugs. That he was neither an advocate of hashish nor a regular user of it is overlooked. Those who would attack hashish have used Baudelaire's general decline as indicative of its insidious evil, but that is misrepresentative. Baudelaire was a tragic figure from early in his life. An opium-addicted alcoholic, he was a failed suicide filled with self-loathing who regarded himself as a failure. His death, on 31 August 1867, was caused not by drugs but by the degeneration of his brain caused by syphilis which he had contracted as a young man.

A third member of Le Club des Hachichins also added to the corpus of hashish literature. Gérard de Nerval (the pseudonym of Gérard Labrunie), a close friend of Gautier's from their time in school together, was the son of an army doctor. His mother died when he was two and he was raised by relatives in the country, only returning to live with his father in Paris when he was twelve. At the age of twenty, he translated Goethe's *Faust*, which was to be the basis for Berlioz's opera *La Damnation de Faust*. After a failed love affair with an actress and her subsequent death, he went to the Levant, writing as a result *Voyage to the Orient*. Appearing as a serial in *La Revue des Deux Mondes* before being published in a single volume, it was not only a travel book but also a study of the society, history, mythology and religion of the region. In the book, de Nerval wrote an allegorical hashish story about a caliph with a double life, the implication being that the man's hashish use prevented him from separating fantasy from reality. He was further to record the effects of hashish eating in much the same tenor as Baudelaire and Gautier. A mystical Freemason, de Nerval additionally studied the history of the Assassins and Sufism – to which Freemasons believed their organization was linked – alarming his brethren by publishing facts about the Master Builder Hiram, a central figure in Masonic ritual, but, at the same time, augmenting his knowledge of hashish.

That de Nerval took hashish in the Hôtel Pimodan seems certain: it is also just as likely he used it on his travels. However, he was also addicted to opium, which he took to fend off bouts of depression, and spent much of his life in penury having frittered away an inheritance on a failed drama magazine. Like Baudelaire a gloomy figure, de Nerval was unstable and finally hanged himself from a lamp post on the rue de la Vieille Lanterne in Paris. He was forty-six.

Whether or not Alexandre Dumas was a member of Le Club des Hachichins, he still wrote about hashish, no doubt aware of the fascination it held for his readers. In *The Count of Monte Cristo*, Baron Franz d'Epinay meets an enigmatic stranger on the island of Monte Cristo who refers to himself as Sinbad. Guardian of a treasure hoard he has found, he lives in a cave which he has decorated in a fantastical manner to greet his guests. Upon his arrival there, Franz is served a meal and, after it, an ambrosial dessert of green paste resembling crystallized angelica. Shortly after eating it, Franz begins to hallucinate, imagining himself to have eagle's wings sprouting from his shoulders. *'Ah, yes,' said Sinbad, 'the hashish is beginning its work. Well, unfurl your wings, and fly into superhuman regions; fear nothing, there is a watch over you; and if your wings, like those of Icarus, melt before the sun, we are here to ease your fall.' He then said something in Arabic to Ali, who made a sign of obedience and withdrew, but not to any distance. As for Franz, a strange transformation had taken place in him. All the bodily fatigue of the day, all the preoccupation of mind which the events of the evening had brought on, disappeared as they do at the first approach of sleep, when we are still sufficiently conscious to be aware of the coming of slumber. His body seemed to acquire an airy lightness, his perception brightened in a remarkable manner, his senses seemed to redouble their power, the horizon continued to expand; but it was not the gloomy horizon of vague alarms, and which he had seen before he slept, but a blue, transparent, unbounded horizon, with all the blue of the ocean, all the spangles of the sun, all the perfumes of the summer breeze; then, in the midst of the songs of his sailors – songs so clear and sonorous, that they would have made a divine harmony had their notes been taken down – he saw the Island of Monte Cristo, no longer as a threatening rock in the midst of the waves, but as an oasis in the desert; then, as his boat drew nearer, the songs became louder, for an enchanting and mysterious harmony rose to heaven, as if some Loreley had decreed to attract a soul thither, or Amphion, the enchanter, intended there to build a city. At length the boat touched the shore, but without effort, without shock, as lips touch lips; and he entered the grotto amidst continued strains of most delicious melody. He descended, or rather seemed to descend, several steps, inhaling the fresh and balmy air, like that which may be supposed to reign around the grotto of Circe, formed from such perfumes as set the mind to dreaming, and such fires as burn the very senses; and he saw again all he had seen before his sleep, from Sinbad, his singular host, to Ali, the mute attendant; then all seemed to fade away and become confused before his eyes, like the last shadows of the magic lantern before it is extinguished, and he was again in the chamber of statues, lighted only by one of those pale and antique lamps which watch in the dead of the night over the sleep of pleasure. They were the same statues, rich in form, in attraction. and poesy, with eyes of fascination, smiles of love, and bright and flowing hair. They were Phryne, Cleopatra, Messalina, those three celebrated courtesans. Then among them glided like a pure ray, like a Christian angel in the midst of Olympus, one of those chaste figures, those calm shadows, those soft visions, which seemed to veil its virgin brow before these marble wantons. Then the three statues advanced towards him with looks of love, and approached the couch on which he was reposing, their feet hidden in their long white tunics, their throats bare, hair flowing like waves, and assuming attitudes which the gods could not resist, but which saints withstood, and looks inflexible and ardent like those with which the serpent charms the bird; and then he gave way before looks that held him in a torturing grasp and delighted his senses as with a voluptuous kiss. It seemed to Franz that he closed his eyes, and in a last look about him saw the vision of modesty completely veiled; and then followed a dream of passion like that promised by the Prophet to the elect. Lips of stone turned to flame, breasts of ice became like heated lava, so that to Franz, yielding for the first time to the sway of the drug, love was a sorrow and voluptuousness a torture, as burning mouths were pressed to his thirsty lips, and he was held in cool serpent-like embraces. The more he strove against this unhallowed passion the more his senses yielded to its thrall, and at length, weary of a struggle that taxed his very soul, he gave way and sank back breathless and exhausted beneath the kisses of these marble goddesses, and the enchantment of his marvellous dream.*

Dumas's idiomatic description did much to publicize hashish and its effects. His novel was extensively read, not only in French but also in translation.

With the death of the core members of Le Club des Hachichins – Gautier lived the longest, dying in 1872 – the mantle of hashish writing passed to a new generation. Both of the poets Paul Verlaine and Arthur Rimbaud, the founder of Symbolism, used hashish in addition to absinthe, a very strong, bitter and highly addictive green liqueur made out of distilled wine and wormwood, the plant *Artemisia absinthium*. Rimbaud, who fled his native Charleville in north-eastern France to get away from a dominating bigot of a mother, immersed himself in the decadent bohemian life of Paris. With Verlaine, who was ten years his senior, he made the most of his freedom, drinking, taking hashish and writing poetry: his first verse was published when he was sixteen. At about the age of eighteen, he wrote a prose poem about hashish entitled 'Morning of Drunkenness', sometimes referred to as 'The Time of the Assassins'.

By the age of nineteen, Rimbaud had fallen out with Verlaine (who had shot and wounded him, being imprisoned for his attempted murder), almost starved, joined the Paris Commune but left it just before it was ruthlessly put down by French troops and been reunited with Verlaine. After being mauled by the critics, however, he stopped writing and thereafter embarked upon a life as an adventurer, crossing the Alps alone and on foot, signing on for (and deserting from) the Dutch colonial army in the East Indies, visiting Egypt, gaining employment as a common labourer in Cyprus, becoming clerk to a coffee merchant in Aden and travelling throughout Ethiopia, being the first white man to visit the Ogaden. Of his own volition, he set himself up as a merchant in Ethiopia, selling anything from coffee to armaments. He may well have used hashish during these years: indeed, this is most likely as he lived in a culture in which hashish taking was a social activity and he was popular with the Ethiopians. He built up a sizeable fortune from his trade but never returned to the literary life, despite having a sound poetic reputation back in France, due to Verlaine's championing and publishing of his work in his absence. Early in 1891, a tumour appeared on his right knee. He returned to France, his leg being amputated almost as soon as he landed in Marseilles. After a brief spell at home, he set off back to Ethiopia but, reaching Marseilles again, he could go no further and died there at the age of thirty-seven.

The legacy of Gautier, Baudelaire, de Nerval and Rimbaud continued, however, hashish established in the consciousness of the public and the literature of France. It also spread across the Atlantic to the USA.

# THE PASTOR'S SON FROM
# POUGHKEEPSIE

BY THE MID-1850S, THE USA WAS EXPERIENCING AN UNPRECEDENTED literary renaissance and whilst most of the work produced was within the moral confines of society, there was much that was not and it caused some disquiet. Writing about drug-taking was one of the more *risqué* subjects, although the intention was, unlike in France, more to educate the reader than entertain him.

The availability of psycho-active substances in America was widespread and there was no control over either their retail or their usage. Most people took them for medicinal reasons, yet there were those who sought to experiment with them, not just in order to enhance imagination or amuse themselves but to scientifically investigate the substances. Even then, many wrote of their researches anonymously, not wishing to risk being regarded as self-indulgent sybarites. In a predominantly austere Christian society, drunkenness and immoderation prompted considerable and universal disapproval.

Bayard Taylor appears to have been the first American to write about eating hashish. A very prolific author and journalist on the staff of the New York *Tribune*, Taylor was first and foremost a poet and travel writer, although his metrical translation of Goethe's *Faust* led to his being appointed US Ambassador to Germany in 1878, the year of his death in Berlin. Sometime in 1851, after the success of two travel books on Europe and the Californian goldfields, he embarked on a journey to the Middle

East during which, having a journalist's curiosity, he tried hashish in Egypt.

In *A Journey to Central Africa*, published in 1854, Taylor described taking what seems to have been a weak dose of hashish for he wrote, *The sensations it then produced were those, physically, of exquisite lightness and airiness – mentally of a wonderful keen perception of the ludicrous, in the most simple and familiar objects . . . I noted, with careful attention, the fine sensations which spread throughout the whole tissue of my nervous fibres, each thrill helping to divest my frame of its earthly and material nature, till my substance appeared to me no grosser than the vapors of the atmosphere, and while sitting in the calm of the Egyptian twilight, I expected to be lifted up and carried away by the first breeze that should ruffle the Nile.*

Upon reaching Damascus, Taylor was to try hashish again, but on this occasion, under the misapprehension that it came in a standardized strength, he took a little more than he had in Egypt to see what would happen. In fact, he was given a much more potent variety and ate at least twice the normal amount. The result he recorded in his next book, *The Land of the Saracens; or, Pictures of Palestine, Asia Minor, Sicily, and Spain*, published in 1855. Not able to altogether abandon his journalistic skills, Taylor started by going into the Assassins' mythology before expanding upon his hashish experience. What began in a hashish paradise ended, however, in his being *plunged into its fiercest Hell.*

The first sensation he received was of a quick pulse of thrills followed by visions of the Great Pyramid of Khufu (which he had recently visited) and riding in a pearl boat over the desert under a multi-hued sky, the air filled with perfume and soft music. On seeing a sweet maker trying to cram a transparent jelly into a mould, he laughed uproariously, his tears transforming into loaves of bread. At this point, the hallucinations took a nasty turn. He felt he was burning up, a pitcher of water failing to slake a terrible thirst. Crying out for help, he thought his mouth was filling with blood which poured from his ears. From the room in which he found himself, he ran onto the flat roof of the house, his head dropping its flesh to leave him a skull. Returning to the room, he sank into a terrible despondency and a fear that he was going permanently insane. Finally, he fell into a troubled sleep for thirty hours, from which he occasionally awoke although without much comprehension. When the hashish finally wore off, he was left exhausted.

Whilst Taylor's literary style was still somewhat flamboyant, the message was clear. He considered he had been lucky to escape with his life and sanity intact and was issuing a warning that hashish was not as wondrous as others might have it. The sub-text was that, if one had to try it, one should be sure one knew what one was doing and did not overdose.

The September edition of *Putnam's Monthly Magazine* the following year carried an anonymous story entitled 'The Hasheesh Eater'. The main character, a lawyer called Edward who has similarly escaped from hashish in Damascus, aided by a former school friend, warns others about touching a box of hashish he has been sent from Smyrna. They, however, want to see the effect of the drug so Edward volunteers to show them. He hallucinates that he has murdered his fiancée and forswears the drug thereafter. It was a moral tale and well received, for it supported the prevailing social condemnation of all forms of intoxication. The anonymous author was Bayard Taylor.

Another year went by and a book appeared under a similar title. Its author was not Taylor but someone who had been experimenting with hashish for at least three years and who had read Taylor's travel books with great interest. His name was Fitz Hugh Ludlow.

A seminal figure in the literature of cannabis in the West, in some respects as important to it as De Quincey was to opium, most of what was known about Ludlow was confused or deliberately misinterpreted by those who wanted to either denigrate or laud the drug. This situation was only finally set to rights in 1998, with the publication of the first comprehensive biography of Ludlow, *Pioneer of Inner Space: The Life of Fitz Hugh Ludlow, Hasheesh Eater*, written by Donald P. Dulchinos.

Fitz Hugh Ludlow was born in New York City on 11 September 1836. His father, Henry Gilbert Ludlow, initially studied law but later abandoned this and enrolled in the Princeton Theological Seminary in 1821. A passionate convert to Christ, he was in 1826 appointed pastor of the Presbyterian Church on Spring Street in what is now the Greenwich Village district of New York. Three years later, he married Abigail Welles and became a committed supporter of and spokesman for the abolition of slavery. The year after the birth of his son, Ludlow took up the post of pastor at the Church Street church in New Haven, Connecticut. When the slaves embroiled in the Amistad controversy were imprisoned in the town and unjustly charged with murder, Pastor Ludlow took their side: a lynch mob severely beat him for his abolitionist views in a street in the state capital of Hartford. By the time Fitz Hugh Ludlow was five the family home had become a safe house on the Underground Railway, the escape route for runaway slaves heading for Canada, and he met his first 'passenger', a male slave called Isidore Smith whom his father baptized John Peterson to hide his identity. In 1842, Fitz Hugh Ludlow's family moved yet again, his father being offered the position as a pastor with the Presbyterian Church in Poughkeepsie, on the Hudson River sixty miles north of New York.

When he was thirteen, Fitz Hugh Ludlow's mother died. She had been in poor health for some time and her death was not entirely unexpected although it must have come as a shock to him. Thereafter, when not at school, the boy was academically and religiously educated by his father with whom he travelled both on Church business and preaching trips.

Now a precocious child, Ludlow read widely, wrote poetry and short stories and sketched accounts of his travels with his father. He also attended a number of educational establishments including Poughkeepsie Collegiate School, where, in 1850, he first had a piece of writing published in the school student magazine, of which he was occasional editor. Not surprisingly, bearing in mind his upbringing, Ludlow espoused a commitment to Christianity but, in his early teenage years, he also developed his own set of personal values, possibly as a rebellion against his father who had since remarried.

Some time in 1853, dividing his time between a seminary in Manchester, Vermont and home, Ludlow met an apothecary called Anderson who maintained his business in Poughkeepsie. How they came to be introduced is unknown but it is probable that Ludlow was sent to him for medicine as he was, like his mother, dogged by ill health. They struck up a friendship which was to have a far-reaching influence on the teenager's life. One day in the spring of 1854, he called on Anderson, whose shop was Ludlow's self-confessed *favorite lounging-place*, to discover his friend had taken delivery of some bottles of an olive-brown extract containing *Cannabis indica*. This was not cannabis *per se* but a medicinal tincture of hashish of which Ludlow had heard, having read about it in *The Chemistry of Life*, a standard reference book of the time. Already making upon himself, as he put it, *the trial of the effects of every strange drug and chemical which the laboratory could produce*, he set to experimenting with the extract.

Taking a two-gram dose, he set off home. As he walked through Poughkeepsie, he found himself *by turns in different places and various stages of being. Now I swept my gondola through the moon-lit lagoons of Venice. Now Alp on Alp towered above my view, and the glory of the coming sun flashed purple light upon the topmost icy pinnacle.* However, these marvels were soon to turn devilish. An incredibly evil face confronted him and he fled, reaching home to the sound of his own blood coursing through his veins. The whole experience terrified him. Although he had read texts on opium, and had studied the pharmacology of hashish, these had not prepared him for what he had undergone. Possibly, he had expected the soporific, lambent narcotic effect of opium but found instead something that truly – and actively – altered his perception. On reaching home, he took himself to bed but, as soon as he closed his eyes, *a vision of celestial glory burst upon me* filled with a crystalline stream of *discoursed notes of music which tinkled on the ear like the tones of some exquisite bell-glass*, a grand temple better than anything the ancient Greeks had built, a *congress of crones* knitting purple yarn, an immense cavern with its roof in cloud and an endless sea. The following morning, Ludlow woke to discover there were no lasting effects but, concerned that the drug might have damaged his mind, he consulted a doctor whom he swore first to secrecy. The doctor confirmed that no permanent impairment had occurred.

The pre-formed subconscious of the taker being the basis for his hallucinations, the images Ludlow received were extrapolated from his devout religious background and his fertile imagination which had been fuelled by his comprehensive reading and almost innate ability to tell stories.

Fascinated by the drug, Ludlow determined to continue experimenting with it, not only taking it in tincture form but also as a bolus, or large pill. His next session occurred about a week later. It ended in *a delirium which, unlike all that had preceded it, was one of unutterable calm . . . a clarifying of all thought, and the flowing in of the richest influences from the world around me, without the toil of selecting them. I looked at the stars, and felt kindred with them; I spoke to them, and they answered me. I dwelt in an inner communication with heaven . . .*

Through the summer months of 1854, Ludlow persisted, uninterrupted, with his experimentation, always in secret and without being found out. That September, however, he enrolled in the College of New Jersey, today known as Princeton University. He stayed six months, leaving in March 1855 after Nassau Hall, the dormitory in which he was resident, burnt down.

For some time, Ludlow had been going off the rails. His behaviour had been erratic, sometimes truculent and often supercilious or arrogant. There have been those who have blamed his drug experimentation for this character shift but this hardly seems likely. He was a clever youth, came from a repressively strict family background, had lost his mother, had had to accept a stepmother and had had a fairly itinerant life, moving from school to school. His behaviour was, therefore, more likely to have been that of a normal – but exceedingly clever – young man than someone whose mind was addled by narcotics.

After his departure from the College of New Jersey, Ludlow was sent to Union College in Schenectady. This was by no means a disadvantageous move for the college, founded in 1795 and the first to be chartered by the Board of Regents of the State of New York, rivalled Harvard and Yale. It also had a reputation for handling gifted but errant students.

The college president, Eliphalet Nott, an eccentric educational genius who was to rule over the establishment for half a century, exerted a great influence over Ludlow. Despite this, Ludlow was not always in Nott's favour, being fined for cutting classes. That said, it appears Nott himself, who was a strict disciplinarian, was not beyond bending the rules. To finance higher education and his college, he instigated a state-wide lottery but was accused of manipulating the results and charged with corruption.

As a student, Ludlow was regarded by his peers as being somewhat odd, sometimes aloof and superior, and at first not overly popular although he was generally found to be amiable, a proficient conversationalist and, on occasion, good company. Part of his detachment from his fellow students may almost certainly be put down to the fact that he was again experimenting with hashish, having found a pharmacist in the town who would oblige him.

Informed by the pharmacist that what he was providing was of a weaker strength than that which Anderson had supplied, one evening Ludlow took a heavy dose of fifty grains, about three grams. By midnight, nothing having happened, he went to bed only to wake in the night to *a realm of the most perfect clarity of view, yet terrible with an infinitude of demoniac shadows.* Soon, a funeral bier bearing a corpse surrounded by candles appeared at his bedside. He tried to crawl away from it only to discover the walls of his room were moving in on him, the ceiling simultaneously descending. After a short time, the ceiling pressed him against the corpse and all went black: then Ludlow found himself in the place of the corpse. A demon of white-hot iron chanted at him, accompanied by others. They vanished and Ludlow, with a powerful thirst, discovered himself by a vast fountain in a European village. Passing through a crystal gate into a rose-covered valley, he was greeted by a multitude proclaiming him their liberator. It was now he realized his soul had left his body but, later, a voice ordered it to return whence it had come.

To what extent the images related to Ludlow's recent reading is unknown but Dulchinos states that he had not long before read Edgar Allan Poe's *The Pit and the Pendulum*, which may well have partially governed his hallucinations. As for the metempsychosis, or extra-corporeal experience, this is not uncommon in near-death situations or under the influence of a number of drugs, including hashish and lysergic acid diethylamide (LSD).

The next morning, Ludlow felt refreshed but concerned by the demonic nature of his experiment. He vowed to *experiment with the drug of sorcery no more*. It was a vow he was soon to break.

After a while, Ludlow let a few of his fellow students in on his secret and they sat in on his sessions, partly to observe and partly to be there to comfort or steady him if required. In a comparatively short space of time, he discovered that continued and regular use of hashish caused his experiences to meld together, one leading into the next which began, as it were, where the last left off. His life became *one unbroken yet checkered dream*.

Ludlow's general academic studies seem not to have been adversely affected by his hashish 'habit', his overall grades neither poor nor spectacular, but there was one subject in which he excelled. It was called Kames and was taught personally by Nott. Based upon the book *Elements of Criticism*, written by Henry Home, Lord Kames, it offered a new approach to aesthetics with which Nott was in full accord. Part of this course involved the students reading their work aloud to their peers. Ludlow, already an accomplished storyteller with a vivid (and hashish-enhanced) imagination, was in his element. As a consequence, his literary skills were honed, aided on occasion by his letting himself and some of his peers into a local church, to which they could obtain the key, where they gave orations that were mutually criticized. He also wrote verse, including love poems to various fellow female students, contributed a poem entitled 'The Hymn of the Soul of Man' to the college student journal, *The New Era*, and penned the 'Union Terrace Song' for a student society. As a result of the latter, he was invited by Nott to compose an ode to the college. This he did. He called it 'Ode to Old Union' and, set to the tune of a traditional drinking ballad, it reads:

> *Let the Grecian dream of his sacred stream*
> *And sing of the brave adorning*
> *That Phoebus weaves from his laurel leaves*
> *At the golden gates of morning.*

> *But the brook that bounds thro' old Union's grounds*
> *Gleams bright as a Delphic water,*
> *And a prize as fair as a god may wear*
> *Is a dip from our Alma Mater.*

*[Chorus]*
*Then here's to thee, thou brave and free,*
*Old Union smiling o'er us,*
*And for many a day, as thy walls grow gray,*
*May they ring with thy children's chorus!*

This is still sung by the Union College student body today. Considering the visual imagery in the lyrics in the light of Ludlow's hashish experiments, this must make it the only college song in the United States to have been written influenced by dope.

With his literary skills enhancing his reputation amongst his contemporaries, not to mention his allowing a select number in on his secret, Ludlow was admitted into the Kappa Alpha Society, the first undergraduate fraternity in the USA. It was also a literary society which held weekly meetings throughout the college term at which literary, political and philosophical issues were debated.

Not only did Ludlow confess his hashish use to a select group of friends, but he initiated them into trying it. In part, he did this so that he might study their responses to it. Observing them under the influence of hashish, he concluded that hashish affected different personalities in different ways. From his research, for this is how he now referred to his experimentation, Ludlow deduced that the more powerful the personality the more intense the drug reaction. Quiet or introverted people – he described them as *lymphatic* – had lesser reactions, if any at all. Only vertigo, giddiness or nausea were, he noted, common to all.

By the time he joined his fraternity society, Ludlow was quite inured to whatever happened to him in his hallucinations. He had come to terms with the unexpected and, after a pleasant experience, would sometimes deliberately take another dose before the first had fully worn off, hoping this might prolong the euphoria. More usually, it turned his mind towards grotesque and terrifying visions. He did not feel guilty at conducting his research, nor for his introducing others to it, but it appears he did feel somewhat shamefaced at the subterfuge involved, his religious upbringing at odds with his newly formed, rebellious intellect.

In the spring of 1856, Ludlow was taking as much as four grams of hashish tincture at a time. Reaching such a dosage made him realize that his research had become more than mere experimentation: it was a habit. He determined to cut his dosage to two grams a day. Yet there was more to this decision than prudence. As Ludlow put it, there came *the appearance of Deity upon the stage of my visionary life.* An awful presence arrived during an hallucination in a vision, a projection from his subconscious of his father's Christian zeal and teachings. He started to see images of Heaven and hell and, in one, he witnessed the death of God which greatly unnerved him. More and more, he interpreted his hashish dreams in religious or spiritual contexts. His suppressed guilt was getting the better of him.

Ludlow graduated from Union College in June 1856. Of his time there, Nott was later to write, *He was considered here a young man of very decided talents, and unimpeachable character. Having completed his college course, he left the institution esteemed alike by his companions and his instructors, as well as distinguished by literary honors.* Clearly, the college president was either unaware of Ludlow's extra-curricular activities or adept at writing perfidious testimonials.

Returning to live with his father and stepmother in Poughkeepsie, Ludlow continued with his hashish taking, trying to keep his dosage down to between ten and fifteen grains a day, but he found it difficult. This made him realize he was addicted to hashish although he was not to know it was a psychological rather than physical addiction, such as he might have acquired from using opiates. On several occasions, he tried to give up hashish altogether but failed. The attraction of its hallucinations was too great for him.

Visiting a local bookshop several months after graduating, Ludlow picked up a copy of the September 1856 edition of *Putnam's Monthly Magazine* containing Bayard Taylor's article. Reading the piece, Ludlow was filled with hope. *For the first time in all the tremendous stretch of my spell-bound eternity,* he later wrote, *heard I the voice of sympathy or saw I an exemplar of escape.* He immediately wrote to the magazine and was put in touch with Taylor from whom he asked help to break his addiction. Taylor replied, offering encouragement. Ludlow did not immediately abandon hashish, but he heeded all Taylor said and a literary friendship commenced.

Now a graduate, Ludlow wanted to find employment, preferably in a job that would give him ample opportunity to read and write. He also hoped that whatever he did might remove the temptation to continue taking hashish. Teaching seemed apposite, so he applied for and was appointed to the position of classics teacher at Watertown Academy, a college preparatory school on the eastern shore of Lake Ontario in upstate New York. A month after taking up the post, he was published professionally for the first time. A poem entitled 'To the Lady with the Black Sail' appeared in a magazine called *The Knickerbocker*. Rich in drug imagery, it is a dark and brooding piece the first verse of which reads,

*As night the rosy bosomed hills unfolding*
*Softens their traces in his weird embrace;*
*So, more ethereal grew the matchless moulding*
*Of thy pure earnest spiritual face,*
*Most pensive maid,*
*Beneath the shade*
*Of that strange veil of melancholy lace.*

Regardless of this success and his new life as a schoolmaster, Ludlow still found he occasionally craved hashish and attempted to sublimate it with tobacco and, bizarrely, by blowing soap bubbles, the colours swirling on them reminding him of the marbling hues of his hashish hallucinations. At Taylor's suggestion, he also wrote down as many details as he could recall of his hashish dreams. Intended primarily as an exercise in catharsis, these were soon shaped by Ludlow into an article that was printed in the December 1856 edition of *Putnam's Monthly Magazine*. Headed 'The Apocalypse of Hasheesh', it was understandably published anonymously and broadly addressed the philosophy of hashish. It was Ludlow's premise that Pythagoras, the ancient Greek philosopher and mathematician, had used hashish with the members of his mystical brotherhood at Crotona.

At the end of his first term at Watertown, Ludlow was finding teaching not as he had anticipated. His responsibilities gave him little time to himself and the work load was grinding him down. Resigning his position, he returned to Poughkeepsie, determined to seek treatment for his continuing hashish craving. For a while, he tried to combat it with laudanum but soon gave this up, fearful of its potential for addiction: he saw no value in giving up one longing for another. Next, he tried alcohol but deemed it as pernicious as opium. Taking Taylor's advice, he settled down to concentrate instead on writing up the full story of his ensnarement by hashish. For four months, he worked constantly on what was to end up as a 365-page manuscript.

When it was done, Ludlow submitted it for publication to Harper Brothers in New York, one of the most prestigious publishers in the country. With virtually no revisions, it was accepted for publication on 1 July 1857. Entitled *The Hasheesh Eater, Being Passages from the Life of a Pythagorean*, it went on sale that November, priced at a dollar. A simultaneous publication was released in London by Sampson Low and Son to whom Harper Brothers had sold the European rights. The authorship was not attributed. By referring to himself as a Pythagorean, Ludlow intended it to be understood that he believed in the principle of metempsychosis and considered himself, like the mystical followers of the Greek philosopher, an outcast because of his convictions. It was his opinion that hashish was good for both body and soul.

As the title implied, the book was autobiographical, narrating Ludlow's hashish experiences in chronological sequence interspersed with lengthy comments on lessons learnt along the way. These included his opinion that hashish proved the existence of the soul and that there was a scientifically substantiated unity to all the senses which are in effect natural forces governed by a single law – his synaesthetic experiences whilst under the influence of hashish verified this theory. In the final chapter, Ludlow justified the attraction of drugs to men of ideas and genius. He demanded that society be *kinder in our judgment of the man who runs to narcotics and other stimulants for relief.*

What Ludlow had set out to do was to write a polemic about hashish, just as Thomas De Quincey had about opium in his *Confessions of an English Opium Eater.* That he had read and was much influenced by De Quincey, and possibly Théophile Gautier as well, is indisputable, although he lacked their more mature literary artifice and stylistic confidence. Graphically describing the misery of the user, Ludlow stressed how what was initially a transport to Paradise became a terrible snare which, in turn, led to a deeper understanding of oneself. The implication was that the rigours – no matter how horrendous – were ultimately a worthwhile price to pay. At the same time, however, one senses he knew he was addressing an audience with its mind already set: a society bound by parochial Protestant ethics which frowned upon alcohol and condemned any impious excess was never going to endorse cannabis.

The book was prominently reviewed in the November issue of *Harper's Monthly Magazine.* The reviewer, bearing in mind he was writing in the publishers' own journal, was hardly going to be too condemnatory, but his comments were not entirely laudatory: *Unequal to De Quincey in literary culture and in the craft of book-making, the author of this work compares favorably with him in the passion for philosophical reflection, in the frankness of his personal revelations, and in preternatural brilliancy of fancy.*

Yet there was more to the review than mere criticism. It aroused considerable public interest. Being one of the trend-setting publications of its day, *Harper's Monthly Magazine* reached many influential readers and was taken seriously. Other reviews followed which considerably swelled Ludlow's literary career. Almost every reviewer followed the original critic's line, comparing hashish to opium and Ludlow to De Quincey.

The book, which ran to a number of editions both in America and

Great Britain, brought Ludlow overnight fame and established his reputation as a writer.

Falling out with his father who could not accept his son's involvement with hashish, Ludlow left Poughkeepsie in 1858 for New York where, through a family acquaintance, he was employed as an assistant to a lawyer under whom it was intended he should also study law. His ambitions, however, were literary and he began regularly to visit Pfaff's Restaurant at 647 Broadway. Also known as Pfaff's Cave, it was a watering-hole for the city's up-and-coming actors, writers, journalists and poets who met there to eat, drink and talk. Their circle became known as the Bohemians. Here, amongst these dissolute, hard-drinking, hard-living literati, Ludlow found his intellectual level. Amongst the group was Walt Whitman, later to be one of America's most outstanding poets.

Resigning from what amounted to a legal apprenticeship, Ludlow turned his hand to freelance journalism but, always in poor health, he was forced to leave New York to convalesce from a bout of pneumonia in a health resort on the Catskill Mountains. There, he met an eighteen-year-old girl called Rosalie Osborn. Despite her parents' misgivings, they were married at Waterville on 15 June 1859. His health again failed and, shortly after the wedding, they moved for a while to Florida where the climate would ease his repeated bronchial illness. The following year, Ludlow's first novel was serialized in the recently founded *Harper's Weekly Magazine* and *The Hasheesh Eater* was reprinted. Continuing to write prolifically, he turned his hand to travel writing, critical journalism, poetry, scientific commentary and even playwriting. His stage adaptation of *Cinderella* was penned to raise money for the treatment of those wounded in the US Civil War. Yet his main forte lay in romantic, stereotyped fiction and short stories. His writing might have brought him increasing fame but it was not very lucrative and he accepted an editorial position on the *New York Evening Post* and a clerical job at the New York Customs House, checking the manifests of in-coming vessels.

By 1863, his health failing and his financial worries continuing, Ludlow decided he had to leave New York, if possible, for good. The most obvious direction in which to head was west.

Amongst Ludlow's friends from Pfaff's Cave was an artist called Albert Bierstadt. His reputation growing, a number of his rich patrons financed a painting trip across the continent. Bierstadt invited Ludlow to document the journey. He accepted, was awarded a commission from the Smithsonian Institution and the *New York Evening Post* to write his chronicle for publication and they set off, travelling by railroad and stagecoach.

*En route*, they hunted bison, met Brigham Young and Mark Twain, descended into a gold mine in a spoil bucket, visited an opium den in San Francisco and camped in Yosemite carving their names and the date on a rock. Reaching Oregon, Ludlow fell ill with the onset of tuberculosis and returned to New York by sea via Cuba.

Ludlow's articles on this odyssey greatly enhanced his reputation and made him a darling of New York society. For Bierstadt, his paintings made him a millionaire. Yet the trip had done Ludlow great harm. Behind his back, the artist had been conducting an affair with his wife. She and Ludlow separated and he quickly went downhill, drinking heavily and, possibly, eating hashish again, which he had abjured for some time. His work suffered, his editors rejected his submissions and he became all but destitute. With considerable self-determination, he pulled himself together and started to publish again, In 1866, he and his wife divorced. In less than six months she married Bierstadt. Ludlow then re-married the widow of a judge and continued to write.

One of his projects, written for *Harper's Monthly Magazine*, was an article on opium addiction, which subject he had been studying for some time, working with opium addicts. In October 1868, he contributed to a book entitled *The Opium Habit* in which he promoted a cannabis extract as a medicine to help overcome opium withdrawal symptoms.

All the while, he worked upon his notes of his trans-continental journey which were the foundation for his book *The Heart of the Continent*, published in 1870. Throughout the text he was meticulous in omitting any reference to Bierstadt.

Ludlow's health continued to decline and, eventually, his family decided to take him to Switzerland, then famous as a centre for the treatment of tuberculosis. He died in a house on the banks of Lake Geneva on 12 September 1870, the day after his thirty-sixth birthday. Five years later, his remains were returned to Poughkeepsie to be interred in the family grave plot. At his death, Fitz Hugh Ludlow's estate was worth less than one hundred dollars.

Although *The Hasheesh Eater* went out of print soon after Ludlow's death, it had a lasting legacy. Through Ludlow's fertile imagination, his detailed descriptions of his hashish experiences and his statement that he was addicted to it, hashish – a comparatively mild narcotic – came to be regarded as akin to the much more powerful and dangerously addictive opium, a misconception that has persisted to the present day.

# 9

# CANNABIS R$_{\text{x}}$

IN THE SECOND HALF OF THE EIGHTEENTH CENTURY, CANNABIS STARTED to appear in dispensatories, textbooks referred to by pharmacists and physicians in much the same way as modern chemists or doctors might consult The British National Formulary or the US National Library of Medicine MEDLINE website. It was most often recommended as an antibiotic and analgesic, the same applications as were suggested by folk remedies. This situation, however, was to change in the first half of the nineteenth century.

Word started to filter out of India about a wonder drug derived from hemp. One of its main exponents was an Irish doctor by the name of William Brooke O'Shaughnessy. Born into a staunchly Roman Catholic family in Limerick, he attended the University of Edinburgh from the medical school of which he graduated in 1830. Three years later, at the age of twenty-four, he went out to work for the East India Company, being appointed assistant surgeon in Bengal and professor of chemistry at the Medical College in Calcutta. From the very start of his employ, he realized the therapeutic potential for hashish and, after a period of intensive study of oriental texts on the matter and talking to native doctors and scholars as far away as Teheran, Cabul and Caudahar (Kabul and Kandahar), he started using animals to investigate it scientifically, especially dogs, of which there was, as he put it, *an over-abundant superfluity* in the streets of the city.

Not surprisingly, he found hashish affected canines much as it did humans. A dog given ten grains of hemp, O'Shaughnessy recorded, *became stupid and sleepy, dozing at intervals, starting up, wagging his tail, as if extremely contented; he ate some food greedily; on being called to, he staggered to and fro, and his face assumed a look of utter and helpless drunkenness. These symptoms lasted about two hours, and then gradually passed away.* Seeing the dogs suffered no lasting effects, he then tried it on human patients, concentrating on those with rheumatism, tetanus, cholera and epilepsy. Whilst the hashish did not offer a cure, it did prove to be an effective and valuable analgesic and sedative: it also, he reported, improved the libido.

Encouraged by this, O'Shaughnessy also dosed a rabies sufferer with two grains of 'hemp resin' an hour. Inevitably, for there was no known cure for rabies at the time, the patient died but O'Shaughnessy noted it seemed *evident that at least one advantage was gained from the use of the remedy – the awful malady was stripped of its horrors; if not less fatal than before, it was reduced to less than the scale of suffering which precedes death from most ordinary diseases.* The patient even took some damp rice, sugar cane and fruit juice. This was a remarkable achievement, for a rabid person suffers acutely from hydrophobia, an intense fear of water.

Six years after arriving in India, O'Shaughnessy presented the first medical paper – in the modern sense, of the research being objective and scientifically collated – to the Medical and Physical Society of Bengal. It was entitled *On the Preparation of the Indian Hemp, or Gunjah (Cannabis Indica): The Effects on the Animal System in Health, and Their Utility in the Treatment of Tetanus and Other Convulsive Diseases.* He was aided in his research by several medical colleagues and his brother Richard, who was also a doctor practising in Bengal. After discussing the history of cannabis and his mostly primary sources, O'Shaughnessy went into detail on his experimentation with animals and then gave case studies of patient trials, determining that hashish was *an anti-convulsive remedy of the greatest value.*

His paper, however, was to do more than medicinally promote hashish. It was also to dispel myths and provide succinct accounts of its use by native peoples. An avid scientific observer, he even went so far as to explain why hashish was greenish in colour (it contained chlorophyll) and to describe at length the method of making *majoon*:

The Majoon, or Hemp confection, is a compound of sugar, butter, flour, milk and sidhee or bang. The process has been repeatedly performed before me by Ameer, the proprietor of a celebrated place of resort for Hemp devotees in Calcutta, and who is considered the best artist in his profession. Four ounces of sidhee, and an equal quantity of ghee are placed in an earthen or well-tinned vessel, a pint of water added, and the whole warmed over a charcoal fire. The mixture is constantly stirred until the water all boils away, which is known by the crackling noise of the melted butter on the sides of the vessel. The mixture is then removed from the fire, squeezed through cloth while hot — by which an oleaginous solution of the active principles and colouring matter of the Hemp is obtained — and the leaves, fibres, &c. remaining on the cloth are thrown away.

The green oily solution soon concretes into a buttery mass, and is then well washed by the hand with soft water, so long as the water becomes coloured. The colouring matter and an extractive substance are thus removed, and a very pale green mass, of the consistence of simple ointment, remains. The washings are thrown away: Ameer says that these are intoxicating, and produce constriction of the throat, great pain, and very disagreeable and dangerous symptoms.

The operator then takes 2 lbs. of sugar, and adding a little water, places it in a pipkin over the fire. When the sugar dissolves and froths, two ounces of milk are added; a thick scum rises and is removed; more milk and a little water are added from time to time, and the boiling continued about an hour, the solution being carefully stirred until it becomes an adhesive clear syrup, ready to solidify on a cold surface; four ounces of tyre (new milk dried before the sun) in fine powder, are now stirred in, and lastly the pre-pared butter of Hemp is introduced, brisk stirring being continued for a few minutes. A few drops of attur of roses are then quickly sprinkled in, and the mixture poured from the pipkin on a flat cold dish or slab. The mass concretes immediately into a thin cake, which is divided into small lozenge-shaped pieces. A seer thus prepared sells for four rupees: one drachm by weight will intoxicate a beginner; three drachms one experienced in its use: the taste is sweet, and the odour very agreeable.

He added that:

Ameer states that there are seven or eight majoon makers in Calcutta — that sometimes, by special order of customers, he introduces stramonium seeds, but never nux vomica; that all classes of persons, including the lower Portuguese, or 'Kala Feringhees,' and especially their females, consume the drug; that it is most fascinating in its effects, producing extatic happiness, a persuasion of high rank, a sensation of flying — voracious appetite, and intense aphrodisiac desire. He denies that its continued use leads to mad-ness, impotence, or to the numerous evil consequences described by the

Arabic and Persian physicians. Although I disbelieve Ameer's statements on this point, his description of the immediate effect of majoon is strictly and accurately correct.

Visiting England in 1842, O'Shaughnessy gave some hashish to a London pharmacist called Peter Squire who owned a chemist's shop in Oxford Street, requesting that he make a medicinal extract from it. Squire duly made the first recorded extract of hashish in alcohol, patented it as Squire's Extract and put it on the market as an analgesic. Other pharmacists took it up and sold it under different names, including the famous James Smith of Edinburgh. It was his extract, made under licence in America as Tilden's Extract, that Ludlow discovered in Anderson's shop in Poughkeepsie a decade later.

Ironically, O'Shaughnessy is not best remembered for his medical work on cannabis, his place in the annals of medical history assured by his invention of intravenous electrolyte therapy, re-hydrating the body with a steady drip of saline, which he completed even before going to India. His major achievement in life, however, had nothing whatsoever to do with medicine. Fascinated by the 'electric telegraph', he published a paper on its potential at more or less the same time as he presented that on cannabis. It was ignored for eight years until the Governor-General of India, Lord Dalhousie, appointed him Director-General of Telegraphs. In this post, he oversaw the building of India's first telegraph network, being knighted for his work in 1856. Changing his name by royal licence to William O'Shaughnessy Brooke, he retired and abjured all interest in medicine, dying in the seaside resort of Southsea, in Hampshire, at the age of eighty in 1889.

Whilst Squire was almost certainly the first person to manufacture a medicinal tincture of cannabis, he was by no means the only pharmacologist experimenting with and investigating cannabis, the work encouraged by the recent successes in isolating morphine, nicotine and caffeine. All these substances, however, were alkaloids but, as cannabis contains no active alkaloidal compounds – and it was these for which the searchers were hunting – little progress was made.

Squire's Extract and medicines like it quickly became widely used. Doctors were keen to prescribe them because the only other effective painkiller they could offer was highly addictive opium and, it was soon realized, cannabis-based extracts were not physically addictive. Furthermore, opium was expensive and produced side effects such as chronic constipation, a lowering of respiratory and heart rates, excessive pruritis (itching) and loss of appetite. Cannabis appeared to have no adverse side effects whatsoever other than feelings of euphoria, drowsiness and hallucinations. By 1850, it was listed in a number of British and European pharmacopoeias and was, that year, included in the *United States Pharmacopoeia* with its application being appropriate for the treatment of neuralgia, tetanus, typhus, cholera, rabies, dysentery, alcoholism and opiate addiction, anthrax, leprosy, incontinence, snake bite, gout, virtually any disease that induced convulsions, tonsillitis, insanity, menorrhagia (excessive menstrual bleeding) and uterine haemorrhaging. This new drug gained much credibility when it was widely rumoured that even Queen Victoria had been prescribed it by her physician-in-ordinary, Sir John Russell Reynolds, who gave it to her to relieve menstrual cramps, but no documentary proof of this has yet come to light.

During the second half of the nineteenth century, scores of research projects were conducted upon, and papers published concerning, cannabis, doctors becoming extremely knowledgeable about the drug. Even before O'Shaughnessy presented his first paper on cannabis, the American Provers' Union, the professional body of North American homoeopathists, published an article on it in its journal in 1839. Seven years later, the editor of the *American Journal of Insanity*, Dr Amariah Brigham, reviewed Moreau's work and, acquiring some hashish from Calcutta, ran trials on some inmates of a lunatic asylum at Utica, in upstate New York. In 1860, the Ohio State Medical Society's Committee on Cannabis Indica reported on the efficacy of cannabis in treating stomach cramps, coughs, venereal disease and 'childbirth psychosis', now known as post-natal depression. Many other treatises followed, some more scientifically sound than others.

Yet, as the years passed, the research became more exacting and specific, meeting higher scientific criteria. In 1889, an article by Dr E. A. Birch in *The Lancet*, then as now one of the world's leading medical journals, outlined the application of cannabis for the treatment of opium and chloral hydrate withdrawal symptoms: the mixture reduced the opium craving and acted as an anti-emetic. The following year, an article appeared in the same publication by Queen Victoria's doctor, Reynolds. He declared cannabis *one of the most valuable medicines we possess* and ideal for treating uterine bleeding, migraine, neuralgia and epileptoid and choreoid spasms. He was not so sure of its use in cases of asthma, depression and delirium tremens and declared it of no benefit in instances of joint pain and epilepsy.

Those researchers not concerned with the purely medical application of cannabis addressed the reasons for its efficacy. An American, Hobart Amory Hare, suggested in 1887 he had found a reason for the analgesic properties of cannabis: *During the time that this remarkable drug is relieving pain a very curious psychical condition manifests itself; namely, that the diminution of the pain seems to be due to its fading away in the distance, so that the pain becomes less and less, just as the pain in a delicate ear would grow less and less as a beaten drum was carried farther and farther out of the range of hearing. This condition is probably associated with the other well-known symptom produced by the drug; namely, the prolongation of time.* He also noted how cannabis calmed the anxiety felt by sufferers of terminal illnesses.

Not all the researchers, however, were necessarily as keen to discover a strictly medical relevance. The foremost English pharmacologist and author of the immensely influential *A Manual of Pharmacology*, Walter Ernest Dixon, wrote in the *British Medical Journal* that *hemp taken as an inhalation may be placed in the same category as coffee, tea and kola. It is not dangerous and its effects are never alarming, and I have come to regard it in this form as a useful and refreshing stimulant and food accessory, and one whose use does not lead to a habit which grows upon its votary.*

For many in the latter half of the nineteenth century, cannabis and laudanum were as readily available as stimulants as coffee, tea or Coca Cola are today. What was more, they were cheaper than brandy, gin, whisky or tobacco and could be purchased freely from any pharmacist, or even grocery store, without prescription. For the poor, who could not afford a doctor's fees, cannabis was a boon, whereas for the middle classes – especially women in Britain – who considered alcohol to be masculine and working class, it was an acceptable tonic when taken as a proprietary or patent medicine. Yet, despite its cheapness and availability, cannabis never caught on as much as the opiates which were the drugs of choice, because it did not have an immediate effect. What was more, opium was considered respectable and widely available as laudanum or morphine in Battley's Sedative Solution or the baby-calming gripe waters Godfrey's Cordial and Mrs Winslow's Soothing Syrup, to mention but a few.

When cannabis was sold, it was in tincture form. One of the most famous British patent medicines of them all, Dr J. Collis Browne's Chlorodyne, contained morphine, chloroform and tincture of cannabis. Invented by an Indian army doctor as a palliative for cholera victims, it was sold as a highly effective cure for diarrhoea. It may still be bought today in Britain, without prescription: needless to say, it no longer contains cannabis and the morphine content, originally 2 grains per fluid ounce, is very considerably reduced.

As it was in Britain, so was it across the Atlantic. In America every pharmaceutical company was busy manufacturing cannabis-based patent cures: E. R. Squibb & Sons marketed their own Chlorodyne and Corn Collodium; Parke, Davis turned out Utroval, Casadein and a veterinary cannabis colic cure; Eli Lilly produced Dr Brown's Sedative Tablets, Neurosine and the One Day Cough Cure, a mixture of cannabis and balsam which was a main competitor for another new cough cure released by the German pharmaceutical firm, Bayer. It was trademarked Dreser and consisted of diacetylmorphine, more commonly known today as heroin.

It was not only in tincture form that cannabis was available. Pills of hashish coated with sugar to sweeten the taste and prevent them from adhering to each other were widely sold as common painkillers, much as paracetamol might be today. A mixture of marijuana and tobacco snuff was on sale as an asthma cure whilst in England in 1887, cannabis and Turkish tobacco cigarettes – in effect marijuana joints – were advertised in *The Illustrated London News* at 1s. 9d. a pack. As in America, where they were manufactured by Grimault and Sons as 'Indian cigarettes', they too were promoted as an asthma and cough treatment which could also dull facial pain and aid insomniacs.

Although the range of cannabis medicines was wide, there were several fundamental problems with them all which, in some instances, made doctors regard them with caution. The usual dose was between a quarter and one grain, but it was all but impossible to judge an exact dosage because the strength of the medicines, even from bottle to bottle of the same brand, could vary greatly. This was due to the difficulties encountered in processing the cannabis used in them. The 1854 edition of *The US Dispensatory* warned of the perceived dangers and consequences of overdosing and it was not until 1900 that a method of assessing strength was devised. Another disadvantage was that cannabis was insoluble in water which meant that it could only be eaten, not injected. This resulted in the effects taking up to several hours to begin. When the hypodermic syringe was perfected by Dr Alexander Wood of Edinburgh in 1853, opiates (which are water soluble) were readily injected intravenously and became the painkillers upon which most doctors and surgeons relied. This, in turn, reduced cannabis' popularity in the medical profession.

A third shortcoming was the fact that any cannabis preparation left standing for a while tended to separate out, with the cannabis forming a residue at the bottom of the bottle. If it was not shaken vigorously, the patient receiving the last inch or so of the contents of the container tended to be heavily overdosed. This led to reports being published in medical journals of cannabis poisoning, which was counteracted by the patient having his stomach pumped or being fed a powerful emetic to promote vomiting, followed by brandy, water, a strong stimulant such as black coffee and acidic liquids such as lemon or lime juice and vinegar. That these instances were not ones of actual poisoning – in that cannabis is non-toxic – but merely overdosing to the extent of creating considerable hallucinogenic reaction, and that not one fatality was recorded as a result, was overlooked. Doctors, already wary of the dangers of opiates, became over-cautious.

There was a method whereby the overdosing problem could be addressed. It was to titrate the cannabis solution to determine its strength. This is a technique in chemical analysis whereby a reagent of known concentration is added to the liquid under test until the moment when the chemical reaction between the two liquids either ceases or commences.

Responding to correspondence in *The Lancet*, Sir John Russell Reynolds, who had been using cannabis on his patients for much of his professional life, suggested any treatment should begin with a very weak dose, the potency being gradually and carefully increased over three or four days, each dose being titrated. *With these precautions,* he wrote, *I have never met with any toxic effects, and have rarely failed to find, after a comparatively short time, either the value or the uselessness of the drug.*

However, titration is a time-consuming process which requires specialized if fairly simple equipment and, for many doctors, it was a procedure with which they could not be bothered, considering the strength of opiates were, if still not exact, more reliable.

Aware of these drawbacks, pharmacists increased their efforts to extract the active ingredients of cannabis which, if they could isolate them, they could use to standardize quality. In 1881, two Americans called Siebold and Bradbury, applying the same method as they had used for extracting nicotine from tobacco, managed to obtain a syrupy yellow liquid which they termed cannabinine. Two other American chemists, Warden and Waddell, repeated their process three years later, confirming their results. A decade later, a pharmacist called Robert separated out a dark red syrup which he found possessed the ability to intoxicate. A number of other substances were extracted and named – cannabene, cannabinnene, cannabin tannin, cannabindon, cannabinon, cannabin, cannabine – but no one was quite sure which if any of these was the substance they sought.

Finally, in 1895, T. B. Wood, W. T. N. Spivey and T. H. Easterfield, research chemists at the University of Cambridge, made a breakthrough. Working with what they termed 'a red oil' extracted by a method of vacuum distillation from Indian hashish, they isolated a relatively impure extract which they named cannabinol. A viscous resin, it turned into an oily liquid on gentle heating and induced delirium if eaten. For the next forty years, this was considered to be the psycho-active element in cannabis. In 1897, further research by an analytical chemist called C. R. Marshall proved that cannabis lost its potency over time due to oxidation. With these discoveries, the stage was set for the pharmaceutical industry to assay accurately any drug but, for cannabis, this all came too late.

What finally put paid to cannabis as a viable medical product was the emergence of synthetic drugs created from the massive advances in chemistry made especially during the last thirty years of the nineteenth century. That these synthetics were often far more harmful than natural cannabis was considered by the way. It was the age of science, optimism and faith in scientific potential and infallibility overruling sensible judgement. When, in the mid-1880s, antipyrine and acetanilide appeared, the writing was on the wall. Five years later, a new drug developed from the research into these was put on sale for the first time. Its chemical name was acetylsalicylic acid but its trade name was aspirin.

For a few years, patent medicines containing cannabis tincture were still taken to alleviate muscle cramps and insomnia but this was not to last. The British Medical Association instigated a campaign against patent medicines with their 'secret' ingredients, thereby striving to eradicate the use of opiates, cocaine and cannabis from non-prescription tonics and potions. Through this campaign, doctors became more aware of the new synthetics and, at the same time, became responsible for the distribution of drugs to patients through organized prescription systems. Dispensing chemists also became more professional and started to issue only quality-controlled substances.

Cannabis had had its medical day and a great medicinal opportunity had been missed.

# 10

# LOOSENING THE GIRDERS
# OF THE SOUL

FOR MOST PEOPLE IN NINETEENTH-CENTURY EUROPE OR AMERICA, cannabis only existed in medicines and, for the vast majority of those, there was little realization that what they were taking in their patent tonics was the exotic plant featured in *The Thousand and One Nights* or the legend of the Assassins. Yet there were those who did know of the connection and, for them, cannabis provided more than a relief from migraine or muscle spasms.

In 1857, a Dr John Bell, writing in the *Boston Medical and Surgical Journal*, commented on the proliferation of articles in the press appertaining to hashish and discussing its effects. He seemed to imply that there were, following in Ludlow's wake, an increasing number of his fellow American citizens experimenting with the drug. His implication was correct. Cannabis was being used by some outside the strictly medical sphere.

When *The Marriage Guide; or, Natural History of Generation: A Private Instructor for Married Persons and Those about to Marry, both Male and Female* was published in 1851, written by a quack doctor called Frederick C. Hollick of Philadelphia, it advised readers to write in for the author's patent aphrodisiac. It contained hashish and, with the book which was re-published in nearly two hundred subsequent editions, made Hollick's fortune. This was not the only time cannabis was recommended to those in wedlock. Some women's temperance societies advocated it in place of alcohol: their reasoning was that drunks hit their wives, but cannabis users did not. At the American Centennial Exposition of 1876, in Hollick's home town of Philadelphia, there was a Turkish hashish stand at which passers-by could try it out: pharmacists throughout the town stocked up in anticipation of an increase in demand.

Confectioners also produced cannabis candy. The Gunjah Wallah Company of 476, Broadway, New York, was the first, offering the *Arabian Gunje of Enchantment confectionised – A most pleasurable and harmless stimulant* in about 1864. Guaranteed to be *a complete mental and physical invigorator* bringing new life and energy to every class of person, it sold in twenty-five-cent and one-dollar boxes and was still on the market in 1900. Dr George Grover Wheelock, the author of *Shadows Lifted or Sunshine Restored in the Horizon of Human Lives: A Treatise on the Morphine, Opium, Cocaine, Chloral and Hashish Habits*, published in 1894, tried a piece of the company's product in Baltimore, walking *en route* for a dinner party. The effects hit him at the meal, during which he described his experiences to his fellow diners, including an hallucination of hundreds of singing canaries in golden cages.

In the decades after the US Civil War, cannabis use in America became accepted. It was seen neither as anti-social nor as a serious weakness of character, such as was considered alcohol abuse. Indeed, drug-taking in general, for other than medicinal purposes, was not universally frowned upon. For example, morphine addiction rates rose rapidly after 1865, partly because wounded or sick veterans of the Civil War were returning home addicted, having been given morphine in military hospitals, and partly because the widows of men killed took to morphine to drown their sorrows, in preference to socially deplored alcohol. Mrs Henry Lafayette Dubose, the widowed neighbour in Harper Lee's novel *To Kill a Mockingbird*, shows how addicts were regarded by society as late as the 1930s when the novel was set: she is portrayed as courageous and a figure of sympathy, not one of derision or disgust.

The prevalence of cannabis soon entered mainstream literature. Louisa M. Alcott, the author of *Little Women*, used cannabis as a centre pin in the plot of her short story *Perilous Play*, published in 1869 when she was fast becoming the darling of the American literary scene. Although the story first appeared anonymously, she was clearly not worried that writing about cannabis would harm her burgeoning reputation. There is no mention in her private papers of her ever having taken cannabis herself, but it is possible. In 1862, she volunteered to serve as a nurse to wounded Civil War soldiers and caught typhoid, from which she almost died. The medication she was prescribed gave her mercury poisoning, but it is feasible to assume she may also have been given cannabis. Her familiarity with the form of cannabis taken by the hero in her story suggests she also knew of it as a medicine, for she describes it as being a white (probably sugar-coated) 'bean' with a green centre, a number being needed to have an effect. Dr Meredith, the fictional supplier of the beans, which he refers to as *despised bonbons*, suggests *any bashful young man to take hashish when he wants to offer his heart to any fair lady, for it will give him the courage of a hero, the eloquence of a poet, and the ardor of an Italian*. And so it is for the story's hero, who gains his true love in such a fashion.

On the whole, although hashish use was not illegal, those who indulged preferred to do so in private, the public munching of candy aside. When stories about hashish appeared in the popular press, they tended to be condemnatory, linking the drug to the titillating and sensationalist exoticism of other substances such as opium with its notorious underworld of dives and dens. The December 1876 issue of *The Illustrated Police News*, a tabloid journal that reported the underbelly of American society, contained an illustration captioned 'Secret Dissipation of New York Belles: Interior of a Hasheesh Hell on Fifth Avenue'. It depicted five upper-class women sprawled semi-conscious on divans. It was the first the general public knew of the existence of 'hasheesh houses' which catered for the well-to-do thrill-seeker.

Such establishments were again the centre of attention in November 1883 when an article appeared in *Harper's Monthly Magazine*. Published anonymously, it was actually written by a well-known doctor, H. H. Kane, who had published a number of texts on what he considered the danger of drugs to American society. Entitled 'A Hashish-House In New York: The Curious Adventures of an Individual Who Indulged in a Few Pipefuls of the Narcotic Hemp', it concerned a house on 42$^{nd}$ Street, between Broadway and the Hudson River in the area of the city known colloquially as Hell's Kitchen. Here, the two men about whom the story revolved entered a shabby-looking building to find a number of wealthy New Yorkers of both sexes wearing masks or oriental costumes and eating or smoking hashish. Paying two dollars for some hashish, the visitors are given silk smoking robes with tasselled hats and felt slippers in place of their street shoes. Shown upstairs, they are ushered into a sumptuously appointed room where, Kane wrote, above deep-pile carpets hung *a magnificent chandelier, consisting of six dragons of beaten gold, from whose eyes and throat sprang flames, the light from which, striking against a series of curiously set prisms, fell shattered and scintillating into a thousand glancing beams . . . upon*

100

*the floor, were mattresses covered with different-colored cloth, and edged with heavy golden fringe. Upon them were carelessly strewn rugs and mats of Persian and Turkish handicraft, and soft pillows in heaps. Above the level of these divans there ran, all about the room, a series of huge mirrors framed with gilded serpents intercoiled, effectually shutting off the windows.* In addition, pots of exquisitely scented plants grew here and there, vines clambered over the walls, the hall lamp was *grotesquely shaped* and even the staircase balustrade was *of curious design.* Kane continued, *Swallowing two of the lozenges, my guide filled our pipes, and we proceeded to smoke, and watch the others . . . As I smoked, the secret of that heavy sickening odor was made clear to me. It was the smell of burning hashish.* How truthful Kane was being is open to conjecture. With an anti-drug agenda in mind, his intention was plainly to highlight the debauchery of the place and there are moments when he seems to be exercising not a little poetic licence. It is highly unlikely that he would have eaten *and* smoked hashish at the same time. The pipe he describes seems more like an opium pipe than a chillum or tobacco pipe and he makes no mention of the burning sensation of the smoke that he must have experienced. And, to cap it all, as well as smoking his hashish pipe and eating his hashish lozenge, he also drinks a cup of 'Paraguay tea', an infusion of coca leaves. When he describes his hallucinations he might be paraphrasing Ludlow. What Kane hoped his article would do was imply that hashish houses were not just degenerate but also widespread. They were not, although by the 1880s, there were a number of such places secreted away in the major cities of America, mostly patronized by the well-to-do professional classes.

In Britain, matters were different. Medicinal cannabis was commonplace but any frivolous use of the drug was rare. There were no hashish houses in London – or any other city – and no outpouring of literature as there was in France or the USA. There did, however, appear in print a number of references to cannabis. In 1848, the weekly *Chambers' Edinburgh Journal* contained an anonymous piece warning against the hashish menace currently sweeping France. Then, in 1850, David Urquhart, Member of Parliament for Stafford, published his two-volume travel book *The Pillars of Hercules, A Narrative of Travels in Spain and Morocco,* in which he outlined his personal experience of hashish, stressing that he was not endorsing it. He was, nevertheless, an *aficionado* of things oriental: in 1862, he oversaw the building of the Hammam, Britain's first Turkish bath, at 76 Jermyn Street in London.

Whether Urquhart approved of hashish or not, other writers were convinced it was not posing a problem to British society. An anonymous contributor to *Little's Living Age Magazine* in 1858 said the English were at no risk of becoming *opium or hashish debauchies* and other writers supported this premise. Indeed, it posed so little concern that it appeared in the best-known children's book of the age. When Lewis Carroll's Alice, in her *Adventures in Wonderland*, published in 1865, *stretched herself up on tiptoe and peeped over the edge of the mushroom . . . her eyes immediately met those of a large blue caterpillar, that was sitting on the top with its arms folded, quietly smoking a long hookah, and taking not the slightest notice of her or anything else*. No major polemicist appeared either, although one anonymous book, *Confessions of an English Hashish-Eater*, was published in London in 1884. As the title might suggest, it was in poor imitation of De Quincey and Ludlow, and declared hashish to be benign. There is a strong chance that the author was Arthur Machen who published his first book, *The Anatomy of Tobacco*, with the same publisher, George Redway of Covent Garden, in that same year. Furthermore, Machen was employed by Redway as an editor on his magazine, *Walford's Antiquarian*. The book did not gain a wide readership and sank without trace.

As a nation the British, whilst not dismissive of drug-taking, preferred alcohol which was not looked down upon as it was in the more puritanical USA. That said, there was some recreational drug use. Sir Richard Burton, the famous Arabic scholar and explorer, mentioned in 1885 having heard of a *hashish-orgie* in London and, indeed, he took it himself on his journeys in the Middle East: he was the first white man to visit Mecca, disguised as a Muslim pilgrim. According to an entry in *A System of Medicine*, published in 1900 and edited by R. C. Albutt, there had occurred an instance in 1886 when some students at the University of Cambridge, obtaining an imported hashish candy called Turkish Delight, had overdosed upon it and fallen ill. Ernest L. Abel, in his seminal study, *Marijuana – The First Twelve Thousand Years*, lists other confections that were being imported into Britain in the late nineteenth century, including Bird's Tongue, Saffron and the intriguingly named Crocodile Penis which played upon the Eastern belief that a crocodile's genitalia were a powerful aphrodisiac if eaten.

The very small number of English cannabis experimenters tended to belong to minority groups such as intellectuals and students. The intellectuals – artists, writers, musicians – were, as has always been the case, seeking illusory truths and pushing on the boundaries of their artistic universes.

It was towards the end of the nineteenth century that the cannabis atmosphere that had infected France fifty years before came to impact upon Britain. The main protagonists of this new direction were a loose association of predominantly writers to whom the Irish poet William Butler Yeats gave the appellation The Tragic Generation. The main players were Yeats himself, Oscar Wilde, Aubrey Beardsley, Havelock Ellis, Arthur Symons, Richard Le Gallienne, Ernest Dowson and Selwyn Image. Conceding to Gautier's principle of art for art's sake, they were keen to establish a new literary order in which morality was not important. Their search used drugs not only as a source of visionary ideas but also as a means to stave off the mundane. As Verlaine and Rimbaud had, they also frequently used absinthe, which was Wilde's favourite tipple. Yeats, Dowson and Havelock Ellis all used hashish at various times, the former two also using mescaline, an alkaloid hallucinatory derived from a cactus, *Lophophora williamsii*, found growing in Mexico and southern Texas.

Yeats may have seen his group of friends as a tragic generation but outsiders dubbed them the Decadents. They lived, by the mores of their day, dissolute lives devoid of moral ethics and rich in self-indulgence and, if not heretical, then certainly irreligious activities: many of them, and especially Yeats, were fascinated by the occult, spiritualism and the mythological history of Britain, particularly the Celtic. Drugs were not a part of their social lives, as hashish had been for Le Club des Hachichins, nor did they write about them. They were considered a chemical means to an artistic end, albeit one that whilst not illegal was still a slap in the face of accepted social convention.

In 1890, Yeats and Ernest Rhys founded the Rhymers Club in London, a literary clique which they intended should be the British equivalent of the French Symbolists and which attracted a large number of up-and-coming writers. They met frequently, to read and criticize each other's work, discuss literature and flout convention, in an upper room at the Cheshire Cheese, a tavern in Wine Office Court off Fleet Street. Only Yeats and Oscar Wilde, who was an occasional rather than a dedicated member, went on to literary fame and the club ceased to exist in 1894.

Whether or not hashish was used at Rhymers Club meetings is hard to determine. Some sources claim it was; others refute it. Much of the activity of the club has become shrouded in literary myth. Whatever the truth, it is certain that Yeats indulged in hashish and, for a short while, laudanum. He and Maud Gonne, his lover, used hashish in an attempt to make themselves telepathic, whilst she used it to counteract bouts of insomnia. Over the winter of 1895, Yeats shared lodgings with Arthur Symons in the Temple, London's select legal enclave across Fleet Street from the Cheshire Cheese. It was at this time that Yeats completed *The Secret Rose*, a collection of stories containing both opium and hashish imagery. Three years later, in Paris in the spring of 1898, Yeats took hashish with a group of Martinists, occultists who followed the French mystic and philosopher Louis Claude de Saint-Martin. The group adhered to a system of mystical Christian Illuminist philosophy which aimed to return mankind to its original divine state. Amongst the members was A. E. Waite, one of a number of occultists whom Yeats came to know closely. Fascinated by the supernatural, Yeats joined The Theosophists in 1887 after meeting its founder, Madame Blavatsky. He was also initiated into the Isis-Urania Temple of The Hermetic Order of the Golden Dawn on 7 March 1890 at 17, Fitzroy Street, London, which used hashish ritually.

Helena Petrovna Blavatsky, the Russian-born daughter of an army officer and a novelist, and the granddaughter of Princess Helena Dolgorukov, began the Theosophical Society in New York in 1875. An eccentric polymath, she had travelled widely, earning her living by teaching piano, working in a circus, acting as assistant to the famous spiritualist medium D. D. Home and becoming a medium herself. She also used hashish which played a substantial role in her attaining the occult visions which formed the foundations for her most important work, *Isis Unveiled*, later famously republished in 1877 as *The Secret Doctrine*. A tomic study of magic, mysticism and religion, it took her two years to write, working long hours every day, almost chain-smoking hashish and black Russian tobacco cigarettes.

For Yeats, drugs were a method of entry into the occult as much as a way of inducing visions of literary value. Symons, on the other hand, was a hedonistic literary drug user whose better poetry is rife with drug imagery. Ernest Dowson, of whom Symons was to become biographer and whom he described as *the archetypal young poet who lived in squalor and produced beauty from his wretchedness*, was steeped in drugs. From a wealthy background, he wasted away his student years at Oxford with alcohol and hashish and entered literary London as something of a dandy, always dressed in the height of literary fashion. Suddenly, however, Dowson abandoned this lifestyle, turning almost hermit-like in a ramshackle house where he drank absinthe and took opiates in abundance. He died in 1900, at the age of thirty-two, consumptive and an addict. Symons recalled visiting his friend one afternoon and being offered a cup of tea, cake, cigarettes and hashish.

Dowson was present in Paris in 1896 when Henri de Toulouse-Lautrec and Leonard Smithers, publisher to many of the Decadents, persuaded the artist Aubrey Beardsley to try hashish for the first time. Beardsley ate a piece of hashish but, finding it had no immediate effect, felt disappointed. Some hours later, however, he came under its influence at dinner in a restaurant with the others. Dowson wrote of the event, *Luckily, we were in a cabinet or I think we would have been turned out – for Beardsley's laughter was so tumultuous that it infected the rest of us – who had not taken haschish & we all behaved like imbeciles.* When Ludlow's *The Hasheesh Eater . . .* was reprinted in London in 1903, Beardsley's illustrations graced it. He, however, did not live to see it, dying in 1898 of tuberculosis at the age of twenty-five.

Of The Tragic Generation, one person was to seriously investigate drugs. It was Havelock Ellis, today remembered for his pioneering studies in the psychology of sex but who, in the 1890s, conducted extensive research into mescaline. Two of his guinea pigs were Yeats and Dowson, given the drug in order that Ellis might study the psychological relationship between dreams and drugs. He also tested hashish on them and on John Addington Symonds, the poet, biographer and Renaissance historian. In time, Ellis built up a small following of people dedicated to joining in his experiments but, for many, drugs had another, equally valid, purpose. It was, as Yeats had discovered, to probe the unknown.

Throughout the later decades of the nineteenth century, interest in the occult had expanded almost exponentially. By the turn of the century, alchemy, mysticism, spiritualism, witchcraft, magic and astrology were all being investigated, practised and performed by a large number of esoteric groups. Some were driven by genuine quasi-scientific or philosophical curiosity, some by a search for an alternative religion or theology and some by way of devising a thinly disguised spiritual opening into the realms of debauchery and sexual promiscuity. Amongst those at the fore-front of the occult use of drugs, along with A. E. Waite and Yeats, was the most famous (or infamous) 'black magician' of them all, Aleister Crowley.

Born on 12 October 1875 in the genteel town of Leamington Spa, Edward Alexander Crowley was the son of a pietistic and prominent Plymouth Brother and teetotaller who, hypocritically, not only invented a brewing machine but also owned a large brewing company. As a young child, Crowley travelled the countryside with his father, proselytizing, preaching on street corners and 'doing the knock', calling on house-holders to sell them tracts and persuade them to follow the Brethren's way towards salvation and away from the demon of alcohol. His father dying when he was eleven, Crowley had a chequered school career under the eye of his sanctimonious mother and uncle after which he went up to the University of Cambridge. Receiving several inheritances totalling over one hundred thousand pounds (the equivalent of £6.5 million in 2002), he embarked upon a life of considerable self-indulgence centred upon his fascination with the occult. Like Yeats, he joined The Golden Dawn, then quarrelled with Yeats and others, split from it and, in time, founded his own occult religion, the Ordo Templi Orientis or OTO, in the magical rituals and sexual magic rites of which a number of drugs, including hashish, played a vital part.

Crowley was probably first introduced to the occult potential of psycho-active chemicals in 1899 by Allan Bennett. Three years older than Crowley, Bennett had been raised by an authoritarian Roman Catholic mother. An enigmatic man, he had piercing eyes and pale skin to the point of translucence, in later years shaving his head thereby giving himself an even more pallid appearance. An asthmatic and always in frail health, he lived his life in a cycle of medication. First, he took laudanum; after a week or so, he switched to injecting morphine; in another week he turned to cocaine and, finally, a week later, took to inhaling chloroform. In later years, Bennett became a Buddhist and was one of the first men to establish the religion in Britain, dying in poverty in London in 1923.

It was Bennett's belief that drugs could produce a simulacrum of mystical and religious experience opening *the gates of the World behind the Veil of Matter*. To find the key to this gate, Crowley began experimenting with a wide range of drugs including ether, cocaine, opium and hashish. It was his aim, with their help, to project his astral body so that he could in essence, if not in material flesh, travel the universe at will. For most of the rest of his life, Crowley was to seek to loosen, as he put it, *the girders of the soul* by means of occult magical practices, meditation, sexual magic and drugs.

By 1906, Crowley was deeply involved in a magical ritual called the Operation of the Sacred Magic of Abramelin, the purpose of which was to converse with one's Holy Guardian Angel, and through it come to know one's inner self. Whilst preparing for the ritual and during the performance of it, Crowley took hashish with which he was magically experimenting at the time. He recorded in his diary that some of his experiments *had been somewhat unexpectedly successful. I found my habit of analysing and controlling my mind enabled me to turn the effect of the drug to best account. Instead of getting intoxicated, I became quite abnormally able to push introspection to the limit*. He also recorded, *Remarkable experiment with hashish. I took some five grains, and smoked a little ganja. I was drinking a good deal of port, too.* He noted how varied the strength could be and that some samples he used were virtually inert: no doubt these were old and had oxidized. Somewhat mischievously, Crowley also on occasion tricked the audiences to some of his public rituals, which he performed to raise money, by feeding them hashish or opium disguised in a preparatory libation.

Just as Ludlow had liked to frequent Anderson's shop in Poughkeepsie, so did Crowley have a favourite hang-out. It was a London chemist's shop in Stafford Street, not far from Piccadilly Circus, owned and run by a pharmacist called E. P. Whineray. Purveyor of drugs to the wealthy of London, Whineray knew all the secrets: who was taking what and when and the substances to which they were addicted. The drugs were, of course, supplied within the law, but many people of position wanted their foibles kept confidential. Later in his life, after various drugs were proscribed, he was arrested on a charge of dispensing irregularities: with Whineray, old habits died hard and he appeared to have become a pusher. What is virtually certain is that he was Crowley's supplier of hashish, amongst other drugs.

Inspired by his hashish use, Crowley was to write an essay under the assumed name of Oliver Haddo entitled 'The Psychology of Hashish', which formed part of an article that was published in 1909 in *The Equinox*, an esoteric magazine of which he was the financier and editor. (When W. Somerset Maugham had published his novel *The Magician* in 1908, which was based on Crowley, he called him Oliver Haddo: with characteristic wit, Crowley borrowed the name.)

The article appeared in two parts. The first, 'A Pharmaceutical Study of Cannabis sativa – The Herb Dangerous (Being a collation of facts as known at the present date)' was written by E. P. Whineray, MPS. It included a section by David Hooper, the Curator of the Calcutta Botanical Gardens, on *charas* growing in India and mentioned Wood, Spivey and Easterfield's work on cannabinol. The second part comprised Crowley's essay, in which he made some highly pertinent comments on hashish, although to find them one has to read through much esoteric or ephemeral verbiage. He noted that hashish was psychologically rather than physically habit-forming, and that previous writers and investigators had been somewhat piecemeal in their studies, especially Ludlow whom he considered too much influenced by De Quincey. He agreed with Baudelaire's opinion that hashish *merely exaggerates and distorts the natural man and his mood of the moment* which he considered justified by Ludlow's experiences. Yet, in the long run, Crowley felt he *had no use for hashish save as a preliminary demonstration that there exists another world attainable – somehow.* For him, hashish was pleasurable and it aided his prodigious sexual life because it suppressed inhibitions in both himself (not that he had many) and his male and female partners, but it was essentially a tool for his exploration of consciousness. Crowley also believed that drugs should be legalized for adult use and that to abuse drugs was foolish and weak. They were, in his mind, too precious as substances capable, under the direction of the individual's will, of developing the human consciousness to be exploited.

Crowley was not alone amongst the devotees of the occult in writing about hashish. Algernon Blackwood who, like Crowley and Bennett, reacted against a zealously evangelistic Christian parent, was introduced to drug taking by a Dr Huebner whom he met whilst living from hand-to-mouth in North America. Returning to England, Blackwood mixed with a number of occultists in London and started to use hashish. In 1908, he invented John Silence, a Sherlock Holmesian character who was a psychologist-cum-detective. When *John Silence, Physician Extraordinary* was published, many of the fictional cases the sleuth addressed had psychic themes to them and one, 'A Psychical Invasion', dealt with psycho-active drug use. John Silence tells a client who has come to him after being bothered by poltergeists that he is in touch with them because the hashish he has been taking has amplified his rate of psychical vibration, thus allowing him to gain access to the spirit world.

Elsewhere, others were also writing about hashish. At about the same time as Blackwood was writing his John Silence stories, the Russian mystic George Ivanovitch Gurdjieff was travelling in the Middle East, studying Sufism. He later wrote of hashish in *Meetings with Remarkable Men* and is reported to have fed hashish to his students at his Institute for the Harmonious Development of Man in Tbilisi and, subsequently, at Fontainebleau.

The American *Medical Review of Reviews* included an article in 1912 written by Dr Victor Robinson, a physician with an interest in medical history. Headed 'An Essay on Hasheesh: Historical and Experimental', it was a series of accounts of hashish taking either by Robinson himself or administered by him. They were not very elucidating and the article said nothing new, but they are worth noting if only for their somewhat facile schoolboy humour. Of one experiment, Robinson wrote, *On May 13, 1910, this world was excited over the visit of Halley's comet. It is pleasant to remember that the celestial guest attracted as much attention as a political campaign or a game of baseball. On the evening of this day, at 10 o'clock, I gave 45 minims to a court stenographer named Henry D. Demuth. At 11:30 the effects of the drug became apparent, and Mr Demuth lost consciousness of his surroundings to such an extent that he imagined himself an inhabitant of Sir Edmund Halley's nebulous planet. He despised the earth and the dwellers thereon; he called it a miserable little flea-bite, and claimed its place in the cosmos was no more important than a flea-jump. With a scornful finger he pointed below, and said in a voice of contempt, 'That little joke down there, called the earth.' . . . He imitated how Magistrate Butts calls a prisoner to the bar. 'Butts,' he explained, 'is the best of them. Butts-Butts-cigarette-butts.' If this irreverent line should ever fall beneath the dignified eyes of His Honor, instead of fining his devoted stenographer for contempt of court, may he bear in his learned mind the fact that under the influence of narcotics men are mentally irresponsible.* Concerned that too few American poets had sung the praises of hashish, Robinson included his own poetical contribution:

> *Near Punjab and Pab, in Sutlej and Sind,*
> *Where the cobras-di-capello abound,*
> *Where the poppy, palm and the tamarind,*
> *With cummin and ginger festoon the ground —*
> *And the capsicum fields are all abloom,*
> *From the hills above to the vales below,*
> *Entrancing the air with a rich perfume,*
> *There too does the greenish Cannabis grow:*
> *Inflaming the blood with the living fire,*
> *Till the burning joys like the eagles rise,*
> *And the pulses throb with a strange desire,*
> *While passion awakes with a wild surprise: —*
> *O to eat that drug, and to dream all day,*
> *Of the maids that live by the Bengal Bay!*

For those who did not realize it, he pointed out it was a sonnet.

Less flippant than Robinson was Jules Giraud, the French author of *Testament of a Hashish Eater*, published in 1913, and the founder of a magazine called *Cannabinologie*, who railed against those who were intolerant towards hashish users.

Giraud had cause to fulminate. Times were changing. Society was becoming less forbearing when it came to drug taking. Although the Victorian era, on both sides of the Atlantic, is considered to have been repressive and authoritarian, it was in fact a time of considerable personal liberty and freedom of expression. For hashish and its disciples, it was a golden age. It would not be long before those publicizing their hashish experiments and experiences would do so with a wary glance over their shoulder.

# CONVENTIONS, COMMISSIONS AND CONTRABAND

GRADUALLY, AS THE NINETEENTH CENTURY ROLLED INTO THE TWENTIETH, concern began to mount about drug taking and attitudes started to harden. What had been regarded as an eccentricity or a bad habit was now being seen as a vice if, at first, but a minor one and governments began to address what they saw as a looming problem.

One of the first was the British administration in India which was deeply implicated in the importation of *charas* from central Asia to meet a shortfall in demand in the northern and Himalayan states. The supply route ran from Afghanistan over the mountains of the Hindu Kush to Peshawar, or via Quetta to Shikarpur, or from Chinese Turkestan, now known as the Xinjiang Uygur Autonomous Region, and the high passes of the Himalayas through Ladakh or western Tibet. It existed before the British arrived in the region, hashish from Afghanistan, Samarkand and Bukhara having had a reputation for quality since the eighteenth century but the trade increased under British rule.

From time to time, the hashish business was interrupted by internecine fighting amongst local tribes or warlords. In the 1860s, with Russian influence expanding in central Asia, and Turkestan in particular, hashish production fell either by design of the Czarist forces or because of the social upheaval they caused. Whatever the reason, production moved south into Afghanistan and further east into the fertile oasis area of Yarkand on the western end of the Takla Makan desert, today known as

Shache (or So-ch'e). Despite these temporary setbacks, however, the *charas* trade continued and flourished.

The hashish cargoes from Shache were carried by mule, human and camel caravan over the eastern end of the Karakoram mountain range to Leh where the British authorities maintained godowns in which the hashish was temporarily bonded, weighed and taxed before being released for import. In Hooper's contribution to Whineray's 1909 article, the trade is succinctly outlined. Once cleared through customs the *charas* trader, he wrote, *obtains a permit allowing him to take the drug to a special market. The zamindars of Chinese Turkestan are the vendors of the drug, the importers being Yarkhandis or Ladakhis, who dispose of it at Hoshiapur and Amritsar principally, returning with piece-goods, or Amritsar merchants who trade with Ladakh. The drug in this way reaches the chief cities of Punjab during September and October. Thence it is distributed over the Central and United Provinces as far as Bombay and Calcutta, and is used everywhere for smoking. Charas, though a drug, plays the part of money to a great extent in the trade that is carried on at Ladakh, the price of the drug depending on the state of the market, and any fluctuations causing a corresponding increase or decrease in the value of the goods for which it is bartered. The exchange price of charas thus gives rise to much gambling. A pony-load (two pais or three maunds* [a woven basket used as a measure]) sells for Rs. 40 or Rs. 50, the cost of transport to Hoshiapur (the chief Punjab depot) is Rs. 100, and there it fetches from Rs. 30 to Rs. 100 per maund. Retail dealers sell small quantities at a price that works out at Rs. 200 to Rs. 500 per maund. Five years ago the Kashgar growers, encouraged by the high prices, sowed a large crop and reaped a bumper harvest, only to find the market already overstocked and prices on the Leh Exchange fallen from Rs. 60 to Rs. 30 per maund.* He went on to note that, in the winter of 1904–5, just under 141 tons of hashish passed through Leh, valued at over twelve million rupees.

The trade was a lucrative one for both the merchant and the revenue collector, but it was coming increasingly under criticism in Britain. This started in earnest in 1874 with the foundation of the Anglo-Oriental Society for the Suppression of the Opium Trade which, in turn, led to the ascendancy of the anti-alcohol temperance movement and drew attention to Indian cannabis. Reports reached London that the discipline and efficiency of *sepoys*, native troops employed by the British, were being eroded by their use of *ganja* which, it was said without any basis whatsoever, led to illness, madness and criminality. The disaster of the Indian Mutiny of 1857–8, which was also referred to as the Sepoy Mutiny, still fresh in the public – and Parliamentary – memory, the risks were exaggerated.

In fact, concern had already been voiced. An official investigation had been set up in India in 1871 to look into the effects of cannabis on all levels of native society, but it concluded there was no proof that using the drug caused insanity or any increase in crime. It was also suggested that a complete ban on cannabis would only lead to smuggling and tax evasion, the best way to reduce consumption being to increase tax levels and, thereby, retail prices. For a while, the issue was avoided, only to come to the fore again in 1877 when another commission was instigated: it drew broadly the same conclusions.

Much of the move against cannabis came from native Indian administrators who, being mostly middle class and upper caste, considered cannabis was causing unrest amongst the lower, working class and the untouchables, upon whom most of the manual-labour tasks were placed. Cannabis, it was argued, was making the work force lazy. The real causes of this were poor housing, medical care, hygiene and nutrition, but this was conveniently ignored. The British *raj* started to agree.

On 16 July 1891, a Parliamentary question was tabled in London by Sir Mark MacTaggart Stewart, Member of Parliament for Kirkcudbrightshire, who had already called for a cessation of the opium trade. The question asked whether *the Secretary of State for India has seen a report in the* Allahabad Pioneer *of 10 May that ganja, which is grown, sold and excised in much the same way as opium, is far more harmful, and that 'the lunatic asylums of Bengal are filled with ganja smokers'? Is he aware that ganja has been made illegal in Lower Burma and that excise reports say this has been 'of enormous benefit to the people'? and Will he call to the attention of the Governor General the desirability of extending the prohibition to other provinces?* The reply was affirmative to the first two questions with a promise to look into the last. Within a month, the administration in India had replied, citing the 1871 report findings and stating that, whilst *ganja* might be considered *the most noxious of all intoxicants commonly used in India*, prohibiting it was impractical. Further despatches enclosed with the papers, dating to 1873, pragmatically pointed out that whilst *ganja* use might be undesirable, it was nothing like as dangerous as opium.

Stewart's question faded into Parliamentary oblivion and his party lost the 1892 general election. The incoming Liberal administration, which was keen to act against opium, sidelined cannabis and appointed a Royal Commission to look into the opium trade. The anti-cannabis faction was incensed and wanted to know why opium was being moved against and not cannabis. Indeed, some thought cannabis to be the more dangerous.

As long ago as 1840, William Bingham Baring, the 2nd Baron Ashburton and Member of Parliament for North Staffordshire, had lobbied that, if opium was banned, it would lead to *an exhalation of the hemp plant, easily collected at certain seasons, which was in every way more injurious than the use of the poppy.*

The anti-cannabis bloc was gaining momentum. In February 1893, the Liberal Member of Parliament for Bradford East, William Sproston Caine, read the despatches sent from India in answer to Stewart's question and, on 2 March 1893, tabled his own: *I beg to ask the Under Secretary of State for India if the Secretary of State for India will instruct the Government of India to create a Commission of Experts to enquire into, and report on, the cultivation of, and trade in, all preparations of hemp drugs in Bengal, the effect of their consumption upon the social and moral condition of the people, and the desirability of prohibiting its growth and sale.* He also wanted reports from the rest of India's provinces.

As an indirect result of Caine's question, Lord Kimberley, the Secretary of State for India, launched the Indian Hemp Drugs Commission under the chairmanship of the Hon. William Mackworth Young, First Financial Commissioner for the Punjab, and consisting of a secretary, three British officials (including the Professor of Chemistry at the Medical College in Calcutta, the post formerly held by O'Shaughnessy) and three native ones including Raja Soshi Sikhareswar Roy of Tahirpur.

The commission was charged, as Caine had requested, with studying every aspect of cannabis in India, from its cultivation and taxation to its effects upon the people and the likely result of prohibition. Over a thousand witnesses were called or responded to questionnaires in the year starting August 1893, ranging from senior civil servants to Christian missionaries, traders to doctors to native farmers. Commission members also travelled widely throughout India researching the situation for themselves. Interestingly, the missionaries were the least helpful of the correspondents, most citing an ignorance of the subject, the commission drawing the conclusion that, if such men were not bothered by or had not noticed cannabis, then it could hardly be a problem. Missionaries, after all, were more in touch with the natives than any other Europeans.

Assessing the results, the commissioners came to several realizations. First, cannabis use was far more widespread than had previously been understood; it was used not merely as a recreational drug but as a medicine and adjunct to religious rituals. Second, it was not as pervasively dangerous as had been mooted and was not a significant cause of crime or mental illness. Third, to ban the use of cannabis would impact upon religious observance and create considerable civil unrest. The impracticality of banning such a widely available substance was also illustrated.

The findings, consisting of over 3500 pages, were published in Simla in seven volumes during 1894. They were specifically unpartisan and objective and remain to the present day the most thorough official study of cannabis ever conducted. In final summary, the commission was of the opinion that the moderate use of hemp drugs produced virtually no *evil results* and recommended against prohibition. If, the commission stated, the Government was determined to restrict cannabis use it was best to attempt to do so by taxation.

Little changed as a result of the commission. Laws and tax levels were standardized between provinces but, otherwise, it was business as usual. Cannabis was grown on government-licensed farms for processing into *ganja* and medicinal hashish. *Ganja* shops continued to be licensed and taxed. *Charas* importation from Shache and Afghanistan increased although, at the same time, so did smuggling, the high level of fines imposed on captured *charas* runners doing little to discourage them. What further affected the trade was that hashish demand in Europe was on the decline. Pharmaceutical hashish was being replaced by synthetic medicines, especially aspirin. Consequently, in addition to the Ladakhi and Chinese *charas* smugglers, farmers who had exported to Europe now turned their attention to selling into a domestic black market. This state of affairs was more or less maintained until 1945, unaffected by the Russian and Chinese partitioning of Turkestan in 1934 but not the subsequent Chinese eradication of cannabis growing in Shache. An Indian government report of 1938 announced that all illegal *charas* traffic with China had ceased but this only meant that hashish production increased in Afghanistan, Kashmir, the wild and inaccessible North-West Frontier Province and Nepal.

While the debate on cannabis was running its course in India, in South Africa it had become a problem. *Dagga* was used much as *ganja* was in India, as a social intoxicant and as part of religious ritual. Europeans considered it an aspect of the primitive Africans' way of life and, as long as it stayed in the bush, it was generally ignored. This *laissez-faire* approach had changed in 1843 when Britain annexed the Republic of Natalia (now the province of KwaZulu/Natal) to the Cape Colony.

Once annexed, the province experienced a surge in sugar-cane production but it was found that the indigenous population was unsuited to the manual labour involved, mainly because they had little awareness of the concept of time and could not be relied upon to turn up for work. To address the problem, 6000 indentured coolies were imported from India. The work was hard and most, as soon as they could pay off their obligations, quit to find other employment as servants and semi-skilled workers. The majority of them came from southern India and, being darker skinned than many of their countrymen, but not black like Africans, they formed an ethnic sub-group which both black Africans and white settlers despised and ostracized.

The white settlers, however, had another reason to abominate the Indian immigrants: they used cannabis which they either brought with them or obtained from the natives. It was soon perceived that the drug was responsible for making the coolies ill and indigent; and, when they were dismissed, or failed to earn money because they were 'ill', they turned to crime.

To compound matters, after the initial waves of plantation coolies, thousands more Indians were imported to work in the gold and diamond mines. These, too, brought cannabis with them and exacerbated the situation which was finally confronted in the 1870s by the passing of a law against cannabis use and possession. It was roundly ignored. Indeed, it was deliberately flouted by mine operators who found their workforce – both African and Indian – became less tired if allowed periodic smokes throughout the shift period. Some mines even took to growing their own supplies exclusively for their employees many of whom, especially in the diamond mines, lived in secure camps to prevent them pilfering gemstones. Such workers were, in effect, a captive cannabis-using community.

In 1887, a commission under the leadership of Supreme Court Judge Walter Wragg declared cannabis dangerous to white rule and stability, fearing it might turn the native tribes into belligerents. Less than a decade had passed since the battle of Isandhlwana and the fanatic bravery of the Zulu impis at the Battle of Blood River was not forgotten either. The law was tightened with still no discernible effect. Enforcing it was well nigh impossible: the authorities could hardly police thousands of square miles of virgin bush.

As the twentieth century began, moves towards the international prohibition of opiates increased as more was understood about their potential for addiction. This, in turn, became a call for the internationalization of drug prevention. The first international gathering, the International Opium Commission, met in February 1909 in Shanghai. The irony of the choice of venue was not lost on many observers: Shanghai was the most opium-addicted city on earth.

The commission had no powers nor did it arrive at even a skeletal agreement, yet it publicized the issue. Two-and-a-half years later, in December 1911, a second convention met at The Hague in the Netherlands. Only a dozen countries were represented but their members were charged with constructing a convention that would allow for a framework for international drugs legislation. At this conference, the Italian delegates asked for cannabis to be included in the discussions but they did not wait for the result of their request, leaving as they did after the opening sessions. The South African representatives pressed for cannabis to be treated as being as addictive as opiates but the main thrust of the meeting was towards opiates, of which the governments represented agreed to restrict the manufacture and sale. It was decided that the matter of cannabis would be looked into – *the Conference is of the unanimous opinion that it is advisable to study the question of Indian hemp from the statistical and scientific point of view, with a view to regulating its abuses* – but nothing was actually done.

The outbreak of the Great War put the debate in abeyance but, once it was over, drugs quickly reappeared on the international political scene. The Treaty of Versailles itself addressed measures concerning opium and, three years after the war ended, the League of Nations established the Advisory Committee on the Traffic in Opium and other Dangerous Drugs. Its aim was to collate international intelligence on drugs and supervise international conventions on control. In 1923, the South African government made another attempt through the Committee to have cannabis banned but the British, protective of their tax revenue in India, vetoed it. In the same year, the International Police Commission, more commonly known as Interpol, was set up with headquarters in Paris to gather and disseminate intelligence on all international criminal activity including drug trafficking.

Such protectionism subverted the November 1924 International Opium Conference convened in Geneva. Actually consisting of two conferences held a fortnight apart, the delegates fell into two camps, the user nations who wanted a ban and producer nations who did not: however, the meetings did create the Central Board, a body to oversee regulation, and established the Geneva International Convention on Narcotic Control. This prohibited the non-medical use of opiates, cocaine and cannabis, the latter included by demand of the Egyptian delegate, Mohammed El Guindy, with the Turkish in accord. Egypt and Turkey were suffering from what Guindy called *chronic hashishism* and wanted it urgently addressed. India complained at this because cannabis was vital to its social and religious culture. Britain fudged the issue, abstaining from voting but signing up to the convention. The British representative, Sir Malcolm Delevigne, a career civil servant who was in fact an international expert on labour reform, stated that not enough time had been given for his country to study the arguments. The French toed the British line. A sub-committee pointed out that a control on cannabis production was not easy because it also produced fibre and oil.

Finally, it was suggested that the export of cannabis resin – in other words, hashish – would be restricted except for medicinal and scientific usage, the importing country issuing an import licence to indicate acceptance. This suggestion was approved but not signed by all the participating nations, both the USA and Egypt withdrawing, thus making it virtually unworkable. Those who did comply only agreed to follow the recommendation to their best ability.

By this time, cannabis use was widespread. In 1924, Louis Lewin published one of the most important studies of drugs, entitled *Phantastica*. A German toxicologist, he was born in 1850 in the West Prussian town of Tuchel, the son of a Jewish cobbler. After studying medicine in Berlin, he worked for several pharmaceutical companies and became a university lecturer in Berlin, rising in due course to a professorial chair. In his book, he gave a synopsis of where cannabis was used. It seemed from his research that, Western Europe, the Americas, Australia, New Zealand and the Pacific islands excepted, there was nowhere that the general population was not familiar with cannabis.

As the discussions at the conference in Geneva had shown, hashish use was a very serious problem in parts of the Middle East. Egyptian society was swamped with it. Hashish possession had been made a capital offence in 1868 but it had no effect on hashish use. In 1874, hashish imports were taxed, even though possession was still illegal. Three years on, the authorities seized and burned all they could find; then it was made illegal to import it; next, cannabis cultivation was banned. To give the local officials an incentive, in 1884 they were permitted to sell overseas any hashish they had confiscated, sharing the profits between themselves and their informers. Many simply sold back into the local market through middlemen, no doubt later confiscating the very same hashish all over again and reselling it in a cycle of corruption. Further weakening the legal process was the fact that non-Egyptian nationals were exempt from the hashish laws and immune to arrest. They could continue to import both hashish and opium with impunity, eroding the fabric of Egyptian society. It was little wonder the laws were ineffectual.

The situation was described by Malcolm Muggeridge, the noted British journalist. As he recorded in his autobiography, *Chronicles of Wasted Time*, in 1928 he went to Egypt to teach at the University of Cairo. Of his students in the Zaffaran Palace in which the university was located, he wrote, *They seemed to be faraway, lost in some dream of erotic bliss; a consequence, no doubt, in the case of many of them, of their addiction to hashish, widespread among the effendi class, and prevalent among the fellahin* [peasants], *especially among the ones who had moved into the towns.* A lifelong opponent of drug use, he was in later life to recall *the stupefied faces and inert minds of so many of the students there; the dreadful instances of the destructive effects of this drug on bodies and minds which any resident in the Middle East was bound to encounter.* The authorities did their best to eradicate the problem, as Muggeridge was to recount: *The deleterious effects of this addiction were, in those days, universally taken for granted; and the Egyptian authorities, following a plan of modernisation and national revival on the general lines of Kemal Ataturk's in Turkey, spent a lot of money and effort in an attempt to stamp it out. Russell Pasha, the head policeman and the last Englishman to hold the post, was particularly active in trying to prevent hashish getting into the country, and in reducing indulgence in it.* It can be argued that Russell was the first senior police officer to move actively against cannabis.

Thomas Wentworth Russell was born in November 1879 and, after graduating from the University of Cambridge in 1902, joined the Egyptian Civil Service, later becoming the founder of the famous Camel Corps. In 1917, he was appointed commandant of the Cairo Police, with the title *pasha*, a Turkish rank given to senior military commanders. Twelve years later, he was made head of the Egyptian Central Narcotics Intelligence Bureau, and ordered to fight the drug trade wherever he found it. This he did, with efficiency and devotion, and he was knighted for it: yet it must be noted he considered opiates, especially heroin, to be the most dangerous drugs he encountered and he was if not apathetic towards cannabis then at least understanding of its place in Arab culture. Indeed, he was sympathetic to the *fellahin* whom he described as taking hashish with a water pipe called a *goza*, made of a watertight coconut shell bound with iron or brass bands. In his autobiography, *Egyptian Service 1902–1946*, Russell said he believed the drug was used because of the malaria, as well as bilharzia (or schistosomiasis) and ancylostomiasis (intestinal hookworm), from which the majority of peasants, particularly male, suffered as a result of contact with slow-moving water in irrigation canals. He considered that cannabis gave them the strength they needed to continue to work whilst suffering these debilitating diseases and, when the price of hashish rose due to effective policing, he noticed how they turned to drinking strong tea and mixing henbane leaves with their tobacco.

After the Great War, Russell Pasha thought it was best to concentrate on what he called white drugs – cocaine, heroin and morphine that appeared commonly as white powder or blocks – and ignore the black drugs, hashish and raw opium. He even mooted legalizing hashish, producing it under government monopoly: this, he said, would not only control the drug but also swell the exchequer and address the balance-of-payments deficit being caused by the smuggling of hashish from overseas. The authorities disagreed and Russell was ordered to tighten his grip on the smugglers.

Russell had his task cut out for him. Hashish was – and still is – comparatively simple to smuggle. It was dense, compact, easily shaped and concentrated, a small amount being readily concealed yet attaining a high price by weight at the end user. It was profitable to smuggle even a small amount. Catching the hashish runners was, therefore, extremely difficult.

Most of Egypt's hashish came from Greece where it first arrived on the Cycladian island of Syros about 1850. By 1880, migrant labour from across the Middle East working the docks in Piraeus, Greece's major sea port, increased the demand for hashish so Greek farmers started to produce it. It was not long before they started to export the surplus.

What made combating the smuggling from Greece all the harder was the strong trade links with Cairo, merchants and traders sailing between Piraeus and Alexandria in such numbers as to make stopping and searching all but a tiny percentage of them impossible. That which did not come direct by sea arrived from Greece at ports such as Benghazi along the coast of Cyrenaica (now north-eastern Libya) to then be transported across the desert by camel. These smugglers were wily desert nomads, the most infamous and ruthless of whom was Abd el-'Ati el-Hassuna who came from Tripoli but operated out of Benghazi.

The camel trains carried blocks of hashish merely wrapped in cloth but other smugglers had to be more artful and the methods used by them to hide or disguise their contraband were ingenious in the extreme and are, in some cases, copied to this day. To suppress the distinctive smell of hashish, especially strong when the consignment was warmed by the sun or confined in the hot cargo hold of a ship, it was often packaged with powdered pine resin which was used to tan leather. On one occasion, hermetically sealed containers hidden inside fake concrete millstones were used, custom-made by a Dutchman in Istanbul. The consignment was discovered by a tip-off, which was just as well as the shipment was a practice run for a future massive bulk shipment of heroin. Another recorded instance is of a shipment of prunes, the stone from each fruit being replaced by an oval nugget of hashish: they were only discovered by a hungry stevedore helping himself to a prune out of a split sack and biting into it. At sea, hashish was wrapped in watertight bags weighted down with bags of salt and thrown overboard at a pre-arranged position. The salt dissolved in time and the hashish floated to the surface to be picked up. An equally ingenious trick was to hide consignments in off-shore navigation or anchorage buoys, most of which were hollow, the space accessed through a removable iron plate. Service staff bringing them onshore to repair or repaint them collected the drop. This means of smuggling was common at Port Said and through the Suez Canal where buoys had to be kept in pristine condition because of the exactitudes of navigation in such constricted sea lanes.

Where there had been hashish users' memoirs, there now came into existence a new genre of cannabis literature – the smugglers' memoirs. Portraying themselves as romantic adventurers, they sought to equate themselves with the eighteenth-century contrabanders who had run brandy or silk from France into England, always one step ahead of the excise men, doing no harm to anyone save the revenue system. Indeed, the public often regarded them more as rapscallions in the Robin Hood mould than purveyors of evil: that classification was reserved for heroin smugglers.

In 1933, a French soldier-of-fortune, yachtsman and writer called Henry de Montfreid published his third book *The Hashish Crossing*, which described his exploits as a hashish smuggler between France, Greece, Egypt, the Sudan and India. Finding himself in the French-administered territory of Djibouti at the mouth of the Red Sea, and short of money, de Montfreid decided about 1915 to start smuggling hashish. Sailing his vessel, a *boutre* or dhow called the *Fat-el-Rahman*, to Athens, he travelled into the countryside of the Peloponnesian peninsula where he purchased his first supply direct from the farmer. Hashish was clearly a major cash crop there for de Montfreid wrote, *All the farms in this district prepared hashish; it was their chief industry. Each estate had its brand, quoted on the market, and there were good and bad years, exactly as for wines.*

New to the game, de Montfreid was ignorant of judging the quality of what he was buying and decided it was wiser to keep his mouth shut and be thought an innocent than open his mouth and prove it. Being given a sample, the farmer sniffed at it then *took a piece and rolled it between his fingers into a slender cone, to which he put a match. It burned with a tiny and rather smoky flame, and when he hastily extinguished it, a heavily perfumed white smoke rose from it. In my turn I took a piece and went through exactly the same manoeuvres, only, having noticed how quickly he put out the flame, I on the contrary let it burn. Then in silence, with a cold and rather disdainful air, I held it out to him.* Playing the deal by ear, de Montfreid demanded a higher-quality product. The farmer *vanished, and returned in a moment with a piece of the same matter, but less brittle and of a greenish hue. He went through the same gestures, but this time the flame was long and very smoky, and he complacently let it burn. That, thought I, is probably the sign of really good quality. Now I knew how to buy hashish.* Purchasing 600 kilos, de Montfreid watched as it was sieved and put into small linen bags sewn by the farmer's wife. Each hashish cake was square and about four centimetres thick with an elephant trademark stamped onto it. Once in their bags, the cakes were packed into zinc-lined boxes that were soldered shut. The cargo was then legally shipped to Marseilles and on to Djibouti from where de Montfreid smuggled it into Egypt. Through the 1920s, he continued in the hashish trade, 'went native', converted to Islam, calling himself Abd el-Hai, and became a prolific author. Of his many titles, three others dealt with hashish, *The Pursuit of the 'Kaipan', The Man from the Sea* and *The Enchanted Cargo: Charas*.

Not long after de Montfreid purchased his first hashish, the cultivation of it was prohibited in Greece, and the centre of production moved to Syria and the Lebanon, nomadic Bedouins from Sinai running it into Egypt across the desert and the Suez Canal. Their opponents were Russell Pasha's Camel Corps. The troops who made up this élite unit were mostly Sudanese, expert camel riders and desert trackers who could tell from a glance at a camel's hoof-print not only in which direction it was heading but also how much weight it was carrying. Fire fights between the smugglers and the Camel Corps were frequent and, at times, fierce but many of the runners escaped capture, Egyptians collecting the hashish from them to give to teams of young boys who swam over the Canal with it. In time, the Camel Corps was issued with desert-going vehicles fitted with special spongy, low-pressure tyres which enabled them to drive over sand without becoming bogged down. In July 1933, the newly equipped cars chased, caught up with and arrested a band of Bedouin, seizing 156 kilos of hashish. Russell offered a bounty of five Egyptian pounds for every smuggler apprehended or shot.

Camels did more than act as mere pack animals. On one occasion early in 1932, a group of Bedouins approaching the frontier post at Qantara-el Sharquiya with a herd of camels going across the Suez Canal for slaughter as meat was stopped by a Camel Corps patrol. A Sudanese corporal noticed that one of the camels, which had not been shorn of their winter coats, had a particularly fine covering of camel hair and decided to buy the creature for his wife, so that she might spin the highly prized fur. The Bedouin owner, however, refused any price. As they bargained, the Sudanese ran his fingers through the animal's coat and discovered something hard. Hidden in the dense wool were one-kilo blocks of hashish. All the camels were carriers. The camel drivers had shorn the hair where it was thickest on the camels' backs, glued the hair to the hashish blocks then glued the blocks to the camels' skin, combing the hair over to look natural. Some years later, at the Qantara-el Sharquiya customs post, camels going for slaughter in Egypt were found to have been force-fed chargers – cylindrical, zinc or zinc-plated tin containers with rounded ends about fifteen centimetres long and four wide, some filled with hashish and some with opium. Each had a lead weight at one end to stop the camel regurgitating it to chew as cud. The plan was that, once in Egypt, the animals would be slaughtered and the contraband reclaimed from their stomachs. Detection was effected by running a military mine detector over the camels' bellies. This was developed at Qantara-el Sharquiya into a camel-sized metal detector of the sort now used to screen passengers in airport security. In modern times, heroin has been run by this method, but using undetectable rubber chargers.

Other smuggling techniques were just as imaginative. Railway trucks heading from Palestine into Egypt had the self-lubricating grease-pads in axle casings removed and replaced by hashish blocks. In the short term, this was successful but if the axle ran dry and started to squeak or seize up the drugs would be discovered. Livestock cargo vessels disposed of dead animals *en route* by throwing them overboard – often with their bellies filled with hashish. As the sun heated the carcasses, the gases within expanded and the animals became buoyant. Fishermen in league with the smugglers collected the floating corpses. Within the Suez Canal, pigs' bladders and the crops of dead chickens were similarly used. It was not unknown for a ship's cargo handler to walk down the gangplank with a charger inserted up his anus.

The innovative mind of the smuggler was not the only problem Russell Pasha and the Egyptian authorities faced. Hashish use and hashish smuggling reached the highest levels of government and corrupted the police and customs officers, many of whom readily accepted *baksheesh* – backhanders. De Montfreid noted that hashish smuggling was *a State institution . . . jealously hidden and kept secret, but with agents everywhere, high up in the police, in the customs service, even in the diplomatic service.* One smuggling ring, known as the Cairo Drug Syndicate, operated a monopoly on traffic coming across the Suez Canal south of Ismailia and included several well-known bankers from the city who provided the working capital.

The most important smuggler was a Greek, Lambros Yannicos, who ran not only hashish but also opium and heroin. When, in the early 1930s, Russell's men smashed his organization, they tried not only Yannicos but also forty-five other Europeans and sixteen Egyptians: despite this, it was still estimated that only 10 per cent of smugglers and contraband was ever discovered. His success in breaking up this ring and others had Russell appointed vice-president of the League of Nations Advisory Committee in 1939, concerning himself particularly with opiate smuggling. He retired from the position in 1946 and died in 1954, the last British officer to serve in the Egyptian administration.

Egypt apart, the other large market for hashish was Turkey, especially Istanbul. Over the years, various legal steps were taken in both Greece and Turkey to outlaw the drug but they were all at least partially, if not totally, ineffective with local consumption being accepted.

In Turkey, hashish was colloquially known as *Esrar* (The Secret) and smoked, although other forms of cannabis were chewed in the same fashion that coca leaves are by Peruvian Indians. The best hashish, which rose to the fore in the 1920s, came from Bursa, 50 miles south of Istanbul, that not used domestically being exported to Greece. Here, there was concern at the rise of hashish consumption, which had begun in the 1890s but accelerated in the immediate post-Great-War years, the growth increased considerably by the return of Greek troops and the repatriation of half a million Greeks from Turkish-held territory at the end of the Greco-Turkish War in 1922.

Hashish was particularly prevalent in the coffee shops, or *tekés*, of Piraeus and Athens, where many of the returned expatriates gathered. Mostly poor and often all but dispossessed, they came together to smoke hashish with water pipes, as they had done when living under Turkish domination, drink *ouzo*, talk and entertain themselves. Especially, they played folk music. Known as *rebetika* – which also came to be the name of the hashish-smoking culture of the *tekés* – the music was highly influenced by Turkish folk songs and, whilst some of it consisted of romantic love ballads, much of it was about the loneliness of living in a foreign land, sex, criminality and drugs. The musicians were usually of an anarchic mind, anti-Fascists for whom this music, often akin in subject matter to the Negro-inspired blues in America, was as much protest as it was entertainment.

With the advent of the Second World War, the days of the *tekés* were numbered. During the war years and the Nazi occupation, hashish consumption slumped dramatically assisted by the severity and persecution of the Metaxas dictatorship between 1936 and 1941. *Rebetika* music was outlawed and remained so until after the 1974 ousting of 'The Colonels', the oppressive military junta.

As the Greeks stepped up their anti-drug legislation, the Turkish hashish smugglers began to target other nearby Balkan countries. Bulgaria was the first, followed by Romania and Yugoslavia but, by 1932, all three countries had imposed blanket prohibition. Throughout this time, the Lebanese continued to produce hashish and, as the Turkish smugglers found it increasingly hard to trade, the Lebanese took their place as the primary Middle Eastern providers. Thousands of acres were put down to cannabis, mostly in the northern region of the Beqaa Valley. This situation remained unchanged until the Second World War when British forces stationed in Palestine joined up with local government agents and, in 1944, destroyed a crop estimated to be worth nine million Egyptian pounds wholesale on the streets of Cairo. The following year, with most British troops deployed to the European theatre of war after D-Day, the cannabis farmers sowed an even bigger crop.

The League of Nations Advisory Committee, however, concentrated on opiates. The 1931 Convention decreed that all heroin exportation cease and all seized shipments be destroyed, with tight regulation on the production and distribution of dangerous drugs from the point of manufacture to the final end user. In 1936, the Conference for the Suppression of the Illicit Traffic in Dangerous Drugs dealt with addressing the criminality of trafficking and, by the outbreak of the Second World War, there was an abundance of international legislative conventions and laws in force although the ratification of them often weakened them because individual countries wanted specific clauses inserted to protect their own interests. Some signatory states ignored the provisions of the various conventions altogether but one nation, which was not even a signatory, carried out most of the League of Nations' recommendations.

It was the USA and the actions it took were to reverberate down the coming decades.

# MARY JANE, COCKROACHES AND
# THE BLUES

AS HASHISH HAD BEEN USED IN AMERICA BY ONLY A SMALL NUMBER OF people, the population as a whole was ignorant of it and it could hardly be said to pose a threat to the social well-being of the country. Yet, in the early twentieth century, the situation was to change dramatically. The cause, which not surprisingly caught on in a society in which tobacco smoking was extensive, was a 'new' way of taking cannabis by smoking the dried leaves and flower heads.

To appreciate why this was viewed as a dangerous social menace one has to consider two factors in the background to American society.

As already mentioned, by the turn of the nineteenth century, there was a growing condemnation of drug use. With an estimated 3 per cent of the American population medicinally addicted to opiates in 1900, there now existed a climate of considerable caution: and with caution came fear. In addition, drugs were identified in the public consciousness with foreigners and ethnic minorities who, in the strongly xenophobic and racist white portion of American society from which the administration and ruling class were drawn, were regarded with suspicion and already subjected to considerable social exclusion and repression. Drugs were, in short, deemed un-American.

Two ethnic groups in particular were disenfranchised: the Chinese and the Negroes. They were the forerunners of the perceived 'enemies of the state' that have, from time to time, historically been seen to threaten to undermine the fabric of the nation, from gangsters to Communists to civil rights militants to rock musicians and now, admittedly with perhaps more justification than any of these forerunners, extremist Muslims. The US government, whilst decrying every group, has also used them to bolster social unity and a sense of nationhood, and slip through its own agenda of discreet social manipulation. Where cannabis is concerned, this has been the case from the early 1900s.

When, with the 1849 Californian gold rush, large numbers of Chinese coolies arrived in America, they brought with them their opium habit. Over the next two decades, tens of thousands more followed in their footsteps to work as indentured labourers on the railways. They, too, smoked opium. The gold rushes over and the railways built, the Chinese stayed and settled and opium stayed with them, smoked in dens in every Chinese quarter in America from San Francisco's Chinatown to lower Manhattan. Abhorred, abused and resented as a degenerate race, they were considered the 'yellow peril', bent on destroying white American society. Opium, perceived to be their insidious weapon of social destruction, was the subject of much vilification but the truth was different. Most Americans who could afford to buy a bottle of painkilling medicine had taken opium in one form or another for it was the most common analgesic available. The real cause of the hatred was racial.

Laws were passed against opium use and possession, first in San Francisco in 1875 then across the nation, state by state. On the face of it, the laws were aimed at preventing white youths from indulging in such an alien, dangerous and corrupting practice, but the reality was that they were aimed first at further suppressing the Chinese and, second, at halting the creeping use of drugs in the white middle classes.

In time, the opium threat was seen as reduced but it was soon to be replaced. By 1900, cocaine was being used by blacks in the southern states where they made up the labour force that drove the predominantly agricultural economy. With its euphoria, it was thought it might make the workers lethargic and consequently indolent. It was also feared that the intoxicated blacks might rise up, shake off their shackles and attack the white folk, a slave mutiny forty years after emancipation. It was even said that cocaine incited black men to molest and even rape white women.

Onto this scene arrived the smoking of cannabis.

Hemp had been grown for its fibre in the USA for a long time but this had not led to an awareness of its psycho-active potential, at least in the white population. Black slaves, however, knew of it from their experience of *dagga* back in Africa and the smoking of dried cannabis flowers was done across a swathe of southern states from southern Virginia to eastern Louisiana. Nevertheless, the practice was not extensive and, even if whites knew of it, they would not have tried it: it was something the *negras* did and therefore totally unacceptable.

The responsibility for the introduction of cannabis as an intoxicant in the Americas rests with the Portuguese and Spanish. Prior to their conquests, native Americans used tobacco in rituals and as a relaxant, but not, it seems, cannabis. Girolamo Benzoni, the author of *The History of the New World*, published in 1565, described tobacco smoking, being probably the first European to witness it: . . . *they retain it* [the smoke] *as long as they can, for they find a pleasure in it, and so much do they fill themselves with this cruel smoke, that they lose their reason. And there are some who take so much of it, that they fall down as if they were dead, and remain the greater part of the day or night stupefied.* Some native North American tribes, such as the Iroquois, also smoked tobacco mixed with intoxicant herbs. Sitting Bull and Great Elk of the Dakotas smoked such tobacco–herb mixtures, including the bark of red willow trees.

The consensus of opinion is that cannabis use came to the Americas with black slaves from Africa arriving in Brazil in the first half of the sixteenth century to work the newly established sugar plantations. It has been conjectured that the seeds arrived in magical talismanic dolls worn by slaves, or that they were carried by Portuguese sailors or deliberately imported from Portuguese settlements in India, especially Goa. Cannabis cultivation occurred mostly on slave-laboured plantations in the north-east of the country, its use understandably most prevalent there, and it was here the native Indians, coming into contact with the slaves, first started smoking it. Interestingly, it was often smoked using a water pipe, the technique introduced by the Portuguese.

Cannabis was not taken up universally by the natives. Competing with other, often far more powerful drugs such as peyote, coca and mescaline, its spread across the northern half of South America and across the Panama isthmus was a gradual process. It did not reach some regions until the twentieth century.

A number of tribes, however, did take to cannabis, mostly in Central America. The Cuna Indians in Panama communally smoked it in pipes at tribal meetings, the Cora Indians in the Sierra Madre Occidental of Mexico used it in sacred rituals and the Tepehuan Indians turned to it when other drugs were unavailable. As the tribes were Christianized, many incorporated cannabis into their quasi-Christian rituals. The Tepehuan even named it Rosa Maria and the flowers Santa Rosa, giving it a sanctity of its own. Some worshipped the plant, claiming it to be of divine origin. As recently as the 1970s, it was in some remote areas still referred to as la Santa Maria.

After the emancipation of slaves, plantation owners and farmers across the Caribbean faced a labour problem. In the USA, the majority of former slaves continued to work for their erstwhile owners but, on the larger islands of the Caribbean such as Jamaica, many withdrew their labour and established their own smallholdings. To make up the deficit in manpower, the plantation owners imported indentured labourers from India. To say they were familiar with cannabis is to state the obvious.

By the 1880s, cannabis was widely used by peasant farmers, plantation and ranch workers across Brazil, Central America and the Caribbean. Mostly indentured and little better than slaves, poor, deprived, ignorant and oppressed, cannabis was their one release from misery and the daily grind of aching muscles and hard toil under a brazen sun.

Whether or not hemp farming had continued unbroken since the days of the conquistador Pedro Cuadrado, by the 1880s the use of cannabis was noted in Mexico. Twenty years later, it was to be found growing rampant in the wild and was commonly cultivated by peasants who mostly smoked it in pipes but also ate or made infusions of it with sugar cane sap, milk and chillies. It was also extensively used by the *curandero*, herbalists-cum-witchdoctors who were repositories of what was termed 'the old knowledge', a mixture of native-American and old Mexican remedies. A decade later and cannabis cigarettes became common, the contents of which were called marijuana. The word was colloquial, its derivation uncertain. One root for it seems to have been the Mexican military slang phrase *Maria y Juana* (Mary and Jane), meaning a prostitute or brothel, but another suggestion has it coming from an Aztec Indian phrase, *mallihuan*, which the Spanish pronunciation altered. Whatever the case, by 1900 the word was everyday parlance in Mexico and the substance itself was creeping north into Texas.

Mexico at that time was in a state of characteristic upheaval. The capitalist dictatorship of General Porfirio Diaz was unpopular and dissent was rife, the economy at best unstable. This caused a large number of Mexican peasants to migrate north, over the Rio Grande into Texas and, to a lesser extent, New Mexico. Here, in border settlements like

Brownsville, Laredo, Del Rio and El Paso, they settled in shanty-towns, pueblos and the poorer quarters of town, eking out an existence as unskilled labourers and living as they had south of the border, which included smoking marijuana. Then, as the migrant workforce made deeper inroads into the USA, they took their customs and habits with them. Soon, cities well inside Texas such as Corpus Christi, San Antonio and the state capital, Austin, had substantial Mexican populations all using marijuana. The revolution that overthrew Diaz in 1910 increased the migration rate – and the use of marijuana. Demand was so high that there were companies that specialized in importing marijuana from Mexico, retailing it through grocery and drug stores in one-ounce packets.

The overthrow of Diaz was engineered by Francisco Madero into whose forces was recruited Doroteo Arango, subsequently to become known as Pancho Villa. Two years later, during a second uprising led by Pascual Orozco, Villa fell foul of one of his commanding officers, General Victoriano Huerta, was arrested and condemned to death. Escaping from prison, Villa joined up with troops loyal to him, called the División del Norte (Division of the North), and fled into the USA where he attacked the military outpost of Columbus, New Mexico, in 1916. It was not his first incursion north of the Rio Grande: Villa had been in the habit of raiding border towns and ranches to obtain supplies for some years.

Villa's troops, almost to a man, came from peasant stock like himself and smoked marijuana both to relax and to prepare themselves for battle. A well-known Mexican folksong immortalizes them. Called 'La Cucaracha' ('The Cockroach'), it tells in its original form the story of one of Villa's foot soldiers, colloquially known as cockroaches:

> The cockroach, the cockroach,
> Now he cannot walk,
> Because he don't, because he don't
> Have marijuana to smoke.

It is from this reference that the modern American slang for a joint butt comes – a roach.

Villa's incursions into the USA led to a force being taken against him under the command of General John 'Black Jack' Pershing who drove the Mexican rebel army back over the border. In the process, some of his soldiers discovered marijuana although, in fact, US Cavalry troops had been smoking it in border posts and forts before this and black troops were known to smoke it in garrison towns such as El Paso. At about the same time, Puerto Rican and American soldiers serving in the newly created Panama Canal Zone were also reported to be smoking marijuana having picked the habit up from the Mexican and native American labourers digging the canal. By 1921, the practice was sufficiently common in the ranks for the commanding officer of Fort Sam Houston in San Antonio to forbid its use on US military property. Two years later, marijuana possession was outlawed in the military in Panama and the Republic of Panama civilian authorities banned cannabis cultivation. This reduced but did not eradicate marijuana smoking so, in April 1925, a military tribunal was set up under Colonel J. F. Siler of the US Army Medical Corps. He ran trials during which a number of soldiers, four military doctors and two military policemen smoked marijuana. The conclusion of the trials was that it was not addictive and had no *appreciable deleterious influence on the individual using it*. It was allowed, however, that it might undermine military discipline or morale. Prohibition was lifted. Some senior officers balked at this and demanded further investigation. This was carried out, coming to the same conclusions, but the higher echelons would not have it and the ban was reinstated in 1930, forbidding marijuana possession on military bases.

The influx of Mexican migrant workers in the first thirty years of the century, not to mention Pancho Villa's occasional attacks, damaged US–Mexican relations which had been historically weak for a century. Many Americans looked on these newcomers with disdain and racial distrust: a Mexican was regarded by definition as a thief and ne'er-do-well. Yet America needed them. The country was expanding and the Mexicans were cheap labour. Traditionally employed as *vaqueros* on the ranches of Texas, they soon spread to become fruit and vegetable pickers in east Texas, Arizona and California, labourers on the Colorado and Montana sugar beet farms, cattle wranglers on the railroad as far north as Chicago and horse wranglers in northern Texas, Oklahoma and Kansas. For a while, this was accepted but it was not long before it was the cause of more racial bitterness. Corporate landowners began to squeeze small farmers out of business by hiring the low-waged Mexicans and labour unions hated them because they were non-union and took union members' jobs. They were commonly robbed, beaten, murdered, driven out of town and generally accused of being un-American because of their language, their willingness to accept poor wages and their use of marijuana which was blamed whenever the Mexicans struck back. As the Chinese had suffered half a century before over their opium use, so now did the Mexicans over cannabis. Marijuana was labelled an alien drug, the fact that it was grown in America and had been an ingredient of patent medicines for decades was conveniently overlooked.

Inevitably, marijuana came to the attention of the law-enforcement agencies and was linked to crime and violence, often without any pretext or proof whatsoever.

It all started at a localized level in the towns on the Texas–Mexico border. In El Paso, a city by-law was passed in 1914 banning the sale and possession of marijuana after a serious fight had occurred involving a marijuana user – in other words, a Mexican – and the town was marked out as a hotbed of marijuana fiends which included not only Mexicans but also blacks, white criminals, native American Indians and all variety of riff-raff, none of which would have been out of place in any rough Texas cow-town. The underlying reason for the law was not to prohibit cannabis but suppress the Mexicans.

Once the potential of marijuana legislation for suppressing the migrants was realized, other cities and districts were quick to imitate it. Soon, the south-western and southern state legislatures started to lobby in Washington for federal action against what was now being termed 'killer' or 'loco weed.'

The US federal government had, in fact, already begun to draft and pass some anti-drug legislation. The Pure Food and Drug Act of 1906, although not designed to address the problem of narcotics, required the listing of them as ingredients on all patent medicines that crossed inter-state borders. Cannabis was therefore included alongside opium, morphine and cocaine as dangerous and the perception accepted. In addition, more legislation was about to be ratified.

Hamilton Wright, the co-leader of the US delegation to the Shanghai Opium Conference in 1909, working in collaboration with the Episcopal Bishop of the Philippines, Charles Henry Brent, urged the US Congress to legislate against opium. He argued that America had to set an example in narcotics control and lead the world in it. Just before the conference, the Smoking Opium Exclusion Act was passed, making illegal all imports of opium save those purchased by registered pharmaceutical firms. Penalties ranged from fines to incarceration with mere possession justify-ing arrest. With this act, for the first time, an 'alien' narcotic was criminalized. Spurred on by this, Wright continued campaigning against drugs. His zeal might have been genuine and justified, but he used scare-mongering, racist techniques to alarm especially the white population. In a pamphlet published in 1910, he forcefully reiterated the old fear that blacks taking cocaine were a sexual threat to decent white women. After the Hague conference in 1911, with much due to Wright and his constant lobbying of Congressman Francis Burton Harrison, new legislation was drawn up. It came into force as the Harrison Narcotic Act of 1914, which did not go so far as to prohibit narcotics but demanded doctors, pharmacists and licensed dealers maintain records of drug transactions and pay a stamp tax on them. The tax was not so much to raise revenue as to give the federal authorities a chance to regulate and control drug dispensing. The US Treasury was given the responsibility of collecting the tax and enforcing the law. To do this, it set up a narcotics division.

In early drafts of the Harrison Act, cannabis had been fully included, but the federal lawyers later excluded it as it was so common as a medicine, especially for glaucoma and migraine sufferers. The drug companies pressured for its exception. It was argued that the availability of a drug used in corn plasters and veterinary preparations should not be so restricted. It was, the lobbyists pointed out, ridiculous for a pharmacist to have to record every sale of a sticking plaster because it contained a listed narcotic. Even some anti-drug reformers allowed the point that cannabis was hardly as significant a problem as opiates and cocaine. The downside to the legislation was that physicians and druggists felt put upon by the bureaucracy and, on the now illegal market, prices rose sharply for opiates and cocaine, so many addicts, who had previously been good citizens, turned to petty crime to meet the rising cost of their habituation.

These moves did not greatly affect marijuana, the use of which – corn plasters aside – remained a low-key priority with federal law-makers. Individual state legislatures passed their own narcotics laws making cannabis illegal except as a medicine, putting them on the statute books only when they perceived they had a problem. By 1934, thirty-three states would have cannabis laws in place.

The 'problem' was often assessed by a census of the Mexican or black population. Surprisingly, the exception was California. Henry J. Finger, a member of the California Board of Pharmacy and one of Wright's delegates at the Hague conference, wrote to him on 2 July 1911: *Within the last year we in California have been getting a large influx of Hindoos and they have in turn started quite a demand for cannabis indica; they are a very undesirable lot and the habit is growing in California very fast.* He went on to say that there was a danger of them *initiating our whites into this habit*, and ended, *it seems to be a real question that now confronts us: can we do anything in the Hague that might assist in curbing this matter?* The *Hindoos* in question were

Sikhs and Punjabis who arrived in San Francisco in 1910 as indentured labourers and caused a furore. They were regarded as the next wave of the 'yellow peril' and hated from the start for their strange culture and food, dirty appearance, dubious morals, drug use and, of course, preparedness to work for low wages. That in all there were only two thousand of them in the entire state, most of them in one agricultural area, that they did not drink alcohol and worked hard — and hardly used any drugs at all — was ignored. They were Asiatics so it stood to reason they used drugs and were a bad lot.

Finger's fear that good white folk might be corrupted was preposterous. Most whites never came across marijuana and those that did failed to comprehend much about it. Even those who should have done, did not. When the Texas state legislature debated the subject, one member declared, *All Mexicans are crazy, and this stuff is what makes them crazy*. A Montana politician went further: *Give one of these Mexican beet field workers a couple of puffs on a marijuana cigarette and he thinks he is in the bullring at Barcelona*. Stories of the effects of the 'loco weed', appeared even in newspapers respected for their objective reporting. The *New York Times*, for example, ran the following article on 6 July 1927, under the headline, 'Mexican family go insane'. Datelined Mexico City it read, *A widow and her four children have been driven insane by eating the marihuana plant, according to doctors, who say that there is no hope of saving the children's lives and that the mother will be insane for the rest of her life. The tragedy occurred while the body of the father, who had been killed, was still in a hospital. The mother was without money to buy other food for the children, whose ages range from 3 to 15, so they gathered some herbs and vegetables growing in the yard for their dinner. Two hours after the mother and children had eaten the plants, they were stricken. Neighbors, hearing outbursts of crazed laughter, rushed to the house to find the entire family insane. Examination revealed that the narcotic marihuana was growing among the garden vegetables.*

The concern that the upper classes might become contaminated by marijuana use was not restricted to the USA. In Mexico, the same thought prevailed in the collective mind of the Government which was wary of the effect it might have on the Army and society in general. In 1925, the recommendations of the Geneva conferences were adopted as law, making the growing of cannabis an offence, but they were ineffectual. Corruption and the remoteness of so much of Mexico made enforcement impossible.

It was not only Mexican migrant workers who introduced marijuana to the USA. So, too, did sailors from the Caribbean and West Indian immigrants who settled in ports around the Gulf of Mexico. Marijuana use was soon established in Galveston, Houston and, particularly, New Orleans where it was readily found in the brothels and bordellos and variously known as *muta* (sometimes spelt *moota*) or *grifa*. The sources of non-Mexican marijuana were usually Havana, Tampico in Guatemala and Vera Cruz in Brazil, some of it imported by sailors whose sole source of income was marijuana running.

In August 1920, the attention of the Louisiana state health authorities was focused upon marijuana by the arrest of a young musician who had obtained it using a forged doctor's prescription. Dr Oscar Dowling, a member of the state health board for whom marijuana prohibition was a personal crusade, wrote to the state governor, copying his letter to the US Surgeon General. A few years later, Dr Frank Gomila, Commissioner of Public Safety in New Orleans, set his own anti-marijuana campaign going. The Louisiana press then got hold of what they thought a juicy story and published a series of articles in 1926 sensationalizing the issue, claiming children were smoking – indeed, were being educated in the smoking of – *muta*, but not pointing out that these were Mexican or black teenagers with whom marijuana use had been common for decades. The intended implication was that alien forces were corrupting white youths. The stories were picked up nationwide and made good copy for some years. Goaded by the spurious reports, the Louisiana legislature banned marijuana at its next sitting, possession or sale being penalized with six months in prison or a five-thousand-dollar fine.

For a while, this *status quo* was maintained then, as the Great Depression hit in 1929, the issue was once more agitated by a new anti-marijuana zealot, Dr A. E. Fossier. A bigot and a racist, he laid out his thoughts on the subject in an article entitled 'The Marihuana Menace', published in 1931 in the *New Orleans Medical and Surgical Journal*, in which he wrote, *The debasing and baneful influence of hashish and opium is not restricted to individuals but has manifested itself in nations and races as well. The dominant race and most enlightened countries are alcoholic, whilst the races and nations addicted to hemp and opium, some of which once attained to heights of culture and civilisation have deteriorated both mentally and physically.* Quite who he was railing against is hard to tell. The Mexican population of New Orleans was, according to a recent census, a mere 991 whilst crime statistics showed that, in 1928, three-quarters of all those arrested for narcotics crimes in the city were whites born and bred in the USA.

The link between drugs and racism was not confined to the USA. In Canada, opium and cocaine importation was banned from 1908 and 1911 respectively. Marijuana was ignored and would no doubt have remained so were it not for a Canadian feminist called Emily F. Murphy, who wrote under the pseudonym of Janey Canuck. Born in Cookstown, Ontario, in 1868, she came from a wealthy family, her grandfather having been a politician, newspaper proprietor and founder of an Irish Protestant Orange Order lodge, with two of her uncles holding posts as a senator and Supreme Court judge. At the age of nineteen, she married a priest and started fighting for women's rights and enfranchisement. In 1916, she was appointed a police magistrate in Edmonton, the first woman magistrate in the British Empire.

When, in 1920, the Canadian government considered redrafting its narcotics laws, Murphy was asked by *Maclean's Magazine* to write some pieces on Canada's drug problem. What did not exist she fabricated, taking her information from American publications. She attacked anyone who was not white or a Christian and had anything to do with drugs, accusing them of seeking to seduce white women as part of an international conspiracy of Orientals and blacks who sought to control the *bright-browed races of the world.* In her articles, she wrote of *an addict who died this year in British Columbia* [who] *told how he was frequently jeered at as a 'white man accounted for.' This man belonged to a prominent family . . . and used to relate how the Chinese pedlars taunted him with their superiority at being able to sell the dope without using it, and by telling him how the yellow race would rule the world . . . They would strike at the white race through 'dope' and when the time was ripe would command the world.* She added, *Some of the Negroes coming into Canada – and they are no fiddle-faddle fellows either – have similar ideas, and one of their greatest writers has boasted how ultimately they will control the white men.* The identity of the great black writer who made this boast is open to conjecture.

Everything Murphy wrote about marijuana, which was virtually unheard of in Canada at the time, was hearsay. *Persons using marijuana*, she warned sagely, *smoke the dried leaves of the plant, which has the effect of driving them completely insane. The addict loses all sense of moral responsibility. Addicts to this drug, while under its influence, are immune to pain, become raving maniacs, and are liable to kill or indulge in any form of violence to other persons.* If she was to be believed, the Assassins had been reincarnated in British Columbia. That she had no first-hand knowledge of marijuana whatsoever was never an issue.

As a result of Murphy's xenophobic ranting, drug users, who had previously been regarded at worst as degenerate, were now classed as dangerous public enemies. From her moral high ground, and with the weight of her legal appointment behind her, she drew the attention of the Canadian authorities which promptly added marijuana to the schedule of regulated substances in the Opium and Narcotics Drug Act of 1923. Yet it was another ten years before marijuana arrived in the country.

Regardless of the anti-drug campaigns, marijuana had continued to be used in New Orleans. As well as the dock labourers or field hands, another group, still black and often poor, were also using it. They were the musicians playing the new music: jazz.

Drugs and music had long been partners. Itinerant musicians attached to circuses, medicine shows and saloons or working the Mississippi paddle-steamers had frequently used drugs for the same reasons slaves and labourers had: to keep them going in a hard life. Most had used opiates or cocaine but, as these became increasingly hard to obtain, they switched to marijuana. Its illegality also gave them a mystique, a frisson of thrill that they were, as artists, beyond the confines of petty law.

New Orleans came to be regarded as the birthplace of jazz. With its sleazy, permissive reputation, its whores and gamblers, cabarets and saloons, dance halls and decadent French past, the town was an ideal breeding ground for a music that was new, invigorating and *risqué*. In Storeyville, the red-light district where most of the musicians worked and lived, drugs had been a part of life almost from the start. Prostitutes had used opiates for decades, not only to keep their stamina up in their physically demanding profession, but also as a form of contraception. They also used drugs to incapacitate some of their customers, known as 'johns', so that they could rob them.

The jazz musicians, who were mostly black and played in the brothels or saloons, avoided alcohol because it dulled the senses and opiates because they sent the taker to sleep. Marijuana, on the other hand, with which they were all familiar, kept them alert and fought off exhaustion. It also enhanced their musical creativity. Jazz and blues evolved with the help of marijuana.

In 1917, New Orleans' city fathers closed down Storeyville. The musicians moved north up the Mississippi, joining a general exodus of blacks heading in the same direction in search of work to such places as Kansas City and Chicago. Jazz and blues went with them, to become the new music of America and, later, the whole Western world. Marijuana went with them, too.

The post-Great War years were a time of sea change in America. As so often happens after a war, there was a realignment of the public psyche. The old order was questioned. The young, regardless of their colour but mostly white, wanted new directions, new challenges, a new world. Many turned towards black culture, attracted by its anti-establishment stance, its idealism, its down-to-earth honesty and its vibrant music. The most rebellious of the seekers became jazz musicians.

One, above all others, was to come to embody this new world of music and marijuana. His name was Milton 'Mezz' Mezzrow. White and of respectable middle-class Jewish extraction, he was born in Chicago in 1899 but he spent much of his formative life on the streets, becoming involved in petty crime. When he was arrested in the act of stealing a Studebaker car, he was sentenced to a period in the Pontiac Reformatory south-west of Chicago. Whilst there, as he was to later reminisce in his autobiography, *Really the Blues*, published in 1946, he *got me a solid dose of the colored man's gift for keeping the life and spirit in him while he tells of his troubles in music. I heard the blues for the first time, sung in low moanful chants morning, noon and night . . .* [it] *hit me like a millennium would hit a philosopher.* He learnt to play a saxophone and, on his release, rejected white society to become a jazz musician. Henceforth, he wrote, *I knew that I was going to spend all my time from then on sticking close to Negroes. They were my kind of people. And I was going to learn their music and play it for the rest of my days. I was going to be a musician, a Negro musician, hipping the world about the blues the way only Negroes can.* In time, he became a noted clarinettist playing with many big-name bands as well as owning his own, The Disciples of Swing, and considered himself to be black. In 1940, the US Army draft board actually listed him as a Negro, much to his delight.

It was inevitable that Mezzrow, living in the milieu of the jazz musician, would come across marijuana, of which he had previously been ignorant. In his autobiography, he was quite open about the subject. His first experience with 'muggles', the colloquial name for marijuana at the time amongst jazz musicians, occurred in 1924 at the Martinique Inn at Indiana Harbor, a small steel town not far from Gary, Indiana, where he was performing. A fellow musician newly arrived from New Orleans offered him a joint rolled like a cigarette but in brown wheat straw paper. Reluctantly, Mezzrow accepted: he had been offered marijuana before but always refused, afraid of what it might do to him. The musician showed him how to smoke it: *You got to hold that muggles so that it barely touches your lips, see, then draw in air around it. Say 'tfff, tfff', only breathe in when you say it. Then don't blow it out right away, you got to give the stuff a chance.* The drug kicked in during Mezzrow's next set. *The first thing I noticed,* he recalled, *was that I began to hear my saxophone as though it were inside my head . . . Then I began to feel the vibrations of the reed much more pronounced against my lip . . . I found I was slurring much better and putting just the right feeling into my phrases . . . All the notes came easing out of my horn, like they'd already been made up, greased and stuffed into the bell, so all I had to do was blow a little and send them on their way, one right after the other, never missing, never behind time, all without an ounce of effort . . . I felt I could go on playing for years without running out of ideas and energy. There wasn't any struggle; it was all made to order and suddenly there wasn't a sour note or a discord in the world that could bother me . . . I began to preach my millenniums on my horn, leading all the sinners to glory.*

He also described with considerable honesty what it was like to smoke marijuana for the first time, his account arguably one of the best ever written: *It's a funny thing about marihuana – when you first begin smoking it you see things in a wonderful soothing, easygoing new light. All of a sudden the world is stripped of its dirty gray shrouds and becomes one big bellyful of giggles, a spherical laugh, bathed in brilliant, sparkling colors that hit you like a heat wave. Nothing leaves you cold any more; there's a humorous tickle and great meaning in the least little thing, the twitch of somebody's little finger or the click of a beer glass. All your pores open like funnels, your nerve-ends stretch their mouths wide, hungry and thirsty for new sights and sound and sensations; and every sensation, when it comes, is the most exciting one you've ever had. You can't get enough of anything – you want to gobble up the whole goddamned universe just for an appetizer. Them first kicks are a killer.*

Jazz musicians believed marijuana aided their creativity because it dulled any musical inhibition and many tried to re-create the abandon they felt when intoxicated, the structures of the music seeking to imitate the way the instruments sounded under the influence of marijuana. Metrical structure was also considered affected by the stretching of the sense of time caused by marijuana. Hoagy Carmichael, one of America's great composers of popular songs such as 'Georgia on my Mind' and 'Lazybones', described the influence of marijuana and gin he experienced while jamming with Louis Armstrong: *the muggles took effect and my body got light. Every note Louis hit was perfection. I ran to the piano and took the place of Louis' wife. They swung into 'Royal Garden Blues'. I had never heard the tune before, but somehow I couldn't miss. I was floating in a strange deep blue whirlpool of jazz.*

Not every jazz musician concurred with these sentiments. John Hammond, producer, promoter, anti-racist and talent spotter – he was to discover Bob Dylan and Bruce Springsteen – declared that marijuana played hell with time while Artie Shaw, the famous clarinettist and saxophonist, believed it actually harmed jazz and resented its influence over his music.

Marijuana in the early years of Chicago's jazz world was plentiful and of high quality, much of it traded by Mexicans who used the profit to supplement their pitifully low incomes. For a while, its use did not even have to be clandestine. Mezzrow remarked how, *There being no law against muta then, we used to roll our cigarettes right out in the open and light up like you would on a Camel or a Chesterfield. To us muggles wasn't any more dangerous or habit-forming than those other great American vices, the five-cent Coke and the ice cream cone, only it gave you more kicks for your money.*

As time went by, marijuana acquired a cultural status amongst those musicians who used it. They saw themselves apart from those who did not indulge, superior in both music and outlook. Mezzrow explained how it felt. *Us vipers* [jazz slang for a marijuana smoker] *began to know we had a gang of things in common,* he wrote. *We were on another plane in another sphere compared to the musicians who were bottle babies, always hitting the jug and then coming up brawling after they got loaded. We liked things to be easy and relaxed, mellow and mild.* Jazz being a symbol of racial liberty and rebellion, marijuana was, as Mezzrow put it, part of a *collective improvised nose-thumbing at all pillars of all communities.*

Louis 'Satchmo' Armstrong, probably the best known jazz musician of them all, who was actually born in Storeyville in 1900, was also a frequent marijuana user. He stated, *It makes you feel good, man. It relaxes you, makes you forget all the bad things that happen to a Negro. It makes you feel wanted, and when you're with another tea smoker it makes you feel a special sense of kinship.*

This was part of the allure of marijuana. The users were a loosely woven clique, an in-crowd who shared not only the experience of drug intoxication but also a whole sense of cultural identity that went with it. In a world that was increasingly uniform, drab and industrial, they were unique, united and unfettered. Marijuana and the free-form expression of jazz was their liberty.

By 1930, marijuana had spread throughout most of the major cities of the USA, being particularly noted not only in Chicago but also Denver, Detroit, Tulsa, San Francisco, Baltimore, Cleveland, St Louis and Kansas City, all cities or regions of heavy industrial activity with substantial Mexican or black working-class populations. Kansas City was a positive den of iniquity where prostitutes, alcohol (during Prohibition) and drugs were readily to be had. This was due to the mayor of the Missouri half of the city, Thomas J. Prendergast, a wealthy brewer and corrupt Democrat who was more than slightly mob-connected. His closest associate-cum-civil enforcer was a local *mafioso* called John Lazia and he counted Charles Arthur 'Pretty Boy' Floyd amongst his friends. In such a libertarian climate, jazz flourished to such an extent that the town was for a while to rival New Orleans and Chicago as a centre of music. Curiously, New York City and its environs were excluded from this expansion. For the time being.

White workers, however, who made up the majority of the labour force, very rarely used marijuana, even if they were keen on jazz. It was still regarded as a substance used only by ethnic minorities and the whites preferred to keep to their beers, whiskey chasers and tobacco.

Those who did use marijuana came to be regarded as renegades, members of a sub-culture which considered itself aloof and exclusive. Along with Mexican migrants and blacks, both black and white jazz musicians were seen in this mould, outlaws who, with their 'primitive' music, were liable to corrupt the young, rob them of their sense and strip them of their morality. The sexual connotations of the lyrics, the primordial beat of the drums, the licentious abandon of the dancing (known as jiving) and the association with blacks and drug-taking was enough to provoke moves to have the music banned from public performance.

Yet there was something far more central to American society as a whole that was banned in the 1920s. The Volstead Act of 1919 was passed by Congress, providing the legal means by which the Eighteenth Amendment to the US Constitution could be enforced – and that prohibited the manufacture, sale and transportation of alcoholic beverages across state borders within the USA. It was in essence a far more draconian version of the Harrison Act and heralded the age of Prohibition, speakeasies and the mobsters who supplied them with illicit booze, defined by the Volstead Act as any beverage with an alcoholic content in excess of 0.5 per cent.

The temperance movement and anti-drug lobbies considered they had scored a vital and significant victory with the legislation, otherwise known as the National Prohibition Act. They were going to clean up American society with it. Denouncing minorities and whipping up racial tension, they prepared to aim at new targets. Tobacco was one of these, jazz was another and marijuana, the drug linked to it and used by those sections of society that allegedly most posed a threat, a third. That most Americans had never come across marijuana, let alone tried it, was immaterial. It was an evil substance that the ethnic minorities had in their arsenal of racial weaponry. It had to be suppressed and the stage was set for a witch hunt.

Into centre stage stepped a man who was to change the future of marijuana. His name was Harry J. Anslinger.

# WHEN THE LEGEND BECOMES FACT, PRINT THE LEGEND

HARRY J. ANSLINGER HAS BEEN PILLORIED AS THE MAN WHO SINGLE-handedly made marijuana illegal in the USA, but this is false. He did not instigate anti-marijuana policies or prohibition, which already existed, but he did mastermind a very efficient national campaign that was to do much to determine public attitudes towards marijuana and other drugs for over three decades. As such, he is probably the most important player in the history of both American and international anti-narcotics law enforcement and legislation.

He was born Harry Jacob Anslinger on 20 May 1892 in Altoona, Pennsylvania, the sixth of nine children in a working-class family. His father, Robert J. Anslinger, was a Swiss *émigré* who worked as a barber and, later, as a railroad security guard. His mother, Rosa, was of German descent. The family had emigrated to America about 1885: Harry was their third child to be born in the USA.

At the age of twenty, to earn money to support himself through his course majoring in agricultural business studies at the Department of Agricultural Economy and Rural Sociology in the College of Agricultural Sciences of Penn State University, Anslinger worked as a trackside maintenance labourer on the railroad, reporting anything suspicious he might see to the senior railroad security captain who was also his father's superior. Several years later, when the security captain appointed a fire marshal, he employed the newly graduated Anslinger as a statistician and arson investigator. Upon the USA entering the Great War in 1917, Anslinger was not drafted into the services on account of being blind in one eye, the result of a childhood stone-throwing incident with his brother, and was instead employed in the War Department in Washington overseeing government ordnance contracts. He then transferred to the State Department and, being a fluent German speaker, was sent in 1918 to The Hague in the Netherlands where he joined the American embassy, part of his responsibilities being to gather intelligence of both military and commercial value. Three years later, he passed the necessary examinations and was promoted to vice-consul in the German sea port of Hamburg where he discovered American merchant seamen being bribed to smuggle drugs into the USA. This was not, however, Anslinger's first encounter with narcotics. According to his own account in a book he published in 1961 entitled *The Murderers – The Story of the Narcotic Gangs*, Anslinger first came across drugs as a boy when he was sent on an errand to a pharmacy to fetch morphine for an addicted neighbour and later lost a choirboy friend to opium smoking.

From Hamburg, Anslinger was posted as consul to La Guaira in Venezuela then, in 1926, to Nassau in the Bahamas. In the former, he investigated pearl smugglers but in the latter he was to come across far bigger game – European merchant vessels running alcohol into the USA in defiance of Prohibition. Meeting with other consuls, he persuaded the British, Canadians, French and Cubans to combat this rum-running, as it was termed. This success prompted the US Treasury Department to appoint him as head of the foreign control section of their Prohibition Unit. In 1929, he was promoted to the post of its assistant commissioner.

The Prohibition Unit had been instigated in 1919 out of a narcotics department founded in 1914 by the Inland Revenue Bureau of the US Treasury Department to collect taxes and enforce the law as laid down by the Harrison Act: it was renamed the Prohibition Bureau in 1927. Within the Prohibition Unit, a separate narcotics division had been founded headed by a Colonel Levi G. Nutt. His reputation and that of many of his fellow officers was to be ruined in 1930 by allegations of sleaze involving the fixing of arrest records and association with the New York Jewish mobster and gambler Arnold Rothstein. Nutt was transferred to a regional alcohol-taxation office.

The scandal prompted a government reassessment of the situation. Republican Congressman Stephen G. Porter, a long-time congressional expert on narcotics and member of the American delegation to the Geneva opium conferences, persuaded a large number of his fellow congressmen to support his move to set up a new Bureau of Narcotics within the US Treasury Department. On 12 August 1930 his plan was adopted and the Federal Bureau of Narcotics (FBN) came into existence. Porter, who was a Congressman for Pennsylvania, did not live to see his achievement for he died of cancer on 27 June in Pittsburgh.

Anslinger was appointed the first commissioner of the FBN, his appointment ratified by President Herbert Hoover the following month and confirmed by the US Senate in December. It seems likely that Porter had put Anslinger's name forward for the latter's wife, Martha Denniston, was politically connected through her uncle, Andrew Mellon, who was Secretary of the Treasury, and moreover her family were exceedingly wealthy steel mill owners and major contributors to the Republican Party. A staunch Republican himself, Anslinger received a salary of nine thousand dollars per annum and the brief to supervise, regulate and enforce the law concerning both licit and illicit habit-forming drugs within the USA. He remained in the post until 1962.

With hindsight, Anslinger had all the attributes for the job. He was diligent, trustworthy, incorrupt, a skilful diplomatist, an expert judge of character and a loyal civil servant. He was also said to be, especially in later years, frightening in appearance. His square head was out of proportion to his body, he had huge ears and his eyes could be staring. In short, he looked the part of the tough law maker and drug buster, this mani-festation of commanding power filtering down through his organization.

Where marijuana was concerned, Anslinger was to develop a fixation. He was sincere, but he was out to get the drug and all those connected with it, almost at any cost and often with blunt disregard for the truth of any facts that were contrary to his argument. To his advantage, the Government gave him and the FBN a free rein for many years and did not discourage him from stepping outside the law in his crusade. It is said that, during Franklin D. Roosevelt's first term as president, Louis Howe, a close presidential adviser, told Anslinger that were he ever to recom-mend the President to show clemency for a drug dealer, he could append his resignation to the document.

Ultimate triumph in the war on marijuana aside, Anslinger had another goad to success. It was the Federal Bureau of Investigation (FBI), run as a bureaucratic fiefdom by his adversary in law enforcement, the devious and secretive J. Edgar Hoover. The rivalry between the two men went to extremes. Hoover, cautious of the murky world of narcotics and its potential to corrupt FBI agents, preferred to go after high-profile criminals such as gangsters whose arrests made good publicity: Anslinger was forever seeking to emulate this to raise awareness of the FBN both with the public and in government circles. Inevitably, there was much rancour and hatred between the two men and each created his own *bête noire* to grab headlines and the moral high ground. For Hoover, it was political enemies of the state, for Anslinger drug addiction and its hand-maiden, organized crime. Hoover was to win this struggle for supremacy by way of publicity. His targets – Nazis, Communists, civil rights activists, spies – were seen as more important and romantic in the public eye than Anslinger's poor Mexicans, ghetto blacks and other marijuana-smoking social outcasts and nondescripts.

To address this shortfall in his drive for publicity, Anslinger worked upon marijuana, building it up in the public consciousness into the 'Killer Weed' with such statements as *If the hideous monster Frankenstein came face to face with the monster marihuana, he would drop dead of fright*, which he declaimed in *The Washington Herald* in 1937. His intention was to strike fear into the heart of the American man in the street. It worked. Yet, when first becoming head of the FBN, Anslinger had been dismissive of a federal ban on marijuana. At the time, he simply did not see it as that great a threat.

From the start, Anslinger revolutionized the approach to law enforce-ment, employing undercover agents and setting up intelligence-gathering networks in the USA and overseas. At first concerned primarily with the enforcing of the Harrison Act, his attention was then drawn to the use of marijuana in the south-western states but he did not take the situation too seriously. Only Mexicans were involved and containing them was not difficult. What was more, as there was no federal marijuana law, there was little he could or should do.

Some attempts had been made to attach cannabis to existing federal narcotics legislation. In 1929, a number of Congressmen led by a Texan senator approached Anslinger to append it to the Harrison Act but this was opposed on the grounds that hemp was a domestic agricultural crop and it was impractical to attempt to control interstate commerce in it. The federal government did, however, take some action that year in establish-ing two centres (called 'farms') at Lexington, Virginia, and Fort Worth, Texas, for the treatment of federal prisoners who were addicted to, as it was put, *habit-forming narcotic drugs* including Indian hemp.

There was another reason for Anslinger's reluctance to address marijuana. It was manpower. He knew he would need many more agents to combat a drug so commonly used amongst Mexicans and blacks. In the early years of the FBN, he had only three hundred full-time agents at his command and they were needed to combat opiates and cocaine. Consequently, he suggested individual states tackle their marijuana problem according to its severity. This was all very well for most states but those in the south-west, where marijuana use was widespread amongst ethnic minorities, pressured for federal legislation. The press and 'concerned citizens' took up the call, driven not only by their zeal but also by their anti-Mexican attitudes, which were strengthened during the Depression when jobs were scarce and migrants seen to be stealing work from the white work force. The Mexicans were accused, without any justification, of spreading marijuana across the nation. State marijuana laws were often used as an excuse to deport or imprison innocent Mexicans. Resistance to arrest was put down to marijuana-induced violence or frenzy.

Marijuana was used – yet again – to attack Mexican cheap labour. In California, where there was by now a substantial Mexican population, the Missionary Educator Movement and the American Coalition of Patriotic Societies lobbied the state government. A leading member of the latter, C. M. Goethe, announced in *The New York Times* in 1935: *Marijuana, perhaps now the most insidious of our narcotics, is a direct by-product of unrestricted Mexican immigration. Easily grown, it has been asserted that it has recently been planted between rows in a Californian penitentiary garden. Mexican peddlers have been caught distributing sample marijuana cigarettes to school children.* He had no justification for this by now well-worn accusation. Newspapers, particularly those owned by William Randolph Hearst, who was a racist, made much of the supposed Mexican threat. Such sensationalist and unprincipled coverage even earned its own soubriquet of 'yellow journalism.'

It was Hearst, or more accurately his newspapers, which popularized the word marijuana, spelt at the time with an *h*. Prior to the 1930s, those who knew of the drug, and were neither Mexican nor black, usually referred to it as hemp. Marijuana, as it gained common parlance, came to stand for a criminal substance, a foreign drug set to undermine mainstream American culture.

Anslinger, who maintained a very substantial file on marijuana even though he was not initially involved in legislating for it, attempted to historically link the word marijuana to the Aztec Indians of Mexico. According to his argument, cannabis was called *malihua* or *mallihuan* in Nahuatl, the Aztec language. This was, Anslinger claimed, constructed of the noun *mallin* (a prisoner), the preposition *hua* (of or suggesting a property) and the verb *ana* (to capture, take or grab). Therefore, *mallihuan* (sometimes spelt *milan-a-huan*) meant the prisoner taken captive by the plant. In other words, an addict.

Within two years of the establishment of the FBN, it was in trouble. The Depression caused a considerable fall in tax revenue and government spending plummeted. The FBN budget was substantially cut. In order to boost his organization, Anslinger had to find a new target – a new drug menace – upon which to peg a budget increase. Although he had previously given marijuana little thought and deferred putting it under federal legislation, he now set about demonizing it, circulating pamphlets and planting stories in the press about murders committed whilst under marijuana intoxication. He also started pushing for marijuana to be included as a dangerous drug alongside opiates and cocaine in the Uniform State Narcotic Acts then widely under consideration by a large number of state legislatures. Under these, there would be a standard approach to non-federal narcotics legislation nationwide, each state having the power to make arrests for possession and use of restricted substances, closing a drugs taxation loophole in the Harrison Act. There was another motive to Anslinger's actions. If marijuana was legislated against at state level, it would relieve the FBN of some responsibility for it and therefore free up a part of the budget. In time, Anslinger won the day, aided by the press, especially the Hearst newspapers which whipped up public opinion. Eventually, by 1936, thirty-eight states would add marijuana to their most dangerous drugs list under the Uniform State Narcotic Acts. Those remaining still passed some legislation governing the sale or possession of it.

The American public was ripe for anti-marijuana press exploitation. Prohibition had been extremely unpopular and anything that diverted attention away from it was welcome. Apart from not being able to get a glass of whiskey, the public was also worried by the crime wave Prohibition had set in motion: indeed, it gave a far greater boost to organized crime than anything before. In 1933, when the Volstead Act was repealed, the emphasis switched from alcohol to drugs, not just in law enforcement but also in lawbreaking.

Prohibition had another effect that concerned the legislators. The well-to-do, who had been used to a café and cabaret society life before Prohibition, took to speakeasy bars and secret drinking dens where they not only drank illicit booze but also came into contact with criminals – and the music of the speakeasy was jazz, the players of which often used marijuana. The link was made. Furthermore, not only the temperance and anti-narcotics organizations grew worried. When Prohibition was lifted, the brewers and distillers became concerned that marijuana – cheap and easily grown – would dent their profits. Marijuana therefore posed not only a legal but also a commercial quandary which had to be tackled somehow.

Towards the end of 1934, Anslinger himself came under censure. He had faced the threat of losing his position in 1933 when Roosevelt won the US presidency and set in motion his Democratically biased New Deal under which all government employment was scrutinized, any whiff of favouritism being sniffed out. Anslinger's wife's family connections had placed his job in jeopardy. Now, he was facing outright dismissal not only for his running of the FBN but also because of an uproar created in Pennsylvania by black community leaders who objected to Anslinger referring to a coloured man in one of his anti-marijuana pamphlets as a *ginger-colored nigger*. He survived but only because of his support base of editors, hardline congressmen and some senior pharmaceutical industry figures.

Late in the year, under pressure to be seen to be proactive, Anslinger began to focus on marijuana, writing articles about how it induced rapes and murders in which the perpetrators were almost always black or Mexican, the victims white. These were issued by the FBN to the press or sourced by the newspapers to Anslinger.

Not surprisingly, public awareness of marijuana increased very sharply and a wide range of lobby groups such as the YWCA and YMCA, the Women's Christian Temperance Union and the national association of parent-teacher associations joined in the demand for the drug to be included in the Uniform State Narcotic Acts. FBN annual reports, which had hitherto concentrated on opiates or cocaine, suddenly started to concentrate on marijuana. The 1935 publication held thirteen pages on the subject, with photographs.

The anti-marijuana bandwagon was now on the road and the US treasury came under pressure to federally legislate against it, the anomaly being widely voiced that opium and cocaine which were produced in foreign countries were banned but a home-grown drug – purportedly just as insidious – was not.

Although he had originally been keen on state legislation, Anslinger was quick to appreciate the advantages of federal law-making. It would very considerably raise the FBN arrest rate, giving the organization a higher standing both in public and government eyes and, consequently, generate a greater budget. He increased his efforts.

So did the press. In 1936, a story went out that is typical of the coverage. Issued by the Universal News Service, it read in part: *Murders*

*Due to 'Killer Drug' Marihuana Sweeping United States . . . Shocking crimes of violence are increasing. Murders, slaughterings, cruel mutilations, maimings, done in cold blood, as if some hideous monster was amok in the land . . . much of this violence* [is attributed to] *what experts call marihuana. It is another name for hashish . . . a roadside weed in almost every State in the Union . . . Those addicted . . . lose all restraints, all inhibitions. They become bestial demoniacs, filled with a mad lust to kill . . .* Also released at about the same time was a letter Anslinger received from Floyd Baskette, the city editor of the *Daily Courier* in Alamosa, a small town in Colorado halfway between Denver and Santa Fe, New Mexico. It was an agricultural area with a substantial Mexican migrant labour population. The letter reported the story of Lee Fernandez who had been responsible for a wave of rapes and murders across southern Colorado. There was no proof that Fernandez had used marijuana, although the odds are that he did: no link between the drug and his one-man crime wave existed. Nevertheless, it was considered enough, as Baskette stated, that he was a Spanish-speaking person *most of whom are low mentally, because of social and racial conditions.*

As if press coverage were not sufficient, Anslinger's campaign spawned several anti-marijuana movies, although several silent two- and three-reelers had appeared on the subject in the 1920s.

*Marihuana*, released in 1935, had the tagline, *Weird orgies! Wild parties! Unleashed passions!* (Another film of the same title was made in Mexico, directed by José Bohr, soon afterwards.) The most famous and widely distributed was *Tell Your Children* (also entitled *Reefer Madness, The Burning Question, The Dope Addict, Doped Youth* and *Love Madness*), released in 1936 and directed by Louis J. Gasnier. The narrative, as told to a PTA meeting by a high-school principal called Dr Carroll, centres around Mae and Jack, played by Carleton Young who was later to star with John Wayne in the seminal western *The Man Who Shot Liberty Valance*. Mae and Jack introduce their fellow students to marijuana. The lives of all are shattered, especially that of one who is committed to an insane asylum for life. The film was partly financed by a major distilling company which would have lost a considerable income had marijuana become more popular than alcohol. The following year, *Assassin of Youth* was released, starring Dorothy Short who had appeared in *Tell Your Children*. It was about a high-school girl involved with teenage marijuana smokers and a reporter who poses as a soda jerk to infiltrate this ring of teenage dope fiends.

A line that Young's character in the western was to utter twenty-six years later might well have applied to Anslinger, his campaign, the press coverage of marijuana and the marijuana movies: *When the legend becomes fact, print the legend.*

All this publicity strengthened the bond between marijuana, crime and violence. It was compounded by arrested criminals agreeing in their confessions that marijuana had played a part in their crime in the hope of a reduced sentence and, of course, whenever violence and marijuana were mentioned in the same sentence, the myth of the Assassins was resurrected as cast-iron proof.

One story in particular was repeated time and again by Anslinger. It concerned a young man called Victor Licata who came from Tampa in Florida. Aged twenty-one, Licata murdered his parents, two brothers and a sister with an axe, allegedly claiming to the police that he had done so when in what he termed a marijuana dream: it was said Licata had been smoking marijuana for six months. That Licata had already been subject to a police attempt to have him committed to a mental asylum, which his parents had contested whilst agreeing to look after him themselves, and was subsequently found under psychiatric analysis to be criminally insane and, according to a psychiatrist's report, *frequently subject to hallucinations accompanied by homicidal impulses* was ignored. When he was finally incarcerated in a mental institution, he was diagnosed as suffering from probably inherited *dementia praecox with homicidal tendencies*. No mention is made in his records of marijuana.

Not only violence was associated with marijuana: so was sex and promiscuity. In the *International Medical Digest* in 1937, an article headed 'The Menace of Marihuana' recounted how a *boy and girl who had lost their senses so completely after smoking marihuana, actually eloped and were married.* Another piece published in the same year spoke of high-school pupils meeting to smoke marijuana and dance sensuously then, *after a time, girls began to pull off their clothes. Men weaved naked over them; soon the entire room was one of the wildest sexuality. Ordinary intercourse and several forms of perversion were going on at once, girl to girl, man to man, woman to woman.*

Quite possibly, there was yet another reason for the outlawing of marijuana. According to Jack Herer, a leading American marijuana activist and the author of the seminal marijuana text *The Emperor Wears No Clothes*, there were economic as well as moral considerations at play. He believes that hemp products posed a threat to established financial and industrial interests. There is much of the conspiracy theory about his premise but it is not at all outlandish. He argues that the petrochemical and pulp paper industries stood to lose billions of dollars if the commercial potential of hemp was fully realized. Experiments, such as those being carried out by the Ford Motor Company, were underway to develop synthetic products from renewable resources, especially hemp, instead of fossil fuels, the possibility being that hydrocarbons of hemp could be used instead of petroleum hydrocarbons. Herer names William Randolph Hearst and Lammont Du Pont, head of the multi-national pharmaceutical and petrochemical conglomerate that bore his name, as the main orchestrators of the anti-hemp movement. At the centre of the hypothesis was the invention of the hemp decorticator, a machine that could strip hemp fibre without retting, making it feasible to use hemp on a large scale.

Many inventors, since the time of Thomas Jefferson, had come up with hemp processors but only the decorticator patented on 1 July 1919 by George W. Schlichten worked effectively at an industrial level. It was able to strip the fibre from virtually any plant, the pulp (known as hurds) discarded for any alternative use that might arise and the fibre ready for treatment.

The first decorticator went into operation in a spinning mill owned by John D. Rockefeller. He tried to buy the patent rights but Schlichten rebuffed him: the economic downturn caused by the Great War also discouraged investors. Yet one, Harry Timken, the owner of the Timken Roller Bearing Company, wanted to develop it and saw its potential as a provider of not only fibre but also paper pulp. He arranged a meeting with Edward W. Scripps, the proprietor of the Scripps Newspaper Company in San Diego. Scripps owned massive timber interests in the states of Washington and Oregon. It did not take a genius to realize that, with the decorticator in operation, the need for wood pulp (in which industry not only Scripps but also Hearst had a substantial holding in addition to huge forestry interests) would be much reduced.

Something had to be done to stymie the industrial march of hemp.

Between 1935 and 1937, Du Pont persistently lobbied Herman Oliphant, chief counsel to the US Treasury Department. Andrew Mellon, by now Secretary of the US Treasury Department and not only Anslinger's uncle-in-law but also Du Pont's banker, also piled on the pressure for federal legislation. He too had vested interests in seeing hemp suppressed as he was a major shareholder in Gulf Oil and a huge coal mining concern in Pennsylvania, not to mention a number of utility companies. Whether or not Herer is right in his assumption is perhaps immaterial. What is a fact is that there was much hypocrisy being exercised in the marijuana debate.

The marijuana propaganda may have made for salacious press stories but marijuana was, throughout the 1930s, essentially unimportant. People did not bother about it. Far from there being an epidemic of marijuana use, it was rarely seen outside the world of seamen, cow hands, jazz musicians, working-class blacks and Mexicans, and gangsters. The spreaders of alarm and despondency produced no scientific evidence to support their claims, although this did little to dilute the reputation of the killer weed that drove you mad. Whenever voices of moderation spoke out, they were suppressed or dismissed.

Anslinger discouraged any unbiased scientific investigation or evaluation. He even prevented marijuana from being provided to respectable research institutions for the purpose of research. From the mid-1930s onwards, he engaged upon a vigorous and sustained anti-marijuana campaign without a reasoned justification other than his personal prejudice. With few experts able to counter his claims, he was at liberty to preach as he pleased. Only once, in the winter of 1936, did he allow, in a letter to the magazine publishers P. F. Collier and Son, that there was no solid, proven link between crime and marijuana.

Not satisfied with his national anti-marijuana stance, Anslinger also started to work on an international campaign knowing that, once marijuana was banned by international law, the USA would have to comply with it.

At the Conference for the Suppression of Illicit Traffic in Dangerous Drugs in Geneva in June 1936, Anslinger urged the international control of cannabis but other countries rejected his approach on the grounds that there was insufficient evidence to support his claims of the drug's iniquity. The following January, however, the US Treasury Department held a conference on cannabis. At this, Anslinger trotted out all the horror stories in his repertoire and stepped up his campaign by accepting speaking engagements all over the USA. Oliphant set to drafting a bill against marijuana based upon the Harrison and National Firearms Acts, applying a punitive transfer tax on marijuana as existed on automatic machine guns. It was the only way to address Anslinger's demands within the US Constitution. The bill was known as the Marihuana Tax Act, 1937.

The various preliminary hearings for the proposed bill commenced in April 1937. Anslinger repeated his shock stories and, with no qualifications whatsoever, gave his own medical opinion of the dangers of marijuana and went so far as to state to the hearings, *Here we have a drug that is not like opium. Opium has all the good of Dr Jekyll and all the evil of Mr Hyde. This drug is entirely the monster Hyde* ... No valid statistics or scientific evidence were put forward. The 'expert' witnesses called all but perjured themselves. When Anslinger asked Dr Carl Voegtlin, chief of the Division of Pharmacology of the National Institute of Health, if insanity was produced by smoking marijuana, the answer came back, *I think it is an established fact that prolonged use leads to insanity in certain cases ...* Witnesses called to speak against the bill included Ralph Loziers of the National Oil Seed Institute, who complained the proposed provisions were too sweeping but accepted them in principle, and a representative of a major bird seed manufacturer who said hemp seed was incomparably the best bird seed available. Consequently, hemp seed was exempt under the Marihuana Tax Act – and remains so to this day. However, the seeds had to be 'de-natured' (sterilized) before sale.

Only one voice was in serious opposition to the bill. Dr William C. Woodward of the American Medical Association (AMA) was a lawyer as well as a physician, and no friend of Anslinger. Under the Harrison Act, FBN agents had apprehended or threatened thousands of doctors, often on trumped-up prescription charges. Dr Woodward stated openly that the whole hearing process was biased, there was a lack of scientific proof for the claims being promulgated, witness testament was vague, the assumption that the medicinal use of cannabis was responsible for the 'marijuana menace' was unfounded and it was all being rushed through with undue haste. Although he concurred with the need to regulate marijuana, Woodward was also at odds with Anslinger on another point. Where Anslinger saw marijuana users as dedicated criminals, the doctor regarded them as patients in need of treatment. That the AMA was mostly Republican and the administration predominantly Democrat did not help. The AMA objections were overruled and, when the Senate committee debated the bill, its passage was given a smooth ride by the chairman who was a close friend of Du Pont.

The bill finally reached the floor of Congress for ratification at the very end of a Friday afternoon session, by which time many of the legislators had gone for the weekend. The debate lasted a matter of minutes, the Speaker – a long-standing Texan Democrat called Sam Rayburn – seemed unsure what the bill was about and no vote was taken. Instead, the teller system was used whereby congressmen walked past a teller who counted the number of people going by him. Only a Republican congressman from New York raised any questions. When he enquired as to what the AMA thought of the proposal, a Democrat supporter replied, *Their Doctor Wentworth came down here. They support this bill one hundred per cent.* He even got the doctor's name wrong.

The Marihuana Tax Act was signed by President Roosevelt on

2 August and came into effect on 1 October, the first federal legislation controlling marijuana.

Under the new law, any person cultivating, transporting, selling, prescribing or using marijuana had to be registered and pay a tax levy of one hundred dollars an ounce every time the drug changed hands. For industrial use, the level was set at one dollar an ounce. To give this some perspective, the price of a brand-new Ford Model-Y saloon car in 1937 was $205. In theory, the Act was a piece of revenue legislation and any infringement a tax violation not a narcotics one. Yet the aim was clear: to control the social use of marijuana. In effect, it was a prohibition and unconstitutional in that the substance itself was not proscribed, just made all but inaccessible by repressive taxation.

The Act might have been aimed at the non-existent drug fiend, but it hit hardest at the legitimate hemp-farming industry. Although this had been shrinking in size over the years, the Act dealt it a death blow, depriving American farmers, who had been hard hit by the Depression, of what could have been a new, multi-million-dollar cash crop. With Schlichten's decorticator, which the inventor had been refining and improving ever since he registered the patent in 1919, hemp could have made the US self-sufficient in natural fibres and reduced, if not removed, the reliance upon imported fabric and thread. Yet the Marihuana Tax Act killed off any chance. Not only was the hemp industry ruined, so too was Schlichten who lost all his money and never saw his machine in widespread use.

As for any wild hemp plants, Anslinger set about eradicating them too, with nationwide itinerant gangs of labourers.

In 1938, Canada prohibited cannabis cultivation. The aim there was not to raise revenue but to prevent the leisure use of marijuana. Doctors were still permitted to prescribe tincture of cannabis, but the bureaucracy that came with every prescription discouraged many from offering it to patients. What further stopped it being prescribed was the imposition of the Marihuana Tax Act south of the border for most medicinal cannabis was grown in Florence, South Carolina and was hit by the new regulations.

Three years later, just before the USA entered the Second World War, cannabis was dropped from the American pharmacopoeia, it is said at Anslinger's request. Although American doctors were still theoretically allowed to prescribe medicinal cannabis, they did not because of the over-regulation and cost in tax.

With the Marihuana Tax Act in force, Anslinger was faced with the problem of controlling the traffic in a substance that was more readily available than any other drug. Indeed, it was a weed and any number of clearance gangs could not totally eradicate it. He also privately admitted that heroin was far more dangerous and far more easily controlled. Yet marijuana had served its purpose. The FBN budget was substantially increased and he embarked once more on a campaign of marijuana vilification, appealing to the nation to help him.

His utterances to the press and on radio were in the best traditions of yellow journalism. In what has become his most famous article, 'Marijuana: Assassin of Youth', published in the *American Magazine* a few weeks before the Marihuana Tax Act was passed, he wrote, *The sprawled body of a young girl lay crushed on the sidewalk the other day after a plunge from the fifth story of a Chicago apartment house. Everyone called it suicide, but actually it was murder. The killer was a narcotic known in America as marihuana, and to history as hashish. It is a narcotic used in the form of cigarettes, comparatively new to the United States and as dangerous as a coiled rattlesnake . . .* He continued with the Licata story before introducing a new case: *In Los Angeles, a youth was walking along a downtown street after inhaling a marihuana cigarette. For many addicts, merely a portion of a 'reefer' is enough to induce intoxication. Suddenly, for no reason, he decided that someone had threatened to kill him and that his life at that very moment was in danger. Wildly he looked about him. The only person in sight was an aged bootblack. Drug-crazed nerve centers conjured the innocent old shoe-shiner into a destroying monster. Mad with fright, the addict hurried to his room and got a gun. He killed the old man, and then, later, babbled his grief over what had been wanton, uncontrolled murder. 'I thought someone was after me,' he said. 'That's the only reason I did it. I had never seen the old fellow before. Something just told me to kill him!' That's marihuana!*

This hysterical approach and the passing of the new Act were to prove problematic for Anslinger. First, as he increased his warnings about the supposed menace so the public came to believe him and demand more arrests which were not forthcoming. Second, he had by his ranting alienated a large section of the ethnic-minority population of the USA which was, marijuana aside, largely law abiding. This in turn caused them to become secretive and closed. Third, with marijuana use widespread in certain geographical and social areas, the FBN found itself under-funded and under-staffed at a local level to deal with the situation. From the very beginning, enforcing the Marihuana Tax Act was a lost battle.

The dubious honour of being the first person to be arrested under the Act fell to fifty-eight-year-old Samuel Caldwell who was tried in Denver, Colorado, on 8 October 1937, accused of selling a small amount of marijuana to Moses Baca, aged twenty-six. The presiding US district judge was J. Foster Symes. Anslinger was also present in court. Caldwell was fined one thousand dollars and sentenced to four years' hard labour in the infamous US federal penitentiary at Leavenworth, Kansas. Baca got eighteen months in the same jail.

It was not long before another dilemma faced Anslinger. Defence lawyers started arguing that their clients' crimes had been 'marijuana induced', the plea being one of marijuana insanity and temporarily diminished responsibility. The attorneys cited Anslinger's article, 'Marijuana: Assassin of Youth', arguing the logic that users were themselves victims of their circumstance since – as Anslinger himself had declared – marijuana was the source of their criminality. The defence lawyers were further aided, and marijuana's poor reputation further strengthened, by Anslinger's public statement that marijuana was *an addictive drug which produces in its users insanity, criminality, and death.*

The argument was first applied in January 1938, in the defence of Ethel 'Bunny' Sohl of Newark, New Jersey, then in the trial of Arthur Friedman of New York City three months later. Both were murderers. The former claimed she grew vampire-like incisors after smoking marijuana whilst the latter started off killing dogs then graduated to two police officers. In each trial, Dr James Munch, a pharmacologist from Temple University, Philadelphia who had been an expert witness testifying for the FBN in the Marihuana Tax Act hearings, was called by the defence. Under cross-examination at one of the trials – and under oath – he outlined his marijuana experiments on dogs, admitting he had tried the drug himself for scientific reasons. When asked what had happened, he answered, *After two puffs on a marijuana cigarette, I was turned into a bat.* He then claimed he flew around the room and down a 200-foot-deep inkwell. The local newspaper ran the headline, 'Killer Drug Turns Doctor to Bat!' Both murderers, although found guilty, had their sentences commuted from death to life imprisonment.

Shortly after it was announced that Friedman had avoided the electric chair, Anslinger wrote to Munch and told him to stop testifying as a defence witness or his appointment as an FBN special adviser would be terminated. He complied.

Anslinger realized that he had, by his vociferous and usually un-substantiated anti-marijuana rhetoric, undermined his own credibility. In an attempt to regain some ground, he began to retrench, greatly lessening the sensationalism he had so blatantly fostered. The link between marijuana and the act of criminality was considerably played down, scare-mongers were actively discouraged and fear tactics suppressed. He did not, however, diminish his own use of such strategies when applying each year for the FBN budget, his report concentrating upon arrest and eradication statistics and case histories.

Whatever successes Anslinger claimed for the FBN drive against marijuana, he and his agents found great difficulty in their task. Unlike with opiates or cocaine, there was no organized trafficking network to hit. Small-time dealers were fairly easily apprehended but the drug barons behind them were not, for the simple reason that there were none. Opiates – heroin and morphine – were substantial criminal businesses. Marijuana was, by comparison, a cottage industry. Although it was never voiced, Anslinger's unofficial policy was that the FBN pursued the inter-national opiate and cocaine runners while state police forces targeted marijuana.

Four years after the Marihuana Tax Act wiped out America's hemp industry, the plant was suddenly in demand. After the attack on Pearl Harbor in December 1941, and the nation's declaration of war on Japan, the US government overlooked any worries it had about marijuana and promoted a *Grow Hemp for Victory* campaign, the usual source of plant fibre, the Philippine Islands, falling under enemy occupation. Approximately twenty thousand farmers in the Midwestern states were registered under the federally funded War Hemp Industries Corporation to cultivate over 30,000 acres of cannabis producing 42,000 tons of fibre and 180 tons of seed annually throughout the war years. Hemp seed oil was used as an aviation lubricant. Whereas, in 1940, cannabis had been all but eradicated so that, amongst other things, children could not be con-taminated by it, in 1942, school children in rural areas were being encouraged to grow it to aid the war effort. To encourage farmers to grow hemp, those who agreed were – with their sons – exempted from military service. A fourteen-minute patriotic propaganda film was made by the US Department of Agriculture (USDA), singing the praises of cannabis which was, as the script read, going *on duty again – hemp for moor-ing ships, hemp for tow lines, hemp for tackle and gear, hemp for countless naval uses both on ship and shore!* In Germany, meanwhile, the Nazi government was spurring its own farmers on to grow hemp, their supplies from Russia having ceased.

A footnote to this is almost as ironic as the plea for children to grow cannabis. In 1980, when marijuana activists led by Herer asked to see the film, the USDA denied it had ever existed. Thorough searches of govern-ment archives could not produce a print. It had been deleted from all databases, most likely on the post-war request of Anslinger and the FBN. Finally, two prints were found in the copyright-holding section of the Library of Congress in which, by law, all intellectual material released in the USA must be represented.

As the tide of the war in Europe turned, America was increasingly able to obtain hemp fibre supplies from European sources. Domestic production was reduced until, from 1946 onwards, the hemp-growing programme was terminated. It left thousands of acres of cannabis growing unharvested. In next to no time, the fecund plant had re-established itself once more as a widespread weed. It may still be found growing in the Midwest where it is known colloquially as 'ditch weed'. It has, however, evolved somewhat and has a very low THC content. Anslinger's eradication drive had been in vain.

Hemp was sought by the US government during the war for more than fibre. In 1942, the Office of Strategic Services (OSS), the forerunner of the Central Intelligence Agency (CIA), investigated the potential of marijuana as a truth drug to be used in the interrogation of enemy agents and captives. The first extract was termed honey oil. Tasteless and made from hashish, it was to be added to the food of interrogation subjects. When it was tested on OSS guinea pigs, they broke out in peals of laughter, talked incessantly, became paranoid or clammed up. The research was abandoned in favour of developing LSD for the same purpose. However, the researchers published a report on marijuana which stated that the commonest effect of honey oil was fits of laughter. Anslinger, who had been attacking marijuana for over a decade as a brain-destroying narcotic, was a signatory to the report.

In retrospect, Anslinger did marijuana a huge service. He mythologized it and nationally publicized it more effectively than an advertising campaign. Certainly, much of his erstwhile sales pitch did alarm people, but there were others who questioned his propaganda and wanted to know the truth.

# 14

# NEW YORK, NEW YORK

FIORELLO 'FRANK' LAGUARDIA, THE MAYOR OF THE CITY OF NEW YORK, was one of Anslinger's main critics. It was not that he was pro-marijuana but he was anti-humbug and a man of considerable political integrity for whom the truth had value.

In 1938, determined to discover the reality about marijuana and defuse the public concern which had arisen from the yellow journalism of the tabloids as well as Anslinger's own propaganda, LaGuardia decided to act. With the assistance of the New York Academy of Medicine he set up The Mayor's Committee consisting of an investigative panel of over two dozen assorted eminent medical practitioners, health experts and sociologists under the chairmanship of Dr George B. Wallace. Much against Anslinger's wishes but with the full co-operation of the New York City Police Department (NYCPD), the committee carried out a full-scale scientific and sociological study of marijuana. Hand-picked police officers were retrained as specific investigators, the medical staff of Riker's Island, the city penitentiary in the East River, assisted and the Goldwater Memorial Hospital provided ward, laboratory and office accommodation. At last, an in-depth and comprehensive scientific study of marijuana was under way.

Marijuana had come late to New York. Despite an article appearing in the *New York Times* in January 1923 announcing that marijuana was the latest habit-forming drug to be found in the city, its use was insignificant for the city had not been a destination for Mexican migrants. Even FBN undercover agents' reports stated marijuana was obvious by its absence and only used by a small ethnic group of Latin-American seamen.

This changed with the Depression. By 1931, the black population of New York, especially in the district of Harlem, exceeded three hundred thousand. Most had come from the southern states and the Caribbean, hoping for work. They did not find it and for many, who had previously lived a rural existence, unemployment only compounded the misery of living in a city. To escape their lot, some turned to drugs, both using and dealing in them. For a minority, this meant heroin but for the vast majority it was marijuana, the one drug with which they were already familiar. Those who were not familiar with it soon came to hear of it through the other escape to which these urban blacks resorted – jazz.

By the early 1930s, New York had taken over from New Orleans and Chicago as the city of jazz and amongst those who moved there was 'Mezz' Mezzrow. He lived in the Bronx but he gravitated to Harlem where, on his own admission, *Right from the start I was surrounded by a lot of wonderful friends, the first gang of vipers in Harlem . . . Before I knew it I had to write to our connection for a large supply, because everybody I knew wanted some . . . Overnight I was the most popular man in Harlem.* His supply was far superior to much of the marijuana then available. *That mellow Mexican leaf,* he wrote, *really started something in Harlem – a whole new language, almost a new culture.* In next to no time, Mezz became known as the man to whom one went, his reputation as a marijuana connection greater than that as a jazz musician. So famous was he that his name entered the local slang: a 'mezzrow' was a large, high-quality joint whilst the adjective 'mezz' meant 'genuine' or 'superb'.

Mezzrow was not a pusher in the traditional sense. He sold marijuana only to acquaintances, not necessarily for a profit, and he did not advocate its use. *Even during the years when I sold the stuff,* he admitted, *I never 'pushed' it like a salesman pushes vacuum cleaners or Fuller brushes. I had it for anybody who came asking, if he was a friend of mine. I didn't promote it anywhere, and I never gave it to kids . . . I sold it to grown-up friends of mine who had got to using it on their own, just like I did; it was a family affair, not any high-pressure business.* He kept to this level of business, despite being approached by gangsters and, in 1933, an entrepreneur thinking of setting up a national reefer manufacturing company. It was enough for him to be an underground, New York, jazz-world celebrity.

Harlem in the 1930s was the world of 'hip', sometimes referred to as 'hep' meaning 'alert' or 'wise to': today, it might be interpreted as being 'trendy' or 'with it'. It was the milieu of jazz, dancing and the newly bur-geoning urban black culture in general of which marijuana was an essential part. Those who were immersed in it were referred to as hipsters, ones who were in the know. (Although it was applied to the marijuana/jazz culture, the term 'hip' actually had its roots in the world of the opium den where to 'be on the hip' meant to be smoking opium, lying on one's side.) It was a word in a whole new vernacular language known as jive and based upon the slang of plantation slaves which in turn derived from var-ious West African languages, particularly Wolof which is spoken in Senegal and Gambia. In Wolof, *jev* meant to insult, hence jive: the lan-guage of the disparaged; *degga* meant to comprehend which gave rise to the phrase 'Do you get it?' meaning 'Do you understand?'. 'Hipi' was a noun referring to one who was wide awake and may have been a partial derivation for the word 'hip.' In his autobiography, Mezzrow wrote of jive that it *is a private affair, a secret inner-circle code cooked up partly to mystify the outsiders, while it brings those in the know closer together because they alone have the key to the puzzle. The hipster's lingo is a private kind of folk-poetry, meant for the ears of the brethren alone.*

Marijuana was frequently smoked in marijuana dens, known as 'tea pads', tea being a street name for marijuana. Whilst a few were permanent premises, the marijuana equivalent of liquor-serving speakeasies, most were just apartments being used for parties, the tenants charging at the door for admission: this was the start of what was to become the famous Harlem 'rent parties' for they were usually not serious business ventures but just a means of getting the next week's payment in hand. They all had one thing in common, marijuana aside: they were meeting places where like-minded users could congregate with their fellow smokers, talk and, often, listen to jazz on records. The ambience of the tea pads was succinctly summed up by one of LaGuardia's investigators: *The marihuana smoker derives greater satisfaction if he is smoking in the presence of others. His attitude in the 'tea pad' is that of a relaxed individual, free from the anxieties and cares of the realities of life. The 'tea-pad' takes on the atmosphere of a very congenial social club. The smoker readily engages in conversation with strangers, discussing freely his pleasant reactions to the drug and philosophising on subjects pertaining to life in a manner which, at times, appears to be out of keeping with his intellectual level. A constant observation was the extreme willingness to share and puff on each other's cigarettes.* As he noted, they were hardly dens of iniquity.

One of the best tea pads was known as Kaiser's. It was approached, speakeasy fashion, through several basements, the entrance in one building but the premises under another further along the street. The joints were served on trays, music was provided by a jukebox and no alcohol was available. The clientele was multi-racial but with more black than white customers. Entry was very selective and not easy. Meyer Berger, a journalist for *The New Yorker* specializing in the seedy side of the city, spent weeks arranging his entrée into a tea pad in a tenement building on 140th Street, writing about it in an article in 1938 entitled, 'Tea for a Viper'. The tea pad he visited, known as Chappy's Place, was far from salubrious. The only light came from the jukebox, the air was thick with marijuana smoke and the only furniture was old settles and armchairs. Some of the smokers danced, others just sat around smoking and languidly talking.

Some tea pads were marijuana shops but most people preferred to buy their supply on the street. Peddlers sold marijuana at between fifteen and fifty cents a joint. Frequently, they hung out round theatres and dance halls in which marijuana was smoked by those not going to a tea pad. In the latter, where jazz was played, the musicians imbibed as well as the audience.

Although Harlem was an almost exclusively black district, whites did venture into it, in ever-increasing numbers as the 1930s passed by. There was no danger for them there, as was to be the case in future decades, for everyone knew why they came – for jazz and marijuana, a taste of excitement and Afro-American food. The main venue to head for in Harlem was the Savoy Ballroom on 141st Street and Lenox, where most of the greatest jazz musicians could be heard.

Mezz Mezzrow may have been one of the first whites to visit the area and become known in it, but another was to have just as lasting an impact. About 1936, a young Jewish high-school pupil from Brooklyn called Bernie Brightman started to hang out round the Savoy, mixing with the vipers and going to tea pads to which he was introduced by a black girlfriend. As had Mezzrow, Brightman considered himself honoured and fortunate to be allowed to join in the black community, and be a hipster with the best of them. Yet, where Mezzrow had provided marijuana, Brightman later founded Stash Records, releasing not only an album called *Reefer Songs*, but, in due course, a substantial body of jazz and minority interest records.

Marijuana produced many of its own reefer songs, sometimes called viper music, which were a sub-genre within the wider body of jazz. Amongst the best-known were 'Muggles' by Louis Armstrong, 'Gimme a Reefer' by Bessie Smith, Cab Calloway's 'Reefer Man', and 'Viper Drag' by Fats Waller. Other tunes included 'Blue Reefer Blues', 'Reefer Hound

Blues', 'Reefer Head Woman', 'A Viper's Moan', 'The Stuff Is Here and
It's Mellow', 'Smokin' Reefers', 'You'se a Viper' and 'Mary Jane'. The lyrics
of the songs were overt. The middle verse of Bessie Smith's 'Gimme a
Reefer' reads,

> Gimme a reefer and a bottle of beer
> Send me, gage, I don't care
> I feel just like I want to clown
> Give the piano player a drink because he's bringin' me down
> He's got rhythm, yeah, when he stomps his feet
> He sends me right off to sleep
> Check all your razors and your guns
> We're gonna be a wrasslin' when the wagon comes
> I want a reefer and a bottle of beer
> Send me 'cause I don't care. Slay me 'cause I don't care

whilst 'You'se a Viper', later released somewhat altered by Fats Waller
under the title 'The Reefer Song', begins,

> Dreamed about a reefer five feet long.
> Mighty Mezz, but not too strong.
> You'll be high but not for long
> If you're a viper.
> I'm the king of everything.
> I've got to be high before I can swing.
> Light a tea and let it be
> If you're a viper.

After 1937, however, and the passing of the Marihuana Tax Act, the lyrics
of viper songs began to be obscure.

Like the Negro spirituals sung by slaves, many reefer tunes were social
statements on the hard life of the urban black in New York. 'All the Jive
is Gone', a song popularized by a band called Andy Kirk and his Twelve
Clouds of Joy, was a lament about a tea-pad client arriving to find the
supply of marijuana had run out whilst one of the famous Ella Fitzgerald's
early songs was called 'When I Get Low, I Get High'. Although about
marijuana, the lyrics had much in common with the archetypal 'the pub's
got no beer' type of drinking song and lacked any real social comment or
awareness. It was more a refrain than a pithy comment on the drug user's
lot.

The Marihuana Tax Act did more than cause jazz musicians to disguise their lyrics. In some instances, the music actually sided with the Anslinger campaign. 'Sweet Marijuana Brown' and 'Knocking Myself Out' by Lil Green dealt with the 'new' view of marijuana and were clearly against it. The former included the lines,

> *Boy, she's really frantic, the wildest chick in town*
> *She blows her gage, flies into a rage*
> *Sweet Marijuana Brown*

and

> *Every time you take her out*
> *She's bound to take you in*

The final verse of 'Knocking Myself Out' concerned the singer, losing her lover and contemplating suicide, killing herself slowly as if with the 'evil drug', rather than outright by a more immediate method.

In 'Working Man Blues', released in 1937, the lyrics stated quite bluntly that marijuana was for fools.

Post-Act songs not concerned with the use of marijuana dealt with the risks involved in being a smoker. Whereas the earlier songs had made a social hero of 'the man', meaning the marijuana supplier, the term came after 1937 to refer to the government agent, or G-man. The song 'Light Up' warned,

> *Don't let that man getcha,*
> *Just puff on your cig and blow those smoke rings*

while the title of the 1945 song, 'The "G" Man Got the "T" Man', sums up the mood of many marijuana users.

In the mid-1940s, many songs contained esoteric references to marijuana, even such standards as 'Tea for Two' – the tea here might have come from India but it was certainly not that with which one brews the 'cup that cheers' – and 'I Didn't Like It The First Time' (or 'The Spinach Song') by Julia Lee and Her Boy Friends, which was not about what it seemed: perhaps this was the spinach Popeye took to punch up his courage and muscles, not the salad vegetable. Drugs even started to appear in songs in a humorous context as in 'Who Put the Benzedrine in Mrs

Murphy's Ovaltine?'Yet, by the end of the decade, references to marijuana disappeared.

What many outsiders did not appreciate about the marijuana culture of Harlem was the fact that it was more than just a subversive or under-ground social swell. It was a seeking for identity by black people who had been displaced from their lives in the south. They had been cast as out-siders and now they revelled in it. Their music, their language and their sense of values were different. When the law took against marijuana, it only served to help the black population to further display its individuality. In 1943, when Meyer Berger reported again on life in Harlem, he noted the development in the culture with fashion now play-ing a part, the zoot suit being the clothing of the *hep-cats or swing-mad kids*. The influence was also spreading out of Harlem and across the black population of America.

The life of one of Harlem's most renowned sons gives a snapshot of how black people felt in what was a ghetto, how they viewed their future and what they thought of the world and its treatment of them.

Known in Harlem as Detroit Red, his real name was Malcolm Little. He hailed from Omaha, Nebraska where he was born in 1925. As a child, his family moved to Lansing, Michigan but there, their home burned down, his father was murdered, his mother had a breakdown and he and his siblings were sent to orphanages and foster homes. A clever boy, he had dreams of becoming a lawyer but was told this was not a *realistic goal for a nigger*. Leaving Michigan, he settled first in Boston before moving south to Harlem where he took a number of low-paid, often unskilled jobs before, at the age of seventeen, borrowing twenty dollars of operat-ing capital and starting to peddle marijuana. He obtained his supplies from sailors and sold to jazz musicians. *I kept turning over my profit*, he later wrote, *increasing my supplies, and I sold reefers like a wild man. I scarcely slept; I was wherever musicians congregated. A roll of money was in my pocket. Every day I cleared at least fifty or sixty dollars. In those days . . . this was a fortune to a seventeen-year-old Negro. I felt, for the first time in my life, that great feeling of free!* Eventually, the police became aware of his activities, not only as a marijuana dealer but also because he was involved in illegal gambling, prostitution and violent crime.

Arresting him for marijuana dealing was not as easy as it seemed. Unless a peddler was caught in possession it was impossible to apprehend him. To overcome this, Detroit Red kept the joints he had rolled in a packet inside his coat, under an armpit. If he sensed he was being followed by a 'narc' – a narcotics agent – he would turn a corner, lift his arm, drop the package through his coat and walk on. If it transpired that his suspicion had been unfounded, he would return and retrieve the packet.

Moving back to Boston, he was arrested in 1946 for armed burglary and sentenced to seven years' imprisonment. Whilst serving his time, he studied the teachings of the Nation of Islam leader, Elijah Muhammad, who urged black Americans to sever themselves from white society and thereby gain their own dignity, political power and economic strength. By the time he was released from jail in 1952, Malcolm Little, aka Detroit Red, was Malcolm X. His anonymous surname indicating his lost, unknown, African tribal heritage, he shunned the hipster world he had previous inhabited and strove to offer a different alternative lifestyle to the ghetto existence of jazz, marijuana and racism.

Malcolm X may have avoided being arrested for marijuana possession but Mezz Mezzrow was not so lucky. He was caught in possession of sixty joints whilst entering the stage door of a jazz club at the New York World Fair in 1940. He was held on Riker's Island in, at his own request, a cell block for black prisoners. During his time there, he came across other convicts who were taking part in LaGuardia's marijuana test and research programme: . . . *they were used as guinea pigs by some city doctors to find out what the score was with marihuana. They stayed over in that hospital smoking all the reefer they wanted at the city's expense, playing records, eating good, and talking up a breeze, while the doctors made all kinds of tests. As the guys came drifting back they told me those doctors had gone over them from stem to stern, not missing a square inch, and hadn't been able to find one harmful effect, or prove that reefer was in any way habit forming. I began to feel pretty sore, doing a twenty-month stretch . . . for being in possession of some stuff the city's own doctors couldn't prove was any more harmful than some cornsilk cigarettes.*

Upon his release, Mezzrow did not return to dealing but he did write his autobiography. It was published in 1946 and became a blockbusting bestseller much to Anslinger's chagrin: he considered it *a glorification of marihuana smoking* and *an advertisement of narcotic addiction.* In part, he was right.

After the Second World War, in common with many jazz musicians, Mezzrow left America and settled in Paris, dying there in 1972 at the age of seventy-three. He is buried in the Père Lachaise cemetery, his grave in the same hallowed ground as those other marijuana users Honoré de Balzac, Honoré-Victorin Daumier, Gérard de Nerval and the rock singer Jim Morrison of The Doors.

As Mezzrow discovered from his fellow convicts, LaGuardia's committee failed to prove marijuana was harmful. The first news of what line the committee would take was published in the September 1942 issue of the *American Journal of Psychiatry*, written by two members of the committee, Dr Samuel Allentuck and Dr Karl Bowman. Their paper, 'The Psychiatric Aspects of Marihuana Intoxication', stated that marijuana was a mild euphoriant and went on to prove the lie to much of Anslinger's propaganda. The actual report appeared two years later, despite rumoured attempts by the FBN to have it censored.

Entitled *The Marihuana Problem in the City of New York*, the report concluded amongst its many and detailed findings that marijuana did not lead to addiction in the medical context of the word, in the same way as did opiates or cocaine, was not a sexual stimulant and was not involved with the committing of serious crime. LaGuardia wrote in the foreword to it, *I am glad that the sociological, psychological, and medical ills commonly attributed to marihuana have been found to be exaggerated insofar as the City of New York is concerned.* In summary, it announced, *From the study as a whole, it is concluded that marihuana is not a drug of addiction, comparable to morphine, and that if tolerance is acquired, this is of a very limited degree. Furthermore, those who have been smoking marihuana for a period of years showed no mental or physical deterioration which may be attributed to the drug.* In other words, LaGuardia's committee had completely debunked Anslinger's proselytizing.

No sooner was the report published than Anslinger waded into it. In his book *The Murderers: The Story of the Narcotics Gangs*, he dismissed the report as *giddy sociology and medical mumbo-jumbo*. He labelled the authors dangerous men and started to rally the right-wing press, religious groups and anyone else he could to his cause. He also destroyed all the copies of the report he could acquire. In fact, LaGuardia's report, although the most thorough, was not unique. Other, smaller studies had been conducted during the war years by the US public health service and the US Army: using mostly black volunteers, both concluded the drug was not a problem but the attitude of the user might be.

The outcome of LaGuardia's report, as well as that of studies recently conducted in Mexico, was considered with interest overseas. At the end of the Second World War, the anti-narcotic organizations set up by the League of Nations in 1919 continued under the newly constituted United Nations, the Advisory Committee renamed the Commission on Narcotic Drugs. At its first meeting in 1946, it was decided no further study need be conducted into cannabis. Not surprisingly Anslinger, in his role as US representative to the Commission, disagreed.

Made to look foolish by LaGuardia, and feeling snubbed by his fellow members of the United Nations Commission, Anslinger continued his campaign against marijuana just as he had before but now, instead of specifically demonizing the drug, he increasingly turned his attention towards one group whom he had already been observing, who used it and who, in his mind, were its missionaries carrying its evil gospel to the world – musicians.

# 15

# STAR-BUSTERS

LAGUARDIA'S INVESTIGATION OF MARIJUANA WAS ONLY ONE THORN IN Anslinger's side as the 1930s came to an end: another was his lack of resources, a third his own zeal. Marijuana use was so widespread in some areas, he found he was too short of agents to hit at it on all fronts. It also became clear that he had to revitalize his publicity campaign but was at a loss as to how to do so. He had already, as it were, run out of epithets of horror. The answer then presented itself: aim for specific targets.

Although they had been using marijuana for years, it was not until 1938 that Anslinger finally came to realize the link between jazz musicians and the drug, despite the fact that the FBN had been keeping open dossiers on a number of them since 1931, particularly those who had been previously arrested. Once the association dawned on him, he set about going after the entertainment industry in general and jazz musicians specifically. They fitted nicely into his racist agenda: if they were not black, they were whites who had come under and been corrupted by black influence. He not only considered them degenerate but he was alarmed that, through their music, they were exerting such an influence upon mainstream America and especially its youth. In Anslinger's mind, the same applied to film stars. Again, because the target group was disparate, Anslinger pinpointed specific people in what was to be known as his 'star-bust syndrome'.

Musicians had been targeted before. Louis Armstrong had been arrested under the Californian law against marijuana back in 1931. He was standing outside the stage door of a night club in Los Angeles, taking a rest between sets and sharing a joint with Vic Berton, considered the best jazz drummer on the West Coast. Two police officers busted them, albeit somewhat reluctantly. They were jazz fans. It also transpired they were acting on a tip-off from one of Armstrong's rival band leaders. The policemen allowed him to finish the show then took him into custody where he faced a six-month custodial sentence for possession of a roach: most of the joint had been smoked. Armstrong was remanded in custody for nine days, pending trial. News of his arrest was leaked to the press, leading to a tabloid feeding frenzy. At the trial, he was given a suspended sentence. The episode was to have a humorous side to it, as Armstrong later narrated. *I laughed real loud*, he reminisced, *when several movie stars came up to the band stand while we played a dance set and told me, when they heard about me getting caught with marijuana they thought marijuana was a chick*. It seems they thought marijuana, or Mary Jane, was the name of an under-age minor from whom he was soliciting sexual favours.

The Great Satchmo was lucky. It was not long before things changed. In an interview given to his biographers, Max Jones and John Chilton, he stated how much he had enjoyed marijuana: *Well, that was my life and I don't feel ashamed at all. Mary Warner, honey, you sure was good and I enjoyed you 'heep much'. But the price got a little too high to pay, law-wise. At first you was a 'misdomeanor'. But as the years rolled on, you lost your 'misdo' and got meanor and meanor, jailhousely speaking*. This, of course, was exactly what Anslinger wanted, liberalism replaced by long sentencing with celebrities being scared off marijuana.

Matters came to a head in February 1938 when two men were sent to trial in Minneapolis for cultivating and distributing marijuana. The local senior FBN officer, Joseph Bell, released a press statement to the *Minneapolis Tribune* which read, *The tempo of present-day music, the big apple dance and these jam sessions seem to do something to the nerves. As a result, use of marihuana is on the increase. Not only is it being used by dance band musicians, but by boys and girls who listen and dance to these bands*. In response, Sidney Berman, the editor of *Orchestra World*, wrote to Anslinger protesting this blanket insult. Anslinger replied that the comments were those of the arrested men, not Bell. He was being disingenuous. Bell had reported to him that his personal knowledge supported the statement although one of the arrested had allowed that some jazz musicians used marijuana. Thereafter, Anslinger pursued jazz musicians.

He and his agents misunderstood much of what they were attacking.

For one, Anslinger took the lyrics of viper songs as literal, but this was nothing compared to his new attitude towards a deviant sub-culture that was predominantly black, played 'hot' music late into the night, lived dissolute lives and exhibited unconventional behaviour, none of which fitted with Anslinger's view of a model citizen. He and his deputy, Malachi Harney, also came to realize that a drug transaction was virtually impossible to police as it was in effect a 'victimless' crime, in that neither party was likely to lodge a complaint with the authorities. Harney came up with the solution, to recruit an army of informers, some of whom were paid up to two thousand dollars for a successful prosecution brought about by their information. Convinced Harney had the answer, Anslinger funded the initiative but he reckoned without the close-knit camaraderie of the jazz musicians' fraternity: stool-pigeons came to account for very few convictions.

In January 1941, Anslinger's feeding of the sensationalist newspapers with more misinformation about the link between marijuana and jazz prompted a response with which he must have been pleased. *The Keynote*, the monthly magazine of the Detroit Federation of Musicians, lambasted marijuana-using jazz musicians for bringing the reputation of their music into disrepute. Two years later to the month, *Down Beat*, the foremost jazz magazine, reported an incident involving some musicians, show-business personalities and soldiers smoking joints. Headlined 'Tea Scandal Stirs Musicdom', this magazine also attacked musicians for their drug use. Encouraged by this and desperate for more publicity, Anslinger doubled his investigation of musicians, contacting the San Francisco FBN senior officer and instructing him to escalate the *volume of reports indicating that many musicians of the 'swing band' type are responsible for the spread of the marihuana smoking vice*, adding, *I should like you to give the problem some special attention in your district. If possible, I should like you to develop a number of cases in which arrests would be withheld so as to synchronize those with arrests to be made in other districts.*

What also intensely annoyed Anslinger was the preparedness of some jazz musicians to openly admit their use of marijuana to the draft boards in order to avoid active military service. An admission of addiction guaranteed a classification of exemption. This, Anslinger considered, was yet another example of jazz musicians being unsuitable citizens and good reason for hunting them down. That so many were using this excuse also reflected badly on the FBN, the military authorities questioning why Anslinger's men were failing in their responsibilities.

Files were kept on every jazz musician who had used marijuana – and their acquaintances. The list was formidable, a real Jazz Hall of Fame including Louis Armstrong, Duke Ellington, Cab Calloway, Lionel Hampton, Dizzy Gillespie, Jimmy Dorsey, Count Basie and Thelonius Monk. Many musicians were kept under covert surveillance and orchestras or bands containing marijuana users were constantly monitored.

According to Harry Shapiro in his fascinating book *Waiting for the Man: The Story of Drugs and Popular Music*, as a result of the musicians' evasion of the draft, a curious experiment was conducted during the war, known as the Carl Seashore's Musical Aptitude Test. A dozen prisoners serving time for marijuana offences were tested for their recognition of pitch, tone and similar innate musical skills. Then they were given marijuana. None fared worse in the test. Eight thought they had done better. Anslinger interpreted this as indicative that marijuana did not improve musical skill, but the test was, to be charitable, unscientific and no one investigated the prisoners whose musical senses improved under the influence of the drug.

When the war ended, the star-bust campaign was generally seen to have been a failure, but it did net one major jazz figure, the greatest jazz drummer of all time, Gene Krupa. In July 1943, acting on a tip-off, the FBN arrested Krupa in Los Angeles for possession of marijuana and for sending a seventeen-year-old teenager working in his jazz band to his hotel room to bring him some joints. According to Anita O'Day, the singer with Krupa's band who was herself jailed for marijuana possession, having already had his dressing-room searched by an FBN agent, Krupa knew his hotel room would be next. He sent the teenager to his hotel room to collect up the joints he had there and flush them down the toilet. Instead, the teenager stole them and was found with them on him. On the possession charge, Krupa was sentenced to ninety days in prison and a five-hundred-dollar fine. Separately, he was tried for involving a minor in the transportation of narcotics and sentenced to between one and five years' incarceration. The latter penalty was rejected on appeal but he still served eighty-four of his ninety days for possession.

The persecution of jazz musicians was not as successful as Anslinger had hoped. Although some leading musicians had been arrested, he had to admit that they were not of the calibre he was after and, besides, not all the public knew, followed or liked jazz. Yet everyone went to movies and he knew that, if he could catch a major film star, the publicity would be enormous. In the fall of 1948, his ambition materialized.

Robert Mitchum, then a thirty-one-year-old screen idol rising fast in the firmament of stardom, was arrested in Laurel Canyon in Hollywood.

Agents raided what they called a marijuana smoking party, charging Mitchum and three others with possession and conspiracy to possess. When he was taken in to custody, Mitchum gave his occupation as *former actor*. He believed his career was finished. Anslinger prayed it was. Facing the press, the film star admitted, *Sure, I've been using this stuff since I was a kid. I guess it's all over now. I'm ruined. This is the bitter end.*

Retaining one of Hollywood's top lawyers to the stars, Jerry Geisler, Mitchum stood trial early in 1949. Mitchum claimed he had been set up. He was judged guilty of conspiracy to possess, the lesser of the charges levelled at him, and sentenced to two years' probation with sixty days in jail. Nine months later, the Los Angeles District Attorney ordered a re-investigation into Mitchum's claim that he had been framed. It was deemed possible the incident had been the work of a blackmailer. Early in 1951, the guilty verdict was dismissed although neither Mitchum nor his studio employers publicized the fact. His career was not affected by the incident: indeed, it did him a favour, casting him as a tough guy outsider both on screen and in real life. Ironically, to advertise that he had been let off the charge would have been damaging. Anslinger had, therefore, done much to enhance Mitchum's screen personality and star reputation.

The Mitchum affair made the studios cautious. Although the FBN did not have the power to censor films, some studio heads of production ran scripts past them, just to be on the safe side. Marijuana and drugs were not mentioned in films unless the FBN approved, as it did in the case of *She Shoulda Said No* (also released as *Marijuana, the Devil's Weed*), starring Lila Leeds in 1949. It was about a chorus girl whose career is ruined by marijuana. The film pandered to Anslinger's opinion: to make a movie that showed drugs in a good light was tantamount to financial suicide as well as being potentially litigious.

Hollywood even went so far as to give Anslinger and the FBN much positive publicity. *Johnny Stool Pigeon*, starring Howard Duff, Shelley Winters, Dan Duryea and the young Tony Curtis in a non-speaking role, told the fictional story of federal agents infiltrating a heroin ring. Even more high profile was *To the Ends of the Earth*, made in 1948 and ostensibly based on FBN files. With this film, Anslinger's hypocrisy reached new heights. He was just as ready to use the entertainment industry as he was to target it for drug abuse and, in fact, he even took part in the film, playing himself.

Regardless of his restricted levels of success, Anslinger stuck by his policies. In 1949, when arguing his case for the following fiscal year's budget with the US Congress Ways and Means Appropriation Committee, he stated, *I think the traffic has increased in marihuana, and unfortunately particularly among the young people. We have been running into a lot of traffic among these jazz musicians, and I am not speaking about the good musicians, but the jazz type. In one place down here in North Carolina we arrested a whole orchestra, everybody in the orchestra. In Chicago we have arrested some rather prominent jazz musicians; and in New York. It is pretty widespread.* There was no justification for this statement whatsoever and, when he continued in the vein that it was time the music industry paid attention to its corrupt members, there was public uproar. The differentiation between jazz and what Anslinger implied was proper music almost immediately drove a wedge between him and the music industry which he had been trying to woo. His next move was to have cancelled the passports of all jazz musicians with a conviction for marijuana but this intention was quashed by his superiors in the US Treasury Department. The suggestion was undemocratic, not that that bothered Anslinger. His ordered harassment of many musicians, Thelonius Monk in particular, verged upon the unconstitutional.

The music industry, if it did not have the last laugh against Anslinger, certainly had the longest. During the war years, a great many show-business people travelled abroad or nationally, putting on morale-boosting performances for the troops. Because of a shortage of vinyl, the plastic used in making records, few were cut during the war but some were sanctioned. Known as V-discs, they were made for use by the US armed forces radio services and were widely distributed to all theatres of the war. In 1943, Fats Waller cut a disc, introducing the song with, *Hey, cats, it's four o'clock in the mornin'. I just left the V-disc studio. Here we are in Harlem. Everybody's here but the police 'n they'll be here any minute. It's high time, so catch this song . . .* The opening words were, *Dreamed about a reefer five foot long.* No one, it seems, understood what the song was about and the record was duly dispatched by the hundreds, much to the hilarity of practically every coloured person in the entire armed forces.

As the 1950s approached, it became clear to Anslinger that a new emphasis had to be made concerning marijuana. The post-war world was changing fast, a new enemy – Communism – replacing the old, bringing with it the witch hunt of McCarthyism. Anyone who did not fit the perceived norm of American society was suspect, particularly if they had a social position.

Seeking to find a new focus for his anti-marijuana drive, Anslinger decided to link it to heroin, the new and truly terrible drug that was beginning to cause serious social problems and was believed to be a pivotal part of the Communist plan – particularly that of Communist China, against which America was to wage war in Korea – to destroy America and its values. Anslinger was not slow in disseminating information that bolstered this perception although, privately, he did not believe in it. Nevertheless, he stressed that marijuana could turn America into a nation of compliant pacifists: this, when ten years before he had been preaching how it induced violence. The label of docility was to remain attached to marijuana for another two decades.

To associate marijuana with heroin, Anslinger stated that the heroin addict's first taste of drugs was with cannabis, from which he graduated to more dangerous substances. That in 1937 he had said quite bluntly, during the debate leading up to the Marihuana Tax Act, that marijuana did not lead to heroin use, was now conveniently forgotten. This was to be a backbone of his anti-marijuana argument for the remainder of his career at the FBN and was given credence in 1951 when a US Senate committee declared marijuana led to a use of other drugs.

Attitudes hardened. Addicts were seen as Communists, pro-Communist or abetters of Communism. Anslinger announced marijuana responsible for rising crime statistics because it gave confidence to criminals – no doubt, as opposed to making them so docile as to not be bothered to commit a crime in the first place – and, testifying before the Senate Special Committee to Investigate Organized Crime chaired by Tennessee Senator Estes Kefauver in 1951, he lobbied for tougher sentences including compulsory imprisonment. It was left to Louisiana Congressman Thomas Hale Boggs, Sr to finally bring in the legislation to counteract what he saw as a climate of leniency.

The Boggs Act, passed in late 1951, rationalized the penalties applicable under the Narcotics Drugs Import and Export Act and the Marihuana Tax Act. For a first offence involving marijuana, cocaine or any opiate the sentence was set at two to five years: a second offence was given five to ten years, a third ten to twenty. From the second offence onwards there was no parole consideration. Even serial killers, rapists and spies were afforded parole. Not everyone was in accord with Boggs' legislation. James Bennett, the head of US penitentiaries, said it was a knee-jerk, hysterical reaction and judges across the USA demanded the minimum-sentence requirement be relaxed.

Apart from Anslinger's theory that marijuana was what was known as a gateway or stepping-stone drug enticing users to experiment with more powerful substances, there was still an aspect of racism to his thinking.

Marijuana was popular with blacks and Hispanics, as the Mexicans were now called, and they were the progenitors of the swelling civil rights movement which, as were Communists, was seeking to topple the traditional, white dominated, American way of life. The marijuana laws, therefore, were a handy vehicle to keep the ethnic minorities in their place. Where the anti-marijuana laws were the harshest was in the southern states. In Louisiana, for example, possession carried a possible sentence of ninety-nine years: in Georgia, a second offence carried the death penalty. In many states, procuring marijuana for a minor was also a capital offence.

Whenever a new president entered the White House, there was sure to be a reshuffle of senior government posts. This was certainly true in 1952 when Dwight D. 'Ike' Eisenhower came to power but Anslinger survived the changes in the administration. Once again secure in his job, he set off rounding up support for even more hard-line policies, supported by a raft of senators who considered even the Boggs Act did not go far enough. When the 1956 Narcotic Control Act was ratified, it reassessed the maximum terms for possession of marijuana as laid down by Boggs and increased them to ten, twenty and forty years. Convictions for dealing were set at five to twenty years for a first offence, and ten to forty years thereafter. The same penalties applied to the far more dangerous heroin and cocaine. Ominously, for the first time, FBN and customs agents were routinely armed.

The year before Eisenhower became president, the FBN budget had been lower in real terms than it had been at its inception but, in the face of the Communist threat, the rise of organized crime with its drug-trafficking association, the increasing civil rights unrest and Anslinger's persuasion, it rose sharply in the mid-1950s. Drugs were not only illegal but even mentioning them became taboo. It became difficult to get books published that mentioned them, no scientific investigation occurred or was permitted and addiction, rarely mentioned openly even in official circles, spiralled. It was not until 1956 that the FBN actually published an estimate of addiction statistics.

When scientists did seek seriously to study the drug problem, they were hounded and harassed by Anslinger. One who was systematically intimidated was Professor Alfred Lindesmith, a sociologist working at the University of Indiana who had for years been pressing for the medical treatment of addicts. His research was solid and humane. In his opinion, drug addicts were not sub-humans but people suffering from physio-logical or psychological infirmity brought on by a dangerous chemical.

When he published articles sympathetic to addicts, attacking the *stereotyped misinformation* on them put out by the FBN, agents tried to suppress his work, tapped his telephone and even planned to plant narcotics on him then arrest him for possession. When these strategies failed, Anslinger went to such lengths as to personally approach his arch rival, J. Edgar Hoover, to ask if the FBI knew if Lindesmith was associated with any Communist organizations. The academic world offered the professor little succour: even those who agreed with him kept their heads down to avoid being similarly persecuted.

In 1948, a thirty-four-minute film documentary was made by the National Film Board of Canada in association with the Royal Canadian Mounted Police (RCMP). Starkly titled *Drug Addict*, it was intended to be a training film for RCMP narcotics agents and doctors, and bluntly addressed addiction and trafficking. It was not that Canada had a major drugs problem, regardless of the dire prophecies of Emily F. Murphy: there were only twenty-five marijuana convictions recorded in Canada between 1930 and 1946, cannabis cultivation being legal until 1938. The Government simply wanted the relevant professionals to be aware of the subject and ready for it if needs be.

The documentary gave credence to Lindesmith's assertions that addiction was a medical or psychological condition, showed that addicts and dealers came from all racial and social groups, that the demonization of the addict as a drug fiend was inaccurate and that the complete control of restricted drugs and policing was an impossibility.

Anslinger targeted the film, requesting the Canadians not to seek to have it distributed in the USA. Lindesmith, whose ideas it vindicated, publicly voiced opposition to this censorship. In a letter to the *New York Times* on 20 January 1950, he accused the FBN and Anslinger of duplicity: they were banning a balanced documentary whilst simultaneously supporting Hollywood movies that sensationalized the issue. He also, with the backing of the American Civil Liberties Union, tried to find out exactly who had banned the film, and questioned the legality of their action, but in vain.

The issue caused many health and legal professionals to come out in Lindesmith's support. The American Bar Association (ABA) and the American Medical Association (AMA) produced a joint paper which was published by the University of Indiana Press. Anslinger also attempted to have this suppressed and, when he could not, published his own rebuttal of Lindesmith's opinions. From this situation was eventually created The Lindesmith Center, an independent drug policy institute founded in

1994 to promote policies based on science, public health and human rights. In 2000, it amalgamated with the Drug Policy Foundation to form the Drug Policy Alliance.

Although Anslinger's star-busting began to lose its impetus somewhat in the mid-1950s, it was still very much on his agenda and a specific piece of legislation greatly assisted him. Called the cabaret card system, it was applied in New York City. Any musician who played for more than three days in a premises where alcohol was served had to carry a cabaret card issued by the police. If that musician had had, or was given, a drugs violation, the cabaret card was withdrawn or withheld, thus preventing him from earning a living in a city that was the world centre of jazz. To increase arrest statistics, black musicians were methodically targeted, their cars or houses turned over while they were subjected to random street searches. In 1951, Thelonius Monk was falsely imprisoned for the possession of drugs and, despite his proven innocence, he was deprived of his cabaret card for six years.

For all Anslinger's efforts, marijuana remained available. From the late 1940s, when the US government encouraged Mexican immigration under the *braceros* (labourers) programme to replace the workforce lost through war casualties, marijuana started to appear on high-school and college campuses. Many were introduced to the drug by one of the thousands of men who, after serving in the military, were encouraged by the Government to enter higher education after their demobilization. A large number had discovered marijuana whilst posted to, or passing in transit through, the Philippines during the Second World War or the Korean conflict.

Within five years, another wind of change started to blow through the schools, colleges and universities of America. Teenagers were becoming established as a social group with their own developing culture, rejecting much of what their parents had stood for or accepted. Self-expression was important to them, as was their own peer identity and individuality. For them, jazz was outmoded but black music was not and they turned towards black folk and gospel music and the blues, marrying this to their own country-and-western music. From this musical melting pot came rock 'n' roll, condemned – just as jazz had been – for its lascivious under-tones, its not-too-hidden sexuality and its sheer unadulterated vitality. With the new music came a new drug called speed. Like marijuana, it had been legal, used by US troops in Korea to combat battle fatigue. Many of the early rock 'n' roll musicians took speed (more correctly known as amphetamine or methamphetamine) which had been used in the pre-war years as a slimming pill for it reduced appetite: Johnny Cash, Jerry Lee Lewis, the Everly Brothers and the king himself, Elvis Presley, were all speed users. Their audiences and followers took it, too. Drugs and popular culture, regardless of Anslinger's efforts, seemed irrefutably inseparable – and not just in America, either.

# 16

## DORA, BEBOP AND THE VIPERS
## OF LONDON

IN 1900, THE NON-WHITE POPULATION OF GREAT BRITAIN NUMBERED considerably less than ten thousand and yet this did not prevent drugs and their prohibition from being associated with racial issues and ethnic minorities. The only real immigrant community was an insignificant one of peripatetic Chinese sailors in the East End of London where they operated several opium dens occasionally visited by Victorian journalists or, surprisingly, tourists looking for sleaze, corruption and vicarious, exotic excitement. With the passage of the Pharmacy Act of 1868, which made chemists and pharmacists the custodians of drugs and poisons, and the founding of the Society for the Suppression of the Opium Trade, opium had come to be regarded as evil and the Chinese, because of their familiarity with and use of it, came to share its reputation. If stories appeared in the press about drugs, the Chinese were always the opiate fiends and blacks the cocaine fiends. Marijuana hardly ever featured and, until about 1910, this remained the case.

The recreational drug use that had existed in literary circles in the 1890s spread outwards into the higher echelons of society in the decade leading up to the start of the Great War in 1914 by which time cocaine was frequently indulged in by the upper classes, especially in Mayfair, Belgravia, South Kensington and the other fashionable areas of London. With the war, this pattern changed and, by 1920, drugs were regarded as a problem across all the strata of the class system.

Two events caused the drug issue to enter the British political agenda. The first was the 1911 Hague Convention at which Britain agreed to legislate against drug trafficking. The second was a scandal in 1916 when it was discovered that Canadian troops posted to Britain were using cocaine. To address this, a most important piece of legislation was introduced, known officially as Regulation 40B of the already existing Defence of the Realm Act: its acronym was DORA 40B and it made the supplying of cocaine or opium to troops during wartime a very serious offence which was later expanded to include civilians, for whom possession without a doctor's certificate was a criminal act. Cannabis, morphine and heroin were not covered by DORA 40B but that was immaterial. What it did do was establish the fundamentals of prohibition. The public were not unduly bothered by this; what caused an uproar was that DORA 40B also introduced strictly enforced opening times for public houses, restricting not only the drinking habits of forces personnel in the interests of the defence of the nation, but also those of the public at large.

During the Great War and the 1920s, a very small underground 'dope' culture arose with its own urban legends concerning evil foreigners, German spies and white slavery. From the latter came stories of dissolute actresses corrupted by drugs into prostitution or 'bachelor girlhood', a synonym for lesbianism. These stories were fuelled in 1918 by the death of a twenty-one-year-old actress, Billie Carleton, who had supposedly died of cocaine poisoning at a Victory Ball. The *Daily Express*, in a style imitative of American yellow journalism, reported that her life had been ruined by a circle of hashish-eating friends. The newspaper followed up her death with a series of drug-inspired articles, mostly fictional but dressed up as fact and reminding its readers of the wartime German intention to subvert Britain with addiction. Cannabis was briefly mentioned in the articles.

Under the terms of the Treaty of Versailles, Britain had to legislate against dangerous drugs. In 1920, the Dangerous Drugs Act was passed. It was DORA 40B adjusted to meet international legislative requirements. By this Act, drug use was separated into two forms, the medical and what was in effect the criminal. Opiates and cocaine were listed. Cannabis was not.

Drug stories continued to titillate and scandalize the public. Whenever possible, xenophobic feelings were stirred into the mix to hype the narratives. Two of the so-called 'dope kings' – the first drug barons – were a Chinese and a coloured man.

Brilliant Chang was a Chinese restaurateur in London's Regent Street who was accused in 1922 of causing the death of a taxi dancer, Freda Kempton. It was alleged that Chang had been dealing in opiates, cocaine and hashish since 1917. At the inquest into Kempton's death, it was decided she had committed suicide by swallowing cocaine. According to the *Empire News*, as soon as the verdict was announced, *some of the girls rushed to Chang, patted his back, and one, more daring than the rest, fondled the Chinaman's black smooth hair and passed her fingers slowly through it.* At trial, Chang was sentenced to fourteen months in prison for aiding and abetting Kempton's death; he was deported at the end of his sentence. That white girls would associate themselves with a Chinese was deemed disgraceful, the outrage increased by another event that same year in which three unconscious, semi-naked sisters were discovered with the body of a dead Chinese called Yee Sing (aka Johnny Hop) in an opium-smoke-filled room over a laundry in Cardiff. The other dope king was Eddie Manning, a Jamaican jazz drummer convicted in 1923 of peddling opium and cocaine: like Chang, he was said to have had bevies of white female admirers whom the press claimed he charmed with a love potion made of hashish. The antidote to the potion was said to have been an extract of geraniums.

Press sensationalism, 'penny dreadful' novelists and the urban rumour mill soon gave the impression that drugs had escaped from London and infected the whole country, ensnaring women and depraving the young. Chinese were blamed, despite the fact that the Chinese population of the whole of Britain in 1921 was not quite three thousand.

It was one thing for a Celestial – as the Chinese were derogatorily known – or a nigger to be involved in drugs, but quite another when it was a white man, and one who already had a dubious reputation.

Between 1920 and 1923, Aleister Crowley continued to experiment magically with drugs at his Abbey of Thelema he had set up at Cefalù in northern Sicily. In this small community, acolytes used heroin, opium, cocaine, hashish, laudanum, veronal and anhalonium. The community draining his financial resources, Crowley decided to try to make a profit out of the press-hyped drug craze. He approached a publisher with an offer that he would *write a shocker on the subject which was catering to the hysteria and prurience of the sex-crazed public; the drug traffic insanity.* The publisher William Collins accepted and the book, a novel, was released in 1922 under the title *The Diary of a Drug Fiend.* The title was intended to be ironic and ridicule the public hysteria. True to his word, Crowley's book was a shocker and remains even now one of the most accurate and detailed accounts of drug taking and addiction ever written. The story revolves around a pair of young lovers who travel across Europe whilst taking heroin and cocaine. Their addiction is finally cured by King Lamus, a master Adept based upon Crowley himself, who uses practical magic and the application of their own true wills to set them free. Crowley believed addiction was due to weakness and was nothing more than a state of mind. Initially, the book was seen as a warning about dangerous drugs but when the *Sunday Express* newspaper delved into Crowley's background, it exposed him as a blatant drug user and experimenter. In a very short space of time, he was labelled the drug fiend of the book's title, the book itself his own confession. The magazine *John Bull* went further and, through a series of lurid features, dubbed Crowley *The Wickedest Man in the World* for his drug use, occult meddling and sexual perversion carried out in the name of what he called Magick. The name stuck but, worse, Crowley became the arch-demon scapegoat the press and the public wanted, the primary example of what evil drugs were capable.

Other authors relied upon drugs as a means of spicing up their fiction. Heroin being over-used as a literary device, thanks in no small measure to Crowley, some turned to cannabis or hashish. Many of the stories were wildly inaccurate and were plainly written by people with little or no experience of cannabis. One author wrote of *burning jute* producing *the soporific fumes of hashish* causing *drowsiness . . . wild dreams and waking ecstasy*, another of Scotland Yard detectives feeding hashish to a murder suspect who then, whilst intoxicated, re-enacts his crime. One novelist, Arthur Ward, visited the Limehouse area of the East End of London and then, under the pseudonym of Sax Rohmer, created the archetypal arch-villain, Dr Fu Manchu. Fu's drug was opium, but Rohmer used hashish in a novel published in 1919 entitled *Dope*, a character in it implying hashish was far more dangerous than opium. To cash in on Rohmer's Fu Manchu success and current anti-Chinese sentiments, the British author Thomas Burke invented his own character, Tai Fu (Big Fu), who was also Chinese but used hashish, whilst the American author Carl Van Vechten created Peter Whiffle, a drug experimentalist. It is likely that Van Vechten was well acquainted with hashish himself for he was an avid promoter of black artists.

As the 1920s progressed, illegal drug-taking remained a predominantly upper-class activity or one restricted to a small coterie of artists, musicians and writers. Cocaine was popular as were morphine and chloroform, the fumes of which were inhaled. Cannabis was rare in the extreme and few even tried it. For those who did, the experience was not necessarily all for which they had hoped. Augustus John, the famously bohemian painter, ate some hashish jam but the only effect he felt, he said with disappointment, was one of uncontrollable laughter.

Cannabis was outlawed in Britain when it was added to the schedule of the Dangerous Drugs Act on 28 September 1928, to comply with the stipulations on international trade in drugs as laid down in the 1925 Geneva International Convention on Narcotics Control. It was not banned from medicinal use but it was gradually being superseded in any case by new, more potent synthetic painkillers.

It was not until the mid-1930s that marijuana smoking became somewhat more prevalent in Britain and then, as in the USA, the association was made with jazz musicians. An article in the 22 February 1936 issue of *Melody Maker*, the British journal of the music industry, first exposed the issue under the headline, 'Dope Cigarette Peddling Among British Musicians'. It read in part, *The time has come for light to be thrown on an astonishing situation which is likely to become a serious menace to the jazz world on two continents. This concerns the 'reefer' or dope habit which is spreading rapidly amongst musicians . . . Drug peddling and drug-taking is growing in this country. It can no longer be denied that jazz clubs have been among the haunts of drug peddlers. It is right that the searchlight of publicity be turned upon clubs of this nature. It is unfortunate that the searchlight should sweep also across the many clubs that are guiltless. This newspaper has consistently championed the avant garde of dance music and its practitioners. It will continue to do so.* Yet it went on to say it would also *hamper . . . those who would make jazz clubs the marketplace of dope.* This was scare-mongering. The so-called menace was minuscule and already declining by the time the article was written.

In general, after the commotion over Crowley's novel, the British press did not follow the sensationalizing of drugs as was the case in the USA. This said, a few lurid articles did appear from time to time. The *Daily Mirror* of 24 July 1939 ran a piece under the headline 'Just a cigarette you'd think, but it was made from a sinister weed and an innocent girl falls victim to this terror'. In part, the text read: *Marihuana . . . Does that word mean anything to you? Perhaps you have heard vaguely that marihuana is a plant that is made into a drug. But do you know that in every city in this country there are addicts of this dangerous drug? In London there are thousands of them. Young girls, once beautiful, whose thin faces show the ravages of the weed they started smoking for a thrill. Young men who, in the throes of a hangover from the drug, find their only relief in dragging at yet another marihuana cigarette. How do they obtain this drug since the police are hot on the trail of all suspected traffickers? They obtain it from so many unexpected sources that as fast as one is closed by the police, so another opens up. Night clubs, reputable hotels and cafes are frequented by agents. They operate from the least likely places — milliner's shops, hairdressers, antique shops. But in Soho, in little lodging houses run by coloured men and women, the cigarette can be had for a secret password, and a very small sum of money. And many terrible tales are told about marihuana addicts. One girl, just over twenty, known among her friends for her quietness and modesty, suddenly threw all cautions to the winds. She began staying out late at nights. Her parents became anxious when she began to walk about the house without clothes. They stopped her when she attempted to go into the street like that. At times she became violent and showed abnormal strength. Then she would flop down in a corner, weeping and crouching like an animal. Soon she left home. No trace could be found of her, but cigarettes and ends in her room were identified as marihuana. How much does a marihuana cigarette cost? Just a shilling! Or in a 'reefer club', the low haunts where men, usually coloured, sell the cigarette, a puff can be had for six-pence. The fumes of the smoke are caressing, but they leave a somewhat acrid taste, and a pungent, sickly smell. That is, to the beginner. The addict likes it. She likes it, not because of its taste or smell, but because it gives her abnormal strength and makes her indifferent to her surroundings. One day, passing a narrow street in Soho, I saw a small crowd gazing at the third floor of a dingy house. A young and lovely woman, her clothes in shreds, stood perilously perched on a window ledge. Behind her was a man. He, too, was wild-looking and dishevelled. Several times the girl made an effort to jump and the man feebly held her back. Soon, a third man appeared, coloured and strong, and hauled them both back. They were both marihuana addicts. As she disappeared, she could be heard screaming: 'I can fly. Well, I don't care if I die!' Unconscious of herself, of any danger, she acted on the impulse to do the impossible. I heard of one case, a nineteen-year-old dancing girl who was taken to a 'reefer club' by a party of friends. Soon a man was at her side, offering her a cigarette, for which he made no charge. It was a decoy. Soon she became one of his best customers, spending half her salary on the weed. She sank lower and lower. Her associates became criminals, drug lunatics, and dope peddlers. Unlike opium, hashish and other drugs, which make their victims seek solitude, marihuana drives its victims into society, forcing them to violence, often murder . . .*

It was the usual mishmash of ill-digested facts, journalistic embellishment, racism, myth and ignorance. Why, bizarrely, it was said to be distributed by antique shop owners, hairdressers and milliners was not explained. Accompanying the article was a photograph of a young woman smoking what was quite plainly an ordinary cigarette.

After the commencement of the Second World War underground clubs, which had existed in London for decades, usually as drinking establishments offering gambling or prostitution on the side, began to proliferate to cater for the sense of *carpe diem* that infected so many people, especially after the Blitz began. Their number further increased substantially once America entered the war and US military personnel came to be based in Britain. Soho established itself as the centre of these dives, jazz the music played in them by visiting black GIs or members of the then very small British West Indian community. Inevitably, servicemen on leave gravitated towards the area bounded by Oxford Street, Regent Street, Leicester Square and Charing Cross Road, the streets still mediaeval in layout with little alleys and mews, courtyards and basements. To cater to and prey upon them were whores, black marketeers, hustlers and drug peddlers, all in their own way offering escape from the reality of war. The most common drugs on offer were speed and marijuana. These did not give rise to any great concern although it was noted that opium was being brought in by Chinese sailors.

It was not long after the war ended that the clubs metamorphosed into establishments playing Bop (or Bebop) defined as Afro-American jazz music performed at a very fast tempo and intensely emotional in content and rhythm: it was the music that was to evolve into modern jazz. Its followers – jazz musicians, West Indians and young whites – came to smoke marijuana because it was a part of the culture of jazz imported from America, the musicians the primary instigators of it.

Marijuana was smuggled into Britain mainly by African and West Indian sailors with Chinese bringing in a small percentage alongside their more traditional contraband of opium. Drug offences, especially for marijuana, increased sharply in the immediate post-war years, most customs' seizures being of flower tops but some involving hashish. The marijuana commonly arrived on banana boats from Nigeria whilst the hashish came from the Lebanon via Cyprus. There was no massive smuggling network in operation. Mostly, the drugs were run by individuals who knew a ready recipient for whatever they had to offer. Most sailors sold drugs as a means of raising some spending money when they reached a British port.

The first country to become Britain's major, organized cannabis supplier was Burma, which was under British rule until 1948. The smuggling was conducted by half a dozen rings using British cargo vessels sailing out of Rangoon. The smugglers were mostly Lascar sailors or Indian ship's engineers who had a thorough knowledge of the structure of their vessels and knew the best places in which to hide sometimes quite sizeable packages, where they would avoid not only detection but also deterioration during the six-week voyage. Upon arrival at a British dock, the smugglers were aided by British stevedores in offloading the contraband and passing it to middlemen who then contacted their distributors. Throughout the 1950s, this was the main route by which marijuana reached Britain, but it came to an end in 1959 with the seizure of 400 pounds of cannabis on a ship in Liverpool and the arrest of the mastermind of the ring in Rangoon.

Nineteen fifty was the first year in which prosecutions for the possession of cannabis were more numerous than those for opium: indeed, they were more than double the opiate figure. Despite these statistics, it was officially believed that marijuana and opium use was restricted to the West Indian and Chinese communities respectively. Yet this was to change.

It all started when the police, acting on information obtained from a ship's steward under arrest in London, decided to 'knock over' the premises of Club Eleven at 50, Carnaby Street, Soho. The club, a co-operative founded by eleven musicians, hence its name, had initially opened in December 1948, the first in Britain to present exclusively Bop. Situated in a basement that had formerly been a nightclub, it quickly gained a wide reputation as the hottest dive in town, the clientele known for its bohemian eccentricity.

On the night of 15 April, forty police officers raided the club which, at the time, was packed with about 250 patrons. Everyone was thoroughly searched and two men found in possession of cannabis. The floor, perhaps predictably, was littered with twenty-three packets of marijuana, a number of joints and small amounts of morphine and cocaine. Amongst those in the club was Ronnie Scott, the eponymous father of British modern jazz, who was found to have a small amount of cocaine in his wallet. He was convicted of possession and fined. Several months later, Club Eleven having closed, the Paramount Dance Club in Tottenham Court Road was raided. Cannabis was found on dancers who, it was noted with a disgusted disquiet, were mostly coloured men and white women.

It was considered that only a certain class of girl was associated with cannabis, *the type*, the *Daily Telegraph* opined in August 1951, *who became camp followers when American troops in large numbers were stationed here during the war*. Once again, the spectre arose of blacks corrupting whites, especially women, with their killer weed, this xenophobia all a part of the then contemporary dislike for West Indians who were beginning to emigrate to Britain in large numbers.

What had been considered a drug threat during the two world wars –

the Germans and, before and between the conflicts, the Chinese – was now replaced by coloured men, this jingoism heightened not only because of the immigration situation but also by the American cant put out since the 1930s by Anslinger and the FBN. Concern was not only voiced about the fate of women in black hands: there was a worry that the young might also come under their spell, this given credence by the arrest, in August 1951, of the first white teenager found in possession of marijuana. Cannabis, the black man's narcotic, was widely regarded as more dangerous than heroin or cocaine, not because of its potential for addiction but for its facilitation of multi-racial sexual communication.

The press, needless to say, were adroit in latching on to this anti-racial mood. John Ralph, writing in the *Sunday Graphic* in September 1951, stated, *After several weeks I have just completed exhaustive inquiries into the most insidious vice Scotland Yard has ever been called up to tackle – dope peddling.* After this example of extreme hyperbole, he added, *One of the detectives told me, 'We are dealing with the most evil men who have ever taken to the vice business.' The victims are teenage British girls, and to a lesser extent, teenage youths . . . The racketeers are 90 per cent coloured men from the West Indies and west coast of Africa . . . As the result of my inquiries, I share the fear of detectives now on the job that there is the greatest danger of the reefer craze becoming the greatest social menace this country has known.* The last of his articles on the subject ended with what was perhaps the greatest underlying fear of them all, a prophecy that the time would come when *this country will be all* [racial] *mixtures . . . There will be only half castes.* Chapman Pincher, addressing the link between cannabis and jazz, went so far in the *Daily Express* as to emphatically declare, *Yes, there is scientific evidence for a much stronger link which involves the basic nature of the human brain. Reefers and rhythm seem to be directly connected with the minute electric 'waves' continually generated by the brain surface. When the rhythm of the music synchronises with the rhythm of the 'brainwaves' the jazz fans experience an almost compulsive urge to move their bodies in sympathy. Dope may help the brain to 'tune in' to the rhythm more sharply, thereby heightening the ecstasy of the dance.* Another supposedly expert observer, Arthur Tietjen, a *Daily Mail* crime reporter and author of crime books, wrote in *Soho: London's Vicious Circle*, published in 1956, *In their flamboyant suits, shirts and ties, these coloured loungers who never worked, but drew their unemployment pay, enhanced their income by peddling 'reefers'. Their chief victims are white girls who, craving excitement, haunt the 'hot' jazz spots in the underground dens in Soho and off the Tottenham Court Road that are frequented by negroes.*

Whatever scare-mongering tabloid journalistic nonsense was released in the name of improved newspaper circulation, it was nevertheless easy to obtain cannabis in London, if one knew where to go. A book which appeared in 1956 illustrated how effortlessly one could enter this *demi-monde* if one so chose.

*Viper: The Confessions of a Drug Addict*, released in 1956 by Robert Hale, a respectable London publishing house, purported to be the story of Raymond Thorp, a twenty-something office clerk who lived in a bed-sitter in Paddington and frequented jazz clubs such as Club Eleven where he started to smoke marijuana so as not to be alienated from his peers. His introduction to the drug occurred in The Boogie Club: *The jazz seeped into my body. I felt the notes running through my veins, slipping through my tapping fingers into the air around me. I could see colours where before I had seen nothing. I stared fascinated, like a blind man given eyes, at white faces resting on brown shoulders. The reds and yellows and blues of the girls' dresses swam like a rainbow before me. And with it all I felt BIG. I felt big physically. I felt big mentally. Raymond Thorp the clerk had been liquidated. I'd tossed the last clod of earth on his grave with the striking of a match. Now I was just 'Ray'. One of the cats. One of the smart people around town, jumping out of the rut and climbing a rocket bound for heaven.* In a short while, he became psychologically addicted and started fencing stolen luxury goods around the clubs where, in an austere country still in the grip of post-war rationing, he found a ready market. This did not provide him with sufficient income to support his habit, so he began dealing in heroin and cocaine on behalf of a London gang, and using heroin himself. Arrested on charges of possessing dangerous drugs and burglary, he was imprisoned and, after attempting suicide in jail, decided to go straight, hoping the proceeds from the sale of the book would support him while he sought a cure.

The book was ghost-written (or, more accurately, co-authored) by Derek Agnew to whom Thorp is said to have told his life story. There was more than a hint of the tabloid press about the narrative but it was not sensationally written and, for that reason, when Thorp says, *like it or not, it is the black races who are responsible for the post-war spread of hemp smoking in Britain . . . the blunt truth is that numbers of them take perverted satisfaction from 'lighting up' a white girl. I know. I have watched it happen. And it is a horrible sight!* one is tempted to take his remarks at face value.

Despite the presence of dangerous drugs in British society, there was no anti-drug police unit. There was, however, one person who took it upon himself to address the issue. Dr Donald McIntosh Johnson published a book in 1952 entitled *Indian Hemp – A Social Menace*. In it, he told of a reputable Mr A who was fed a Mickey Finn which drove him insane and necessitated him being held in an asylum until the effects wore off. He said the drug used had been cannabis. Years later, including nearly a decade serving as a Conservative Member of Parliament, Johnson admitted the anonymous manic had been himself and that he was not certain what drug had been administered to him. In his book, he also blamed cannabis poisoning as a possible cause of an outbreak of mass hallucination that had occurred in the small French town of Pont-Saint-Esprit in 1951. In fact, it was subsequently proved to be caused by ergot of rye, a fungal disease on the flour from which the town baker made his bread. Accepting this explanation as feasible, Johnson went on to claim that the Russians, from whom Britain imported flour, might contaminate it with cannabis to indoctrinate the country's population, borrowing Chapman Pincher's argument that cannabis altered the electrical impulses in the brain. *For the rhythm of the bass drum,* he wrote, *substitute the rhythm of totalitarian propaganda and the point which I wish to make will be appreciated.*

Johnson's book was generally ignored by both the Government and the public. The police targeted black immigrant communities in their search for marijuana and other illegal drugs, and magistrates and judges handed down increasingly long custodial sentences. Yet, as Thorp mentioned in his story, most policemen and officers of the court would not recognize marijuana if they saw it. Thorp describes deliberately smoking a joint in front of a policeman standing on a street corner because he knew he would not identify the odour. This naïvety went well beyond the ignorant bobby on the beat. The BBC, which censored itself for sensitive material deemed not suitable for broadcast, permitted the eminently respectable Edmundo Ros and his dance orchestra to play 'La Cucaracha', not realizing what lay behind the lyrics.

By 1960, the authorities still exhibited no real concern for marijuana or any other dangerous drug. Her Majesty's Customs and Excise and the police were keeping a tight lid on the situation. They were not to know it, but this was the calm before the storm.

# 17

# THE BEATS

IN THE SECOND HALF OF THE 1940S, A DISPARATE GROUP OF YOUNG, mostly white intellectuals and writers began to frequent the jazz clubs and bars of New York City. In common with many of those around them, they were followers of jazz who used marijuana and other drugs but, for them, these substances were not just a means of getting 'hot'. Eager self-seekers and expressionists keen to reassess the society in which they lived, they evolved a genre that was to unequivocally and irredeemably alter the direction of Western literature, their lives becoming iconic. In time, they were known as the Beats.

Aware of the European tradition of experimentation with hashish, they approached cannabis in a different way from the jazz musicians and their audiences, using it not only as an amazing device to alter or enhance their literary visions but also as a vehicle for their dissension against the banality of the bourgeois society in which they lived. For them, convention was not something to be blindly accepted but rigorously questioned and, if found wanting, overturned so that an alternative might be formed. In this quest for a different world, they were determined to live life to the full, test its boundaries, stretch its values and see how far they could go before it broke.

The Beats adopted the cultural rebellion of the black population of New York City, of which Bop was the most obvious manifestation. Yet there was more to this new music than its fast tempo and clever improvisation. To the untrained or unwilling ear, it might have sounded like a cacophony but it was in fact highly structured and required expert musicianship. The black musicians who played it came to be well respected for their skill and, through them, the social standing of the urban black began to rise and take on a racial identity. Followers of Bop saw themselves as distinctive. They were 'cool' as opposed to 'hot', restrained and refined as opposed to wild and loud. They had their own patois, dressed in their own style of berets and dark glasses ('shades') and sported goatee beards. Seen as affectation by the previous generation of jazz musicians, this seeking for uniqueness angered many of them. The Boppers resented their forebears for pandering to white musical taste and wanted to re-invent jazz so that it might become a black musical form as good as the white man's jazz, which they believed was their own music in hijacked form.

This exclusivity led to many of the Boppers withdrawing into an introspective bohemian lifestyle which involved self-imposed cultural iso-lationism and divorce from everyday reality. The best way to achieve this was through drugs. Some relied upon alcohol. A substantial number, both black Bop musicians and the white musicians who shared their musical vision and social aspirations, turned to heroin. And there was marijuana. The Beats – they were later referred to as the Beat generation – shared this deep affinity for black culture, revelling in its subversion and the underbelly of New York City life around Times Square.

The central figures of the Beat generation, who first met in and around Columbia University in New York at or about the end of the Second World War, were Allen Ginsberg, William Burroughs, Gregory Corso, Lucien Carr, Dave Kammerer and Edie Parker who introduced into the group her boyfriend, Jack Kerouac. Kerouac and the older Burroughs apart, they were university undergraduates by day and hipsters by night.

If the Beats had had an elected leader, it would have been Ginsberg. The son of a left-wing Jewish high-school teacher from Patterson, New Jersey, and an ardently Communist mother who was not infrequently committed to mental institutions, Ginsberg was an English major at Columbia who was confused by his emerging homosexuality and angry in a perplexed way at the society against which his parents spoke but within which they lived comfortably. Of the Beats, Ginsberg was the primary intellectual thinker but this is not to imply he was selfish for he was also an avid promoter of his friends. It is arguable that, without him, neither Burroughs nor Kerouac would have had literary careers and a good many other writers such as Gregory Corso, Gary Snyder and Peter

Orlovsky would have been largely ignored. He also introduced his friends – at least those who had not already discovered them for themselves – to drugs.

Determined from a young age to be a writer, Ginsberg was a keen experimenter in every sense. He pushed at the bounds of his sexuality, of literary form, of narcotics and morality, and was always ready to test how far he could go. In his second year at Columbia, he was suspended for writing *Butler has no balls* in the dust on his room window along with *Fuck the Jews*, decorated with a piratical skull and crossbones. His aim was to draw attention to the lackadaisical cleaning habits of the Irish woman who was supposed to clean his university lodging but Nicholas Murray Butler, the university's president, took umbrage and suspended him. That he had also shared his room overnight with Kerouac, who had previously been a student at the university and was now forbidden access to the campus, did not help. Consequently, Ginsberg moved out of his room and into an apartment with Burroughs and Kerouac owned by another student, Joan Vollmer Adams, who was later to marry Burroughs.

As for William S. Burroughs, he was a Harvard graduate, older than the others, extremely well read and erudite, and an avowed bisexual who had drifted from job to job, living off the meagre proceeds of a family trust fund: his wealthy grandfather, after whom he was named, was William Seward Burroughs, the inventor of the adding machine. Where Ginsberg opened his friends' eyes to his intellectual world, Burroughs opened them to the criminal world of New York, in which he had many contacts provided by Herbert Huncke, a petty thief and drug addict whom Burroughs had first met when he bought a hand gun and some heroin from him in Times Square. When Huncke was jailed for fencing and Burroughs arrested for counterfeiting prescriptions to obtain heroin to feed his own addiction, he left New York and settled in New Waverly in East Texas, 50 miles north of Houston. Here, on a fairly basic farmstead of 97 acres, he established a hidden plot in dense woodland where he tried unsuccessfully to grow opium poppies. With marijuana he was much more successful, cultivating it as a cash crop and sending it up to New York.

Whereas Burroughs came from a background of wealth and Ginsberg from the middle class, Jean-Louis 'Jack' Kerouac came from the exotic. Born in 1922 in Lowell, Massachusetts, he was an American of French-Canadian and Mohawk-Caughnawaga Indian extraction. His father was a failed businessman who turned to gambling to try to recoup his lost income then sank into alcoholism. Gaining a football scholarship to college and working for an insurance company, Kerouac hoped to restore his family's fortunes and, when his success as a football player became evident, he was given a scholarship to Columbia University. Here, disillusioned by his father's drinking, he began to go off the rails, dropped out of the university and, during the war, worked as a merchant seaman. While on leave in New York, he fell in with Ginsberg and his set. Well educated and intellectually astute, Kerouac had a rebellious soul which would not accept the safe basis of the American way of life that had, in his eyes, sucked in and spat out his father. He became a wanderer, describing himself as a strange, solitary, crazy, Catholic mystic.

Before meeting the other Beats, Kerouac drank and took speed, his first experience with marijuana being in a jazz club in Harlem. Jazz and, later, Bop were central to his life not only because he liked the music but because he was also influenced by its intrinsically spontaneous structure which he adapted into his literary style and, in turn, very significantly influenced Western literature. His words did with meaning what jazz musician's instruments did with sound.

No sooner was Kerouac established as one of the Beats than Burroughs introduced him to morphine and heroin. He also discovered mescaline and peyote and, like his father, became an alcoholic. Drugs were to be central to his existence, psychologically, physiologically and creatively. Much of his writing was done under the influence of drugs, coming to him as a stream of consciousness, one idea sparking off the last much as, in the jazz he listened to, one musical phrase led organically into the next. The third of the trio, Ginsberg, used morphine, opium, codeine (another opiate), cocaine, speed and marijuana which he first smoked with some Puerto Rican seamen in New Orleans.

As far as marijuana was concerned, Ginsberg was to say that their *original use was for aesthetic study, aesthetic perception, deepening it. I was somewhat disappointed later on, when the counterculture developed the use of grass for party purposes rather than for study purposes. I always thought that was the wrong direction.* An indication of his marijuana use was how, when studying the work of Paul Cézanne, Ginsberg would smoke a joint then go to the New York Museum of Modern Art and look at the artist's paintings. *I got a strange shuddering impression looking at his canvases,* he wrote, *partly the effect when someone pulls a Venetian blind, reverses the Venetian — there's a sudden shift, a flashing that you see in Cézanne canvases* which he later referred to as *eyeball kicks.* The aim of much of his writing was to achieve the same technique with words.

In 1947, the Beats were joined by a twenty-seven-year-old itinerant car thief from Denver, Colorado, by the name of Neal Cassady. The charismatic, rebellious and eccentric son of a down-and-out drunk, he had a string of arrests behind him for stealing cars and was employed as the parking valet at the Hotel New Yorker on 34<sup>th</sup> Street. He and Kerouac became close friends: Cassady was hungry for an intellectual existence and Kerouac wanted a kindred spirit who was as wild and liberated as he was himself. In Kerouac's books, Cassady was the basis for the characters Dean Moriarty and Cody Pomeray whose rebellion and thirst for freedom epitomized the Beat view of existence.

The affinity that existed between Kerouac and Cassady involved more than friendship. They drank and used peyote, speed and marijuana together, Cassady's incessant talking giving life to the stream of consciousness so central to Kerouac's work. In 1948, they took to the road together travelling across America fuelled by booze, speed and marijuana. It was the ultimate act of ecstatic revolt against the uptight, homogenized, sterilized, paranoiac world of the American dream and the Cold War.

With Burroughs already gone, Ginsberg was left on his own in New York City. He rented an apartment in East Harlem, immersing himself in the works of the eighteenth-century English mystical poet William Blake. While reading Blake's visionary poetry, he had a revelation of, as he put it, almost being swallowed by God which made him think he had been chosen for a mission to seek a higher intellectual and spiritual existence. Blake's religious visions, at times influenced by opium rather than cannabis, appealed to him for they contained imagery similar to those which Ginsberg had received from his taking of drugs, which he was using to expand his mind. Huncke, upon his release from prison, used the apartment to store stolen goods he was fencing. The police raided it and Ginsberg was arrested, only saved from incarceration by his university professors who declared him mad and had him committed to the Columbia Presbyterian Psychiatric Institute for seven months.

In the meantime, Kerouac and Cassady had reached Mexico where the marijuana was plentiful, and came in the form of *a tremendous Corona cigar of tea*, and the women compliant. Kerouac, however, fell ill with dysentery and the pair headed for Mexico City where Burroughs was now living with his wife, having skipped Texas to avoid a drug-dealing indictment. Nursed by Joan Burroughs, Kerouac regained his health and embarked upon a smoking routine of fifteen joints a day. Cassady, who criticized Kerouac's over-indulgence, reported to Ginsberg, *He was really stoned consistently for long periods, alone,* adding, *When one is alone on this stuff the sheer ecstasy of utterly realizing each moment makes it more clear to one than ever how impossibly far one is from the others.*

In October 1950, Kerouac returned to New York, physically and emotionally exhausted. Ginsberg was concerned Kerouac was using too much marijuana but decided he was not at risk from addiction to drugs as he only infrequently used morphine, which was physiologically habituating. Burroughs was more afraid Kerouac would become so introverted that he would withdraw from society like an hermetic Buddhist monk walled up in a cell and fed through a crack in the wall.

By 1952, Cassady was living in San Francisco with his wife, deeply involved in marijuana and determined to enrol as many people as possible into its joys: it was the time of the birth of the San Francisco counterculture that would become the hippy movement. Cassady found work on the railroad, travelling to Mexico and smuggling very substantial quantities of marijuana back across the border in boxcars, but giving it away rather than selling it. It is fairly accurate to say that it was Cassady who introduced large-scale marijuana use in California and, historically, to the future hippy generation.

Early that year, Kerouac went to live with the Cassadys for a while. In his most explicit drug novel, *Visions of Cody*, Kerouac wrote of Cassady's roach kit which he kept in the kitchen: *a dish, glass, deep dish, small, with rolling paper, tweezers, roach pipe (hollow steel tube), roach pipe ramrod came with the tube, attached, an art tool actually, bottles of seeds* . . . The Cassadys found Kerouac's presence a strain. He relied entirely upon them to feed him and provide him with the prodigious quantities of marijuana he demanded. They simply did not have the money and, after a falling-out, Kerouac headed for Mexico City and Burroughs in May. From Nogales, the border town where Cassady dropped him off, Kerouac continued on his way by long-distance bus, teaming up with a young Mexican called Enrique who smuggled marijuana inside a home-made radio set. They spent the trip smoking joints and drinking mescal, breaking the routine in Culiacan with opium.

When he reached Mexico City, Kerouac found Burroughs a widower. Two months previously, he had killed Joan whilst trying to shoot a glass off her head, William Tell-style, with a pistol. He was stoned at the time. Settled into Burroughs' apartment, Kerouac started to write whilst permanently intoxicated by marijuana and, on occasion, morphine. The book, *Doctor Sax*, which he worked on in Burroughs' lavatory so that, if the police called, they would not smell the smoke in the living quarters, relied heavily upon marijuana-induced memories of his childhood and adolescence in Massachusetts.

At the same time, Burroughs was writing his autobiographical confessional novel, *Junky*, about a young man's life high on opiates in the society of addicts. It was the first truly great literary novel about the sub-world of drugs written in America, which he was to follow later with the even more astonishing, surreal and often abhorrent *The Naked Lunch*. While the other Beats were concentrating on their art, Burroughs was becoming without doubt the most authoritative modern literary writer on drugs and addiction.

Late in 1952, Kerouac returned once more to New York where his friend John Clellon Holmes had received a twenty-thousand-dollar advance on his novel *Go*, which was set in contemporary New York and was being feted by the critics. It complemented another recently published novel by Chandler Brossard, *Who Walks in Darkness*, a narrative about a writer living in the bohemian quarter of Greenwich Village. Kerouac dismissed the latter book as pretentious but the former he greatly admired, even envied. Brossard, who was not a Beat, wrote from outside the bohemian experiences but Holmes came from within it. He wrote with authority about the drug-taking and chaotic lives of the Beats, Kerouac the basis for one of the book's characters, Gene Pasternak.

As a result of his novel, Holmes was commissioned to write a feature article for the *New York Times Magazine* on the lives of his New York contemporaries. In it, he credited Kerouac with coming up with the term 'the Beat generation', which Holmes had used in his novel. He recalled, *One evening as he* [Kerouac] *described the way the young hipsters of Times Square walked down the street – watchful, cat-like, inquisitive, close to the buildings, in the street but not of it – I interrupted him to say that I thought we all walked like that, but what was the peculiar quality of mind behind it? Jack answered: 'It's a sort of furtiveness . . . Like we were a generation of furtives. You know, with an inner knowledge there's no use flaunting on that level, the level of the "public", a kind of beatness – I mean, being right down to it, to ourselves, because we all really know where we are – and a weariness with all the forms, all the conventions of the world . . . It's something like that. So I guess you might say we're a beat generation.'* Holmes gave the impression that this was a recent conversation but it had actually happened three years earlier. Kerouac had got the word from Huncke who used it to describe this habitual state of being: he was always beat, meaning tuckered out. Later, Kerouac was to claim it had its roots in the word 'beatific'.

By 1955, Kerouac was back in Mexico City, smoking excessive

amounts of marijuana and shooting up with morphine. In this all-but-permanent condition of intoxication, he wrote the 242-chorus poem 'Mexico City Blues', much of it reading like a literary sort of jazz improvisation, drawing upon immediate stimuli and stringing them loosely together:

> *By the light*
> *Of the silvery moon*
> *I like to spoon*
> *To my honey*
> *I'll croon*
> *Love's dream*
>
> *By the light*
> *Of the silvery moon*
> *We'll O that's the*
> *Part I dont remember*
> *ho ney moon –*
> *Croon –*
> *Love –*
> *June –*
>
> *O I dont know*
> *You can get it out of a book*
> *If the right words are*
> *important*

What was of tremendous importance eighteen months later was the publication of what are probably the two best-known books produced by the Beat generation. One was Ginsberg's *Howl and Other Poems*, the other Kerouac's semi-autobiographical novel *On the Road*.

Ginsberg's book was published by the City Lights bookshop in San Francisco, founded in 1955 by the poet Lawrence Ferlinghetti as a book store-cum-coffee shop where writers and bohemians came to talk and browse the shelves as well as buy the latest books. After a literary magazine of his failed, Ferlinghetti began publishing what he called the Pocket Poets Series, producing books in inexpensive paperback formats. Within a year, City Lights was at the forefront of a West Coast literary renaissance in which poetry, as the critic Richard Eberhart noted, *had become a tangible social force, moving and unifying the auditors, releasing the energy of the audience through spoken, even shouted verse, in a way at present unique to this region.* Ginsberg, by now living in California, frequented the bookshop and his book was the fourth to be released. Shortly after publication, the police obtained a copy of the book and charged Ferlinghetti with publishing and selling obscene and indecent material.

What Ginsberg had done was criticize American society and display his personal search for liberty through drugs, jazz and sexual – and homo-sexual – freedom. Bearing in mind that America was in the throes of extremist right-wing witch hunts of McCarthyism at the time, it was a brave book to write and publish.

When the case came to court, the defence lawyer pleaded the First Amendment on the right of freedom of speech. The trial lasted some months, with many leading American literary figures being called, and ended in a not-guilty verdict. Overnight, City Lights and Ginsberg – and the Beats – were nationally famous. So too, by association, were drugs and marijuana.

*Howl and Other Poems* raised the public consciousness of the Beats but it was Kerouac's *On the Road* that cemented their presence in American culture. Published only months after Ginsberg's collection, it shocked the middle classes and fascinated the young. Probably the most influential American novel of the twentieth century, it centred upon the life and wanderings of a young man, Dean Moriarty, based upon Cassady but not unlike Kerouac. A foot-loose traveller, he became the archetypal American hero, a spiritual extension of the liberty-seeking pioneers of American nineteenth-century expansion. The novel was criticized for its hedonism and degeneracy, but founded an entirely new youth culture in which drugs were an accepted norm. It might be said to have given birth to, or at least been the progenitor of, the modern drug culture.

After its publication Kerouac, who had previously largely lived out of the limelight, became a public literary figure, sought after for interviews and appearances at many of which he tried hard to debunk the perception that the Beats were just rootless and violent, drug-addicted bums. Yet the truth of what they truly were escaped him. His stock answers were that he was *waiting for God to show his face* or, somewhat flippantly, *Man, you gotta stay high, that's all.* He denied using drugs and more often than not appeared for an interview drunk – or, as he recommended, high. After the publication of *On the Road*, Kerouac went downhill fast. Thrice married, he wrote more but his work lacked the verve for which it was previously admired. He died of cirrhosis of the liver in 1969, aged forty-seven, a genuinely remarkable talent extraordinarily wasted by an over-indulgence of drink and drugs.

Yet the anthem had been sung and the Beat gospel, including the use of drugs, had been preached.

From the Beats developed a new breed of youth, the Beatniks. The name was coined by Herb Caen, a journalist on the *San Francisco Chronicle* who first used it in April 1958. How he arrived at it is conjecture but the first-ever satellite, the Russian Sputnik, had recently been launched. 'Sputnik' translated from the Russian as 'friendly traveller' and whether or not it had been Caen's intention, this derivation for 'Beatnik' stuck. According to Jerry Kamstra, in his book *Weed: Adventures of a Dope Smuggler*, published in 1974, it was taken to mean 'beautiful traveller' by those who considered themselves Beatniks, drawing upon Kerouac's definition of Beat deriving from 'beatific'.

Like their forebears, the Beatniks rebelled against the accepted mores of society. The men grew beards and wore old clothes, shades and black turtleneck sweaters, the women jeans and sweaters, often with a Beat-style beret. And they smoked marijuana. In Beatnik clubs, they listened to the new cool jazz, wrote free verse, generally hung out and were soon a cultural phenomenon. Tens of thousands of middle-class students, who would never have let themselves become as degenerate as the Beats, saw themselves as Beatniks and followed the Beatnik way of life. It might be said that the Beatniks were by and large middle-class, bathed-and-washed Beats.

As far as the history of cannabis is concerned, however, the Beatniks were a major force for, by sheer weight of numbers, they disseminated marijuana across the campuses of America.

One of the favourite Beatnik haunts was the North Beach area of San Francisco where Neal Cassady, who had faithfully kept to the Beat way of life, was the primary marijuana supplier. Still working on the railroad, he achieved what must be one of the greatest Beat rebellious actions of all time when he got high on marijuana whilst working as the brakeman on President Eisenhower's campaign train. Early in 1958, he was caught in a police drugs-sting operation and sentenced to two years' to life imprisonment: he served two-and-a-half years in San Quentin followed by three years on probation.

Ginsberg's international literary reputation as one of America's foremost poets was sealed by *Howl and Other Poems* and made him virtually untouchable. He went on to publish work that not only unequivocally stated his homosexuality but also declared his belief that the mind should be expanded by Hinduism, Zen Buddhism, meditation and drugs. He admitted to using peyote, marijuana, mescaline, ether and LSD to *open up an awareness of the supernatural, of the god-head, and free the soul.* By late 1958, he had embarked upon a personal social and intellectual crusade which included pressing for the legalization of all drugs such as opiates, cocaine and marijuana. He even went so far as to imply that he was a heroin addict, which he was not, although he had used it along with many other substances in his search for spiritual advancement and an altered consciousness. This pursuit took him across the world, from the Amazon to take *ayahuasca* with shamans to the banks of the Ganges in India where he smoked hashish with *sadhus.* He maintained this quest until 1963 when, in India, he met Kyabjé Dudjom Rinpoche, considered the most beloved of the great twentieth-century Buddhist lamas of Tibet. Rinpoche instructed Ginsberg to surrender to his search on the grounds that he was now so involved in thinking about obtaining a vision that he was divorced from directly perceiving it.

The Beats were not the only people experimenting with drugs. Aldous Huxley, the English novelist and writer of *Brave New World*, described his 1953 experimentation with mescaline in *The Doors of Perception* and *Heaven and Hell*, both published in the mid-1950s and now considered vitally important texts in the annals of drug literature. Coming from a distinguished intellectual family – his grandfather was T. H. Huxley, the eminent biologist – and with a considerable education behind him, Huxley's judgement was taken seriously. It was his opinion that the human brain automatically restricted the perception of reality, allowing only a small fraction of it to be assimilated. Mescaline, and other drugs, removed this constraint.

Simultaneously, in France, the Belgian-born French painter and writer Henri Michaux devoted much of the later years of his life to a study of drugs, drug-induced fantasies and their effects upon his inner self, concentrating upon mescaline, ether, cannabis and other substances. He wrote extensively on the subject but his critics found his style of writing obscure and dismissed his work as uninhibited hallucination. His best-known book, *Light Through Darkness*, translated into English in 1963, addresses particularly the habit of all hallucinogens to promote laughter: *With hashish, laughter comes after a kind of sinuosity, extremely relaxed, which is at the same time like a wave, like a tickling and like a shudder and like the steps of a very steep stairway . . . Everything stimulates* [the imagination], *and immediately it begins to embroider, to fabulate, to place and to displace. One thing leads to another, there is then an interminable succession of bursts of laughter, cascades of release which release nothing at all, and the laughter, ever racing, after a moment's halt to get its breath, starts off again, impossible to satiate. Laughter on conveyor belts. Laughter without any subject for laughter. Subjects are found at the beginning. Thereupon the imagination wearies but laughter goes on running.*

During the summer of 1960, the American sociologist Ned Polsky spent several months in Greenwich Village studying the way of life of the Beats, publishing his findings in a book entitled *Hustlers, Beats, and Others*. As far as drugs were concerned, he discovered that most of the Beats used only non-addicting drugs, of which the main one was marijuana, and very few – he estimated one in twelve – went on to use 'harder' substances. A number of those Beats with whom he smoked complained that supplies were dwindling because of the increase in use of marijuana across society. Supply had not yet caught up with the demand prompted by Ginsberg's and Kerouac's books. Polsky also realized that not only had the Beats diffused a knowledge and use of marijuana across society but they had also convinced many to question the myths promulgated about it by Anslinger and the FBN. As Ginsberg commented, the idea that marijuana made one dopey, retreatist and defeatist was a CIA, FBI, FBN concept and totally without justification. His remark was vindicated in 1961 when J. Edgar Hoover was credited in the *New York Daily News* with stating at an FBI convention, *The three biggest threats to America are the Communists, the beatniks and the eggheads.*

What the Beats did was not restricted to advertising drugs – more specifically if not intentionally, marijuana – and bringing them into the mainstream of cultural life. They created a climate of personal liberty, challenged traditional values, altered concepts of sexuality, countered hypocrisy, politicized literature and undermined censorship. Their ideals continued to be at the forefront of society until about 1964 when what they stood for started to undergo a new metamorphosis.

# TURNING ON, TUNING IN AND
# RIDING THE BUS

ANSLINGER CONTINUED TO PRESS HIS THEORIES ON THE INTERNATIONAL stage as well as at home. At the UN Commission on Narcotic Drugs, he tried to bring cannabis under the control of a proposed Single Convention which would amalgamate all previous conventions.

He utilized all the old arguments, spurious or otherwise, of the dangers of cannabis then rammed home his message by essentially covertly black-mailing the UN into agreement if it wanted the USA not to veto any forthcoming decisions. In 1954, Anslinger finally forced the UN to agree that cannabis had no medical use whatsoever and it was, consequently, proposed to be internationally banned. Most member states, except India, supported some sort of restriction. Seven years later, the UN Single Convention on Narcotic Drugs was ratified on 10 March 1961. Under it, by international agreement and along with many other drugs, cannabis was fully prohibited throughout the world: even if an individual country wished to legalize it, it could not. An important point to bear in mind, however, is the fact that it did not specifically forbid the medical use of cannabis as such, recognizing that some illicit drugs may have medical applications although conclusive evidence of medical efficacy would be required before they were allowed to be applied. It also did not prohibit cannabis cultivation for industrial and horticultural reasons. The International Narcotics Control Board (INCB) was established to police the convention.

Sixty member states signed the Single Convention. The USA was not amongst them. Anslinger, who had tried to engineer the whole process, refused to agree to some of the terms because he saw them as ambiguous. What particularly annoyed him was a stipulation that *the use of cannabis for other than medical and scientific purposes must be discontinued as soon as possible, but in any case within twenty-five years.* This was a loophole which some countries exploited, especially those in the Third World where cannabis farming was an important part of the peasant economy.

The Americans finally ratified the Single Convention in 1967. In 1971, the UN set up the Fund for Drug Control, today known as the UN International Drug Control Programme. That same year, the Single Convention was amended by the Convention on Psychotropic Substances and then again a new protocol the following year. In 1988 another convention, the Convention Against Illicit Traffic in Narcotic Drugs and Psychotropic Substances, known as the Vienna Convention, was passed.

By the time the US ratified the Single Convention, Anslinger's intolerant reign of disinformation and prejudice was over. He retired in July 1962, aged seventy, the maximum statutory retirement age. Leadership of the FBN fell to Henry Giordano. Anslinger, however, was not out of power for he remained the American representative on drug control to the UN. Rumours persist that Anslinger was forced to resign by President John F. Kennedy.

In September 1962, as he had promised in his presidential campaign manifesto, Kennedy held a Conference on Narcotic and Drug Abuse in the White House. The five-hundred-strong body of delegates accepted that there was much blether spoken about cannabis. Within eight weeks, a paper was published called 'The Prettyman Report', named after its author, E. Barrett Prettyman, a retired US Supreme Court of Appeal judge. Prettyman stated bluntly that marijuana was not proven to be linked to criminality and that reports of its dangers were grossly overstated, and suggested that federal drug laws be rewritten as far as marijuana was concerned, removing the harsh mandatory sentences for being *in poor social perspective.*

Early the following year, Kennedy appointed a Presidential Advisory Committee on Narcotics and Drug Abuse which roundly condemned the prevailing attitude towards marijuana. Some put this radical change of thinking down to the fact that Kennedy was a young man with new ideas but he may have had a secret, long-term, personal agenda regarding cannabis. Kennedy suffered from excruciating back pain for much of his adult life and was said to have used marijuana to alleviate it. It begs the one question that has lingered ever since: had Kennedy had the foresight to move slowly towards the medical application of cannabis?

The stance of Kennedy's committee greatly surprised the American public and there had already been those who were beginning to suspect the FBN and anti-drug lobbies' opinions but their voice had been stifled. That changed on the evening of 12 February 1961.

John Crosby was a syndicated columnist who anchored his own television chat show for Metromedia Network. That evening, his guests were Allen Ginsberg, the novelist Norman Mailer, and the anthropologist Ashley Montagu. Ginsberg, predictably, raised the subject of marijuana and spoke of his experiences of it on his travels overseas in India and Morocco. Mailer is said to have admitted he had tried it and Montagu outlined its cultural status in some countries. The conversation roundly condemned the laws on marijuana: even the show's host agreed they were far too stringent. The following day, the press coverage was extensive. Anslinger, still head of the FBN, demanded equal air time and got it three weeks later, but he had been plainly wrong-footed and was very much on the defensive. Crosby derided Anslinger's refutation in his newspaper column and the FBN set about planning to frame Ginsberg on a marijuana charge.

The current of change was running. Marijuana was no longer a poor Mexican or black drug: it was now being used by rapidly increasing numbers of young middle-class whites. Those in the more educated sections of society, unable to purchase even a bottle of beer before the age of twenty-one, saw marijuana not only as a way to get intoxicated but also to display their ridicule for the alcoholic drink laws. Yet there was much more to it than that. America was entering a new era in which it was not only questioning the validity of its traditional values but doing something about them, addressing the perceived injustices of racial segregation and inequality and political corruption. Marijuana use was just one of the subjects under scrutiny and discussion.

It was not alone. Another drug, lysergic acid diethylamide (LSD), was also at the centre of attention.

Aldous Huxley's writings on mescaline had had a great impact but it was another Englishman, Alan Watts, who wrote of LSD in his book *The Joyous Cosmology*, published in 1962. Watts, born in 1915, was an Oriental theologist and philosopher who had become fascinated with eastern religions while still a pupil at the prominent King's School, Canterbury. On leaving school, he became a Buddhist, married an American and settled in the USA. For him, drugs were not recreational but a means towards redefining intellect and understanding. Both Watts and Huxley, although influential in furthering interest in drugs, were eclipsed by an American whose name has become synonymous with drugs. His name was Timothy Leary.

Born in 1920, Leary was raised a Roman Catholic but turned his back on the Church, and the West Point military academy in which he was enrolled, to become a psychologist. In 1960, at the age of forty, he was a professor of clinical psychology at Harvard University. That year, on holiday in Mexico, he ate seven small black and desiccated toadstools purchased from a doctor and underwent his first psychedelic experience. The fungi — later universally nicknamed 'magic mushrooms' — were locally known as *nanacatl* and contained a drug which Aztec and Mayan Indians had used in religious ceremonies. Back at Harvard, Leary experimented scientifically with an artificial derivative of the fungi, psilocybine, which he hoped might be developed into a therapeutic psychiatric treatment.

In November, Ginsberg visited Leary and brought into his clinical studies his coterie of mind-expansionist writers and musicians. Many of them assisted Leary with his work, finally testing LSD. When the Harvard authorities found out in 1963 what was going on, Leary and a colleague, Richard Alpert, were dismissed, the former settling in California after being deported from Mexico for attempting to establish a drug-research community there.

The idea of a research community was resuscitated the following year when the millionaire William Mellon Hitchcock and his sister financed the Castalia Foundation on his 2,500-acre estate near Millbrook, 10 miles north-east of Poughkeepsie, Fitz Hugh Ludlow's home town. Leary was invited to join it. He did and became the centre of a psychedelic culture, commenting upon LSD, lecturing about it, publishing material on how to use it safely and coining one of the best-known axioms of the twentieth century — *turn on, tune in, drop out*.

Predictably, the authorities watched Leary carefully and, just before Christmas 1965, he was arrested for possession of marijuana. It happened at the US–Mexico border crossing on the bridge over the Rio Grande at Laredo, Texas. Leary, with two members of the Castalia community, his son and his daughter, were prevented from entering Mexico. They turned their car around, recrossed the bridge and were promptly searched by US Customs. Leary's daughter Susan was said to be in possession of half an ounce of marijuana. Leary declared it his. He and his daughter were tried on charges of smuggling marijuana, transporting it and failing to pay tax upon it. They pleaded not guilty. The smuggling charge was dropped – they could hardly have smuggled the marijuana: they had not actually crossed into Mexico – but Leary was found guilty of transportation and tax evasion and sentenced to thirty years' imprisonment, a thirty-thousand-dollar fine and ordered to be committed to a mental institution for psychiatric assessment. The sentence was overturned on appeal but Leary was arrested the next year in Laguna Beach, California, for the possession of two roaches and sentenced to ten years in a low-security prison at San Luis Obispo.

No sooner was Leary in prison than Ginsberg instigated an international Timothy Leary Defence Fund and advertised in the *New York Times* for changes in federal law. In 1970, Leary was sprung from prison by the Weathermen, a radical underground urban terrorist group, and fled into exile.

Leary was now on the run with the US government applying considerable diplomatic pressure on every country in which his foot touched ground. Meanwhile, the District Attorney of Orange County, California, indicted him *in absentia* on nineteen counts of drug trafficking, at the same time naming him as the brain behind one of the world's biggest drug-smuggling rings. Eventually, in the company of a girlfriend called Joanna Harcourt-Smith, Leary reached Afghanistan. He was apprehended at Kabul airport in 1973 by an attaché from the US Embassy. Handed over to the jurisdiction of DEA agents, he was flown back to the USA and into custody and prison. He was finally given his liberty in 1976. By then Leary, who had written extensively on drugs, the apex of his literary output being *High Priest*, published in 1968, was considered the marijuana messiah.

Ginsberg, Huxley and Leary were a new breed of drug writers. Unlike De Quincey, Coleridge, Ludlow, Baudelaire and all their predecessors, they actively encouraged people to take certain drugs, predominantly marijuana but also other hallucinogens. Their writing was objective and measured, promoting a natural herb not as an escapist drug but as a way to increase personal awareness and acuity. For many, especially the educated, middle-class young, this was a new liberation which demanded legal recognition and spawned legalization campaigns.

The first, LeMar (Legalize Marijuana), was begun in 1964, fronted by Ginsberg and a fellow poet, Ed Sanders. On 27 December, the organization staged its first, small demonstration in New York. Nineteen people took part. Within twelve months, there were branches across America.

Ginsberg's FBN file grew steadily thicker. A report was appended to it in March 1965, written by an agent digging into his past at Columbia University and concluding, *From what I have read and heard it would appear that the reported increased and widespread use of marihuana by college students could be attributed in part to the influence of Allen Ginsberg and persons of his ilk. It appears that Ginsberg's writings and poetry readings on the many college campuses and avant-garde meeting places have had a strong appeal and have provided a rationale to many college students and persons in intellectual life here and abroad.* The harassment continued.

When Ginsberg, who was abroad at the time, returned, he was subject to a strip search by US Customs. Officials even studied the detritus in his pockets with a magnifying glass. Ginsberg wrote to his congressman complaining that he was likely to be subjected to either entrapment or a frame-up. His suspicions had been aroused by the arrest of a musician friend for marijuana possession who had been threatened with an increased sentence if he refused to help get Ginsberg. Returning to Paterson in the fall of 1966 to give a poetry reading, Ginsberg mentioned visiting a local beauty spot, Passaic Falls, earlier in the day and smoking marijuana there to appreciate its beauty. The press reported the remark. On his next visit to the town, the mayor ordered his arrest for the act but the charge was dropped for lack of evidence.

As Ginsberg's literary fame increased, his views on marijuana were gradually taken more seriously. He was asked to appear before a government sub-committee studying juvenile delinquency, at which he urged research into hallucinogens. Appointed to a prestigious Guggenheim fellowship, he was able to use the platform of his fame to continue his vociferous and often well-orchestrated campaign. The FBN, unable to get Ginsberg, harassed his associates instead. Such was his position that even the prominent and usually conservative *Atlantic Monthly* magazine commissioned him to write a major article in November 1966 on the subject. Entitled 'The Great Marijuana Hoax: First Manifesto to End the Bringdown', Ginsberg wrote the first pages while smoking marijuana, in order to illustrate the difference between the *habitual shallow, purely verbal guidelines and repetitive second-hand ideological interpretations of experience to more direct, slower, absorbing, occasionally microscopically minute, engagement with sensing phenomena during the high moments or hours after one has smoked.* He believed there was *much to be revealed about marihuana especially at this time and nation for the general public, for the actual experience of the smoked herb has been completely clouded by a fog of dirty language by the diminishing crowd of fakers who have not had the experience and yet insist on being centers of propaganda about the experience . . . Marijuana is a useful catalyst for specific optical and aural aesthetic perceptions.*

In the mid-1960s, America was in social turmoil. John F. Kennedy's assassination in 1963 had radically altered the socio-political landscape. Conflicts escalated. Civil rights marchers became militant and the authorities addressed the fight against their own citizens with loaded rifles. Race riots were commonplace. The National Guard was more active than it had ever been. Racially motivated crimes soared. The long-downtrodden were seeking their rights. The title of a headline article in *Newsweek* on 22 February 1965, about the spread of marijuana, 'Narcotics: Slum to Suburb', might have applied to society as a whole.

As if this were not enough, American society was very different from that experienced by previous generations. Half the population was under the age of thirty and agitated, alienated from its elders. Their lives were in a state of flux. Sexual morality was altering fast, thanks to the invention of the contraceptive pill, and the hypocrisy of religion was under attack. Student activism and feminism were born. Freedom of speech, set in motion by the Free Speech Movement founded on the campus of the University of California at Berkeley, and the rights of the individual became central issues and the basis for considerable dissent. Sit-ins and demonstrations were frequent and often reacted against with heavy-handed, officially sanctioned violence. The gradual involvement of the US in Vietnam, where a French-colonial uprising was developing fast into a major ideological war against Communism, caused millions to question their patriotism and created a youth backlash in the loosely knit and leaderless but coast-to-coast anti-war love-and-peace movement. It was an exciting, invigorating time. America – ironically, like its sworn enemy Communist China which was at the time reeling under the oppression and upheaval of the Mao Zedong-inspired Great Proletarian Cultural Revolution – was simultaneously undergoing its own seismic cultural revolution. The old order was either under attack or on the defensive, and changing fast.

Marijuana was the battle flag of this cultural upheaval and the attitudes of those against it and hashish shifted slightly. The drug was no longer regarded just as a cause for criminality but also associated with a dissolute and un-American lifestyle which was dubbed an existence of sex, drugs and rock 'n' roll. For those who chose this alternative to material-istic, mundane America, it delivered emancipation the like of which they could never have dreamed.

When, in 1966, the federal government decided to make LSD illegal –

which until then it was not – Timothy Leary was asked to address the US Senate hearing discussing the matter. He did, criticizing the senators for being out of touch and stuck in a time warp in which the word drug was equated to crime. To most of America, he pointed out, the noun drug had a positive connotation and it was pertinent that they realized it.

The mood of many was succinctly expressed by Jerry Rubin, an early member of the Free Speech Movement and, with the anarchic activist Abbie Hoffman, co-founder of the radical Youth International Party (YIP): *Drug use signifies the total end of the Protestant ethic: screw work, we want to know ourselves. But of course the goal is to free oneself from American society's sick notion of work, success, reward, and status and to find oneself through one's own discipline, hard work, and introspection.* Rubin's Yippies, as they referred to themselves, used ridicule as a means of protest: as well as marching on the Pentagon, they lobbed pies instead of bombs, wore Uncle Sam suits and put up a pig as a candidate in the 1968 Presidential elections on the grounds it was a viable alterative to Richard Nixon or his presidential opponent, Hubert Humphrey.

From about 1966, the marijuana-smoking, pacifist, alternative youth started to be known by two names. The first was the Flower People, who exercised 'flower power'. The name came about when, at demonstrations where the demonstrators were confronted by the National Guard, young women walked up to the soldiers and placed flowers in the barrels of their rifles. The second, which came to be universally used, was the Hippies.

The origin of the word is confused. It may have derived from hip or hipster, in turn from the old opium slang or from the African–jive word *hipi*, referring to one who was wide awake from becoming self-aware with drugs. In Malcolm X's autobiography, he recalled using the word in the 1940s: *A few of the white men around Harlem, younger ones whom we called 'hippies', acted more Negro than Negroes. This particular one talked more 'hip' talk than we did.* It may have been a bastardization of Yippy. Wherever it came from, by 1967 it had firmly entered the vernacular of the Western world.

The hippies had two spiritual leaders – Timothy Leary and Ken Kesey. The latter was born in La Junta, Colorado in 1935, moving with his family at the age of eleven to Oregon where, after an illustrious high-school career, he eloped with his girlfriend, enrolled in and graduated from the State University of Oregon, was awarded a Woodrow Wilson Fellowship and joined the Creative Writing Program at Stanford University. Whilst there, he experimented with hallucinogenic drugs and got a job as a psychiatric ward orderly at a local Veterans' Administration hospital. This and his experiences of hallucination gave rise to his first, best-selling novel, *One Flew Over the Cuckoo's Nest*. In 1964, he invested his royalties from the book in a company he called Intrepid Trips, Inc., which funded the Merry Pranksters. A group of hippies, they bought a 1939 International Harvester school bus, resprayed it with psychedelic art, fitted it out with beds and a powerful hi-fi system, and drove it from California to New York. In the window where the destination school would have been displayed, their destination read simply, *Further*. The driver on the first trip of what was to become nicknamed the 'magic bus' was Neal Cassady. The odyssey sparked Kesey's hippy axiom, *You're either on the bus or you're not on the bus*. You were with it, or you were outside it . . .

What Ginsberg did for marijuana, Kesey did for LSD, conducting acid tests at happenings across the US. The audience were all given a drop of the drug on a sugar cube then subjected to extreme stimuli of sounds and colours. The difference was that whereas Ginsberg promoted drugs for intellectual reasons, Kesey did so for fun, for kicks and, in doing so, altered the perception of hallucinogenic drugs. He was later twice arrested on marijuana possession charges, fled to Mexico, returned and served a short sentence on a work farm.

In 1968, four years after he drove Kesey's magic bus, Neal Cassady, the other great exponent of marijuana, died. He was walking along a railroad track outside the town of San Miguel de Allende, 6,000 feet up in the central Mexico mountains, when he met a wedding party and joined it. During the festivities, Cassady took some Seconal tablets washed down with a large amount of *pulque*, an Aztec brew made by fermenting the maguey plant. It was early February. After the party, he set off down the railroad and was found dead the following morning: wearing only jeans and a T-shirt, he had passed out under the influence of the drugs and drink and died of hypothermia.

As the Beats had before them, the hippies – and especially those who had not only turned on and tuned in but also dropped out of their studies or the society from which they felt so alienated – tended to gravitate towards specific places with which they became synonymous. As well as settling into usually rural hippy communities – communes – across the country, they moved to Big Sur, on the coast of California between San Francisco and Los Angeles, the Lower East Side of New York City and the run-down, nineteenth-century Haight-Ashbury district of San Francisco, to which the bohemian community of Beats and cool hipsters had been forced from North Beach by avaricious realtors, grasping entre-preneurial landlords and over-zealous police officers. Within a short time, the hippy alternative society had established its own media, social and legal services, places of entertainment and a largely agrarian economy: the health food shops of today are descended from the hippy interest in natural medicines and health.

In the domain of the hippy, marijuana smoking was a social activity. Joints were shared. There was a certain thrill not only from the effects of the drug but also from participating in an illegal group activity. Marijuana formed a fraternal bond. Special equipment was invented for the smoker. One was the steamboat pipe, developed in Los Angeles, consisting of a glass funnel and a reservoir in which the smoke was concentrated before being inhaled: another type pressurized the smoke and blasted it into the lungs. Roach holders – tweezers for holding the last few millimetres of a joint so that as much as possible could be smoked – evolved from hair-grips and paperclips. Many pipes and roach holders were decorative and designed as jewellery as a way to disguise their function. Belt buckles, amulets, keyring fobs, money clips and bracelets were all available as camouflaged marijuana tools.

In 1968 Lewis Yablonsky, Professor of Sociology and Criminology at the California State University at Northridge, published *The Hippie Trip*, a sociological study that estimated there were two hundred thousand hippies in America with the same number again who lived a hippy existence when they could and hundreds of thousands more young pro-fessionals, students and middle-class executives who used psychedelic drugs, occasionally LSD but most commonly marijuana, but did not become hippies *per se*. This was still less than 0.2 per cent of the American population but, because of press attention, they were considered to be a substantial minority with millions of sympathizers.

Hippies and marijuana were indivisible. The drug's spirituality and use in India and amongst 'primitive' cultures prompted a rise in the study and acceptance of Hindu, Buddhist and Taoist philosophy and the religions of the American Indians. From these sprang a plethora of cultural interests in everything from sustainable energy resources and anti-nuclear power protests to the Tarot and astrology, the latter leading to the contemporary period being dubbed the Age of Aquarius. The anti-Vietnam War peace movement is also considered to have been affected by marijuana. The drug afforded its users a feeling of well-being and benevolence which predisposed them towards non-violence. Flower power came to mean more than stuffing daisies in rifle barrels. It was symbolic of the elemental, creative forces of nature versus the inherent destructiveness of mankind.

The hippy–marijuana culture expanded at a remarkable and almost exponential rate until it was no longer an American phenomenon. By 1967, there were hippies in practically every Western country or in every substantial white society. It produced its own psychedelic art and fashion. Both sexes wore their hair long, burned incense (to mask the smell of marijuana rather than devotionally) and candles and wore beads. Psychedelic films were made and psychedelic literature published from a very active underground press although it must be admitted that some of it was unreadable, being pretentious and esoteric in the extreme. Yet there was one strand that held all the others together and brought millions into the hippy and therefore marijuana sphere. It was rock music.

To fully comprehend the structure of the music scene at the time, a differentiation must be made between rock 'n' roll, pop music and rock music. Pop music tended to be light in both content and form whereas rock 'n' roll, whilst harder and more gutsy, still centred upon the teenage life. Rock music dealt with raw life itself. A few examples might explain the differences. If pop music is represented by Herman's Hermits' 'I'm Into Something Good' or Adam Faith's 'Someone Else's Baby' then rock 'n' roll was Elvis Presley's 'Blue Suede Shoes' or the Everly Brothers' 'Peggy Sue' and rock music was The Rolling Stones' 'Satisfaction' or The Who's 'My Generation'.

As had been the case previously with jazz, drugs were an intrinsic part of rock 'n' roll and rock music. Amphetamines were used in the 1950s and early 1960s, as well as the slimming drug Preludin (phenmetrazine), LSD (colloquially referred to as acid), heroin (used by black musicians such as Marvin Gaye and many white musicians such as Hillel Slovak of the Red Hot Chilli Peppers, Eric Clapton, Janis Joplin and, most famously of all, Keith Richards) and cocaine (used by David Bowie, Paul Butterfield, Jim Morrison of The Doors and many others).

Overriding all these drugs, however, was marijuana. Again, as with jazz, its sharpening and expansion of perception affected the music. Lyrics became more intellectually based and the music itself took on complexities and new depths. One no longer just danced to popular music – one listened to it. As recording studio multi-track technology developed, so was it possible to refine and reproduce on vinyl what the musician was hearing in his head. A good example is the music produced by Brian Wilson and The Beach Boys. 'Good Vibrations', perhaps their most enduring song, illustrates just how marijuana influenced the structure of rock music. The lyrics of the song are simplistic but the complex harmonies, multi-layered sound and sudden changes in tempo are all reminiscent of a mellow marijuana intoxication. The wide range of emotions and perceptions drugs offered caused the rock music genre to fragment into sub-genres and styles. As well as acid rock, there was rhythm 'n' blues, folk rock, hard rock, progressive rock, glam rock, southern rock, punk rock, and heavy metal, with further splinter genres such as heavy blues rock, space rock, free rock and funk rock. And more. In addition, there were bands and musicians that cut across the whole spectrum – The Beatles, The Rolling Stones, Cream, The Eagles, Eric Clapton, Bruce Springsteen, Tom Petty and Lou Reed.

Yet above all these stood one figure who was indubitably the most influential musician of the second half of the twentieth century. His music, evolved from the American folk-music tradition, altered the face of popular music.

Born into a middle-class Jewish family in Duluth, Minnesota, in 1941, his name in Hebrew was Shabtai Zisel ben Avraham but in the wider community he was known as Robert Allen Zimmerman. Later, he changed this to Bob Dylan.

In the spring of 1960, Bob Dylan was a student at the University of Minnesota in Minneapolis where he met Dave Whitaker, a well-travelled socialist who knew Ginsberg and Ferlinghetti, had gone drinking with Kerouac and met Burroughs in Paris, and was chairman of the local Fair Play for Cuba Committee.

It is with Whitaker that the Bob Dylan and marijuana myth was born. In the apartment he shared with his wife in Dinkytown, the bohemian quarter of Minneapolis, Whitaker supposedly gave Bob Dylan his first experience of marijuana. As Whitaker was later to admit, *We were the first ones – out of thirty, forty thousand students at the University of Minnesota – the first circle of real pot smokers.*

Determined to become a musician, Dylan dropped out of university, went to New York City and reinvented himself. He immersed himself in the city's very active folk music world, met his hero Woody Guthrie, read Ginsberg and Kerouac and started not only to perform traditional folk music but to write his own songs. And, it is said, he used marijuana. However, it must also be stated that Bob Dylan has always publicly and emphatically denied using any drugs, including marijuana.

And yet, *Grass was everywhere in the clubs*, he remarked in 1978. *It was always there in the jazz clubs and in the folk music clubs. There was just grass and it was available to musicians in those days. And in coffee houses way back in Minneapolis. That's where I first came into contact with it . . . If he did use it,*

Dylan was simply joining the long musical drug tradition. *Being a musician*, he declared, *means — depending on how far you go — getting to the depths of where you are at. And almost any musician would try anything to get to those depths, because playing music is an immediate thing — as opposed to putting paint on a canvas, which is a calculated thing. Your spirit flies when you are playing music. So, with music, you tend to look deeper and deeper inside yourself to find the music. That's why, I guess, grass was around those clubs.* His attitude to drugs, whether he imbibed or not, was purist. He might have been echoing the Beats when he said in an interview in 1966, *I wouldn't advise anybody to use drugs — certainly not the hard drugs . . . I think everybody's mind should be bent once in a while.*

Many of Dylan's songs, although he was to deny it in 1969, seemed distinctly influenced by marijuana. Two of the most obvious are 'Subterranean Homesick Blues' and the ubiquitous 'Mr Tambourine Man' from the 1965 album *Bringing It All Back Home.* The former describes the life of the marijuana user in New York, whilst the latter is a lyrical account of marijuana intoxication. Dylan has frequently insisted that the latter song was not influenced by marijuana, but it was supposedly written during a trans-US driving trip on which, so the myth has it, he and three friends had packets of marijuana mailed ahead to them at their various stopover points. Much of the imagery was lost on the FBN and the police although the next year, when Dylan released 'Rainy Day Women #12 & 35', it was banned from radio air-play for containing the ambiguous line *Everybody must get stoned.* (As, indeed, the myth goes, were most of the band when the track was recorded.)

Spurred on by his subversive rebellion, his voice that of exquisitely accurate protest, his musical dexterity and his sheer genius, others followed in his footsteps, attempting, as Michael Gray has pithily stated in his book, *The Art of Bob Dylan: to learn from drugs . . . to* [attempt to] *recreate drug experiences, the rejection of common-sense logic and the acceptance of mystery — Dylan accelerated the awakening to all this.* This statement seems hard to accept if Dylan did not use marijuana. And yet, throughout his musical career, Dylan has maintained an artistic integrity as rare as hen's teeth in the music industry. If he says he has never used marijuana, one must take him at his word.

Be that as it may, according to rock-music legend, Dylan introduced The Beatles to marijuana in 1964, during their first American tour, but this is not quite true. John Lennon and George Harrison had already tried marijuana. The story goes that Dylan met The Beatles in their suite of rooms at the Hotel Delmonico in New York, the introduction being engineered by the *Saturday Evening Post* journalist Al Aronowitz. Allegedly, Dylan told the band they should not use synthetic drugs (they were whisky and Coke drinkers at the time) but natural ones and he is said to have rolled a joint, passing it to John Lennon who handed it to Ringo Starr, who he said in jest was his taster. Starr, apparently not realizing marijuana etiquette demanded the joint be shared, smoked it himself. Another joint was then allegedly rolled by Dylan's right-hand man, Victor Maymudes. Eventually, everyone present is said to have fallen into a characteristic outburst of uncontrollable marijuana giggling. Paul McCartney started to write down his thoughts.

The Beatles' use of marijuana was to impinge itself upon their music. In 1994, Paul McCartney commented upon his use of marijuana: *I'd been a rather straight working-class lad, but when we started to get into pot it seemed to me quite uplifting. It didn't seem to have too many side effects like alcohol or some of the other stuff, like pills, which I pretty much kept off. I kind of liked marijuana and to me it seemed it was mind-expanding. Literally mind-expanding. So 'Got To Get You Into My Life' is really a song about that. It's not about a person, it's actually about pot. It's saying, 'I'm going to do this. This is not a bad idea.' So it's actually an ode to pot, like someone else might write an ode to chocolate or a good claret* . . . (Another myth says that The Beatles smoked marijuana in a lavatory in Buckingham Palace prior to attending their investiture as Members of the Order of the British Empire.)

Nineteen sixty-seven was an astonishing year. American involvement in the Vietnam War escalated sharply, a Summer of Love was proclaimed in San Francisco as a backlash, thousands of young Americans dodged the military draft, the *Apollo* space programme was set back by the tragic deaths of three astronauts in a launch pad fire, the world's first oil pollution disaster occurred and The Beatles released their *Sergeant Pepper's Lonely Hearts Club Band* album.

Influenced by marijuana and LSD, the album took the world by storm and ruffled more than a few establishment feathers. Where Bob Dylan's drug lyrics had been mostly ambiguous or, at least, indirect, The Beatles' were unmistakable.

The spiritual world centre of the hippy universe was Haight–Ashbury in San Francisco. Here, marijuana and LSD were the crucial ingredients of a psychedelic sub-culture from which arose acid rock. Greatly influencing The Beatles and The Rolling Stones, the main proponent of the genre was a band called The Grateful Dead, the members of which lived as an extended family and were very heavy drug users. The aim of their music was to take the audience out of themselves and onto a higher level of consciousness. Listening to their music was, it was hoped, a voyage into the unknown.

Jerry Garcia, the leading light of The Grateful Dead, had been using marijuana for years. *I was fifteen when I got turned onto marijuana*, he stated in an interview in *Rolling Stone* magazine. *Finally there was marijuana. Wow! Marijuana! Me and a friend of mine went up into the hills with two joints . . . and just got high and laughed and roared and went skipping down the streets doing funny things and just having a helluva time. It was great, it was just what I wanted, it was the perfect, it was – and that wine thing was so awful and this marijuana was so perfect.*

Inevitably, just as Anslinger had targeted jazz musicians and film stars, so did law-enforcement agencies now go after rock stars, looking as much for the publicity as the need to uphold the law. Members of The Grateful Dead were arrested for marijuana possession on 2 October 1967 when the band's communal house was raided. Many others followed, pressure groups like MOTOREDE, The Movement to Restore Decency, proclaiming rock music to be Communist inspired and glorifying drugs, destruction, revolution and sexual promiscuity.

The year was also to be remembered for events that were held, often involving a good deal of marijuana and other drugs. In January, there occurred the Be-In, a rally of several tens of thousands of hippies by the Golden Gate Bridge. They gathered to make love, smoke marijuana and attend a rock concert with a line-up headed by Jefferson Airplane, one of the main acid rock bands. The proceedings ended with Gary Snyder blowing on a conch shell and Allen Ginsberg calling for the litter to be collected, and the huge television coverage of the event turned Ginsberg into a household name, not so much as a poet as a political activist. Other events and be-ins followed then, in June, the Monterey International Pop Festival was held. It lasted three days and featured, amongst others, Jimi Hendrix, The Who, Otis Redding, Jefferson Airplane, The Grateful Dead and The Animals. It was a forerunner of probably the greatest rock music gathering of them all at Woodstock, near Bethel in upstate New York in the August of 1969 when many of the same performers made repeat appearances. Half a million people attended the weekend-long event, thousands of them carrying and smoking marijuana. The whole weekend passed off peacefully – if somewhat chaotically, with 20-mile traffic jams and deep mud caused by a rainstorm – in a mood of self-indulgent promiscuity and hedonism. A comment made by a doctor manning a voluntary medical aid post summed up the hippy ethos and mood of the time. During the whole weekend, he had not had to treat one single violence-induced injury – not so much as a bloody nose – and he won-dered aloud what it might have been like had the five hundred thousand people there been alcohol-drinking sports fans.

It was not always quite so peaceful, however: 1969 saw the curtain start to fall on what the press were dubbing the hippy, peacenik, flower-power, free-love decade. A number of events occurred that showed the world was changing yet again and cast an ill light upon hippies. Ronald Reagan, then Governor of California, ordered the authorities to *drive criminal anarchists and latter-day Fascists off the campuses*, prompting massive student unrest which forced him to declare a state of emergency. A week before Woodstock, Charles Manson and his hippy 'Family' murdered Sharon Tate and others, The Weathermen (who took their name from a line in Bob Dylan's song 'Subterranean Homesick Blues') organized Days of Rage in Chicago, leading to three deaths and three hundred arrests and finally, on Christmas Eve, The Rolling Stones gave a free concert at the Altamont Speedway, north-east of Livermore, 20 miles due east of San Francisco, where the Hell's Angels, employed as security guards, lost control of the audience and themselves and killed an eighteen-year-old called Meredith Hunter.

The hippy era might have been coming to an end but its primary spokesperson, Allen Ginsberg, was as vociferous as ever. Manipulating the media, he stridently advocated an end to the Vietnam War and the legaliz-ation of marijuana, regarding the hippies or their philosophy as a means to transforming American society. To those in the counter-cultural world, he was an elder statesman, a voice speaking on their behalf from a position of unbiased authority. For the establishment, he was a prominent pro-drug subversive. He was not, however, alone in his subversion.

The album cover for *Sergeant Pepper's Lonely Hearts Club Band* consisted of a montage of famous people designed by the artist Peter Blake. Many of the figures represented had been radical outsiders in their time and included T. E. Lawrence of Arabia, Marlon Brando, Dylan Thomas and, with drug-using or -experimenting rebels such as Aldous Huxley and William Burroughs, were also comedian Lenny Bruce, Bob Dylan, Oscar Wilde, the Marquis de Sade and Aleister Crowley.

Crowley's inclusion was indicative of a rise of interest in his work and philosophy which the hippies had rediscovered whilst trawling drug and esoteric literature.

Although Crowley had developed most of his philosophy over half a century before, and had died in virtual obscurity in 1947, his alternative lifestyle held much that appealed to the free-living hippy. That he had experimented with a variety of drugs, had been critical of the society of his time and hounded by it, and had lived a sexually diverse existence, only served to further endear him to the newly liberated, intellectually curious hippies. His credo, *Do what thou wilt shall be the whole of the Law*, seemed apposite in that it allowed one to do as one pleased, with the proviso that no one else suffered as a result.

Not only was Crowley's free-thinking philosophy taken to heart but so too was the body of his writing on drugs, particularly the essay 'The Psychology of Hashish', which offered a depth of understanding of the spiritual and mystical potential of drugs that had escaped other modern writers such as Huxley and Leary.

In addition to Crowley, the work of Fitz Hugh Ludlow also resurfaced although there had briefly been shown interest in his work in 1937 when Dr Robert Walton of the University of Mississippi had studied *The Hasheesh Eater* as part of the federal investigation into marijuana. In his findings, published in 1938 under the title *Marihuana: America's New Drug Problem*, he considered Ludlow's book a thorough and perceptive medical assessment.

The resurrection of Ludlow occurred in the early 1960s when Michael Horowitz, a writer, publisher, bookseller and drug littérateur, who was a close friend of Timothy Leary and was to be the father of the actress Winona Ryder (for whom Leary was to stand as godfather), discovered a copy of Ludlow's book in a second-hand bookshop. Amazed at the contents, he promoted it widely. Ten years later, he founded the Fitz Hugh Ludlow Memorial Library in San Francisco, amalgamating three collectors' archives into what was then the largest private collection of drug-related literature and associated material in the world. City Lights Books republished *The Hasheesh Eater* in 1979 and it has remained in print more or less ever since.

Drug information, along with any other material that was of interest to hippies, was disseminated by the underground press which is considered to have come into formal existence in 1966 with the publication of *The San Francisco Oracle* in the USA and *The International Times* (usually just called *IT*) in Britain. That said, *The Village Voice*, based in Greenwich Village, New York City, was founded in 1955 and was really the true precursor. This alternative press provided a drug debate, from a reasoned platform, which the establishment press ignored, providing balanced comment and advice which was not necessarily in favour of drug use. Dangerous drugs were often as vigorously campaigned against as soft drugs like marijuana were supported. In addition to the underground press, more mainstream but still comparatively seditious publications appeared such as *Rolling Stone*, founded in 1967 by a twenty-year-old dropout from the University of California at Berkeley called Jann S. Wenner. At first, it was a rock music publication but it soon extended its brief to cover articles of interest to the music world and its typical reader, categorized as young, intellectually curious and rebellious. Wenner addressed the interests of the young and, in doing so, altered the face of American journalism, employing such writers as the often outspoken and sparkling Tom Wolfe and Hunter S. Thompson. Where drugs were concerned, *Rolling Stone* had its own pseudonymous contributor, Smokestack El Ropo, whose drug stories and articles were later collected into a book innocently entitled *Smokestack El Ropo's Bedside Reader*. The material ranged from the serious through to the hilarious, such as keying out the tune of the song 'Bad Moon Rising' on the buttons of a tone-activated telephone. The identity of Smokestack El Ropo was never firmly stated but many thought he was Ken Kesey.

The underground press was not just concerned with news and information. It also gave rise to a completely new form of humour: underground comics referred to as comix. These were predominantly satirical and, being free of the censorship that applied to the ordinary comic, were outspoken and frequently *risqué*. Marijuana was the driving force behind many of them, as one title more than amply illustrates – *Tooney Loons and Marijuana Melodies*. The most famous underground cartoonist was Robert Crumb. Creator of Fritz the Cat and *Zap* and *Snatch* comix, marijuana was one of his favourite topics and, in 1971, he founded *Home Grown Funnies* in which one of the main characters was Mary Jane. In his *Fabulous Furry Freak Brothers*, the comic artist Gilbert Shelton told screwball stories about a sort of marijuana Marx Brothers whose motto was, *Dope will get you through times of no money better than money will get you through times of no dope.*

At its height, it was estimated the underground press in America alone had a readership of thirty million. The publicity this afforded marijuana can only be guessed.

By and large, the underground press had two main subjects. Marijuana and drugs was one; the other was the Vietnam War. In the initial stages of American military involvement, with the sending in of ground forces in 1965, the nation was persuaded that the war was just, a valid fight against the evil of Communism. However, as the casualty figures rose so did opposition, particularly amongst the young who not only saw their friends dying but considered the war unjustified and unjust. Anti-war demonstrations and rallies were held across the nation including a march on the Capitol in Washington. Universities conducted teach-ins telling the truth about the war. Two separate incidents shocked the nation: first, an eighty-two-year-old Quaker, Alice Herz, immolated herself in Detroit, then another of her faith, Norman Morrison, a thirty-two-year-old father of three, did likewise below the Pentagon office window of the Secretary of Defence. J. Edgar Hoover, in charge of the FBI, declared the demonstrations *represented a minority for the most part composed of halfway citizens who are neither morally, mentally, nor emotionally mature.* By this, he meant the peace-loving hippies who used marijuana.

As the war progressed, reports of American military might being targeted at civilian villages made of thatched huts, stories of atrocities, carpet bombing, the use of napalm (banned by the Geneva Convention) and chemical defoliants that wiped out whole swathes of virgin forest, caused rage amongst America's young who saw the hypocrisy in their government's stated desire to find peace with honour. Smoking marijuana became a potent expression of dissent. In the theatre of war, where marijuana grew by the roadside, it had another use.

For the US troops in Vietnam, smoking marijuana was not a political statement. It was an escape from the horror of fighting and a recreational drug in place of alcohol, which is prohibited to American forces. There had been a sort of marijuana tradition amongst American regular troops, especially those serving in the Philippine Islands or the Panama Canal Zone, but the vast majority of the soldiers sent to Vietnam were draftees who may have come across marijuana back home but were certainly to discover it in the paddy fields and fox-holes of South-East Asia.

Whilst on 'R and R' in secure bases, on patrol in the jungle, riding in Huey helicopters on medical evacuation flights or into drop-off zones, flying in Chinook gun-ships on strafing missions and in the girlie bars of Saigon, US troops smoked marijuana. Many troops made their own customized pipes out of cartridge cases, bamboo, copper hydraulic piping and, in some cases, the arm or leg bones of dead Vietcong. Marijuana was also smoked through the barrel of a carbine. Drug use was so overt that little effort was made to hide it. Zippo lighters could even be purchased in the official army PX stores engraved with drug poems such as *Always ripped/Or always stoned/I made a year/I'm going home.* In many units, the officers turned a blind eye to marijuana and other drugs so long as they did not affect discipline. It was also accepted that marijuana gave the troops Dutch courage. Those serving in units with more conscientious officers could, in most PX facilities, buy joints (known as 'doobies') under the counter: real cigarettes from which the tobacco had been replaced with marijuana, reinserted into the original packet, which even had the cellophane seal reapplied to make them look untampered with; the price was two dollars for a pack. An alternative, at a higher price, was a joint called an OJ (or o-jay) in which the marijuana had been soaked in liquid opium. The military authorities made light of the situation. They had to. In 1971, it was officially accepted that marijuana and opiates were more plentiful than chewing gum and ordinary cigarettes. Thirty thousand American troops in-country were addicted to heroin. Had the military police applied military law, at least half the men serving in Vietnam would have been in a military lock-up. Adrian Cronauer, the famous US Air Force military radio presenter whose life was the basis for the Robin Williams hit movie *Good Morning Vietnam*, joked on his show, *Speaking of things controversial, is it true there's a marijuana problem here in Vietnam?* And replying to himself in a different voice, *NO, it's not a problem. Everybody HAS it.* Even the normally comparatively staid Bob Hope, on his morale-boosting tours of the troops, made marijuana jokes.

The Vietnam War further politicized marijuana, turning it from a symbol of dissent into one of freedom of expression and deliberate, calculated civil disobedience. Ginsberg considered it a massive political catalyst because, in its way, it gave a clearer vision through which the user could see and interpret the duplicity of the state and question the very basis of its laws. His hypothesis was that, if the law on marijuana was at fault, which clearly it was, then what of the other laws . . .

Yippie Jerry Rubin remarked in 1970, *Smoking pot makes you a criminal and a revolutionary. As soon as you take your first puff, you are an enemy of society.* Within the letter of the law, he was correct. This meant that, legally speaking, American society contained millions of unapprehended criminals involved in what a journalist in *Life* magazine called *the greatest mass flouting of the law since Prohibition.*

Regardless, the federal agencies continued to caution blindly against the menace of marijuana. A 1965 FBN publication declared, *It cannot be too strongly emphasized that the smoking of marijuana is a dangerous first step on the road which usually leads to enslavement by heroin.* It ended, *Never let anyone persuade you to smoke even one marijuana cigarette. It is pure poison.* To anyone who read it who had smoked marijuana, the inference was plain. The FBN did not know what it was talking about.

They were not alone in their ignorance and deliberately alarmist stance. Just as twenty years before, when Anslinger cameoed in *To the Ends of the Earth*, a film was released in 1968 to drive home the message, exploiting the situation as it was officially perceived and giving a grossly distorted and exaggerated view of it. Entitled *Mary Jane*, it starred the heart-throb pop singer Fabian as a high-school teacher who finds out his pupils are smoking marijuana, the pupils' suppliers being none other than his girlfriend, a fellow teacher, and the school football team's star player. He is then framed and arrested on a possession charge. The moral is that anyone can push dope and everyone has to be on the alert for their evil presence.

Henry Giordano may have been responsible for the FBN but, behind the political curtain in Washington, Anslinger was still a force with which to be reckoned. In 1967, he told a US Senate committee that the lobbyists seeking to liberalize the marijuana laws were really out to legalize it. If, he argued, America were to sign the 1961 UN Single Convention on Narcotic Drugs, it could use its obligations to it to quash the legalization of marijuana. Without a debate, the Senate passed the motion with a vote of eighty-four to none. That President Lyndon B. Johnson's Commission on Law Enforcement and Administration of Justice had recently criticized the drugs laws for including marijuana in with heroin and cocaine was ignored.

A year later, Giordano appeared before Congress and announced, *The traffic in marijuana has increased sharply within the last three or four years. Many areas which were formerly almost free of drug abuse now report a small but persistent traffic, centering on the 'hippie' elements and college campuses. Our reports show that more than 40 per cent of the new marijuana users reported to the Bureau in 1967 were under the age of 21 years.*

Marijuana offences rose by 94.3 per cent between 1966 and 1967, even the possession of minuscule amounts bringing sentences of ten years. Some of the arrests were deliberately politically motivated, one of the most notable being the apprehension of Lee Otis Johnson, a student leader and member of the Black Panthers militant group. He was sentenced to thirty years by a court in Houston, Texas, for giving a joint to an undercover agent in a sting operation. The federal district court dismissed the conviction on grounds of political motivation.

If marijuana had become politicized, it was no wonder the attack upon it followed a similar path. When, in 1968, J. Edgar Hoover sent a directive to FBI field officers stating, *Since the use of marijuana and other narcotics is widespread among members of the New Left, you should be alert to opportunities to have them arrested by local authorities on drug charges,* the point was made and the Cointel (counter-intelligence) programme set in motion, relying upon paid informers, illegal telephone taps, false media releases, blackmail, entrapment and false arrest. Even innocent people were being ensnared, framed and given inordinately long sentences. White, middle-class young people and anyone with even a modicum of celebrity were especially treated badly, to act as a deterrent. It did not work. In the 31

October 1969 edition of *Life* magazine, the cover story stated that at least twelve million Americans had smoked pot.

The philosophies, trends, fashions and tastes of the 1960s have lingered ever since in Western culture. Environmentalism, human-rights issues and an abiding interest in and use of cannabis remain. It might be argued that the hippy era deserves to be condemned for promoting widespread drug abuse. On the other hand, it can be said that it gave people the freedom to make their own choices about their lives, informed or ill-informed, for better or for worse.

# ASHRAMS AND THE AGENTS
# OF CHANGE

YOUNG PEOPLE SUDDENLY FOUND THEMSELVES PRESENTED WITH unprecedented liberty in the 1960s and, with Western economies mostly recovered from the depredations of the Second World War, many had money to spend. Clothes, records, cosmetics and books were all targeted at the wallets of the young who also turned to one pursuit that, unless they came from very wealthy backgrounds, had been denied their parents and their grandparents and probably every generation before them. They travelled.

A new type of tourist appeared, assisted by the increase in air travel and the use by airlines of the first mass-produced jet airliner, the Boeing 707. For some, a holiday overseas was the chance of a lifetime but, for a great many others, the opportunity to travel did not mean embarking on a vacation. They were setting off on a quest, to romantic, exotic, far-flung lands only dreamed about a generation before, searching for new truths, new ideas and new experiences. The ever-changing route they took, which often headed through or led directly to countries where cannabis was readily available, came to be known by the late 1960s as the Hippy Trail.

When the first cannabis adventurers set off is unknown but it was probably with the Beatniks in the late 1950s, their first stop Morocco and the city of Tangier. Just across the Straits of Gibraltar from Europe, it was readily accessible by ferry yet had all the allure of a strange and dangerous land.

Tangier's reputation as a mysterious and vibrantly risky city had been well earned from the seventeenth century but, by the 1920s, whilst it was still a somewhat seedy and salacious city to which men on the run might go to hide, it had become a haunt not so much for outcasts and soldiers of fortune but for intellectuals, artists and writers. Many writers visited the city for its louche atmosphere of easy, particularly homosexual, sex and drugs. William Burroughs based the city of Interzone in *The Naked Lunch* on it. Other literary visitors included Joe Orton, Allen Ginsberg, Tennessee Williams, Truman Capote, Timothy Leary and the photographer Cecil Beaton. The social whirl was ruled over by The Hon. David Herbert, the unconventional socialite second son of the Earl of Pembroke, who was a permanent expatriate resident there.

The modern perception of Tangier was more or less created by the American novelist Paul Bowles, author of *The Sheltering Sky*. He first went to Tangier in 1931 for a holiday in the company of the American composer Aaron Copland, under whom he was studying music, and stayed for much of his life. His literary work became steeped in the culture of north Africa and his knowledge of hashish frequently asserted itself in his fiction. Whilst writing *The Sheltering Sky* and working upon the chapter in which his hero died of typhoid, he tried hashish for the first time. *The Moroccans*, he later wrote, *were constantly talking about majoun, which might otherwise be described as cannabis jam. Often I had accepted a pipe of kif when it was passed to me, but since I had never inhaled the smoke, I had not received the effect and still thought of kif as a bad-tasting tobacco. Thus the idea of majoun interested me, particularly after listening to certain vivid accounts of the wonders seen under its influence. I got the address of a house in the Calle Ibn Khaldoun where you could go and knock on the door and hand in your money and a few minutes later would be given a small package. It all worked as it was supposed to; for ten pesetas I bought a big bar of it. It was the cheapest kind and therefore tasted like very old and dusty fudge from which all flavour had long since departed. However, this in no way diminished its power.*

Bowles went up a hillside above his small house looking out towards Gibraltar, lay in the sun and ate a bit. The effect was startling. After a while, he wrote, *my mind was behaving in a fashion I should never have imag-ined possible. I wanted to get off the boulders, down the mountainside, and back home as fast as I could* [in order to complete the chapter]. The next day, he recorded, *Very consciously I had always avoided writing about death because I saw it as a difficult subject to treat with anything approaching the proper style; it seemed reasonable, therefore, to hand the job over to the subconscious. It is certain that majoun provided a solution totally unlike whatever I should have found without it.* Later, in the town of Fez, he found a permanent source of *majoun* and *felt I had come upon a fantastic secret: to change worlds, I had only to spread a bit of jam on a biscuit and eat it. I began a series of experiments with the still unfamiliar substance to determine my own set of optimum conditions regarding the quantity to be ingested, the time of day for the dose, the accompanying diet, and the general physical and psychological ambiences most conducive to pleasure during the experience.* By experimentation, he realized, *Large quantities of hot tea were essential. Twilight was the best hour for taking the dose; the effect came on slowly after an hour and a half or even two hours had passed, preferably at the moment of sitting down to dinner. A clear soup followed by a small steak and salad seemed to interfere the least with the majoun's swift circulation. It was imperative to be unmitigatedly content with all the facets of existence beforehand. The most minimal preoccupation, the merest speck of cloud on the emotional horizon, had a way of italicizing itself during the alteration of consciousness and assuming gigantic proportions, thus completely ruining the inner journey. It is a delicate operation, the taking of majoun. Since its success or failure can be measured only in purely subjective terms, it is also a supremely egotistical pastime. Above all, there must be no interruptions, no surprises; everything must come about according to the timetable furnished by the substance itself.*

Bowles was not the only writer to discover *majoun.* Gertrude Stein and her partner, Alice B. Toklas, had first visited Tangier in the 1920s. Then, in the early 1950s, Toklas, an avid cook, was asked by the American publishers Harper and Row to write a cookbook. They hoped it might contain salacious stories of her life with Stein, who had died in 1946, and their hopes were realized but Toklas, short on recipes and long on anecdotes, thought she needed to pad the book out a bit. To that end, she asked friends to contribute some recipes. One of these, a poet and writer called Brion Gysin, a friend of Bowles and Burroughs and one-time Tangier resident, sent her a recipe for fudge. In his introduction, Gysin mischievously suggested it might be an ideal snack for a ladies' bridge club. The recipe contained black peppercorns, nutmeg, sticks of cinnamon and coriander which were pulverized in a mortar and mixed with chopped dates, dried figs, blanched almonds, peanuts and *canibus sativa*, as he spelt it. This was then folded into melted butter and sugar before being kneaded and rolled into walnut-sized balls. She innocently included it in the book but the American editor's sharp eyes spotted what it was and excised it. The British edition, however, retained it.

William Burroughs moved to Tangier in 1953, attracted by the hashish, *kif* and accessibility of young catamites. For a while, he moved from lodging to lodging, including a notorious homosexual brothel, but finally settled in the Villa Muniriya in the old French quarter, which Burroughs referred to as the Villa Delirium. He was by now addicted to heroin and considered cannabis little more than a light recreational pastime. In February 1957, he was joined by Kerouac who occupied a terraced room on the top floor of the villa overlooking the sea. Kerouac only stayed for three months during which time he was almost constantly under the influence of either opiates or marijuana and claimed to have been made ill by hashish adulterated with arsenic. As Kerouac departed, Ginsberg and his homosexual partner, Peter Orlovsky, arrived and took over Kerouac's room. Ginsberg was captivated by Tangier, explored the older quarters, visited Fez, smoked *kif* in the cafés and frequently partook of a powerful *majoun* Burroughs made. He wrote to Neal Cassady, *The way they do it here, everybody smokes, all the Arabs, all day, young kids and old . . . bearded grandpappys in white turbans and brown robes . . . they mix the kif and tobacco, finely ground tobacco, and also with another dash of what seems to be snuff, and they carry around a little pouchful in a small leather pouch about the size of a small change purse. The pipe is about a foot long, the bowl is a little clay cheap bowl that fits on the bamboo pipestem – you can buy the pipestem, plain for 30c, a fancy painted one costs 50c – and the clay bowls you buy anywhere, at tobacco stands or open air pushcarts . . . 2c each, they break all the time and are replace-able. So they sit down for a glass of mint tea and little music over the radio in this cheesy one-table tearoom with a big brass urn in niche in dirty concrete wall in some hole in the wall in the casbah; and light up a pipe or two or three – or else just setting down in their robes under a tree or by a fence downtown to rest – squatting – but they don't get high, they just get a buzz off this mixture, and they smoke maybe 25 to 50 pipes a day, a continual buzz – sort of like smoking straight tobacco cut with a little tea, they use it for tobacco smoking not for tea purposes. They don't dig getting a real high, just makes them sleepy or dizzy like drunk, bugs them.*

What Ginsberg was observing, and what so fascinated him as an American, had been culturally well established for several centuries. No record exists of when cannabis first reached Morocco but it probably arrived during the fourteenth-century Arab invasion. Legend says an ascetic Sufi hermit called Sidi Hidi brought the first seed from Asia (*hidi* is an ancient Indian term for cannabis as opposed to hemp) to cultivate it in the Rif mountains. Another myth has him being a twelfth-century Algerian Sufi sheikh. Bowles, however, stated he was actually a Moroccan trader-cum-peasant philosopher of the nineteenth century. Whatever the truth, cannabis has been grown in Morocco since the early 1800s, and in the Rif Mountains.

The rugged Rif mountain range runs parallel to the Mediterranean coast east-south-east of Tangier, with the mountain town of Ketama a centre of cannabis farming for at least two hundred years. Cannabis, with the coarse tobacco used in *kif*, has provided the only viable crops for the local Berber tribes, who were first legally permitted to grow it by Sultan Hassan I in about 1890.

Cannabis is grown in the valleys, on small plateaux or on the steep mountain slopes which are cut into terraces. The lower the altitude, the earlier the sowing and harvest, this ensuring cannabis-farming activity over almost seven months of the year. Female blossoms are mixed with variable proportions of tobacco, the resulting *kif* being coloured from gold-green through to brown depending upon strength. Usually, the mixture is two parts tobacco to one part cannabis. The pipe used to smoke it consists of two pieces, the *sebsis* (a wooden stem) and the *chqafa*, a small clay bowl; water pipes are also common.

Between 1912 and 1956, most of Morocco was a Spanish protectorate. Due to rebel fighting in the Rif Mountains, the Spanish made no effort to control cannabis farming partly because it was impractical and partly because non-intervention kept the Berbers from supporting the rebels, which many did in any case. After Morocco gained independence in 1956, the government of King Mohammed V permitted limited sales of *kif* but, for the most part, attempted to eradicate it. Muslim fundamentalists argued that if *kif* was to be banned, so too should be alcohol, which was legal despite Morocco being a predominantly Islamic country. The government could not afford to lose the tax revenue from alcohol so it backed down.

Morocco signed the UN Single Convention upon ratification in 1961, which obliged it to take action to suppress cannabis production. Failure to do so meant a reduction or cessation of much-needed foreign aid. The following year, the Moroccan army invaded Berber areas in the Rif Mountains. The Berbers put up a fight and drove the army out. The eradication campaign was cancelled because it was realized abolition was unattainable. *Kif* smoking was a cultural pursuit, especially amongst the lower classes, and to do away with it would be to deprive the Berbers of their economy. Fiercely independent and often belligerent, the Berbers were an ethnic group, like the opium-poppy-growing Shan State hill tribes of Burma and Thailand or the peasant coca farmers of Colombia, for whom growing narcotics was to develop into an international mercantile activity. Since 1961, also the year in which King Hassan II came to the throne, Morocco has remained a cannabis producer, although the plant can be legally grown only around Ketama; cultivation is prohibited elsewhere.

By the early 1960s, Tangier had been transformed by expatriate Beatniks and prototype hippies. Burroughs was infuriated by them: they had changed the city, in his opinion, into a suburb of Greenwich Village. He left in disgust, returning in 1963 to find the rot even further advanced. The Beats, the renegades, the soldiers of fortune were gone. What was worse, this new breed of expatriate was undermining the long-term expatriates' standing with the authorities and the local people. They had respected Moroccan customs, fitted in with the culture, to an extent 'gone native' and accepted the world in which they were foreign visitors. The newer travellers lacked this respect, behaving little better than blinkered, self-indulgent tourists.

Worse still, they did not just leave their mark upon the city of Tangier. Until the middle of the 1960s, the hashish consumed in Morocco came from the Middle East, local cannabis being used only for *kif*. The cannabis farmers were largely ignorant of how to make hashish. However, hippies who had been to Afghanistan and were returning home to Europe or the USA showed them how to collect and process the resin. Thereafter, hashish production soared, over-reaching local demand and creating a surplus that could be exported. Through the 1970s, despite government restriction, cannabis farming spread outside the Rif Mountains. The Moroccan authorities publicly stated that the hashish trade was illicit and cannabis was being grown only for manufacture into locally sold *kif*. Off and on, small-time dealers were arrested to appease international concern and it was declared the country was trying to enforce a ban, but the reality was different. Hashish exports earned huge amounts of valuable foreign currency.

The Moroccan government turned a blind eye. In fact this was, and remains, common practice in any country where local growers are well established, the local trade sanctioned, the national economy reliant largely upon foreign investment or aid and there is a thriving overseas market not too far away. As, in North America, all that separates Mexican farmer from American user is the Rio Grande river and a fairly permeable desert border, so in Morocco there are only the Straits of Gibraltar between the terraces of the Rif slopes and the coasts of Seville and Granada.

In the years up to 1957, during which time Tangier was a free-trade entrepôt port, the export cannabis business had been limited to a casual trade, with European expatriates and tourists taking a small amount back for personal or friends' use. When the hippy trail reached the city, smuggling increased manyfold. Algeciras and Gibraltar were the main points of entry of Moroccan cannabis into Europe. Cars owned by tourists coming across on the ferry were found to have cannabis stuffed into spare tyres, hidden in roof linings, stuffed into leather pouffes and native cushions, and woven into raffia ware. For those lacking the courage to risk an inquisitive customs official, there was always the air-mail parcel service: HM Customs and Excise in British postal sorting offices always investigated any parcel arriving from Morocco labelled simply 'gift.' Hundreds of packages were intercepted annually between 1962 and 1972.

From Tangier, the hippy trail headed east to Istanbul, which was one of the major hashish markets, then across Iran to Afghanistan. From Kabul, it spread out into the Indian sub-continent, to Srinagar, Kathmandu, New Delhi, Bombay and Goa. Those who went as far as India sought not only cannabis but an alternative and enlightened way of life that included it. Many immersed themselves in the Hindu religion which had used hashish in ritual for centuries. Here, in the ashrams and rural villages, they discovered the fulfilment about which Ginsberg, Leary and others had been preaching. Over the space of a year or two, Indian mysticism, music, meditation and even dress came to be central to the youth culture of the West. Men took to wearing beads and embroidered cotton kaftans, grow- ing beards and their hair long like the Indian gurus: young women also took to wearing kaftans or sarong- or sari-like dresses and grew their hair long, dying it with henna and applying heavy eye make-up. Some even took to placing a *bindi* (a red spot signifying the presence of the mystic third eye) on the centre of their foreheads. When The Beatles arrived in India in February 1968 to study transcendental meditation under the Maharishi Mahesh Yogi, following George Harrison who had gone to India in 1966 to learn to play the sitar from the world's best exponent, Ravi Shankar, the hippy seal of approval on the sub-continent was finally set.

Hippies arriving in Nepal found themselves in a land that had used cannabis for aeons not only as an aid to meditation or communication with the gods but, as it had been in the West until the early twentieth century, also as a medicine for both human and animal. Indeed, Nepalese *charas* had been regarded as the best available since the 1700s, tradition- ally smoked using an often highly decorated *narghile*, or water pipe, made out of a coconut shell. Cannabis was also given to the elderly to help them while away their retirement, but, significantly, Nepalese intake was self-regulated so that society did not suffer from an over-abundance of intoxication.

This happy *status quo* changed dramatically with the arrival of the hippies. Realizing they could readily obtain hashish, not to mention opium, and at a comparatively very low price, a resident community of Westerners began to form in Kathmandu. To cater for their narcotic needs, several dozen shops were set up: although the Nepalese government started taxing and licensing cannabis cultivation and sale in 1961, this had little effect on the business which was otherwise unregulated. The shops quickly became famous hippy meeting places. The best-known were the Central Hashish Store, The Cabin and the Eden Hashish Centre, each selling their own narcotic specialities from a menu, including Temple Balls of hand-rubbed *charas* and Chinese Crackers, which were joints with opiates laced into them.

The influx of Westerners destabilized what was, in many ways, a previously stable but fragile, semi-medieval society ruled by a divine monarch. They brought with them, by local standards, vast sums of money which sent up prices of not just cannabis but everything else and they adversely influenced the younger generation of Nepalis who, not traditionally cannabis smokers, took to over-indulging because it was seen to be Western and chic. Their corruption of the local culture went further, with their political ideas unsettling the local social *status quo*, whilst their demand for cannabis caused a loss of food production, as farmers turned to the more lucrative cannabis crop and organized cannabis-smuggling networks south into India. By 1972, Nepal had joined Morocco as one of the major hashish exporting countries.

The UN and the US government both applied pressure on Nepal to put its house in order. Consequently, on 16 July 1973, all cannabis shop, dealer and farming licences were cancelled. The economy bent to the shockwave as the government suddenly lost a $100,000 per annum tax windfall and the subsistence farmers lost their income. At the same time, heroin was outlawed. However, possession and use of cannabis was not made illegal. It was, therefore, hardly surprising that cultivation continued if on a smaller and less overt level. Six years later, to address the plight of the farmers, a part-internationally funded crop-substitution programme was started, but it failed and cannabis growing increased once more.

Afghanistan also rapidly suffered as a result of hippy intrusion, although the numbers who went there were far smaller than in India or Nepal. In Afghanistan, the most ancient hashish-using culture on earth, the hippies were to come across the most potent form of the drug available. Wherever one went, hashish was openly available in the *chai khana*, tea houses that frequently offered accommodation as well as a café-like facility. Smoking rooms were common, strewn with cushions and equipped with water pipes. When they first arrived, the hippies were welcomed into a hashish culture which had changed little over the last four centuries. Indeed, once the Afghan government realized the export potential for hashish in the late 1960s, it encouraged cannabis growing using artificial fertilizers to boost production. By 1973, huge acreages were under cannabis in the regions around Kandahar and Mazar-e-Sharif.

The high quality of Afghan hashish prompted Westerners to set about smuggling it in bulk. An American smuggling syndicate known as The Brotherhood of Eternal Love was key to this illicit trade. Followers of the teachings of Timothy Leary, they dealt in hashish, powdered resin and hashish oil, beginning in 1968 with a 50-kilogram shipment smuggled into California. Later the same year, an American named Glen Lynd purchased a Volkswagen micro-bus in West Germany, drove it overland to Afghanistan, loaded it with 60 kilos of hashish hidden in body panels, drove it on to Karachi and then shipped it to the USA. This smuggling method was much favoured by the Brotherhood. In 1971, Canadian customs officers in Vancouver seized a Brotherhood-owned vehicle containing 320 kilos of hashish; another was caught in 1972 with a staggering 600 kilos in it. During this time, a Brotherhood member, Robert Andrist, set up a small hashish-oil refinery in California, the product dubbed honey oil. So successful was the process that the Brotherhood took the principle back to Afghanistan and began manufacturing the oil there. Being exceedingly concentrated, it was easier to smuggle in smaller units yet still fetched a high price. The wholesale price in the US was ten thousand dollars a litre; the street value could be as high as two hundred and fifty thousand dollars.

The American authorities became so concerned over this wholesale smuggling and manufacturing network that they sent agents to Kabul in 1971 and, in the same year, an explosion occurred near the city which led Afghan police to a honey-oil factory operated by the Brotherhood. It is unknown if the factory experienced an accident or an agent blew it up. In California, several Brotherhood members were arrested but others soon filled their vacancy in the network and hashish continued to be smuggled.

Whilst the Brotherhood were professional smugglers, amateurs were also busy in the field but were far more readily caught. Russian customs officials routinely searched passengers and baggage flying from Afghanistan to the West when they changed aircraft at Tashkent. Many had their luggage confiscated, including the innocent: the customs officials seized this opportunity to pilfer Western goods which they could then sell on the Russian black market. Those who made it through Russian airspace had to run the gauntlet of European customs officers who studied not so much the incoming cargo as the tickets and passports of the passengers. An Afghanistan stamp or visa was sufficient to arouse immediate suspicion. In time, both semi-professionals and amateurs learnt to 'dead ticket', buying their flights in two legs so that their original point of departure was obscured.

The demand for hashish altered the agriculture of Afghanistan. Until about 1970, most cannabis farming was labour intensive and done by hand with beast of burden. With large-scale production becoming necessary, and the cash returns being substantial, the farmers started to mechanize. Most of the cannabis areas being irrigated by spring melt-water flowing from the peaks of the Hindu Kush, canals were cut. In places, tractors, ploughs and even artesian well-drilling equipment and pumps were provided by the smuggling syndicates. The Western smugglers also brought in metal sieves which were more efficient than traditional methods in the production of the resin powder.

Early in 1973, the US government paid the Afghan authorities forty-seven million dollars to destroy hashish and opium, the country's other main narcotic, within their borders. One of King Zahir Shah's last decrees before he was overthrown, posted throughout Afghanistan, outlawed cannabis and opium poppy farming with immediate effect. It was largely ignored, especially as far as the cannabis farmers were concerned. They had been doing it for centuries and they were not going to stop now. In the summer, Afghan army units fanned out across the cannabis-growing areas, burning crops and homes, intimidating, arresting and killing the farmers. Most of the 1973 crop was lost but not all of it: farms owned by government officials were conveniently ignored. The king's forty-year reign came to an end when he was deposed by his brother-in-law in the autumn. Few farmers regretted it. For two years, little cannabis was grown, the *chai khana* were forced to close and the surviving cannabis farmers relocated to remote areas. The Western smugglers left but hashish production gradually increased again with supplies being smuggled into Pakistan which, in addition to being a large producer in its own right, also became a major international distributor nation.

Some countries in which hashish was traditionally to be had were overlooked or bypassed by the hippy trail. Egypt, the Balkans, Persia, Iraq and Syria tended to be countries of transit, if they were visited at all. Civil war and Muslim fundamentalism or conservatism made them unattractive to the free-wheeling hippies. Turkey and Lebanon were exceptions.

Even then, Turkey was a risky place. There was much anti-Western feeling there and possession of drugs was a useful reason to arrest, imprison or deport. The film *Midnight Express*, made in 1978 and starring John Hurt, Randy Quaid and Brad Davis, shows how antagonistic the Turkish authorities could be. It was based upon the true story of Billy Hayes, an American apprehended smuggling drugs out of the country and thrown into a fetid Turkish jail for twenty years.

Hayes was one of the amateur hashish runners who chanced their arm on their way from Pakistan, Afghanistan or Lebanon. Some brought their contraband with them from their country of departure whilst others had picked it up in south-east Turkey where high-quality hashish was being made around Gaziantep. It was not plentiful and, from 1975 onwards, became even rarer after Turkey banned all cannabis cultivation and the farmers, aware of the brutality of the police, usually decided not to risk planting it.

Lebanon was the most prolific hashish supplier in the region during the 1960s to 1980s, despite hashish being officially prohibited. It was distinctively contained in white cotton or linen bags stamped with simplistic brand marks such as a lion, a crescent moon and star or the cedars of Lebanon, the best hashish being known in the West as Lebanese Gold. As early as 1950, the Lebanon and Syria were jointly producing 300 tons of hashish annually, this for a population in which, in 1976, less than 1 per cent were consumers. As was common in all Muslim societies, only men smoked it, using water pipes, and in secret. The main growing region was the Bekaa Valley where Danadji tribesmen made up the farming community. They were – and remain today – staunchly independent Shiite Muslims whom the Lebanese Suni and Christian ethnic majorities marginalized to such an extent they were almost autonomous. Attempts were made in the mid-1960s to get the Danadji to grow substitute crops such as sunflowers but the farmers were unenthusiastic. Even with subsidized prices, they preferred cannabis which took less effort and cost to raise. Cultivation continued, sometimes in the centre of fields of tall sunflowers which disguised the true crop from all but aerial observers.

Hashish trading, both domestically and, more significantly, by export, earned very substantial sums of money for various religious and political factions in what was a socially and ethnically divided land. When, in 1975, civil war broke out between the Muslim and Christian blocs, the various combatant groups had large war chests with which to fight. After the war took hold and the economy collapsed, the only real currency earner was hashish. Cannabis cultivation became virtually the only item of gross domestic product and financed the armament trade and fighting.

Export was essential and a good deal of it travelled to Egypt. Much was smuggled out to the West, particularly to Europe. The Shiite cannabis farmers, who were supposedly staunchly pro-Islam, were also selling their product to Israel, the sworn enemy of their fellow Shiites, the Hizbullah, the militant Arab group who were fighting for a Palestinian Arab homeland. An article published in *The Times* in 1996 outlined how the Israeli secret service, Mossad, hatched a plan after the 1967 Six Day War with Egypt, to buy hashish in Lebanon and distribute it in Egypt. Codenamed Operation Lahav (Operation Blade), the hashish was sold to Egyptian dealers near military bases who dealt with conscript soldiers. The aim was to weaken the Egyptian army. The operation continued right through the Lebanese civil war and well after it ended in 1979, Israel therefore being responsible for funding the combatants before the war began, prolonging and indirectly part financing the fighting and, at the same time, being actively involved in the international narcotics trade in violation of the UN Single Convention. However, as the Israeli government had already chosen to ignore innumerable UN resolutions and censure concerning the rights of Palestinian Arabs, and dismissed charges of terrorist atrocities against them, to disregard the Single Convention seemed hardly a matter for serious consideration.

Hashish was often carried by migrant Turkish workers in Europe, particularly in Germany, who purchased it from Lebanese merchants in Syria. They did not smuggle the hashish just for profit but also for their own recreational use. Freelance smugglers like them were plentiful. Students, tourists and part-timers ran hashish by air out of Beirut or by road through Turkey and Greece. In 1978, a massive 22-ton consignment of Lebanese hashish was found on board a Liberian registered cargo ship, in New York. This, however, was nothing compared to the discovery that would be made by the crew of the US Coast Guard Cutter *Rush* who were deployed on the US Navy destroyer, USS *Ingersoll*. On 1 July 1991, the destroyer stopped a St Vincent-registered ship, *Lucky Star*, 600 miles west of Midway Island in the Pacific. On board was found a cargo of 70 tons of hashish, the largest single amount ever taken by the US Coast Guard.

In 1970, Afghanistan accounted for approximately 30 per cent of the world's hashish production, Lebanon 25 per cent and Pakistan 20 per cent. Ten years later, the figures revealed Lebanon providing 35 per cent followed by Pakistan (25 per cent) and Morocco (20 per cent).

Between them, the war-mongering governments and peace-loving hippies created a well-organized, sustained, international cannabis trade. They caused what had been a cultural phenomenon in Muslim and eastern countries to spread across the planet, altering the economies of those countries and even changing agricultural and production practices. Whilst they liked to see themselves as benign, the hippies were, in effect, *agents provocateurs* for the global capitalism they so abhorred.

# THE TIMES THEY WERE ADJUSTING

MARIJUANA WAS, BY 1975, THE MAIN RECREATIONAL NARCOTIC USED IN America and many other Western countries. The users were no longer just hippies, dropouts, draft dodgers and the disaffected young but a wide spectrum of people, from matured hippies now in establishment jobs and positions to blue-collar workers who had been enlisted men (known as grunts) serving in the US Army in Vietnam. No longer just a tool of enlightenment-seekers, it became a social relaxant like alcohol, much as it had been in the years when poor Mexicans and blacks took it. In other words, marijuana had moved up-market.

The Vietnam War had done much to promote marijuana. As well as using it widely in combat and afterwards, thousands of grunts sent supplies back home to friends through the US Army mail system. Others being sent home wounded or after the completion of the tour of duty took supplies with them. A small number of more enterprising individuals took top-quality Laotian or Cambodian seeds in order to set themselves up with a lucrative cash crop back on the farm. Military personnel also commercially smuggled drugs back to the US, utilizing the mail service and supply and equipment shipments. Although they concentrated mostly on the more lucrative heroin some cannabis was also run. One small group, connected to organized crime in California, shipped marijuana back home in body bags, normally used for the corpses of those killed in action.

Despite this and the overwhelmingly obvious prevalence of marijuana use in the USA, the federal government seemed blind to the reality of the situation. When Richard Nixon became President in 1969, he made drug prohibition one of his main priorities, not just in domestic but also foreign policy formulation. On 14 July, eager to bolster his standing as a tough crime-fighter, he launched what he called a national attack on drug abuse. He was convinced drugs and crime went hand in hand. In the case of heroin, which was expensive and highly addictive, and cocaine, this was substantially true but with marijuana it was not, because marijuana was cheap, very readily available (either from peddlers or self-grown) and non-addictive. A user might want some marijuana but he did not, as with heroin, have an insatiable physiological need for it.

Twenty-three months later, Nixon announced to the US Congress a war on drugs, declared the situation was tantamount to a national emergency and instituted the Special Action Office for Drug Abuse Prevention and the Office for Drug Abuse Law Enforcement (ODALE). These were given the right to freeze suspected drug dealers' assets and seize property and bank accounts. US embassies abroad were told to target drug producers and millions of dollars were put aside for crop-substitution programmes, replacing opium poppies, coca bushes and marijuana with commercial fruit or vegetable crops.

Administratively, the war on drugs also restructured the American law-enforcement system.

By 1968, the FBN was in turmoil. It had become inefficient and, worse, corrupt. Additionally, it was also at permanent loggerheads with the Bureau of Drug Abuse Control (BDAC), the enforcement arm of the Food and Drug Administration (FDA). In 1968, these two bureaux were combined into the Bureau of Narcotics and Dangerous Drugs (BNDD) in the US Justice Department. In 1973, Nixon amalgamated the BNDD, ODALE and all other drug-associated offices, such as the Office of National Narcotics Intelligence (ONNI), into one unit. It was called the Drug Enforcement Agency (DEA) which, by the mid-1970s, had about ten thousand agents operating world-wide.

The DEA was given extraordinary powers, gathering intelligence on anyone it chose, organizing wire taps and postal (later e-mail) inter-ceptions, searching without warrant, sequestering and confiscating property, freezing assets, arresting on suspicion and taking any other steps it deemed necessary to apprehend suspects and attack the drug trade. Publicity was specifically aimed at the young, a drive that had begun several years before when the Federal Communications Commission

(FCC) persuaded national radio stations to increase *drug education programming and to curb pro-drug music and jargon of disc jockeys*. Records and song lyrics had to be screened before they were broadcast, the implication being that non-compliance might lead to the cancellation of operating licences. Some radio stations banned selected songs. Bob Dylan was a widely targeted musician: one radio station, it is rumoured, banned all Bob Dylan's songs because no one could fully interpret the intellectual or poetic content of the lyrics. The MGM record label even went so far as to void the contract of eighteen groups they considered musically involved in drugs.

The most farcical action, however, occurred in late 1971 when Nixon accepted Elvis Presley's suggestion that he be made a BNDD Federal Agent-at-Large. Nixon, eager to enrol any high-profile figure who might influence the young, seems not to have understood that the young had long since created new idols, and that Presley was past his musical (and physical) prime; more pertinently, he did not know the singer was severely addicted to barbiturates and many other prescription drugs.

One of Nixon's main problems was the amount of marijuana coming in from Mexico. In late 1969, under Operation Intercept, the US–Mexico border was theoretically sealed with all vehicles and pedestrians entering the USA being searched. The idea was to make marijuana so scarce that the street price was forced up to make the drug financially inaccessible. At the same time, it was hoped that by restricting cross-border traffic and therefore trade, the Mexican government would be obliged to heed US demands that they move against cannabis cultivation.

Cannabis grown in the provinces of Chihuahua, Coahuila, Durango and Zacatecas accounted for a substantial proportion of cross-border trade. Much of the marijuana produced went through border towns such as Tijuana, Mexicali, Nogales, Ciudad Juarez, Ojinaga, Del Rio, Piedras Negras, Nuevo Laredo and Matemoros. The Mexican government saw drug use as an American national problem, not theirs, and they were loath to deprive their peasant farmers of their minimal income. Furthermore, the authorities did not want to antagonize many of their police, border and federal law-enforcement officers who were corrupt and aided the trade.

Jerry Kamstra, himself a marijuana smuggler, defined the history of the cross-border operator. First, there was the Texas Syndicate, organized by a group of interrelated families on both sides of the border, who bribed officials and smuggled bulk consignments of marijuana and, not infrequently, heroin. Second, there were the Beatniks who brought across small amounts, up to 20 kilos, who were hardly ever apprehended. They were not smuggling so much for profit as to provide for their bohemian friends. In time, some of these developed into entrepreneurial smugglers. Kamstra included himself in this category. He started trading in luxury consumer goods, cars and guns but moved into marijuana after striking a deal with two of Mexico's most successful dealers, Roberto and Juan Hernandez. After four years, he was arrested at the border crossing of San Luis Rio Colorado in Arizona on 30 August 1966 in possession of 200 kilos of marijuana which he had purchased for five thousand dollars and intended to sell for forty thousand dollars. His problem, one common to all marijuana smugglers, was that in order to make a good profit one had to deal in large amounts which were bulky. Even tightly compressed, 200 kilos filled the trunk of a large saloon car. His cargo, however, was hidden in the door panels. He was given a two-year suspended sentence and placed on probation, later becoming a journalist for *Life* magazine and writing about marijuana.

Third were the hippy smugglers who began by carrying supplies for themselves and their immediate friends but later became highly organized and well financed, sometimes by rock bands and wealthy liberals. Finally, there were the part-timers, students, surfers or tourists who went for weekend breaks to Mexico and returned with a few kilos each. They originated predominantly in California and, in Kamstra's opinion, accounted for more marijuana reaching the USA during the 1960s than by any other method. Few were caught simply because of the numbers involved: in 1969, it was estimated 80-110,000 private vehicles crossed the border each way every weekend, through border control gates that were up to eighteen lanes wide.

Vehicular transportation was the most common smuggling method. Smugglers just loaded marijuana blocks into their car and hoped for the best. Others hid it in door panels, roof linings, spare tyres and under seats. Many regularly used vehicles that were especially adapted by Mexican 'upholsterers' who could reconstruct a petrol tank, chassis unit or seat frame. Made to appear like ordinary family saloons, they were developed with hermetically sealed compartments to foil customs drug-sniffing dogs and which could only be opened with specialist tools. Although many drivers were employed and trained to make the cross-border run, some were tricked into it. An advertisement might appear in the press for a driver to return a car to the USA because its owner had fallen ill, was too elderly to drive it or had had to leave it in Mexico because it had broken down. Anyone applying for the job became an unwitting drug runner.

Some smugglers were in league with garages and would use genuinely broken-down cars, the owner driving it back with a hidden cargo only to have the car stolen back in the USA so the contents might be recovered. One Tijuana dealer in 1969–70 was running three and a half tons a week in three cars a day. If the drivers were pulled over for a customs inspection, they simply abandoned the vehicle and ran back over the border. Their employer accepted this, as his mark-up on selling prices was so significant he could afford to lose the occasional load.

Further east, in New Mexico and, more especially, Texas, the marijuana was hidden in commercial deliveries of frozen fish, vegetables and fruit. One gang, operating between Ciudad Juarez and neighbouring El Paso, smuggled tons of marijuana a week wrapped in plastic and hidden under huge loads of slaughterhouse offal being sent across the border for rendering.

Where the border ran across wild country, such as in southern New Mexico and west Texas, pre-arranged drops were made at remote locations in the desert wherever there was vehicular access. Any bush landing strip, isolated length of road or even flat area of ground allowed for undetected smuggling by light aircraft that flew at zero feet below radar and air-traffic-control coverage.

In southern California and, to a lesser extent, Texas, marijuana was smuggled in by sea. Part-time, weekend smugglers not only went south by vehicle. Thousands of pleasure craft headed for Mexico every week-end or holiday, often making for the Mexican port of Ensenada, only 75 miles from San Diego. Policing this maritime traffic was well nigh impossible, as was catching the large-scale smugglers who either used dummy leisure craft (as they did cars) or delivered supplies at rendezvous points in international waters, passing them to US-registered speedboats.

Once safely over the border, the organized smuggler was not necessarily safe. He could be followed across the US by law-enforcement agents, sometimes for days. To prevent his being caught or divulging information, he either had another smuggler 'watching his tail' for him or he was obliged to telephone back to his employer every few hours to receive the next part of his itinerary. It was not unknown for professional smugglers to be well armed and ready to resist arrest or capture.

Regardless of law-enforcement measures, seizures of marijuana soared from 5 tons in 1965–66 to 35 tons in 1967–68. In 1965, a 50-pound confiscation was hailed as a success; three years later, according to Kamstra, it was considered the mark of a part-timer.

It is also worth realizing that most of the smuggling methods described continue to the present day, running not just marijuana but also heroin, cocaine, other illicit drugs, illegal immigrants from all over the world and more recently, it is thought, possibly terrorists.

The sealing of the border by Operation Intercept annoyed the Mexican authorities who formally complained to the US government. They held firm and the Mexicans were forced to agree to comply with American demands. Nevertheless, after less than a month, the operation was cancelled. In that time, hardly any marijuana had been seized despite over five million border crossings. The only people affected by the operation were the small-time or part-time smugglers. The professionals, knowing of the likely disruption to legitimate cross-border trade and the political ramifications this would cause, had simply stopped operating for a few weeks.

Operation Intercept gave rise to a new type of marijuana runner which Kamstra dubbed the granddaddy smuggler. This was typically an elderly man or couple, perhaps influenced by a hippy or part-time smuggling grandchild, who smuggled marijuana for fun or profit. Some were liberally minded senior citizens or redoubtable old rebels who recalled the days of Prohibition when they had smuggled booze.

In time, Operation Intercept was superseded by Operation Co-operation. The Mexicans agreed to target drug trafficking within their borders and the Americans would provide the means to do this in the form of financing, manpower, intelligence gathering and equipment including weapons. They would also assist with crop eradication by aerial spraying, with electronic sensors being installed along the entire length of the US–Mexico border.

In theory, it seemed a sound move. In practice, it played into the marijuana smugglers' hands. The small-time runners were driven out of business whilst the big players consolidated their efforts and grew more sophisticated than ever, setting up syndicated operations that included not only dealers but also farmers.

Although the US government was making strident efforts to combat drug smuggling, it was by 1970 having to admit that domestic drug control was not only a failure but also causing anger in the middle classes. Thousands of otherwise respectable citizens, most of them under the age of twenty-five, were being given prison sentences and criminal records for what many con-sidered either a petty offence or nothing more than a moment of youthful foolishness. Under such pressure, legislators started to re-assess the criminality of marijuana taking and the penalties attached to it.

From 1969, for nearly two years, a series of Congressional committees addressed the situation which culminated in the passing of the 1970 Comprehensive Drug Abuse Prevention and Control Act which removed mandatory minimum sentences and reduced possession of marijuana to the level of a misdemeanour. All drugs were organized into five schedules according to their potential for abuse and accepted medical value. In short, it was a standardization of levels of perceived danger. Marijuana, although still erroneously considered to be highly addictive, was deemed less dangerous than heroin, use of which was sharply escalating both in the US and amongst GIs serving in Vietnam. In the light of this, marijuana was seen as an occasional recreational drug as against a full-time addiction as was caused by heroin.

Part of the provision of the Act was the founding of the National Commission on Marijuana and Drug Abuse, later known as the Shafer Commission after its chairman, former Governor of Pennsylvania Raymond Shafer. The commission studied claims as to the dangers of marijuana going back fifty years, funding original research to assess the findings. It also reckoned twenty-five million Americans had used marijuana, including 40 per cent of all Americans aged between eighteen and twenty-five. In its final report, released in 1973, it recommended that marijuana possession for personal use should be decriminalized, as should the selling or gifting of small amounts. No conclusive evidence was found that marijuana was a cause of crime, insanity, sexual aberration, promiscuity or led to other drug use. It also stated, *a careful search of literature and testimony by health officials has not revealed a single human fatality in the US proven to have resulted solely from the use of marijuana . . .* and that it *. . . is of the unanimous opinion that marihuana use is not such a grave problem that individuals who smoke marihuana, or possess it for that purpose, should be subject to criminal procedures.*

National legal, medical, religious and public health professional bodies agreed. President Nixon did not. He had personally hand-picked nine of the thirteen commissioners in order to bias the findings. Furious, he ignored the report, accusing it of liberalist tendencies, and increased anti-drug policing budgets.

At the same time, the Canadian government appointed a Commission of Inquiry into Non-Medical Use of Drugs. It was known as the Le Dain Commission, the chairman being Gerald Le Dain, the dean of the Osgoode Hall Law School at Toronto's York University. It was felt a re-assessment of the situation was required. There were no reliable statistics or accounts of cannabis use in Canada and, since it had been included with dangerous opiates in the 1961 Narcotic Control Act, it carried the same severe sentencing criteria.

Prior to 1960, Canada did not have an extensive marijuana-using population, only pockets of marijuana smoking existing in the bohemian circles of Vancouver and Toronto. By the late 1960s, this had changed, due to the exodus northwards of hippies and young Americans avoiding the Vietnam draft, and the not uncommon imitation of American fashions and tastes by young Canadians who, living in a nation with no binding cultural identity, looked south for one. Marijuana use consequently expanded very rapidly indeed across the university campuses of Canada, for much the same reasons as it had in the US.

The Le Dain Commission published two reports, *Cannabis* in 1972 and its final report the following year. Like the Shafer Commission, it argued that marijuana possession should not be a criminal offence but, somewhat illogically, that distribution should remain a criminal act as a means of discouraging use. The Canadian government compromised, affording judges the discretion of dismissal or probation for those charged with possession with an additional option of a minimal fine which was, in practice, usually applied. Over time, the Royal Canadian Mounted Police spent more of their resources attacking serious organized heroin and cocaine rings, with the resultant drop in marijuana arrests.

Throughout the 1970s, although the hippy era was over, marijuana smoking in the US continued at about the level estimated by the Shafer Commission. Whilst still used predominantly by those under the age of thirty, marijuana was no longer regarded just as a symbol of liberty, protest or rebellion but as a commonplace recreational drug. Nevertheless, the subject of marijuana use remained a high-profile thorn in the side of the authorities. It was also bringing up a new breed of marijuana activist.

John Sinclair was born in Flint, Michigan in 1941. At the age of twenty-two, he enrolled in the graduate school at Wayne State University, the subject of his thesis being Burroughs' novel *The Naked Lunch*, but he dropped out the next year and was arrested for the sale and possession of marijuana. He then became deeply involved with an artists' workshop, the underground press and producing and promoting jazz and rock bands.

In 1965, he was again arrested for sale and possession of marijuana and sentenced to six months in the Detroit House of Correction. Two months after his release, he was arrested a third time in a mass police raid on a dance hall and shortly afterwards started to manage rock bands and establish a commune in Ann Arbor, Michigan. He also founded the White Panther Party. In July 1969, he was sentenced to ten years' imprisonment for possession of two marijuana joints and a movement was started to quash this conviction. At a protest rally and free rock concert held in the Crisler Arena at Ann Arbor in December 1971, John Lennon and Yoko Ono took the stage alongside Allen Ginsberg and Jerry Rubin to sing their recent song, 'John Sinclair', which was certainly not great song-writing but achieved world-wide publicity and, within a week, Sinclair's conviction was overturned and he was released.

Sinclair went on to become a major marijuana reformist, ran his own pro-marijuana radio show called *Toke Time* on the Ann Arbor WNRZ-FM station, managed a nightclub, organized music events, became a journalist and, in time, editor-in-chief of the *Detroit Sun*, and was active in community arts projects and prisoners' rights organizations. Highly respected, he came to be regarded as a pillar of the arts community.

As for John Lennon, his part in the rally only served to bolster the case for FBI surveillance which had been going on for some time. An under-cover agent attending the rally actually quoted in his report every line of 'John Sinclair' verbatim, including – in its entirety – the facile chorus, which repeated the word 'gotta' fifteen times.

The US government was concerned about Lennon's presence in the country. His left-wing political views were regarded as dubious and he was considered a risk to the nation. At every turn, he was harassed and perpetually threatened with deportation, potential leverage being a previous arrest in Britain for marijuana possession. Nixon specifically instructed J. Edgar Hoover to try to ensnare Lennon with a drugs charge which would have given grounds for immediate deportation. Hoover duly ordered the New York FBI office, *Careful attention should be given to reports that subject is heavy narcotics user and any information developed in this regard should be furnished to narcotics authorities and immediately furnished to bureau in form suitable for dissemination.*

Three years after Sinclair was set free, residents of Ann Arbor voted to change their city's charter. The result was the most liberal marijuana law in America – possession earned a fixed penalty five-dollar fine. Annually, on 1 April, the city has a Hash Bash to protest against federal marijuana laws.

Whilst marijuana itself remained illegal, businesses peripheral to it boomed in the 1970s. Stores known as head shops, selling everything the smoker needed, did a roaring trade: of course, they did not actually sell cannabis itself. A glossy drug users' monthly magazine was published entitled *High Times*.

The founder was an Arizonan former marijuana smuggler who called himself Thomas King Forcade to protect his family from association with him. Politically active as a Yippie, he started smuggling small amounts by car and ended up flying substantial loads over the border with Mexico in a light aircraft which he often piloted himself. On one flight, his navigation at fault, he accidentally landed on another marijuana runner's remote airstrip and had to persuade those on the ground he was one of them, not an undercover narcotics agent.

At its most successful, *High Times* had a monthly print run of four hundred thousand copies with an estimated 9.4 people reading each copy. One reporter, A. Craig Copetas, proudly declared he was the only full-time drug journalist in America. Despite his magazine's inordinate success, Forcade was a tragic figure. Hounded by the DEA, harassed by the FBI, paranoid from a cocaine habit and dependent upon medically prescribed valium, depressed by the politics in his editorial office and the death of a close friend in a plane crash in Florida, he shot himself in the head in October 1978.

The peripheral marijuana trade of magazines and head shops became very big business with an estimated turnover reaching one billion dollars per annum. It developed its own fashions and its own merchandizing techniques. The range of items available was astounding: hand-carved wooden marijuana/tobacco mixing bowls, pocket scales like those used by gemmologists, camouflaged marijuana containers (which looked like beer, cat food or Heinz Baked Beans tins, paperback books, assorted ornaments and even a telephone – priced at one hundred dollars in 1976), silver- and gold-plated roach tweezers and clips, hydroponic growing kits and sun lamps, marijuana leaves coated in gold and made into pendants, earrings and cufflinks, hand-sculpted stone chillums, brass and glass bongs, coloured and flavoured cigarette papers, printed T-shirts, recipe books and marijuana cooking utensils, incense sticks and stick holders, playing cards and calendars and, perhaps most bizarrely of all, electronic detectors for FBI and DEA listening devices. One entrepreneurial smoker, realizing that ordinary cigarette papers were too small for a joint, invented E-Z Wider rolling papers in 1972: the name was a pun on the 1969 cult film *Easy Rider*. Six years later, the company's annual turnover was seven million dollars and the papers could be bought not only in head shops but over the counters of convenience stores and even K-Mart supermarkets. A later development created by a competitor incorporated a thin steel strip in the rolling paper, like the counterfeit-proof strip in a bank note. As the joint was smoked, the wire was exposed and warped so that, when the joint was burnt down to a roach, it had a built-in roach holder. Just as housewives had Tupperware or lingerie home parties, marijuana users had tokerware parties, the organization run by a New York-based businessman called Ralph Garcia.

It was all a far cry from hippies rolling a loose joint on a table top or jazz musicians dragging on muggles by a Harlem club stage door.

In 1971, a new marijuana lobbying group was founded in Washington by a lawyer named Keith Stroup. Called the National Organization for the Reform of Marijuana Laws, it is more commonly known by the acronym NORML.

There had been marijuana lobbying groups in the past such as LeMar, but whereas they had sought to legalize marijuana use, NORML had a different aim. It did not promote marijuana use but attacked the legislation governing it. Stroup believed there were more effective ways to curb usage than by criminalizing it.

To finance NORML, Stroup had already approached a number of liberal foundations but they were reluctant to be involved. Finally, he called upon Hugh Hefner, the founder of *Playboy* magazine, who regarded himself as a new moralist and hedonist. Seeing the marijuana issue as fitting his moralist brief, he gave Stroup five thousand dollars seed capital. A year later, he donated one hundred thousand dollars to NORML's cause and the organization began in earnest.

When the federal government began to reduce the penalties for marijuana possession, individual state legislature nationwide started to follow their lead. NORML played a major part in this shift of emphasis. By 1980, eleven states had removed all criminal penalties for possession. Alaska went so far as to declare that marijuana possession by adults in their own home was constitutionally protected under the laws of privacy. This remained in force until 1990 when the administration of President George Bush threatened to withhold major federal funding if the state did not reverse the decision. With this federal gun to its head, it did.

Harry J. Anslinger died on 14 November 1975, in Altoona, Pennsylvania. He was eighty-three, blind and reliant upon morphine as a painkiller. He must have been disillusioned. Everything for which he had striven seemed to have come apart and he could not understand how Middle America had become so besotted with the idea of marijuana and, to a lesser degree, LSD.

One of those demanding the reassessment of Anslinger's and his successors' policies was President Gerald Ford who did not share the views on drug abuse held by his predecessor, Richard Nixon. Ford preferred that federal policy should admit the reality of drug abuse and ordered yet another commission to look at the issue. In 1975, it reiterated the previous findings that marijuana was not a threat to society, the elimination of drug abuse was unlikely and government actions could contain the problem and limit any adverse effects. It also suggested that federal funding should target the big international drug cartels not small domestic growers.

Two years after coming into office, Gerald Ford was faced with a new drug problem. In the Sierra Madre mountains of Mexico, the marijuana farmers were planting opium poppies alongside cannabis. The Mexican government was worried.

The Sierra Madre is an inaccessible region over twenty thousand square miles in extent. Always lawless and seldom coming under central government control, it provided almost all America's marijuana, the trade worth two billion dollars a year. The Mexican government had long promised land reforms in the region, but they were never delivered and the peasant farmers were restless. It was wondered in Mexico City if the marijuana trade was not likely to finance a revolution. Worse, if the farmers were now growing opium, which could be processed into heroin, their incomes would soar, exacerbating the problem and the risk of rebellion.

It was decided to wipe out the marijuana and poppy farms but, to do this, the Mexican government needed American funding and technology. The DEA was only too pleased to oblige and a multi-million-dollar pro-gramme was rushed through to aerially spray the farms with paraquat, a powerful non-specific herbicide which was rain-resistant, quickly absorbed by leaves, rapidly biodegraded in sunlight but was dangerous to humans. Contact with the skin caused blistering even in very dilute solution whist higher dosages could lead to potentially fatal respiratory and kidney failure. It could adversely affect livestock and wildlife. Being non-specific, it also killed every plant it touched within hours.

Regardless of this, the programme went ahead. NORML filed a suit against the US government to halt it. The marijuana farmers soon found a way to avoid the loss of their crop. As soon as a field was sprayed, they harvested it, shipped it over the border and sold it.

The story was broken by Copetas writing in *High Times* and posed a serious quandary. Ingested paraquat was lethal. Suicides used it quite frequently. The question was, what happened if it was smoked? Government laboratories tested marijuana and discovered 13 per cent was contaminated and that, if smoked, permanent lung damage ensued. The American government – now under the administration of President

Jimmy Carter – promptly ceased funding the purchasing of paraquat for aerial spraying but the Mexicans, still worried about a possible revolution, obtained it elsewhere and continued using it in the eradication programme.

The Mexicans achieved their objective: Mexican marijuana sales in the US dropped sharply. Marijuana use did not. In the late 1970s, the supply chain merely shifted to Colombia.

Marijuana had been cultivated in Colombia for decades but on a small scale. In the mid-1950s, however, it increased to supply a rapidly growing local market. The government legislated against it but policing was ineffectual either because of the remoteness of the countryside or because of the corrupt nature of the poorly paid police officers. By 1965, large marijuana crops were being harvested and, within five years, there was a thriving export trade which the government ignored because it earned the substantial amounts of foreign currency required to maintain the national economy. The farmers were pleased. Coffee, the other main agricultural staple, at best earned fifteen pesos a kilo at the time. Marijuana fetched up to twenty times that sum and required less effort to grow. By 1980, Colombia was producing more marijuana than any other country, its cultivation employing over seventy-five thousand people and bringing in more foreign exchange than coffee or the nation's other cash crop, cotton.

Most Colombian marijuana reached the US by sea on cargo vessels which could carry a hundred tons or more at a time. They dropped anchor in international waters off Florida to unload their cargo in small consignments onto leisure craft which then took it in to any of the hundreds of beaches, keys, harbours and marinas that lined the coast. Although organized-crime bosses preferred to deal in heroin and cocaine because they were easier to smuggle and more profitable, some, like the Florida mafioso Santo Trafficante Jr, who operated a large and sophisticated cocaine ring, also imported marijuana. Amongst those smuggling marijuana, one of the best known and most successful was Allen Long. It is reckoned he brought into the US nearly one million pounds (weight) of Colombian marijuana in addition to supplies from Mexico, Thailand and Jamaica, concentrating on the finest quality such as Santa Marta Gold, flying it in on his own decrepit ex-military Dakota DC3. He was finally apprehended and sentenced to five years' imprisonment in 1991.

The election of Jimmy Carter to the White House in 1977 seemed to suggest there would be a move towards legalizing cannabis in the USA. In a speech to the US Congress on 2 August, in his first year in office,

Carter was quite forthright: *Penalties against possession of a drug should not be more damaging to an individual than the use of the drug itself . . . Nowhere is this more clear than in the laws against possession of marijuana in private for personal use.* He wanted to remove all federal penalties for possession of less than an ounce of marijuana.

In charge of Carter's drug policy was a British-born psychiatrist, Peter G. Bourne. He was appointed the President's Special Assistant for Health Issues, with the specific responsibility of reorganizing federal policy. All started well, then scandal struck. In 1978 Bourne, who was a qualified physician, wrote an illegal prescription for one of his assistants for Quaaludes. The trade name for methaqualone, this was a physically addictive, synthetic hypnotic sedative similar in effect to barbiturates and used to treat anxiety, but also to be had on the street as an illegal drug known as ludes, soaps or quacks. Bourne was accused of taking drugs himself and forced to resign. The anti-marijuana lobby seized on this set-back and Carter's administration back-tracked.

In the aftermath of the Bourne fiasco, there was a swing against marijuana although it must be said this had been gathering momentum before the incident.

This backlash against liberal attitudes towards marijuana had started in 1976 in Atlanta, Georgia, Jimmy Carter's home state of which he was then governor. Ron and Marsha Manatt had gone out into their yard after their daughter's thirteenth birthday party and found roaches and rolling papers on the ground. Disgusted, they set in motion an anti-marijuana crusade by writing to Robert DuPont, head of the National Institute on Drug Abuse (NIDA). Sympathetic to the Manatts' plight, he asked Marsha Manatt to write a guide for parents which was duly published by NIDA under the title *Parents, Peers, and Pot*. Other parents in the Atlanta conurbation grouped together and forced the state legislature to close down all the head shops.

Elsewhere in America, other parents started to voice protests and form action groups, eventually coalescing into the national Families in Action, the Parents' Resource Institute for Drug Education and the National Federation of Parents for Drug-Free Youth. They were spurred on by a government survey of high-school students which discovered that, in 1979, 10 per cent of them smoked marijuana daily and some went on to try stronger substances. A new phrase entered the anti-marijuana vocabulary: amotivational syndrome, a scientific-sounding phrase for feeling alienated and being lethargic as a result of using marijuana.

So powerful did the parent lobby become that its voice was to be heard in Washington, DC. Even DuPont, who had tended towards being pro-marijuana and had instructed NIDA to conduct research into adverse claims against the drug, was swayed and turned his coat, becoming an anti-marijuana supporter.

What helped change DuPont's mind was the fact that marijuana was being used by younger and younger people. Testifying before a Congressional Select Committee on Narcotics in 1979, Sue Rusche, one of the most active parental activists, drew attention to chillums shaped like *Star Wars* laser guns and spoke of comics that *taught the fine points of smoking dope and snorting cocaine. We are witnessing*, she warned, *the emergence of an industry that glamorizes and promotes illicit drugs* [to] *our twelve- to seventeen-year-old children*. In response, the Justice Department passed a template for anti-drug paraphernalia laws that did away with head shops, although some firms continued to operate legally by mail order out of the few states that did not ratify the law.

To add fuel to the abolitionist fire, publications and articles started to appear stressing the social, psychological and physiological dangers of marijuana use, always emphasizing the negative issues and conveniently ignoring any research that pointed to the contrary. Anslinger would have been pleased.

In November 1980 Ronald Reagan was elected to succeed Jimmy Carter, becoming the fortieth President of the USA. From the start, he took a tough line on illegal drug use. In 1982, he instigated the White House Drug Abuse Policy Office and thereafter reintroduced mandatory minimum sentences for drug offences. First-time marijuana offenders could receive a sentence ranging from probation to life imprisonment and the sequestration of their entire property. It also became an offence to own a roach holder or even a packet of rolling papers. The severity of penalties varied from state to state but, nationwide, the prison population exploded. In 1970, 16 per cent of those held in federal penitentiaries were in for drug-related crimes. By 1994, the figure would be 62 per cent. It was ludicrous. Someone arrested for owning an ounce of marijuana for personal use was metaphorically in the same cell – and certainly in the same prison – as major heroin dealers, smugglers and other organized-crime felons. What was more, the new laws did little to reduce marijuana use. They simply made it more covert.

Reagan's administration was prepared to bend the rules as much and as often as it pleased. In 1878, an Act of Congress had been passed called the Posse Comitatus Act. It prevented the public from being subject to government militarism. In other words, it prevented the government from using federal troops to enforce civilian law. In the war on drugs, the Act was roundly ignored and, in 1982, Reagan had it redrafted to allow him to use the military in his fight on narcotics in general.

This was not the only example of US government heavy-handedness and intransigence in the fight against drugs. In one incident, a $2,500,000 yacht, the *Ark Royal*, was sequestered by the US Coast Guard when one-tenth of an ounce of marijuana was found on board. The boat was later returned after the owner paid a $1600 fine. Another even more ridiculous example was the confiscation of one of America's most important research vessels, the *Atlantis II*, owned by the world-renowned Woods Hole Oceanographic Institution in Massachusetts. US Coast Guards seized the ship because a minute amount of marijuana was discovered in a crew member's shaving kit. The boat was retained for two months, greatly hampering a major oceanographic research programme. A Scripps Institution of Oceanography vessel was also impounded after a sniffer dog uncovered a small amount of marijuana hidden in a deck hand's bunk.

To combat domestic growers, an exceedingly small number of whom were raising cannabis plants in remote areas, Reagan authorized the DEA to spray national forest areas in three southern states with paraquat, under guidelines laid down by the Domestic Cannabis Eradication and Suppression Program but in direct contravention of federal environment legislation. The dangers of the herbicide to wildlife and humans were ignored. In July 1984 the Colombian government bent to US demands and sprayed over twenty thousand acres of cannabis with glyphosphate, another herbicide far less dangerous than paraquat but still non-specific.

As well as the President, First Lady Nancy Reagan joined the anti-drugs campaign, coining the bland slogan *Just Say No*. The White House publicity machine worked hard to affirm that both the President and his wife were at one with concerned parents and, when a thirteen-year-old Californian girl surrendered her parents' cocaine and marijuana stocks to the police, the First Lady was quick to make as much as was possible out of it. That the child's parents were then sentenced to three years' imprisonment and the girl herself taken into care is seldom mentioned. Nancy Reagan praised the girl but the law still broke up her family and there were those who voiced the opinion that it was better to have marijuana-using parents than a broken home, or children being en-couraged by the law to inform on their parents to the authorities.

Not only parent groups were concerned. Employers' associations were worried about lost production, absenteeism and work-related accidents caused by drugs. In 1979, a train driver smoking marijuana had gone through a signal and hit another train and, in 1983, the pilot of a cargo aircraft that crashed at Newark International Airport near New York was found at autopsy to have very recently used marijuana. Companies across the US soon obliged all job applicants to submit a urine sample for testing. The US military did likewise.

Through the 1980s, marijuana use declined but only at the expense of a rise in heroin and cocaine abuse which, unlike marijuana, ignited a sharp rise in violent crime and robberies. Marijuana dealers, who were mostly non-career or part-time criminals for whom the drug was their only criminal activity, withdrew from the market leaving their business open for take-over by hardened career criminals. Some of them continued to sell marijuana but most dropped it as uneconomic. Now, marijuana was in the hands of the heroin and cocaine pushers.

Keen to avoid association with real gangsters – as opposed to friendly marijuana dealers on street corners – as well as being under pressure from the threat of harsh legal retribution and the antagonism of employers, the middle classes eased back on their use of drugs, particularly marijuana. Yet this was a short-term phenomenon. Despite the most costly and extensive publicity campaign in American history, marijuana use began a re-surgence amongst the young in the 1990s. Drug-education programmes, both in the US and elsewhere in the Western world, failed to drive home the message that marijuana was harmful. What the various governments failed to appreciate was the fact that the young were much more street-wise than before. The publicity campaigns had not scared them off drugs. On the contrary, they had educated them in the subject. Teenagers knew heroin was dangerously addictive (and needle-sharing could transmit HIV and hepatitis) and cocaine could rot your sinuses away. Marijuana, they knew from reading, was nothing like as harmful.

In 1989, the forty-first President of the United States, George Bush, formerly Director of the CIA, declared another war on drugs. On 17 December, he set in motion Operation Just Cause under which US forces invaded Panama to oust from power and capture General Manuel Noriega, the country's leader whom the Americans accused of drug running and money laundering on a gargantuan scale. After evading capture by seeking political immunity and asylum in the Vatican nunciature, Noriega surrendered, was extradited to Florida and stood trial after which, being found guilty, he was sentenced to forty years in jail, although the sentence was later reduced by ten years.

While Noriega was holed up under the protection of the Vatican, the US Army was at a loss as to how to winkle him out. They could hardly storm the building of the Papal nuncio. Instead, psychological warfare tactics were decided upon. Knowing the deposed general was an opera buff who abhorred rock 'n' roll, the Americans pointed huge loudspeakers at the building and bombarded it with rock music at full volume, for seventy-two hours without a break. Amongst the performers Noriega was obliged to listen to on record were Bob Marley and The Wailers.

# 21

# ISLAND IN THE SUN

THE ONGOING RELATIONSHIP BETWEEN MARIJUANA AND MUSIC BECAME even closer in the 1970s when the music industry realized that there were profits to be made in providing music for the millions of record buyers using the drug.

One genre of music in particular took marijuana to its soul. It was called reggae and it originated in Jamaica.

When cannabis, not indigenous to the island, was first imported into Jamaica is not known for certain. At some time early in the nineteenth century the British, who administered the island, sent a Russian expert in hemp production there to assess the viability of a commercial planting programme. The plan failed and the plant went feral. The black slaves from Africa seem not to have been aware of it as there is no record of it being used either as food or as medicine. However, when indentured labourers from India arrived in the mid-1840s to take the place of the by now emancipated slaves, the situation changed. They knew what the plant was and what it could do, and their legacy continues to this day.

The Jamaican word for marijuana, *ganja* (sometimes spelt *ganga*) comes from the vocabulary of the Indian plantation workers. Similarly, a marijuana pipe in Jamaica is called a *chillum* whilst the word *colley* (also spelt *colly* and *collie*) meaning a rich, potent marijuana made of female flower buds, comes from the Hindi word *kali*, meaning fierce or strong.

Within a very short space of time, the Indians taught the former slaves

258

all about marijuana and it was soon used widely amongst the black population, as it still is. Yet there was more to it than just showing the locals how to smoke marijuana. The Indians also passed on how to cultivate it and improve it.

Jamaica possessed the ideal climate for marijuana growing and two harvests were possible every year. What was more, it was an ideal crop for the black population to grow, many of whom farmed smallholdings in the hills where large-scale plantation farming was not viable. There began an agricultural pattern that continues to this day, with thousands of farmers growing marijuana for their own use and selling the excess.

In the 1970s, it was estimated that about 70 per cent of the working-class black population of Jamaica used marijuana, either smoking it or ingesting it as a tea, tonic or food additive. It was also used medically in poultices amongst other applications. This usage, the highest of any population in the world, spanned all the age groups. It was not used specifically as an hallucinogen but as a social relaxant and a relief for the aches and pains of a hard working life. In some instances, it was used magically as it was believed to dispel evil powers.

Although marijuana is sometimes added to a baby's milk or juice drink to help it sleep or address any fractious behaviour, for most Jamaicans marijuana enters their lives in their early teenage years, the first joint being regarded as a moment of significance much as might be a first sexual experience. The smoker may not, however, become a regular user, this depending upon how he reacts to his first joint.

The drug being so very widely used on the island, despite being illegal, the Center for Studies of Narcotic and Drug Abuse of the US National Institute of Mental Health sponsored a medical anthropological research programme in 1970 to assess how chronic users were affected by it. The final results were published in full in 1975, written by Vera Rubin and Lamros Comitas and entitled simply, *Ganja in Jamaica*. The conclusions were fascinating.

It was found that marijuana use was the reason for substantially lower levels of alcoholism than anywhere else in similar societies in the Caribbean, it did not cause any measurable brain or chromosomic damage, was not psychologically dangerous and there was no link between marijuana usage and crime, accepting that growing and using it were in themselves illegal acts. More interestingly, the study stated that the culture had in-built restraints which controlled the social effects of marijuana. The teenagers' decision as to whether or not a peer should join in smoking marijuana after his initiation prevented those who might suffer adversely from the experience from continuing with it. There were also widely held social rules which said that, for example, one should avoid the drug if not in a calm state of mind; another advised that *ganja* should never be used on an empty stomach.

Although the programme was conducted with all the necessary scientific rigour, it was all but ignored by international governments because it did not endorse the preferred view of marijuana having negative aspects to it. Another study conducted concurrently by the University of Florida in Costa Rica, which drew more or less the same conclusions, was similarly suppressed and would have remained unknown were it not for one of the very few copies printed being leaked to NORML.

The Jamaican report did little to change the status of marijuana on the island. It was and remained illegal as it had been for decades.

Originally ruled by Spain, Jamaica became a British colony by the terms of the Treaty of Madrid in 1670. By 1700, its primary exports were sugar, cocoa and indigo, grown on plantations worked by slaves. When the Indian indentured labourers arrived, and marijuana started to be used, the colonial authorities and plantation owners at first paid it no regard whatsoever. So long as agricultural production was not affected there seemed no need to do anything about it. However, in time, it was stated that marijuana was undermining the efficiency of the work force and, in 1913, legislation was passed which made it illegal. The foundation for this was not based on truth for the drug did not make the plantation workers less efficient. Indeed, quite the opposite: it enabled them to work longer hours of physical toil. The real motive for the prohibition was to establish a form of social control over the workers rather than addressing any alleged drug-induced indolence. Yet the prohibition was a failure. Marijuana continued to be grown in remote areas and used and all the law did was sow the seeds of a dissension that has reverberated down the years of Jamaican history ever since.

Twenty-four years later, in 1937, the colonial government was harangued by the Americans and Anslinger who expended some effort in promoting their propaganda. The aim was to have Jamaica stop producing marijuana, some of which was reaching US shores. It was a timely campaign for Jamaica was in turmoil with crippling strikes by sugar cane workers leading to rioting. Anslinger stressed how marijuana drove people to psychopathic behaviour. The British authorities, without questioning him and under pressure from Church and sugar-interest lobby groups, rewrote the dangerous drugs laws in 1941 and introduced

American-style mandatory minimum sentences. This only added fuel to the fire of dissent, the plantation owners remaining too blinkered to see how marijuana actually helped their workers maintain production quotas.

The law didn't just anger the workers. It gave disparate social groups a focus that brought them together, and from this adhesion was born the Jamaican trades union movement. There was another group, already in existence, that also benefited from this coming together. They were called the Rastafari or Rastafarians.

Their roots went back to 1655 when the Spanish, in order to hassle the British who had recently invaded and captured Jamaica, released a number of slaves who promptly fled into the mountainous hinterland, from which they waged a guerrilla war against the new colonists. Known as Maroons (from the Spanish word *cimarrón*, meaning wild), they were from time to time joined by runaway slaves and fought sporadically until the late 1730s. Thereafter, they continued as a number of groups which lived by a complex Afro-Jamaican code of ritual, magic and morality. From the mid nineteenth century, this included marijuana.

In the turmoil of the 1930s, as the black society of Jamaica began to assert its independent spirit and identity, Rastafarianism emerged as the umbrella under which the aspirations of Jamaican blacks could be amalgamated. At the forefront of this was one Marcus Garvey.

Born in St Ann's Bay on 17 August 1887, and claiming to come from Maroon stock, Garvey was the youngest in a family of eleven children. At the age of twenty, he organized a strike of print workers, became a social reformer and founded a newspaper, the *Watchman*. After travelling throughout the Caribbean and Central America and seeing the plight of black labourers, he left for Britain in 1912 to seek funding for a social reform group of which he dreamed. In England, he was introduced to an Egyptian Sudanese journalist called Duse Mohammed Ali who encouraged him and prompted him to read Booker T. Washington's *Up From Slavery*, a book which declared that black people would get nowhere, and remain oppressed, if they did not help themselves to rise up from their condition. Inspired, Garvey founded the Universal Negro Improvement Association (UNIA) and the African Communities League. In 1920, after a highly successful convention in New York, UNIA expanded rapidly, establishing branches across the Caribbean and in west and South Africa. To raise funds, Garvey embarked upon a number of ambitious business ventures of which the best known was the Black Star Shipping Line. Over the next five years, UNIA began to disintegrate. Officials embezzled its funds and Garvey was jailed in Atlanta, Georgia, on fraud charges. His sentence commuted halfway through, he was deported back to Jamaica where he entered politics but was unsuccessful in gaining office. In 1935, he returned to Britain and died of a stroke in obscurity and near poverty in a small house in West Kensington on 10 June 1940.

Although a Roman Catholic, Garvey also encouraged Jamaicans of African descent to think of Christ as black and to organize their own church which they did, at first calling it the Garveyite African Orthodox Church. In his teachings, Garvey predicted that a mighty ruler would be born in Africa to bring justice to the oppressed blacks of the world. Looking towards Africa for a symbol of freedom and a location from which this black saviour might arise, he found Ethiopia, then known as Abyssinia.

In November 1930, Ras Tafari Makonnen was crowned Emperor Haile Selassie of Ethiopia. His name translated into English as Prince Tafari, Might of the Trinity, for he was a member of the Ethiopian Church, the Ge'ez Tewahdo, and a Coptic Christian who had been the symbolic head of the Christian community in the country which had deposed the previous, pro-Muslim emperor, Lij Yasu. In Jamaica, Haile Selassie was seen as the fulfilment of Garvey's prophecy. Taking the new emperor's name, the Rastafarians came into being.

There was, however, another facet drawn into Rastafarianism in its early stages. The Jamaican Hamatic Church had been founded around 1925, its teachings based upon the Holy Piby, otherwise commonly known as the Black Man's Bible, which had been compiled in Anguilla by Robert Athlyi Rogers a decade before. The founders of the church, the Revd Charles F. Goodridge and a woman called Grace Jenkins Garrison, were persecuted by the other, more orthodox Christian sects in Jamaica and forced to flee into the forests, accused of occult practices. In hiding, they joined up with the followers of Ras Tafari and began to formulate the doctrines of Rastafarianism. These included a rule that the followers should never cut their hair, should follow a strict code of diet and should reject gambling and alcohol. Yet, because of references in the Bible (and Piby) to herbs, marijuana was considered sacramental.

The main justification for this interpretation came from three sources. First was the Book of Psalms, 104:14: *He causeth the grass for the cattle, and herb for the service of man*; second, the Book of Genesis, 1:11: *And God said, Let the earth bring forth grass, the herb yielding seed, and the fruit tree yielding fruit after his kind, whose seed is in itself, upon the earth; and it was so*; and third, the Book of Revelations, 22:2: *In the midst of the street of it, and on either side of the river, was there the tree of life, which bare twelve manner of fruits, and yielded her fruit every month; and the leaves of the tree were for the healing of the nations.* Additionally, the Rastafarians believed marijuana cleansed the spirit and body in readiness for prayer and communion both with God and with one's fellow man. Rastafarians also considered marijuana to be a good medicinal tonic and analgesic, a provider of physical strength and aphrodisiacal qualities, and an important part of their strict diet, in which it is used much as it has been in Jamaican cuisine since the Indians illustrated its potential by adding it to curries.

The Rastafarians were not the only ones who believed in the holy aspects of marijuana. The Ethiopian Zion Coptic Church, which grew up in Jamaica around the same period, looked on marijuana as having been specifically created by God and referred to it as angel's food, the weed of wisdom or the tree of life. Claiming a direct lineage from the earliest form of Christianity as practised in Jerusalem, a founding member being Kuftaim, son of Mizraim and a grandchild of Noah, they believed marijuana was taken at the Last Supper and that the baptism of fire and the Holy Ghost was actually a ritual in which Christ smoked marijuana with anointees. They differed from Rastafarians in that they did not believe Haile Selassie was divine and also did not abide by the same rules such as that which dictated that their hair could not be shorn.

Once the Rastafarian movement was well under way, it was regarded as dissident. Being racially charged, its aim being the freedom of blacks from oppression by others, most especially the white colonial power, it was seen as a threat to social stability. That it drew almost all of its followers from the poor and working class also discomforted the authorities who saw in it a native uprising in the making. It had to be suppressed but the question remained as to how this might be done without seeming to be racist. The answer appeared obvious. Hit at the Rastafarians through the marijuana laws. By 1950, the suppression of drugs was synonymous with keeping down the Rastas.

January 1958 saw Jamaica move towards independence by becoming a founding state in the West Indies Federation. Four years later it gained full self-dominion. Under international pressure as well as a local determination to stamp out marijuana smoking, the laws that the British colonial administration had put in place remained on the statute books. Within five years, they were strengthened, the arrest rate climbing by 300 per cent. At the same time, political unrest and violence increased dramatically. Gangs roamed the streets intimidating voters. With limited justification, for some of the gangs did consist of their followers, the

Rastafarians were associated with this violence and political terrorization. Yet what caused them to become more fully associated with it was the fact that many of the gangs sourced their financing from marijuana, not just selling it locally but exporting it.

By 1974, the violence reaching epidemic proportions, the Jamaican government, now a member of the Organization of American States, asked America to help stamp out marijuana. The DEA was keen to assist. It meant it would put a halt to exports to the USA and the Jamaican authorities would see a commensurate reduction in violence. The gangs had not only been selling marijuana in America but buying guns with the proceeds. For several years, the trade ceased, although in time it started up again. With it much reduced, Jamaica was left with a problem. Like many poorer countries, it needed foreign exchange. Marijuana provided it. Furthermore, much of the country's rural economy depended upon the cannabis crop. To wipe it out would cause hardship and considerable social upheaval. On the other hand, Jamaica was a signatory to the UN Single Convention and bound by its treaty. In 1980, the country's gross domestic product (GDP) consisted of bauxite, marijuana and tourism, the government tacitly but unofficially acknowledging the place of the drug in its GDP statistics.

Some of the primary exporters of marijuana to the USA were members of the Ethiopian Zion Coptic Church, by no means all of them black. According to the DEA, the church became exceedingly rich on this trade, investing in and operating a large number of legitimate businesses including an automobile importer, a large container transport firm and a number of farms in Jamaica with another in Florida under which tunnels were excavated to hide marijuana. In 1977, a seizure of 10 tons was made from these underground chambers. Nine members of the church were convicted in Miami of importing 105 tons of marijuana, their lawyer arguing that their prosecution was unconstitutional on the grounds that the marijuana was a religious sacrament. This defence has been attempted since, the church claiming that it is an established religion and citing the exemption American Indians have been given for peyote, on the same grounds. They have been unsuccessful.

The Rastafarians might well have remained known only to Jamaicans were it not for their music, reggae. A form of folk music which now incorporates many of the facets of rock music, it may by default be said to be the music of marijuana, for a good number of the lyrics are about traditional herbal medicine practice. Those which are not comment upon Jamaican or black culture, history, politics or religion. It is also the protest music of the poor blacks, railing against poverty, injustice, corrupt politicians and leaders (of which Jamaica has had more than a few), oppression by the state and the laws on marijuana. Its leading exponent, who took the music out of the socially deprived areas of Jamaica and onto the international music scene, was Bob Marley.

Born in Santa Anna on 6 February 1945, Robert Nesta Marley was the son of a young black woman, Cedella Malcolm, and 'Captain' Norval Marley, a middle-aged white Jamaican who worked for the Royal Navy in Kingston, and who abandoned her shortly after the baby's birth, although he did send her money from time to time. When Bob Marley was a child, the 'Captain' returned briefly to try to persuade Cedella to have the boy adopted but she refused. The father then agreed to educate his son in Kingston, taking him away and lodging him with a woman but otherwise having nothing to do with him. Cedella reclaimed him and, in 1957, they moved to the Trenchtown ghetto area of Kingston, built in 1951 to provide lodgings for squatters who had lost their flimsy shanty homes in a hurricane. The houses, constructed around courtyards known as government yards, were very basic but sound, built of concrete with communal cooking and water facilities but no sewage system.

Life in Trenchtown was hard. Bob Marley dropped out of school at fifteen and, with two friends, Peter Tosh and Bunny Livingston (nicknamed Bunny Wailer), formed a trio called the Wailing Rudeboys. Marley also met a successful singer and songwriter called Joe Higgs, who was writing songs about marijuana and the Rastafarians.

Jamaica at the time was in a state of flux. Recently independent, it was fast developing its own post-colonial identity which included the evolution of the traditional Quadrille semi-bluegrass music bands, the players of which used marijuana and drank rum. Through a series of metamorphoses, drawing on the influences of rhythm 'n' blues, American soul music and calypso, a new musical form appeared, called ska. In this new genre, Bob Marley made a local name for himself.

In 1966, Haile Selassie paid a state visit to Jamaica. For the Rastafarians, this was an event of astonishing proportions. For the Jamaican government, it was a problem. As far as they were concerned, the Rastafarians were a dangerous anti-social, marijuana-smoking under class. Yet they had to be accommodated. To have excluded them from meeting the emperor would have meant considerable social discord if not active unrest. Suddenly, the Rastafarians had to be officially recognized as a quasi-religious group.

After the state visit, Bob Marley and his band, known now as the

Wailers, began to turn away from ska and adopt the self-disciplined Rastafarian way of life. His music altered, becoming more idio-syncratically African, the beat slowing, the lyrics growing more consciously provocative. Leaning towards Rastafarianism meant that Bob Marley also started using large amounts of marijuana on a regular basis.

In 1968, Marley was arrested for possession of marijuana and jailed for a month. It was a revelation in some respects. He identified with his fellow prisoners and used the time to increase his knowledge of Rastafarianism. After his release, he increasingly attended Rastafarian prayer meetings, called groundations, and, at one of them, met a young black American singer called Johnny Nash who declared he would get Marley and his band international recognition.

The music Marley was by now playing contained a moderate, rhythmical beat and was referred to as reggae. The derivation of the word is confused: it is said to refer either to the ghetto slang word 'streggae,' meaning uncouth and rude, or to the regular basic beat. Marijuana purists tend towards the latter, claiming the slowed beat was promoted by the laid-back effects of the drug.

By 1971 reggae was the sought-after music on the local scene. Bob Marley became an immediate national hero and *de facto* spokesperson of the poor in the ghettos. Politicians, especially the charismatic and ambi-tious Michael Manley who became prime minister the following year, wooed him. Marley carried the popular vote. However, later that year, Marley and his band moved to London where they were signed to Island Records, then one of the most important independent record companies in the world. Chris Blackwell, the owner, financed Marley to return to Jamaica to record the first reggae album. When it was released, entitled *Catch a Fire*, it was an immediate international hit. The band toured Europe and America, playing the music and thereby simultaneously promoting not only the message of the lyrics but Rastafarian ideals and marijuana.

In 1975, Bob Marley and the Wailers conducted an American tour, fans delivering marijuana at the stage door for them. When the tour ended in Los Angeles, Marley gave a press interview in which he admitted he had smoked marijuana for nine years. *When you smoke herb*, he said, *herb reveal yourself to you. All the wickedness you do, the herb reveal it to yourself, your con-science, show up yourself clear, because herb make you meditate. Is only a natural t'ing and it grow like a tree*. He restricted his comments to the context of Rastafarianism, which was appropriate. He did not use marijuana hedonistically.

When it was rumoured the following year that Michael Manley might legalize marijuana in Jamaica in the light of its extensive usage, and Marley was asked for his comments, he referred to it as the herb that healed the nation, but was otherwise generally noncommittal. Manley may have wanted, politically, to delegislate cannabis but the US – which was a strong trading nation with Jamaica – and the UN treaty obligations prevented it.

Marley and one of the band, Family Man Barrett, were arrested in Britain in 1977 for possession of marijuana. Their car was stopped by the police in Ladbroke Grove, West London, and searched. Two joints were found. It seems as if the halting of the vehicle, the driver of which was not violating any traffic laws, was simply an excuse to search Marley's home. There, a pound of marijuana was discovered. Marley and Barrett appeared before magistrates at Marylebone Magistrates Court on 6 April and were each fined fifty pounds. The chairman of the magistrates warned them, *Whatever the approach or attitude in your own country you must really appreciate that here it is still an offence. While you are here it would be very unwise to use or have possession of cannabis.*

Throughout his musical career, Marley was tempted to use other drugs but always declined. Marijuana was in his opinion not a drug in the accepted sense. It was a divine substance. He recorded several songs about it including 'African Herbsman' and 'Redder than Red'. Another was called 'Kaya', which meant marijuana for *kaya* is the Rastafarian term for *ganja*. Often now called marijuana's greatest ambassador, Marley died of cancer in 1981. At his funeral, his widow placed some sinsemilla in his coffin. This was not just an act of gentle emotion but also a snub to those anti-marijuana activists who had been quick to blame his early death on his smoking habits. Legend states he smoked joints the size of ice-cream cones.

Other artists followed Marley's example in lauding marijuana. Peter Tosh released a song starkly entitled 'Legalize It'. It was banned in Jamaica. Some not only sang about marijuana but included it in their album jacket design. Two Californian musicians, Richard 'Cheech' Marin and Thomas Chong, had giant rolling papers in their record sleeves and in 1978 made a bizarre movie entitled *Up in Smoke*, in which the two of them meet by chance on a Californian freeway and wind up having to drive into the USA from Mexico in a van made entirely of marijuana.

Marley was not the only international show business personality to be arrested for possession of marijuana. Paul McCartney was arrested in Japan in 1980. He and his post-Beatles band, Wings, were on tour in Asia. Because McCartney already had two drug convictions, the Japanese government had refused him and his band entry visas but had relented at the request of the promoters. On arrival, Japanese customs officers searched McCartney's baggage and discovered approximately half a pound of cannabis. He was immediately arrested, spent ten days in jail and was deported after paying the tour promoters considerable compensation for lost earnings.

McCartney's previous convictions had been for carrying marijuana into Sweden and for possession and growing five cannabis plants at High Peak Farm, the property he owned on the Mull of Kintyre in the Scottish highlands. For the latter, he received a small fine. He was lucky. By the time he was arrested in September 1972, British anti-cannabis laws were stringent and rigorously applied.

# SWINGING IN LONDON, STONED
# IN AMSTERDAM

DRUG USE IN BRITAIN, EVEN AS LATE AS 1960, CAUSED NO REAL CONCERN.
In 1961, when the Inter-departmental Committee on Drug Addiction,
known as the Brain Committee after its chairman, Sir Russell
Brain, published its report, it stated, *In our view cannabis is not a drug of
addiction; it is an intoxicant.* Four years later, it reiterated the point
but also noted there was *a risk that young people may be persuaded to turn to
cannabis.* Some observers wondered upon which far planet the committee
members lived for the situation in those few years had changed
dramatically.

Whilst cannabis had long been used in British West Indian communities, by 1965 it was being used increasingly by white youths as a
social drug. Some blamed Caribbean immigrants for this rise, but they
were wrong. The young were aping their American counterparts and,
travelling more widely overseas, became increasingly aware of cannabis of
their own volition. Particularly, the drug was found to be used by students
and those in the creative arts: musicians, artists, advertising writers,
poets and novelists, film and television personnel. Yet it was also used
increasingly outside this sphere and across the upper half of the social
spectrum by those who regarded it as an alternative to alcohol. Unlike in
the US, where cannabis was traditionally a drug of the poor, in Britain it
was primarily one of the educated middle class.

When, in 1965, the British government complied with the UN Single

Convention, it equated cannabis with opiates and established tough penalties under the Dangerous Drugs Act. The maximum sentence was ten years in prison and a fine of one thousand pounds, this applying to both possession and trafficking. The level of sentencing was appropriate in the case of heroin, use of which was sharply on the increase, but seemed otherwise heavy-handed in the extreme, for cannabis was not even the drug of choice for many. For example, the Mods, the first of the Sixties' youth-culture groups along with the Rockers, preferred speed to cannabis. They lived a fast life and considered cannabis more likely to slow them down.

Interest in hallucinogenic drugs was boosted when the British writer Michael Hollingshead who was to publish a book on the drug culture entitled *The Man Who Turned On the World* in 1973, introduced the theories of Timothy Leary to Britain. He also set up the World Psychedelic Centre in the fashionable King's Road, in Chelsea, the epicentre of swinging London. Celebrities, especially famous rock musicians, attended it and afforded it and drugs an effective publicity platform. In the summer of 1965, a huge poetry festival held at the Royal Albert Hall, at which Ginsberg and Ferlinghetti read their work, gave drugs a further impetus.

It was not long before musicians started to be arrested on cannabis charges. Donovan, the bland British Bob Dylan clone, was found in possession, fined £250 and given the customary establishment warning, *I would like you to bear in mind that you have a great influence on young people and it behoves you to behave yourself.* In February 1967, however, the authorities caught a much bigger fish in their net.

A police raid took place on Redlands, the West Sussex home of The Rolling Stones guitarist, Keith Richards. What the police found was a standard rock-music party in progress, an assortment of drugs and the singer Marianne Faithful dressed in nothing but a bearskin rug. Richards was arrested and held on remand in Wormwood Scrubs prison. Mick Jagger, also arrested, was put into Brixton prison. The raid was not fortuitous. The police had been tipped off, it is thought, by a national newspaper that wanted the scoop. Police accusations that both musicians were intoxicated with marijuana on their arrest were strenuously denied. Richards was charged with permitting his premises to be used for the smoking of marijuana and Jagger with the illegal possession of speed. They were found guilty in court, Jagger and Richards being sentenced to three months and one year in jail respectively. Examples, the judge felt, had to be made.

The sentences created a furore. The musicians' legal team decried the severity of the sentences. Parliamentary debates considered the situation. Even the normally staid and ultra-establishment *The Times* newspaper ran an editorial declaiming, *Who breaks a butterfly on a wheel?*.

Far from creating an example for the young, the judge presented them with two martyrs or heroes and two champions for marijuana. Almost immediately, a pro-cannabis lobby group was created called The Society of Mental Awareness (SOMA). The acronym made the name of the drug distilled from magic mushrooms in Huxley's writings and the omnipresent mass tranquillizer-cum-hallucinogen used by society in his novel *Brave New World*. SOMA announced that it was to address *the examination, without prejudice, of the scientific, medical, legal, moral, social and philosophical aspects of heightened mental awareness, with special reference to the effects of pleasure-giving drugs*. Founded by Stephen Abrams, it took out a full-page advertisement in *The Times* endorsed by sixty-five famous signatories, including not only rock-music personalities but also Francis Crick, the Nobel Prize-winning chemist; the noted psychiatrists David Stafford-Clark, Anthony Storr, Ronald Laing and David Cooper; photographer David Bailey; novelist Graham Greene; artist David Hockney and the critic Kenneth Tynan. The advertisement, in the form of an open letter, demanded law reform. It cost £1800; Brian Epstein, The Beatles' manager, paid the bill.

Two Members of Parliament also signed the document, Brian Walden and Tom Driberg. The latter was a controversial figure. As an undergraduate at the University of Oxford in 1925, he had written a letter to Aleister Crowley in which he said, *I have for a long time been interested not only in drugs and the possibility of using them moderately and beneficially, but also generally in the development of latent spiritual powers and questions of occultism.* They met for lunch, at Crowley's invitation, probably because Crowley hoped he might find a wealthy disciple in the young student. Always fascinated by the *risqué* – he was himself a widely practising homosexual at a time when homosexuality was illegal – Driberg's curiosity about cannabis was awakened by Allen Ginsberg. In his autobiography, Driberg wrote that Ginsberg asked him to look up a report in the House of Commons Library. There he discovered the evidence his father, John James Street Driberg, Chief of Police and Inspector of Jails for the province of Assam, had given to the Indian Hemp Drugs Commission. *I found*, he wrote, *that my father had given evidence before this Commission, putting forward strongly the view that people living in a damp, cold climate needed the traditional consolation of ganja, as the stuff was called then. The climate referred to was that of Assam rather than England; but I felt it was almost an act of filial piety to sign a full page advertisement in* The Times *calling for a liberalization of the laws on pot.*

As 1967 was termed the Summer of Love in America, in Britain it could have been renamed the Summer of Action. SOMA held a march in Fleet Street, the centre of Britain's press, and a sit-in in London's Hyde Park. The latter was more of a smoke-in attended by several thousand people. A Youth for Peace rally occurred in Trafalgar Square, protesting against the Vietnam War. A Festival of the Flower Children, Britain's first major hippy gathering, took place in the grounds of the Duke of Bedford's stately home, Woburn Abbey. Demonstrations were held for the legalization of marijuana. At the beginning of June, The Beatles released their *Sergeant Pepper's Lonely Hearts Club Band* album and, later in the month, their song 'All you Need is Love' was beamed worldwide in the first-ever global communications satellite broadcast.

In the middle of all this, Keith Richards' High Court appeal against his conviction was successful on a legal technicality and he was released from prison. Jagger's conviction remained but he was given a conditional discharge. The Establishment had had to cave in not only to legal argument but also to public opinion. That many in authority had little idea about drugs was another factor, as was amply shown by an appearance on *Top of the Pops*, the weekly BBC television music show, by a Mod band called *The Small Faces*. On the nationwide broadcast, watched by at least 80 per cent of all teenagers, they sang 'Here Comes the Nice'. 'The nice' was Mod slang for an amphetamine dealer. No one in authority realized the song was a paean to a drug pusher. All the Mods did, though.

It was evident after the Redlands raid that the police had an easy target in rock musicians, one at which they felt obliged to aim for both assured publicity and possible convictions.

One man in particular, Detective Sergeant Norman 'Nobby' Pilcher, came to epitomize the police anti-drug stance. With an Anslinger-like zeal, he raided Eric Clapton's flat but the guitarist was out. Twice, he targeted Brian Jones of The Rolling Stones. Accompanied by forty officers, he arrested John Lennon and Yoko Ono in Ringo Starr's home for the possession of hashish. Lennon pleaded guilty and was fined for *an offence of moral turpitude*, this being the charge over which the FBI harassed him to try to find or create reason to deport him from the USA. Yoko Ono was discharged.

The raid raised questions. First, it was asked why it took forty policemen to arrest two people who were unarmed and famously non-belligerent. Second, it was wondered how news photographers knew to be outside Starr's home at the right time. Third, Lennon later claimed he was framed and had only pleaded guilty to protect Ono. At the time, this was dismissed but, in 1972, Pilcher was charged with other police officers of conspiring to pervert the course of justice. He was accused of planting evidence in another case, was convicted and sentenced to two years' imprisonment. Credence to Lennon's claim is given by another raid upon the home of his fellow Beatle, George Harrison. On this occasion, sniffer dogs dug up cannabis in the garden. Harrison was adamant it had been placed there by the police.

Stung by the criticism of its attitude towards marijuana, the Government set up the Advisory Committee on Drug Dependence under Sir Edward Wayne, Regius Professor of the Practice of Medicine at the University of Glasgow. It did not have statutory powers but it did report direct to the Home Secretary. Wayne in turn set up a sub-committee to study hallucinogens, led by Baroness Wootton of Abinger, a prominent sociologist, with a panel which included a very senior police officer, a magistrate (who happened to be Chairman of the Poisons Board), a psychiatrist, a pharmacologist and others. Their report, which has become known as the Wootton Report, was published in January 1969.

The Government may have hoped for a controversial report that supported their line but they were to be disappointed. It confirmed earlier studies, announcing, *Having reviewed all the material available to us we find ourselves in agreement with the conclusion reached by the Indian Hemp Drugs Commission appointed by the Government of India (1893–1894) and the New York Mayor's Committee on Marihuana (1944), that the long-term consumption of cannabis in moderate doses has no harmful effects.* It went on to say that cannabis was *very much less dangerous than the opiates, amphetamines, and barbiturates, and also less dangerous than alcohol* [and] *it is the personality of the user, rather than the properties of the drug, that is likely to cause progression to other drugs.* The report recommended that the Government *bring about a situation in which it is extremely unlikely that anyone will go to prison for an offence involving only possession for personal use or for supply on a very limited scale.*

Politicians, the press and anti-marijuana activists were enraged. The *Daily Express* called it a pot-smokers' charter and most of the other newspapers agreed, with the exception of the *Daily Telegraph*, which was surprising considering it was a pro-Conservative Party newspaper and the government of the time was a socialist Labour administration. In the professional press, the *British Medical Journal* attacked the report but the independent *The Lancet* supported it. After a long parliamentary debate the Home Secretary, James Callaghan, expressed his opposition and promptly perched on the political fence, stating that he believed the committee had been nobbled by the pro-marijuana lobby. This was abundantly not the case. The integrity of the members was beyond reproach and Baroness Wootton rejoined with a letter to *The Times* which stated that Callaghan's remarks were offensive.

The Government ignored the report and, in 1971, increased the penalties for all cases involving cannabis under the Misuse of Drugs Act. In this legislation, which was reinforced in the mid-1980s and has remained in force ever since, illicit drugs were categorized in three classes: Class A included heroin, cocaine and morphine; Class B codeine, amphetamines, barbiturates and cannabis; Class C substances were such drugs as the stimulants pemoline and mazindol, steroids and antidepressants. Although the penalties for possession of cannabis were marginally lower than for Class A drugs, those for trafficking in it were not. The Misuse of Drugs Regulations 1985 would define who was permitted to possess, use or prescribe controlled drugs for medicinal purposes. These were divided into five schedules. Those in Schedule 1, such as raw opium, LSD and cannabis, were completely prohibited except under very exceptional circumstances, such as strictly monitored scientific research. Schedule 2 drugs, such as heroin and morphine, could be prescribed by a doctor, but a licence was needed to import or supply them. The other three schedules applied similar rules but with decreasing bureaucratic control. Cannabis was classed in the first schedule because it was considered to have no medicinal value whatsoever, despite the fact that it had been a widely used patent medicine in the nineteenth century and a folk medicine and analgesic for centuries before that. Regardless of the law, however, cannabis use in Britain rose steadily. By 1972, estimates of user numbers ranged between five hundred thousand and two million.

The real drug problem developed in the 1980s and centred upon heroin. The police were at first unequipped to deal with it. Arrests in largely black ethnic-minority areas in London, Birmingham and Bristol led to rioting. The black population were not so much against the crackdown on heroin but those who used cannabis were incensed at being compared to heroin dealers.

They had some justification for their ire. Cannabis, it seemed, was not all that bad. In 1982 the British Advisory Council on the Misuse of Drugs published a document entitled *The Report of the Expert Group on the Effects of Cannabis Use.* It announced, *There is insufficient evidence to enable us to reach any incontestable conclusions as to the effects on the human body of the use of cannabis . . . there is a continuing need for further research* [especially] *on the effects of its long-term use by humans,* adding, *there is evidence to suggest that the therapeutic use of cannabis or of substances derived from it for the treatment of certain medical conditions may, after further research, prove to be beneficial.*

To tighten the law, the 1986 Drug Trafficking Act was passed, giving the police the power to seize all the assets acquired by a drug dealer over the previous six years if he was unable fully to account for their acquisition. The seizure was not dependent upon the quantity of drugs involved. Some cannabis users, accused of supplying, were to lose their property over the possession of just one joint.

Even this extremely harsh measure failed to slow the rise in cannabis use. In 1990, there were more than forty thousand convictions and cautions issued for cannabis use. This figure was over 90 per cent of all drug arrests.

Almost all the cannabis used in Britain was smuggled either as what was officially termed herbal cannabis (marijuana) or as cannabis resin (hashish). The latter made up roughly 65 per cent of all cannabis use. The methods of smuggling ranged from the commonplace to the extremely ingenious. As with vehicles crossing the Mexican border, those travelling into Britain carried contraband in floor and door panels, air and ferry foot passengers carried it in baggage and some was sent by mail. Marijuana, being bulky, tended to arrive by vehicle or boat, sometimes being off-loaded in secluded stretches of coast, but more often disguised in large commercial consignments of fruit or vegetables. Hashish, being particularly dense and malleable – as well as being more potent and there-fore more profitable – was smuggled hidden inside anything that contained a cavity (tennis racquet handles, cricket gloves and pads, beads and nuts manufactured or grown in Pakistan or India) or could be used to camouflage the drug (toothpaste tubes, cricket balls, scuba diving tanks, shoe heels, condom packets, ball pens, tourist ornaments and trinkets, camera film cassettes). At least one artful smuggler imported hashish in radio-controlled model aircraft launched from pleasure craft off-shore. A hi-tech adaptation to the weighted bag of salt system used in Egypt now has weighted watertight packets being thrown overboard with transponders attached: on receiving the transponder signal, the collecting vessel – which may arrive weeks later – transmits a return signal to it which triggers a release mechanism, the package then floating to the surface. Diplomats from Pakistan and some West African countries also smuggled hashish by customs-exempt diplomatic courier.

Large-scale organized traffic in cannabis to Britain began in the 1960s, with Asians keen to acquire the drug for the same reason the blacks in New York had thirty years before. It alleviated their misery in an alien land. At first, only cannabis for personal or friends' use was smuggled but, in a short time, ethnic Asian gangsters took over the trade, increasing their business amongst immigrants and selling out into the white population. In time, the smuggling became a two-way illicit exchange. Many Asians, eager to send money back to relatives they had left behind, used the underground banking network set up by smugglers, especially Pakistanis. The business then became sophisticated. Utilizing the immigrants' deposits, the smugglers bought cannabis in Asia and sent it to Britain, using the proceeds of sale there to purchase consumer goods that were smuggled back to Asia. Once in Britain, the hashish was usually retailed by West Indians.

The main point of departure for the hashish was the Pakistani city of Lahore, its couriers being mostly legitimate Pakistani British passport holders resident in Britain. In exchange for a holiday back home, these Pakistanis were supplied with hashish which they carried either to Britain or to a half-way point in Europe – usually Frankfurt – where another courier took over the last leg of the journey. This split journey became essential after British customs started to target flights from Pakistan.

Gradually, as their systems were discovered, the smugglers became more devious. In April 1967, 89 pounds of hashish was found packed in a cargo of twenty-five crates of oranges arriving at London Heathrow on a Pakistan International Airlines flight. As a result, the Pakistani proprietor of an import–export business in Walthamstow in the East End of London was put under surveillance. A year later to the month, after a tip-off, customs officers intercepted a consignment of mango chutney arriving by sea addressed to the firm. Hidden in the cargo were nine sealed tins containing 164 pounds of hashish. Replacing the hashish with sand, they allowed the consignment through and arrested the importer when it was delivered to him. This case led HM Customs to the ingenious mind behind the operation: an Indian physicist employed on secret military laser technology for both the British and American governments.

In addition to the Asian smugglers, some West Indians trafficked in marijuana but their trade was comparatively insignificant as was that of the freelanders, hippies or students who ran hashish to make a small profit or supply themselves or their peers.

As cannabis use increased in the 1970s, the profits from smuggling started to draw the attention of London's English criminal gangs known as 'firms'. They were attracted not just by the high profits on offer but also by the fact that, compared to their usual activities of armed robbery, bank or jewellery heists and the hold-up of armoured cars and cash couriers, the penalties for those caught were significantly lower. Most of their hashish came from Morocco along more or less established runs.

Supplies purchased in Tangier were taken by small pleasure or fishing boat to Spain. On the Costa del Sol and Costa Brava, the smugglers mingled with the tens of thousands of British holidaymakers, either selling directly to them or passing consignments to couriers amongst them. From there, they distributed across Europe. The itinerary the smugglers took was known as the Carmen Route, named after the opera by Bizet which was set in the Spanish city of Seville.

Customs officers at British ports of entry were faced with a tide of cannabis carriers and resorted to using trained sniffer dogs as, increasingly, did customs authorities around the world. Two types of dog were trained, one from active breeds such as spaniels which were employed to scurry through cargo and baggage holds on aircraft or scamper over the contents of an articulated lorry, the other from more docile breeds like Labradors which sauntered through passenger terminal buildings. If the former scented drugs they barked, whilst the latter simply sat down next to their discovery. Once dogs came into service, the smugglers had to find ways of foiling them. Hashish became vacuum-packed like supermarket food, was surrounded by camphor balls, ground coffee, black pepper, paprika, cayenne or insecticide powder. This fooled many but not all of the dogs.

As in Mexico, there were vehicle bodywork specialists in southern Spain who were adept at hiding hashish in vehicles. Spare-wheel, windscreen-washer-bottle and body-panel hiding places were easily discovered so more intricate and integral parts were used such as chassis members. If saloon cars were used, they were always legitimately purchased and licensed in Britain. The courier–driver was specially trained and his passengers either specifically recruited or picked up *en route*. It was not unknown for husband-and-wife teams to work together, their children acting as camouflage. On one occasion, two English grandparents and their grandchildren were searched by French customs: the grandchildren were sitting on 40 kilos of hashish under the back seat. The grandparents were sentenced to six years in prison.

Exploiting Spain's reputation as a popular holiday destination, caravans and mobile homes were – and still are – frequently used. Toilet and water storage tanks were reconstructed to hold two internal tanks, cooking gas cylinders were rebuilt with false bottoms; if a customs officer flushed the toilet or lit the stove, both would be seen to work normally. As most caravans are made of fibreglass and plastic, it was also easy to hide packets of hashish in the bodywork, resealing any incisions with plastic welding guns. Insulation was often replaced by hashish and, being light and with many structural cavities, caravans were also used on occasion to smuggle the more space-consuming marijuana. Another advantage of using a caravan was, because of its flimsy construction, to search it meant destroying it. Customs officers were loath to risk not finding anything and having to reimburse the owner so they tended to ignore the trailers.

Since the setting up of the European Community, smuggling drugs of all sorts has become much easier. With the removal of internal borders, the smuggler has only to get his contraband into any European country and he is free to distribute across all the member states. As many have porous and often poorly patrolled external borders with non-member countries, this is not an obstacle. Britain is somewhat protected by the natural border of the English Channel, but even this is now easily breached by the Channel Tunnel and the huge volume of traffic using it. The removal of border posts also allows migrant workers considerable freedom of movement and the ability to transport drugs with virtual impunity.

Heroin and cocaine smugglers are often armed, well connected to international organized-crime groups such as the Colombian cartels, the Chinese triads and the Russian mafia, and ruthless. Cannabis smugglers, like their cargo, are often more mellow, more laid back, less prone to violence and more likely to run than fight. The reason for this is partly historical, in that cannabis users are less likely to be criminally inclined than hard-drug addicts, and partly because the financial risk is not as great. Kilo for kilo, 40 per cent pure heroin is up to fifteen times more valuable than even the best grade hashish.

Perhaps the most famous cannabis smuggler of them all is the Englishman Howard Marks whose autobiography, *Mr Nice*, was an international bestseller. It has not gone out of print since its publication in 1996.

The son of a merchant navy captain, Marks was born and educated in South Wales. The epitome of a middle-class boy, he attended Garw Grammar School, was academically bright, appointed Head Prefect and, in 1964, went up to Balliol College, Oxford. As a student, he dressed as a Beatnik, read the Beats and began to smoke marijuana. During his holidays, he hitch-hiked around Britain and western Europe, romantically seeing himself as a sort of British Dean Moriarty or Neal Cassady and, in 1965, went to the Royal Albert Hall to hear Ginsberg and Ferlinghetti read. By the time he graduated in 1967, Marks was smoking twenty joints a day and had built up a substantial network of contacts who came to him for their cannabis or were his own suppliers. Gradually, it occurred to him that he could make a good profit by smuggling hashish himself. Going to Kabul in Afghanistan, he purchased hashish which he then carried on Pakistan International Airlines flights to London, transiting through to Shannon in Ireland with Aer Lingus. Irish customs were very lax. Cannabis use in Ireland was so low as to not be worth their bother. From there, he transported the hashish by car across the Irish Sea into Britain. As this was not considered a cannabis-smuggling route, the customs did not search the vehicles. Nicknamed Narco Polo after his frequent journeys to the Orient, by 1972 he was making so much money he had to set up front companies to launder the proceeds. At this point, he was also recruited into the British secret service because he had contacts with the IRA which was beginning to launch its terrorist military offensive against the British in Northern Ireland, partly funding their activities from drug dealing.

Expanding his smuggling operation, Marks then started sending Afghan hashish to the US hidden in the sound equipment of alleged rock groups going there on tour. His contacts in America were the Brotherhood of Eternal Love in California. In 1974, however, he was arrested in the Netherlands on drug charges and extradited to Britain where he was charged with aiding and abetting the commission of a criminal drug offence in the USA. In fact, he had narrowly avoided arrest in Newport Beach, California, the year before when he happened quite by chance to see the television news breaking the story of his courier's capture.

Given bail, Marks fled, changed his appearance, acquired an increasing number of false identities and returned to business. By this time, he was using forty-three aliases and owned twenty-five legitimate companies across the world. In July 1975, he smuggled 500 kilos of top-quality Nepalese hashish from Kathmandu to New York via Tokyo. Amongst many other cargos, he went on to run a ton of hashish onto a remote Scottish island, import Thai sticks (joints laced with opium) into Britain from Bangkok via Dublin, collaborate with the Mafia in Florida to import Colombian marijuana into the US and, in December 1979, use an ocean-going salvage tug, the *Karob*, to bring 15 tons of Colombian marijuana into the United Kingdom. In 1980, he was arrested in Suffolk and sent to Brixton prison on remand but was found not guilty at trial, having produced a Mexican secret-service officer to support his defence claim of his being a British agent. When, in the mid-1980s, publications about him started to appear, the British and US authorities were not pleased. Now based in Majorca, he was living and travelling under the assumed name of Donald Nice. (Some thought this name was chosen by Marks because it was the slang word for a dealer but this was not the case: he had purchased a redundant passport from someone of that name.) Marks was put under constant surveillance, his telephone in Britain was tapped and an associate compromised by the police and forced to 'wear a wire'. Finally, in 1988, Marks was arrested and extradited to the USA where he was convicted and sentenced to twenty-five years' imprisonment in the US Penitentiary at Terre Haute, Indiana. He served seven years of the sentence and was released in April 1995, since when he has ceased to be involved in smuggling and has become an author and international celebrity. His smuggling of cannabis might have been illegal, but many have come to regard Marks in a different light from the smugglers of harder drugs, his fame based upon his charisma and image and the fact that he was considered more a rip-roaring buccaneer who tilted his hat at the authorities than someone selling substances that would ruin lives and kill.

The history of many countries concerning cannabis echoes that of the US and Great Britain. Laws were brought in because of international agreements. There was an upsurge of cannabis use in the 1960s and a hardening of the line on drugs in the 1970s and '80s. At the same time, enquiries and commissions were held but mostly ignored by the governments instigating them.

In the Netherlands, however, a controversial policy was being adopted. Believing that if they could not stop cannabis use the next best thing was to attempt to contain it, the Dutch government reassessed their narcotics laws.

Drug laws were first introduced in the Netherlands with the Opium Act of 1919 and amended in 1928. Under this, sentencing was strict across the board for any drug but, in the 1960s, it seemed inappropriate to punish the possession of 10 grams of cannabis on the same punitive tariff as for 50 grams of heroin or morphine. Law reformers began to press for a realignment of sentencing to suit the crime. In 1972, a Dutch government commission headed by a noted psychiatrist and addiction expert, Pieter A. H. Baan, was appointed which divided illicit drugs into two categories with cannabis listed among the less dangerous. The law was then altered making possession of up to 30 grams of cannabis a misdemeanour. The figure was determined as the amount needed by an average smoker for three months' usage. Penalties for possession of larger amounts were significantly reduced but, simultaneously, those for heroin, cocaine and similar drugs were increased. After further consultation, the law was again revised in 1976 in respect of the possession and sale of cannabis, with certain provisos.

Cannabis was not legalized. It could not be because the Netherlands was a signatory to the UN Single Convention. Yet minor possession was ignored and it became permissible for specific outlets to supply and retail cannabis without prosecution. The government was being pragmatic by addressing the reality of the situation. The advantages of the *de facto* licensing of cannabis use were seen as considerable. Consumption could be controlled, drug education given, sales monitored, dealing done on officially specified premises and cannabis distribution separated from harder drugs. Furthermore, cannabis was no longer seen as deviant and anti-social by the predominantly young users.

Cannabis sales were permitted in licensed coffee shops (soon to be colloquially known as cannabis cafés) which sprang up in towns across the Netherlands. The first opened in 1972 at Weesperzijde 53 in Amsterdam and was called Mellow Yellow, after the hit song by Donovan. Some sold alcohol as well as cannabis but no other drugs were allowed. The café owners were rigorous in their application of the law. In effect, they were policing cannabis on the government's behalf. As the average cannabis café by the late 1990s had a turnover of about $450,000, which could rise to $3 million near the German border, where they could be visited by non-Dutch nationals, it is no wonder the proprietors were particularly law abiding. It was in their interest not to buck the system or strangle the goose that was laying their golden eggs.

One drawback, of course, was that although the cafés were legal, the dealers from whom the owners obtained their supplies were still criminals, so the trade was not divorced from the smuggler or organized-crime system.

The Dutch policy was unpopular with neighbouring countries which complained about it but the Netherlands government was not for turning. It maintained that an open, if technically illegal, policy reduced addiction to more dangerous drugs, allowing people to become educated in the risks involved. Without any moralistic campaigning which was certain to alienate many, particularly the young, the message that opiates and the like were highly damaging was more successfully heeded. It seemed as if considered expediency was the best weapon of control.

# 23

# THE UNIVERSAL FRIEND

WHEN JACK HERER PUBLISHED *THE EMPEROR WEARS NO CLOTHES* IN 1985, he set in motion a re-evaluation of hemp as an industrial commodity in America. Within a year, what had for many decades been seen as a corrupter of youth, promoter of crime and destroyer of life was being thought of as a possible environmental boon of unprecedented possibility. The cannabis leaf, so long a symbol of social dissent, started to appear as one of conservation.

It was ironic in the extreme that this rebirth of interest should begin in America. Although there was virtually no hemp grown, except for that producing illicit marijuana deep in the backwoods, ecologically minded businessmen began to import hemp products from overseas. At first, the level of importation was very low and limited to little more than twine, specialist rolling tobacco papers (favoured by some for joints) and sterilized bird seed. Yet, at the same time, research into the potential of hemp was being conducted.

The situation began to evolve in 1989 when a group of entrepreneurs with foresight founded Business Alliance of Commerce in Hemp (BACH). They discovered that US Customs rules specifically eliminated both sterilized seed and plant stalks from restriction. In short, if one kept clear of the THC-containing parts of the plant (and one did not import actively fertile seed), one was not breaking the law. With this realization, BACH and other environmental groups started considering hemp as an alternative source of the vital Three Fs – food, fuel and fibre.

Countries where hemp fibre was already grown and used were investigated and manufactured hemp products imported. One company was at the forefront of this development. Based in Portland, Oregon (the state with the unofficial motto *Don't Californicate Oregon*), the House of Hemp started to import Chinese hemp canvas which was retailed to furniture makers and carpet weavers as well as to hat, bag and niche-market tailors. Willie Nelson, the famous Texan Country and Western singer, endorsed a range of cotton–hemp mix fabric shirts and started promoting hemp at his concerts for Farm Aid, a charity originally proposed by Bob Dylan to give support to America's small family-owned farms in the face of unequal competition from corporate farming syndicates.

Interest escalated. The American Hemp Council was founded in Los Angeles in 1991, organizing rallies and trade fairs at which hemp was promoted and products sold. The firms running stands soon expanded their horizons to exhibit at environmental, craft and agricultural shows and fairs. They also attended large music gatherings. Within a year, there were two dozen companies trading, drawing much attention to themselves and hemp. The fact that this was the plant that produced marijuana was played down. With the growth in business and interest, an industry trade journal appeared in 1993 entitled *HempWorld*, to be followed the next year by the foundation of a trade association, the Hemp Industries Association (HIA), which was dedicated to representing the interests of the hemp industry and promoting research into the potential of the plant. In addition, as its mission statement declared, it set out to *maintain and defend the integrity of hemp products and advocate and support socially respon-sible and environmentally sound business practices*. By 1996, there were over three hundred American companies manufacturing a staggering range of hemp-based products including luggage, clothing, cosmetics and soap, blankets and pillows, a wide range of paper and cards, seed grain, skate- and surfboards, rope and yarn, textiles and toys.

For all their success, the hemp companies were still faced with a major problem. They could import hemp materials but they could not grow the plant under the Marihuana Tax Act, which did not differentiate between high-THC-containing plants and those cultivars that had been bred with virtually none. As far as Anslinger had been concerned, and as DEA policy still affirmed, hemp was marijuana and therefore anathema.

Then, in 1996, an unlikely hero appeared who would have driven Anslinger to paroxysms of rage. It was the film star Woody Harrelson, who overtly planted four certified industrial hemp seeds on his land in Lee County, Kentucky, on 1 June, videotaping the act. His intention was to provoke the authorities and test the state law. He was arrested on the misdemeanour charge of possessing marijuana and set off on a four-year-long legal battle to force the state legislature's hand. At the time of his arrest, he told the press, *Industrial hemp can help meet our fibre needs while also revitalizing our struggling rural economies*. The irony of his action and its location could not have been lost. Kentucky, which had produced twenty-four million pounds of hemp a year just over a century before, was now reduced to four plants illegally sown on a film star's rural property.

After several court hearings, in which Harrelson argued that hemp prohibition was unconstitutional because it did not distinguish between hemp grown for marijuana or that for fibre, the denouement was reached on 24 August 2000. Going into court for trial, Harrelson was nervous but he had on his defence team an ally of considerable experience in the form of Louis B. Nunn, a former Republican state governor and state court judge. The prosecution offered a last-minute plea bargain of a month in jail and a five-hundred-dollar fine but Harrelson rejected it, arriving in court dressed in a suit made of hemp cloth. The prosecution asked the jury for a sentence of not less than thirty days and the maximum fine of five hundred dollars. The maximum custodial sentence possible was a year. The jury deliberated for just twenty-five minutes and declared Harrelson not guilty. The trial over, Nunn told the press, *Now it's time to start promoting the growth of hemp so we can have a great economic future in Kentucky. We need to educate people about the distinction between marijuana and hemp . . . We're already losing tobacco and farmers are suffering, and this would be an alternative crop*. Needless to say, the local press headline read 'Woody Harrelson's Trial Goes to Pot'.

Harrelson is not alone in being at the end of the vagaries of the US legal system as regards cannabis. In August 2000, in contravention of treaties existing between the US government and certain native American Indian tribes, armed DEA agents entered the Oglala Lakota Pine Ridge Indian Reservation to destroy two hemp crops near Porcupine, South Dakota. No differentiation was made, of course, between hemp being cultivated for fibres and that for drugs. The hemp was in fact to be turned into fibre for use in a community economic development building project being conducted by the Slim Butte Land Association. It did not escape many of the critics of this action that it took place less than twenty miles from Wounded Knee, the site of the infamous massacre of Sioux Indians in December 1890.

Since Harrelson's public planting, there have been signs of a gradual shift in policy in some American states. In 1999, the first hemp-growing permit to be allowed in the US for four decades was issued in Hawaii. This has been followed by legislation being introduced in ten states to support research and cultivation. The Marihuana Tax Act, however, stays in force.

America might have lost its hemp industry as a result of the Act but elsewhere, countries continued to cultivate hemp. In 1995, the UN Food and Agriculture Organization estimated there were 650,000 acres under hemp in China (the main world supplier of hemp fibre to the industrialized countries), India, Russia, Romania, Hungary, Canada, Australia, Great Britain, the Netherlands, Poland, the Ukraine, Korea, Germany, France and Spain.

What made this large-scale farming of hemp possible, without creating a massive upsurge in marijuana production, was the development of cultivars with exceedingly low levels of THC, the agreed maximum limit of which is internationally set at 0.3 per cent.

France was the only country in western Europe that had an unbroken hemp-producing industry going back decades and only interrupted by the Second World War. In the mid-1980s, Spain began the cultivation of hemp and, early in 1993, the British government followed this lead, lifting its ban so that UK farmers could *gain a share of the market currently occupied by our EC partners*. In other words, here was a potentially lucrative market from which British farmers were loath to be excluded. They were actually at a distinct disadvantage not only because they might miss out on the earning power of hemp but also because, under the Common Agricultural Policy agreed between European Union nations, hemp carried a subsidy.

No sooner was the restriction lifted than a company called Hemcore Ltd contracted thirty farmers in East Anglia to grow approved strains of industrial hemp. Since then, it has expanded to contract over eighty farms across southern England, the hemp core (or pith) being used for animal bedding with the fibre being sold into the paper and insulation industries. In the long term, it is intended to branch out into hemp grain seed production.

The 1998 European hemp harvest was divided between ten countries, France accounting for over half the total with Spain being the next biggest producer. It was found that hemp is an ideal rotation crop which improves soil friability and quality, does not deplete soil nutrients, absorbs heavy-metal soil contaminants, suppresses weeds and is cheaper to grow than most agricultural plants because it does not require expensive fertilizers (being self-mulching) and is largely disease- and pest-free, requiring little or no herbicide and pesticide application which in turn endears it to ecologists and conservation-minded farmers. It is also quick growing, reaching up to five metres in 110 days and yielding between 3 and 8 tons of dry stalks per acre. Almost the entire plant can be utilized. Although in the past it had been a labour-intensive crop, modern agricultural machinery alleviates this problem, especially when the fibres are dew ret or tank ret with newly developed enzymes which speed up the biodegrading process.

It is estimated there are over twenty-five thousand products that can be made from hemp and the scale of the increase in its use can be shown by world trade statistics. In 1993, it was estimated the global turnover in hemp was five million dollars. In 1995, this sum had risen to seventy-five million dollars and, in 2000, to just below two hundred million dollars.

As well as being environmentally beneficial, hemp has distinct advantages over its main competitor fibres, especially cotton which is prone to a multitude of diseases and pest attack and requires heavy fertilization. Hemp fibres can be up to four or five metres long, whilst those of cotton are rarely more than half a centimetre, and they have up to eight times the tensile strength. Always thought of as coarse, hemp can be spun more finely than cotton or wool and yet can still be just as easily fast-colour dyed. Whilst it has been used for durable work clothing since the nineteenth century, it has more recently been used in designer fabrics. Ralph Lauren began using it in the mid-1980s whilst in 1997 Giorgio Armani added jeans, jackets and women's clothing to the Emporio Armani catalogue. Calvin Klein used hemp linen in 1995 for designer duvet and pillow covers.

Yet hemp has far greater advantages when viewed against the environmental destruction caused by deforestation. Wood is used as building material, fuel and as pulp in paper making. Half of the trees felled worldwide are pulped for paper. A utilizable tree can take forty years to reach felling size and requires a comparatively substantial area in which to grow. Virgin forests, euphemistically called the lungs of the world, can take a hundred years to regenerate. A tree is also prone to pest and disease damage and as much as 20 per cent of it is wasted in the processing and preparation of the product. Hemp, of which the whole plant except the roots may be used, provides an immediate and ecologically friendly alternative to deforestation.

From the time when the Chinese first made hemp paper until the middle of the nineteenth century, much paper was made from hemp or a hemp–cloth amalgam. As recently as the 1940s, textiles made from hemp have been used in paper making in Europe. In the immediate post-war years when paper pulp was in short supply, the British paper manufacturer Robert Fletcher and Sons, now a subsidiary of the Imperial Tobacco Group, purchased large numbers of Nazi concentration camp inmates' uniforms which were made of hemp and converted them into paper. Since then, however, textiles have ceased to be used in paper manufacture because synthetic yarns are inappropriate to the manufacturing processes.

Fewer than three dozen hemp paper pulp mills now operate anywhere in the world and most of these are in India and China. They produce about 150,000 tons of pulp annually between them, against the output of one wood pulp mill which can produce 250,000 tons in the same time.

Hemp pulp is usually manufactured into filter bags for vacuum cleaners, tea and coffee bags, fine-art drawing and watercolour parchments, banknotes and cigarette papers. Imperial Tobacco owns the famous Rizla brand, most favoured by marijuana smokers everywhere.

Historically a fibre or pulp source, developments are now underway which considerably extend hemp's viable uses. As long ago as the 1930s, Ford Motor Company research-and-development staff realized that hemp hydrocarbons could be used and were successful in extracting creosote, ethyl acetate and methanol from hemp in a cracking plant at Iron Mountain, 250 miles north of Chicago. It was some years before Ford publicized his work in this field, when the bodywork of a car was made from hemp and sisal fibres and wheat straw bonded by hemp resin. The substance resembled modern fibreglass in appearance, was a third of the weight of steel but was claimed to have ten times its integral strength. As an experiment the 'plastic' was decades ahead of its time but was not developed further because of the stringent restrictions imposed by the Marihuana Tax Act.

Further research in recent years has centred upon hemp hurds, the broken sections of the core of the plant. As well as the animal bedding material produced by Hemcore in Britain, it can also be used in fine filters (such as in anti-pollen and gas masks), bandages and as a substrate in market gardening or hydroponic horticulture. It is also very useful as a source of cellulose in the making of rayon and cellophane.

Modern building materials, being increasingly environmentally friendly either by customer demand or by legislation, are constantly being reinvented. Block, chip and fibre boards are now common but, when made with wood, these lack strength. Medium density fibreboard (MDF), a cellulose composite often used in lieu of wood and made from wood waste or wood cellulose bound by resin, similarly lacks strength, relying for its integrity on the quality of the resin. When made with hemp, however, with its long fibres, it is so strong it may be used not only for ordinary carpentry but for flooring and roofing. It can support up to three times the load of wood-based MDF but can flex without fracturing. A French firm, Isochanvre, which started trading in 1989, now markets hemp-based building materials for walls, cladding, insulation, acoustic control and weather protection. It has even built brand-new houses either entirely out of Isochanvre (which is also the trade name of its hempen product) or Isochanvre on wood or brick frames. The material is also now being used to renovate ancient and historic buildings across western Europe. New buildings made with Isochanvre are not only environmentally sound but can also be built at affordable prices and offer cheap but substantial residential housing. In America, hemp fibre has been mixed with a hemp resin and stone powder to create lightweight building bricks which can be cut to any size or shape with an electric saw. They are impermeable and so strong they can be used as foundation stones to domestic frame houses. The stone powder is only added as a colorant to make them look like concrete blocks.

Hemp seed is a valuable source of vegetable oil which can be refined into diesel fuel, or thinned into use as flammable fuel oil or non-viscous lubricant. The plant stalks can be used as a burning fuel (much as wood might be) and experiments have discovered that these can be thermally processed to produce a natural gas. This could have a very significant impact in Third World countries where deforestation occurs due to the demand for firewood. There is, however, a drawback to growing hemp as a hydrocarbon fuel source. The plant is too valuable for its other properties for it to be used as a fuel source and the acreage required to address the modern need for petrol or diesel would be impractical. It has been calculated that 21 per cent of America's current farmland would need to be put down to hemp just to equal that nation's present fossil-fuel consumption.

Hemp oil has other applications too. It is used in cosmetics as an emollient, a substance that softens hair or skin, causing it to retain water by stopping evaporation. Whilst other natural oils such as almond, coconut and olive oil have been used for centuries in this way, these are expensive to produce and modern emollients such as butyl stearate, zinc oxide, petrolatum or diglycol laurate have tended to be relied upon instead. Hemp oil offers a cheaper and more ecologically conscious alternative. Anita Roddick's famous Body Shop chain launched a range of hemp-based beauty products in 1998 with the slogans *It's hope not dope* and *Hemp revival for skin survival* printed on the packaging and marketing material alongside a cannabis leaf.

Despite this, and the fact that the products had no THC content at all, the company still fell foul of the law. In Hong Kong and Italy, the authorities objected to the use of a marijuana leaf on posters but the ultimate act of stupidity and hypocrisy occurred in France where hemp farms are fairly common and, in some provinces, line the sides of the Routes Nationales with plants up to six metres high in full view of passing traffic. On 28 August 1998, French police raided the Body Shop store in Aix-en-Provence, confiscating all products in the new hemp range. The authorities claimed the promotional material for the hemp products (which did feature a cannabis leaf) encouraged drug abuse. Roddick's retort was, *I know the French have perfected the art of irony in the past, but right now I'd like to see them get a better grip on the future.* The paradox of the situation was further compounded by the fact that, in the USA where hemp control is at its most extreme, her hemp range of toiletries had gone on sale with great success without any official objection, and the hemp oil used in the cosmetics was partially sourced in France. Although the police report reached the local prosecutor, no further action was taken and the matter was conveniently forgotten by the authorities.

Research into hemp as a foodstuff has, in recent years, revealed that the seed contains a wealth of minerals, vitamins (especially vitamin A), amino acids and unsaturated fats and is, on average, 28 per cent protein. Included in this is a globulin known as edestin which is similar to the globulin in human blood plasma which is essential to the operation of the human immune system. The unsaturated fat content includes the omega 6 linoleic (LA) and omega 3 linolenic (LNA) fatty acids: 15 grams of hemp oil provides the adult daily dietary requirement of these essential compounds.

It is fair to say that hemp seed as a nutritional substance is potentially of considerable importance but it is not as readily available as it might be. Cost of production aside, in the US, the government's insistence that hemp seed be sterilized affects its quality. Imported seed has not only to be rendered incapable of germination but is also fumigated with methyl bromide which is thought to affect its chemical composition. The argument given by the DEA for this treatment is that any substance with even the most minute trace of THC has to be regarded as a prohibited material. As of March 2002, all food products containing hemp seed or hemp oil in the US had to be destroyed or exported and all production or distribution of them halted, an appeal being lodged against this decision in the San Francisco federal appeals court by HAI and seven food companies.

Japan has no such official paranoia. In July 1999, on the third floor of the Kitazawa Building in the fashionable Shimokita district of Tokyo, the Café-Restaurant Asa opened for business. Food with hemp additives is served on hemp table mats while a browsing library of hemp publications is available for customers. On the menu are, amongst other dishes created for the restaurant, *kenchijiru* soup (of which the base is hemp milk), *gamodoki* (a fried fish cake with hemp sauce), hemp beer made under licence in Niigata and hemp-seed crackers. The proprietor, Koichi Maeda, claims his establishment is unique but, in fact, hemp seed has long been used as a constituent of Japanese *shichimi* pepper.

Jack Herer claims that hemp could save the world. This is somewhat optimistic and yet it has been assessed that if hemp were to be used as the only source of natural fibre or pulp, the deforestation of the planet would be completely halted and the reliance on hydrocarbons created by the international petrochemical industry to make modern plastics and other materials would at least be halved. Just growing hemp on polluted former industrial 'brown field' sites would reclaim the soil in urban areas, permitting safe re-use of the land whilst avoiding the huge costs involved in chemical soil-decontamination treatment. The beneficial effects upon the environment would be very considerable indeed.

To take advantage of the environmental and commercial windfall hemp offers will, however, require a considerable shift in political thinking, both internationally and within nations like the USA where the legacy of prohibitionists and bigots still clouds an issue that has changed out of all proportion with scientific advance.

It may be premature to think that hemp might save the world but it is not an overstatement to say that it can save lives.

# 24

# THE BALM OF HOPE

THE POTENTIAL OF HEMP AS A HEALING PLANT HAS BEEN KNOWN FOR centuries wherever cannabis was grown and it is still a folk remedy in many countries. Chinese herbal doctors frequently prescribe *huo ma ren*, which is hemp seed, as a laxative and to lower fever. Hemp oil is also a common laxative in China and used on open wounds and burns as an antiseptic as well as being ingested as a cough remedy. Others claim that it eases rheumatic pain and migraine and suppresses internal pain caused by peptic ulcers and cancer.

In India, cannabis is extensively used in the traditional Ayurvedic ('Knowledge of Life') system of medicine which is allied to the Hindu religion. A tenth-century medical treatise, the *Anandakanda*, which is commonly referenced today by Ayurvedic doctors, calls cannabis either *vijaya* or *bhanga* and suggests its inclusion in many standard preparations. The list of ailments it is used to treat ranges from diarrhoea to diabetes, tuberculosis to elephantiasis, asthma to haemorrhoids, anaemia and even rabies. This is to give it an almost miraculous capability but it must be realized that it is often seen not as a cure but as a palliative addressing some of the symptoms, easing the patient rather than healing them.

Elsewhere, cannabis features in Islamic Unani Tibbi medicine to be found in most Muslim countries or communities and in Africa where many sub-Saharan tribes still use it as a painkiller in childbirth or even as a treatment for snake bites. In the latter, it does not work as an anti-toxin but as an antiseptic at the site of a wound.

Throughout Europe and in the Americas, cannabis has a long tradition as a herbal medicine but any investigation of its efficacy was well and truly thwarted by Anslinger and his policies and opinions, which were adopted not only by the USA but also, through his role as a representative to the United Nations, by many other countries. For decades, cannabis research was prohibited or so burdened with bureaucracy as to make it impractical. This situation, however, began to change in the 1960s, caused by two events. The first was Anslinger's retirement in 1962, the second a concern at the rise in hallucinatory-drug use and a realization that little was known about it.

Amongst the first major research conducted was that by Andrew Weil and Norman E. Zinberg at the Psychopharmacology Laboratory of the School of Medicine at the University of Boston. Their study concentrated upon the effects of intoxication and their results were published in 1968 under the title *Clinical and Psychological Effects of Marijuana in Man*. At around the same time, occasional stories started to surface from recreational users about how cannabis assisted with certain medical conditions. Spread initially by word of mouth, they were gradually given wider credence in the popular or underground press.

Bit by bit, scientific interest was aroused. Researchers started to test the effectiveness of cannabis as anecdotally claimed in the nineteenth century, to find that the claims were by and large valid.

Through the 1970s and '80s, as much by chance as scientific design, people became increasingly aware of medicinal uses and cannabis started to acquire a sort of technological-age folk tradition. Patients undergoing chemotherapy for cancer found cannabis was an effective anti-emetic, counteracting the nausea of the treatment. It also reduced pain and stimulated appetite. For sufferers of muscular dystrophy (MD) and multiple sclerosis (MS) in addition to other spastic ailments, it was found to be a very efficient anti-convulsant. Epileptics, paraplegics and quadriplegics also discovered it helped them to control their muscular spasticity whilst arthritics used it as an analgesic muscle relaxant. Not only was cannabis found to be effective on its own but many sufferers came to realize that, if used in conjunction with regular prescribed drugs, it enabled them to take very much reduced doses of these drugs which were otherwise harmful or had distressing side effects.

By the mid-1990s, large numbers of MS, MD and arthritis sufferers throughout the world were using marijuana or hashish and thereby criminalizing themselves, their only source being illegal dealers. In one case in

Britain, that made press headlines and illustrated the sad irony of the situation, a policewoman and former drugs-squad officer, invalided out of her police force by MS, was buying cannabis from those she had previously arrested. Angered by the attitude of the law towards medicinal cannabis use, she did not turn in her 'new' acquaintances.

Statements from cancer patients addressing the issue of marijuana use are not only touching but highly pertinent. The difference, one cancer sufferer has said, between not using cannabis and using it is that without cannabis one is dying of cancer whilst with it one is living with cancer. This is the nub of the matter. Marijuana is not a cure but it alleviates suffering and allows the terminally ill patient a significantly better quality of life.

In one instance, cannabis almost offers a cure. There exists a Jamaican folk story that states that a concoction of rum and marijuana aids night vision. Fishermen were said to use it. Researchers at the Department of Pharmacology at the University of the West Indies investigated the tale. They discovered that the alcohol in the rum dissolved a constituent called canasol from the marijuana which greatly reduced intra-ocular pressure thus improving night vision. The application of this in the treatment of glaucoma, a disease of the eye in which the flow of the aqueous humour is restricted with pressure building up within the eyeball causing permanent damage and blindness, was soon realized. Nothing cures glaucoma except surgery but *ganja* can halt the symptoms as effectively as other expensive miotic drugs. In addition, inhaled vapours of cannabis have also been found to dilate bronchial passages and aid asthma sufferers, whilst ingested cannabis can treat insomnia and depression.

The dilemma facing legislators and medical practitioners concerning the pros and cons of permitting the medicinal use of natural herbal cannabis (as medicinal marijuana is often referred to) is really quite simple. As a British doctor, Dr William Notcutt, a consultant anaesthetist at the James Paget Hospital in Great Yarmouth and director of the hospital's Pain Relief Clinic, stated in 2000, there appears to be a Puritanism concerning the use of cannabis in medicine, a reluctance to use it in case it leads to intoxication and a psycho-active reaction. This objection seems irrational to him. His argument is that, if someone is in pain and depressed, living a miserable life because of pain, why should a medicine that made them happier be proscribed. He pointed out that anti-depressants like Prozac are prescribed almost with abandon and yet they are also mind-altering drugs with a risk of severe side effects. Marijuana has few contra-indications and yet it is prohibited.

Considerable research effort has been put into the creation of synthetic THC and cannabinoids. What made this possible was the synthesis of THC by Israeli chemist Raphael Mechoulam and a co-worker in the early 1980s, the 1988 discovery of the cannabinoid receptor system by a research team in the USA led by Allyn Howlett, and the discovery of anandamine (from the Sanskrit word for bliss), the natural substance that activates and binds to the receptor, by William Devane (a member of Howlett's team) and Mechoulam in 1992.

The results of this research are extensive and on-going but some drugs containing synthetic THC have already been developed from it, although not entirely satisfactorily. They can have considerable and alarming side effects and in some patients offer no benefits whatsoever. It seems likely that synthetic THC cannot offer what herbal cannabis can because the natural substance has other factors in it without which the THC is not effective or acts differently. Some work has gone into developing extracts of cannabis but this, although more efficacious than synthetic THC, still does not have the efficacy of the raw natural substance. Furthermore, as some researchers admit, the patients are hardly likely to purchase an expensive medicine when they can get an equal or better reaction from smoking a cheap joint, even though that is illegal. (Those in favour of cannabis being medically available argue, with some validity, that some-one dying of cancer is hardly likely to give much thought to being arrested on a misdemeanour charge.)

Of course, all this research effort is being expended to prevent the user from becoming intoxicated – in other words, 'high' – which, under the UN Single Convention, is unacceptable.

Regardless of its therapeutic potential, there is reluctance amongst some doctors and patients to use herbal cannabis yet this is often based upon ignorance of the subject. Whilst prolonged smoking might do respiratory harm (as would inhaling any fine particles), it is accepted that cannabis is far safer than most drugs. Overdosing on it, the worry some doctors have because it is hard to assess the potency of one sample over another, is virtually impossible. Cannabis has a lethal-to-effective-dose ratio of 40,000 to 1. For aspirin, for example, the ratio is 10 to 1.

Research may be proving otherwise, but many countries and the United Nations refuse to accept that cannabis has a medical application. Particularly in America, the line being taken is strictly enforced although NORML and other pro-marijuana lobby groups have sought to force the government to reclassify cannabis so that doctors can prescribe it. Under the US Controlled Substances Act of 1970, it was listed in Schedule I, the most restrictive category forbidding its use in medicine. In 1972, NORML began a legal battle but this ended in vain in 1994. The DEA won the day.

In the meantime, many patients suffering chronic pain took the law into their own hands. In 1975 Robert C. Randall, a glaucoma patient, was arrested with his partner, Alice O'Leary, for cultivating cannabis at their home in Sarasota, Florida. When tried, he offered as his defence a plea of medical necessity. Where NORML had failed, Randall won, as a result of which the US government had to set up the Investigative New Drug (IND) programme to supply marijuana legally to qualifying patients. Acquiring qualification, however, was a deliberately lengthy process intended to deter applicants and their doctors. The marijuana officially provided to Randall was grown on a University of Mississippi farm, made into joints at a government facility in North Carolina then sent in sealed tins to a chemist near Randall's home. He found it was of poor quality, lacking, as he put it, *the fine, almost perfumed taste of street marijuana.*

After Randall's court victory, some state governments started to legislate in favour of medicinal cannabis use. New Mexico became the first to do so after a cancer patient admitted his cannabis use to his elected state representative. The authorities heard testimony from other patients and their physicians and, in 1978, ruled in favour of controlled prescription. Sadly, the originating patient, Lynn Pierson, did not live to benefit from his action.

In 1992, after a rush of applications from AIDS sufferers, the administration of President George Bush shut down the IND programme, the director, James O. Mason, stating, *If it is perceived that the Public Health Service is going around giving marijuana to folks, there would be a perception that this stuff can't be so bad.* At the time of its cessation, fewer than two dozen patients had qualified for state-issued marijuana in the entire USA.

Through the 1990s, more terminally ill cancer, arthritis and MS patients broke US federal law. Some were jailed. In one case, a paraplegic was sentenced to life imprisonment plus sixteen years. In another, William Foster of Tulsa, Oklahoma, severely crippled with rheumatoid arthritis, was sent down for ninety-three years for growing ten cannabis plants and fifty-six cuttings, despite his defence proving that the Society of Neuroscience in Washington, DC, had shown marijuana to be an effective treatment for his disease.

Faced with such federal intransigence and insensitivity, there sprang up in some states cannabis buyers' clubs. Members could join after providing personal identification and a bona fide doctor's certificate stating that marijuana would be of benefit to their condition. California, in particular, had a large number of such clubs founded after November 1996 when the state passed its Compassionate Use Act after the public had voted for it. The clubs being technically still illegal, federal authorities have closed down every one they have uncovered. This has not, however, prevented states from considering or passing medical marijuana legislation. The DEA has opposed all this legislation on the grounds that marijuana is too dangerous for safe medicinal use and those states where marijuana is issued medicinally have been warned that they are not protected from federal prosecution. Where the clubs have been shut down, patients have been obliged, as before, to resort to consorting with criminals to buy their supply. There has been, however, a development in that, in late 2001, the DEA sanctioned two neurologists in the University of California at San Diego Medical Center to conduct a research study into the application of marijuana in cases of AIDS-related neuropathy and multiple sclerosis.

This pattern of prohibition of medicinal marijuana, and challenges to it, has been repeated in other countries. In Britain, the British Medical Association (BMA) recommended in 1997 that medicinal cannabis be made legal. Twelve months later on 11 November 1998, the House of Lords Select Committee on Science and Technology released a report entitled *Cannabis: the Scientific and Medical Evidence*, having taken both verbal and written testimony from physicians and patients. The report included the statement that clinical trials of cannabis treatment for multiple sclerosis and chronic pain should be urgently conducted and the recommendation that cannabis be removed from Schedule 1 to Schedule 2 of the Misuse of Drugs Regulations, allowing it to be provided by doctors under prescription. The Government rejected it.

In reality, however, many British courts have tended to take a relaxed view of the law. A number of chronically ill patients have been arrested and tried for growing cannabis plants but have been found not guilty at trial by jury. In July 1999, Colin Davies (who, on the occasion of the royal opening of the Lowry art gallery in Salford in 2000, presented the Queen with a cannabis plant made into a bouquet) was acquitted at Manchester Crown Court – for the second time in just over a year – of cultivation and supplying cannabis which he had been growing as an analgesic. A former carpenter, he had severely injured his back in an industrial accident in 1994 but found the drugs he was prescribed for the chronic pain he had continuously experienced ever since gave him muscle spasms and made him nauseous. He raised the plants in his apartment.

After his first acquittal, at the trial for which his defence had been one of medical necessity, Davies founded the Medical Cannabis Co-operative, a British equivalent of the Californian cannabis clubs, the aim being to supply cannabis to multiple sclerosis, cancer and paraplegia victims on a non–profit-making basis. The plants grown were from seeds of known high-THC-content strains. There was no subterfuge involved and, once word of the co-operative reached the police, they raided Davies' home in Stockport, Cheshire, confiscating twenty-six plants, growing equipment and the co-operative members' list. When he was acquitted for the second time, to cheers from terminally ill customers in the public gallery of the court, Paul Flynn, the Member of Parliament for the Welsh constituency of Newport West, a former industrial chemist and a dedicated campaigner for the legalization of medical cannabis, proclaimed the verdict illustrated *the common-sense of the jury in overcoming an outdated law*. In the summer of 2001, another man was sent to trial for the second time for growing cannabis in his garage to give to his wife who was crippled by arthritis. He was given a two-year conditional discharge with a warning from the court that a third offence would incur a custodial sentence.

There is a humorous side to the tale of Davies' plight. When he presented the Queen with her bouquet, there was a police officer standing very close by on crowd control. The Queen smiled warmly at Davies, graciously accepted the gift, and handed it to an equerry. He, in turn, passed it to the chauffeur of the royal limousine to place in the car with other floral tributes. Had the policeman known what was going on and arrested Davies, a hilarious chain of events would have legally presented itself. Davies would have been guilty by law of distribution. In turn, Her Majesty the Queen would have been technically guilty of possession and, by handing the bouquet to the equerry, also of distribution.

Parliament may have chosen to dismiss the House of Lords report but research into medicinal cannabis continues apace. In April 2000, the British Medical Research Council (MRC) funded clinical trials run by Dr John Zajicek of the University of Plymouth Postgraduate Medical School in partnership with the local regional National Health Service hospital, the study directed at MS sufferers. Twenty months later, MRC-funded clinical trials were expanded to include terminal cancer victims. In the spring of 2000, Notcutt commenced trials of cannabis-based medicines at his hospital. With a small group of patients suffering pain from inoperable nerve damage, he found 80 per cent received some easing of pain with a few experiencing almost total relief.

Other trials were soon to follow at the Rivermead Rehabilitation Centre in Oxford, the Princess Elizabeth Hospital on the island of

Guernsey and the National Hospital for Neurology and Neurosurgery in London, the latter receiving a grant from the Medicinal Cannabis Research Foundation (MCRF).

All the trials have run with the assistance of GW Pharmaceuticals, a company founded in Salisbury, Wiltshire, in 1998 by Drs Geoffrey Guy and Brian Whittle, to develop a range of therapeutic medicines derived from cannabis to meet patient needs in a wide range of indications. The licence issued to Dr Guy to permit him to grow forty thousand cannabis plants stipulated that his cultivation site, which is under glass, be at a secret location, ringed by high-security electric fencing and patrolled by guard dogs. Dr Guy is consequently the only person in Britain who is legally allowed to grow cannabis with a higher than 0.3 per cent THC content. Ironically, the company's head office and research facility is on the Porton Down Science Park, close to Britain's secret biological warfare laboratories.

GW Pharmaceuticals is attempting to develop an extract of marijuana which is delivered by mouth spray and intended to treat multiple sclerosis, rheumatoid arthritis and spinal-cord injuries. The spray is used because smoking is not suitable for all patients and ingestion too un-reliable. Another branch of the research is to try to produce a cannabis-based analgesic which does not cause hallucination or intoxi-cation. (An indication of what the future might hold for medicinal cannabis is shown by the firm's share dealings. When the company floated on the London Stock Exchange in 2001, its flotation was over-subscribed six times. Within a year, an ordinary one penny share was trading at £1.10.)

In May 2002, the first cannabis-based drugs to be developed were delivered to the British government's National Institute for Clinical Excellence (somewhat incongruously known as NICE) for evaluation as a painkiller in lieu of morphine. Even so, supporters of medical cannabis have expressed misgivings. Should cannabis be passed for medicinal use, it will still be illegal unless obtained from a registered supplier who will, in turn, have to acquire their stock from drug companies. Whilst this means the quality or strength of the drug will be standardized, it also means that, as some objectors believe, the drug companies will have hijacked what is in fact an ancient and natural folk remedy. It is also believed by some that the pharmaceutical multinationals are secretly lobbying governments to keep cannabis on a restricted drug schedule so as to keep it exclusive and maintain their monopoly on whatever they might develop in the future. Rumours have also circulated that some companies are seeking to patent the natural constituents of cannabis.

Irrespective of the legality of the situation, a number of British doctors have for some years recommended their patients to use cannabis, if they can find a supplier. This, of course, is not difficult. Most towns in Britain have a local Mr Nice in a pub: it is just a matter of knowing which one. In 2001, it was unofficially estimated that about three thousand MS sufferers in Great Britain used marijuana medicinally.

Some countries have already cleared cannabis for medicinal application. The government of New South Wales in Australia has, since November 2000, permitted the terminally ill to grow up to five cannabis plants for personal use. In Belgium, cannabis is permitted to treat the side effects of chemotherapy, glaucoma, the symptoms of AIDS and MS but it may only be administered in a hospital, on a trial basis and under continual review. Canada has also lifted restriction on growing and taking medicinal cannabis for patients for whom other drugs cause discomfort. For those who cannot grow a plant, the state health service will supply them with marijuana. The decision was made after an AIDS victim successfully pleaded in court that the prohibition on his using marijuana as a medicine was an infringement of his civil rights. There are provisos, however. The patient must have less than a year's life expectancy, be certificated by a doctor and two corroborating medical experts and be suffering from a specific list of ailments including AIDS, MS, cancer and several other incurable degenerative conditions. The Canadian federal government has contracted a Saskatoon-based firm, Prairie Plant Systems, to grow pharmaceutical marijuana to be issued by the national health service. The product, to be worth six million Canadian dollars over the five-year contract period, is deliberately spelt marihuana – as opposed to the now more common marijuana – the letter *h* standing, they say, for health.

The plants are grown under artificial sunlight in subterranean chambers 1000 feet under Flin Flon, Manitoba, in what were once the galleries of copper and zinc mines operated by the Hudson Bay Mining & Smelting Company. The environment is computer controlled and the staff as closely monitored as those in diamond mines, with random security checks and full RCMP vetting. However, in January 2002 it was reported that there had been a hold-up because of the UN Single Convention. The UN Office for Drug Control and Crime Prevention has complained that, although the Single Convention allows for countries to use restricted substances for scientific or medical purposes, Canada has yet to produce *conclusive evidence of* [the] *medical usefulness of marijuana*. In the meantime, a Canadian civil-rights lawyer in Vancouver has pointed out that the Canadian constitution prevents the country from being a signatory to any international agreement that affects the civil rights of a Canadian citizen. Canada has also been embroiled in a cannabis trade war. In 2001, the government of Cameroon, which is an illegal cannabis-producing country, announced it was legalizing medicinal cannabis but importing it from Canada. Local illicit growers were infuriated.

In the Netherlands, the ill have been able to buy cannabis in one of the many cannabis cafés for well over a decade. For those who would or could not go to a café, a company called Maripharm started packaging cannabis in 1994 but the Dutch government moved against this and, in an attempt to further regulate medicinal use, acted in 2001 to prepare the way to permit chemists to supply medicinal marijuana against a doctor's prescription, paid for by the state under the country's health-care system.

Whatever legal or scientific successes or pitfalls may arise in the future, it is certain that the use of medicinal marijuana will increase. Dr Lester Grinspoon, Associate Professor Emeritus of Psychiatry at Harvard University Medical School, one of the world's leading exponents of and experts on cannabis, states that it will eventually be commonly used by millions.

When this happens, Grinspoon declares, it will alter the public perception of cannabis and bring into question the attitude and dogma of governments such as that of the USA which has doggedly opposed the idea of medicinal marijuana because it is supposedly a dangerous drug, as evil as heroin or cocaine. The legacy of Harry J. Anslinger will come under intense scrutiny and when *people learn that its harmfulness has been greatly exaggerated and its usefulness underestimated, the pressure will increase for drastic change in the way we, as a society, deal with this drug.*

# THE INDUSTRY OF DREAMS
# AND DOLLARS

ACCORDING TO THE UNITED NATIONS INTERNATIONAL DRUG CONTROL Programme (UNDCP), the agency charged with overseeing the international control of narcotic and psychotropic drugs, cannabis is the most widely produced, trafficked and used illicit drug on earth, accounting for over 50 per cent of all customs seizures. Little firm knowledge exists, however, of the true extent of cannabis cultivation or the statistics involved. Estimates of global production run from 10,000 to 300,000 tons per annum but the actual figure is guessed to be between 30,000 and 50,000 tons. In the 1990s, 120 countries reported cannabis being cultivated – that is, 65 per cent of all UN nation states – compared to 20 per cent growing opium poppies and 4 per cent coca bushes. The economic value of the annual crop cannot be even guestimated, but it certainly goes to many billions of dollars.

Despite international pressure and eradication initiatives, the producer countries continue to meet the annually increasing worldwide demand, each producing either hashish or marijuana.

In 1995, the main producers of hashish were Morocco (35 per cent), Pakistan (30 per cent), Lebanon (20 per cent), India and Nepal (5 per cent) and Afghanistan (5 per cent), with the remaining 5 per cent coming from various minor sources such as Kazakhstan and Kyrgyzstan. Of the 772 tons of hashish sequestered worldwide, approximately 400 tons was of Moroccan origin whilst 50 per cent of all hashish seizures occurred in Europe.

Morocco, which has filled the vacuum in hashish supplies caused by the disintegration of Afghanistan, trades widely not only with Europe but also the Middle East and North America. Nationally, so much hashish is produced in Morocco that the local tradition of smoking *kif* has waned, with the preference to smoke just hashish increasing.

Throughout the 1980s, the Moroccan authorities took few steps to suppress the trade and cultivation became even more extensive in the Rif Mountains. The wealth this has generated is considerable and standards of living, especially around Ketama, have been raised beyond expectation for many land-owners, traders and farmers. Sadly, the quality of the product has deteriorated with the rush to make a quick buck. Once considered amongst the best hashish in the world, it is now adulterated with wax, fat or vegetable oil to produce bars of hashish disparagingly referred to as soaps. (A semi-liquefied viscous hashish is also available known as squeegee black.)

As demand increased and the industry grew, the farmers required more land and started to spread down from the mountainsides where the government had, unofficially, given them permission to operate. Some moved out of the Rif Mountains altogether and commenced cultivation in the Atlas Mountains to the south. With this blatant expansion, the government felt it had to act and, in 1987, moved against lower-altitude farmers in the Rif Mountains. Five years later, with US financial aid, another drive was made against those farming in the valleys. All that happened, of course, was that the farmers retreated once more to higher altitudes and there were still an estimated 248,000 acres under cannabis.

Until 1979, Afghanistan had been a major hashish-producing country but once the Russian invasion was under way, production plummeted. Farmers could grow only small amounts in secluded areas away from the conflict, and although the Russians withdrew in 1990, the subsequent sectarian fighting prevented them from re-establishing their business. When the Taliban took power in 1995, they were keen, for both economic and political reasons, to enter the international drugs trade but they preferred to grow opium for refining into heroin, which was much more profitable.

As hashish production declined in Afghanistan so it increased in neighbouring Pakistan which had, in any case, been a major conduit for the Afghan dealers for decades. When the supply of Afghan hashish began to diminish, what was available was blended with poorer-quality Pakistani product in the refugee camps along the countries' mutual border where the few family clans that traditionally monopolized the trade were by then living. Cannabis cultivation is widespread but is particularly concentrated in the north of the country with shipments being sent out through Karachi or Mumbia (Bombay).

Although, as elsewhere, cannabis farming is officially banned in Nepal, it continues unabated, once again taking advantage of the collapse of Afghanistan to grab a piece of the international trade. Nepalese hashish is made from both cultivated and wild plants, some of which are also used to make *ganja* for the local market. On occasion, the government destroys a crop but, by and large, it is officially ignored as a major source of foreign currency. Crop eradication is a risky business, for police or troops are frequently beaten off by gunfire. This may not be the action of the farmers themselves, however, for Nepal also has a small army of Maoist insurgents seeking to overthrow the monarchist government and they partly fund themselves from hashish sales.

The largest per-capita population of cannabis users in the world is, as it has been for many years, in India where it must be remembered cultivation and consumption were legal until 1945. After independence, there were moves in India to prohibit it both by confiscation and taxation, and a system of control was introduced, but it simply led to smuggling from surrounding countries and made no impact upon use. Today, most *ganja* originates from the south-eastern Indian state of Kerala where large cannabis farms are run by organized criminals, selling both nationally and internationally. At first grown in small plots, it has since the mid-1990s been cultivated in jungle plantations, difficult to find and harder to eradicate. The criminal proprietors have private armies to defend their crops and any attack is met with fire-power. What protection is not afforded by the gun comes from that created by the corruption that is endemic at all levels of Indian bureaucracy.

Across the Gulf of Manaar in Sri Lanka, cannabis is also cultivated in the jungles but here the authorities have specialist jungle commando units which can move against the farmers, being already trained to fight the Tamil Tiger separatists. As in Nepal, and in Kashmir where rebels fighting for autonomy from India finance themselves with hashish, these insurgents also raise money from cannabis production. To destroy their cannabis crop is to deny them sustenance.

Across the world, the eradication of cannabis from a region where its consumption and cultivation have been traditional for generations has proven to be well nigh impossible. The opportunities cannabis offers for making money are simply irresistible.

Lebanon is a case in point. In the bitter civil war between 1975 and 1991, hashish from the Bekaa Valley and, later, much more lucrative opium in the form of heroin, financed the various factions. When, around 1985, Syrian forces came to control the Bekaa Valley, Syrian traffickers took over the trade, exporting much of their hashish to Canada by sea. Packed into containers, it was usually routed through Cyprus where the consignments were re-certificated with new waybills to disguise their true origins. However, not all the product went out by way of commercial trade routes. At the height of the civil war, some American criminal entrepreneurs built a landing strip in the Bekaa Valley, flying in shipments of arms and flying hashish out.

Annual hashish production in the mid-1980s was conservatively estimated at 700 tons from approximately 49,000 acres of cannabis plants. At the end of the civil war in 1990, one-third of all arable land in the Bekaa Valley was put down to either cannabis or opium poppies, a total of approximately 75,000 acres, generating an annual income of $80 million, equal to $1500 per head of the population.

It did not last. With the war over, both the Syrian and Lebanese governments took the opportunity to have themselves removed from the US government list of pariah nations by jointly destroying narcotic crops. After a concerted campaign, the UN reported no illicit drugs being produced in the area whatsoever. This created considerable poverty. The UN set up crop-substitution programmes promoting tobacco, tomatoes, water melons, wheat and dairy farming but these were either under-funded or inappropriate for the conditions. By 2001, some farmers had returned to raising cannabis protected by Hizbullah. Once again, Lebanese hashish appeared on the market. Lebanese Gold (a reference to its quality not its colour, which is black) was produced from about 37,000 acres in the summer of 2002, double the acreage of the previous year. The sentences of life imprisonment with hard labour, advertised by government air-drops of leaflets, have done little to discourage the farmers who have said they will fight if the government seeks to destroy their crops. The gamble the producers are taking is that the authorities will not dare to move against them for fear of political unrest linked to Muslim fundamentalism. It is also thought that the farmers will be left unmolested because of the influence and investment of senior political figures in the hashish trade.

Although it is substantial, the world trade in hashish is dwarfed by that in marijuana. Countries involved in this industry are to be found in every geographical region other than the Arctic and Antarctic. Over half the marijuana confiscated every year is seized in North America, predominantly the product of Mexico. Other large seizures occur in South Africa and Malawi. Elsewhere, customs officers impound marijuana sourced from Brazil and Colombia (known collectively as the Emerald Triangle or Strip), Jamaica and other Central American countries, the border region overlapping Cambodia, Laos and Thailand (originally known as the Golden Triangle of the opiate trade but now confusingly renamed as another Emerald Triangle), Indonesia, the Philippines, Nigeria and Ghana although not all of these seizures are of marijuana for export.

In South America, Colombia, infamous as the main global source of cocaine, is also one of the major marijuana producers, sometimes exporting through neighbouring Venezuela to the Caribbean. As in so many places, whilst the trade is officially prohibited it is, in fact, either ignored by the authorities or only acted against in a token manner. Venezuelan law-enforcement officers frequently ambush vehicles carrying marijuana towards Caracas: in 2001, they seized 9 tons of cocaine and 5 of marijuana *en route* for Europe and the USA. Brazil is also becoming an important producer nation, the plantations lost in the vastness of the Amazon basin, the product coming down river to Manaus. Jamaica continues to be a sizeable producer with seizures and crop destruction frequent but insufficient truly to dent the trade. The police are also now increasingly involved in counteracting cocaine smuggling and the gang warfare associated with it, Jamaica being one of the most important staging posts between Colombia and North America. The situation has, as of 2001, turned Kingston, the capital of Jamaica, into the most violent city on earth with the highest murder rate. Against this background, the marijuana trade is not a top priority and is being somewhat ignored. It has also been suggested that personal use might be decriminalized for adults and for religious purposes, which will please the Rastafarians. The US government opposes the move but it seems the most pragmatic solution: yet again, it is seen to be impossible to stamp out marijuana where use is part of a cultural tradition.

Mexico, more corrupt than lawless, remains a very big marijuana producing country, the trade earning an estimated thirty billion dollars per annum in foreign exchange. Corruption concerning marijuana has now permeated through the government, to the highest levels. To address this state of affairs, the administration of US President Bill Clinton offered twenty billion dollars in aid in exchange for co-operation on action against the so-called Mexican Federation, a loose association of drug barons with connections to the Colombian cocaine cartels. It had only a limited impact and, in March 2001, Mexican President Vicente Fox annoyed Washington by stating the only way to combat the drug trade was to legalize sections of it.

One *modus operandi* of the smugglers was laid bare on the completion in April 2000 of Operation Green Air, run jointly by the DEA and US Customs. It concentrated on a marijuana-trafficking network run by the Mexican Arrellano-Felix organization which had been supplying a Jamaican syndicate.

In years past, syndicates had used ordinary commercial courier services such as DHL, UPS and FedEx but, in a move to stop both the drugs and money-laundering industries, these companies ceased to accept packages from customers that were not known to them. Furthermore, they insisted random packages be open for inspection when collected. To overcome this hurdle, this network had compromised and bribed a number of key personnel in the Los Angeles FedEx centre. Marijuana was smuggled from Mexico into Los Angeles for onward transportation by FedEx to parcel-handling and distribution centres in Boston, Orlando, Atlanta, Fort Lauderdale, New York and Newark. Bent FedEx personnel saw the packages safely onto the courier's own aircraft, entering them into the guaranteed overnight-service containers by issuing them with regular bar-coded waybills. To camouflage the packages and make tracing more difficult, the staff manipulated corporate billing and accounting records so the consignments not only passed through the computer system un-detected but also usually for free. After an eighteen-month investigation, 104 people were arrested, 34,000 pounds of marijuana was seized and $4.2 million in cash and assets sequestered. It was estimated that, over two years, the ring had smuggled a minimum of 121 tons of marijuana.

It is hardly surprising that, as an awareness of the profit margins to be made from cannabis becomes more widely known, more countries are awakening to the advantages of cannabis growing.

After the Second World War, Albania became a completely closed society with no contact to the outside world save, at a very restricted diplomatic level, with the Communist bloc. The country's paranoid dictator, Enver Hoxha, ruled through the Sigurimi, the Albanian equivalent of the KGB. Political executions and regular Stalinist purges kept the people oppressed, overseas travel was forbidden and all religion suppressed. Then, in 1985, Hoxha died. The country underwent several changes of government and leadership and, by 1991, its borders were open. In essence, Albania was a third-world country in Europe. It had virtually no industry, few roads and an agrarian economy. It was also ripe for the picking. Organized crime moved in fast, much of it from Italy with which Albania has a long historical connection. As drugs and illegal immigrants started to flow through the country and across the Adriatic

Sea, local farmers began to consider what crops they might grow to try and drag themselves and their country into modernity. Western government aid did little to help the farmers. Although thousands of citrus and olive trees were planted, it would be years before they were productive.

Then, in 1991, Greek criminal elements entered southern Albania from Greece and Corfu bringing cannabis seeds, and a new cash crop commenced. Foreign governments saw this trend and put pressure on the Albanians to stamp it out before it developed. In 1995, a concerted effort was made to eradicate the crop. It led to running gun battles between the farmers and the police. Not only criminals were financing the cannabis. So, too, were former Sigurimi officers and they had friends in the police. Two years later, Albania became once more politically unstable and Western aid was withheld, unsettling the economy. The farmers took the only course open to them: they grew food for their families and cannabis to sell.

Much of the cannabis, which is processed into marijuana, is grown in mountainous southern Albania. At first, it was taken over the hills into Greece by teenage boys carrying sacks on their backs and selling to Greek dealers, but this soon gave way to smuggling by sea in speedboats and leisure craft stolen from Corfu or Italy. The Italian mafia now organize the business, running marijuana into western Europe along the Italian Adriatic coast. Once ashore, and in the European Community, it can travel across the continent without let or hindrance from border controls. In 2001, it was estimated Albania exported marijuana worth forty million dollars.

Another country engaged in significant cannabis cultivation is Cambodia, which the UNDCP now considers one of the world's primary producers with marijuana grossing approximately one billion dollars in 2000, as much as the country's other main industry, garment manufacturing, in which over one hundred thousand people work. The international smuggling of the product is controlled by Vietnamese Chinese organized-crime gangs assisted by corrupt Cambodian and Vietnamese officials, some of very senior rank. The marijuana is baled at collecting points, taken down the Mekong River and exported by sea from Ho Chi Minh City, primarily to Europe and Australia. To the west, Thailand is also a producer but not of the same magnitude.

For many years, cannabis has been cultivated in southern Africa, particularly in the South African provinces of Natal and the Transvaal as well as in the tribal homelands of KwaZulu and Transkei. The trade, however, was not organized and little was exported beyond neighbouring countries. This has now changed and South Africa is regarded as a main producer smuggling mostly to Europe. In the spirit of post-apartheid times, the business is operated by black farmers and traders selling to both black and white smugglers often working together. Elsewhere in Africa, the main producer countries are Nigeria and Ghana, which sell to Europe, and Malawi and (increasingly) northern Zambia which sell into other regional countries for domestic use.

Examples in Africa prove the theory that the poorer a country the more likely it is to produce cannabis. This is hardly surprising. The cash return is enormous and more or less immediate as the crop grows quickly and the farmer is paid in ready cash the minute he has harvested it. Furthermore, the plant is cheap to grow, does not require a rich soil or extensive irrigation, needs no agrochemicals and is not labour intensive except at sowing and harvest time. It is an ideal peasant farmer's cash crop.

Whilst many producer nations illegally export, they have also traditionally grown cannabis for their own domestic markets and this pattern is now becoming increasingly common in countries that were historically only consumers and not cultivators.

The trend began in the USA where, over the last twenty years, a thriving illegal cultivation industry has developed in a number of states but, primarily, in California. For a while, the centre of this was the northern counties of Humboldt, Mendocino and Trinity where the farmers concentrated on producing sinsemilla. Today, however, cannabis cultivation is so widespread that the UNDCP classifies the USA as a main producer. It is estimated that a quarter of all marijuana smoked in America is grown in the country. The DEA conducts a national cultivated-crop eradication programme but, even with this in full-time operation, it is still reckoned that cannabis is the fourth largest cash crop in the country, generating fifteen billion dollars a year wholesale. In California, Kentucky and Virginia, the traditional home of tobacco, it is thought to be the main cash crop.

It is also believed that a substantial percentage of the marijuana smoked in Britain, the Netherlands and other western European countries is home produced, although the overall amount is much smaller than in the USA because European cannabis users prefer hashish. Some observers believe that Britain and the Netherlands now produce half of their domestic marijuana requirement. Almost all home-raised cannabis is turned into marijuana but a very small amount is actually used to produce hashish.

In much of the USA, cannabis can be grown out of doors. The climate is amenable and, the country being vast, it is easy to hide even a fairly large acreage. In all but southern Europe, the opposite is true. The climate is not always clement and, much of the land being highly settled, it is not easy to disguise a crop. Where open cultivation is not possible, cannabis is raised either in glasshouses or indoors.

Very limited home cultivation was conducted in Britain on an exceedingly small scale in the 1960s, usually by students and hippies. The plants were raised in pots or window boxes and were, generally, a failure because they produced few if any flowers and had a very low THC content. The seed was often obtained from packets of cage bird food.

By 1990, however, home cultivation in Britain had become a sophisticated art, much of it learnt from the Dutch. Cultivars were developed to produce multiple flower tops and very high THC levels, some specifically suited for indoor growing. One of the first of these strains was known as skunk because of the strong and easily identified scent the plant gave out. This often caused problems for the secretive indoor farmer, the more professional of whom had charcoal filters fitted to extractor fans to kill the tell-tale odour.

Different types of skunk have individual names deriving from its potency, such as Mindblaster, AK47, Jack Flash, White Widow and Red Dragon. Skunk plants are usually shorter and bushier than normal cannabis, seldom growing above two metres in height. The best cultivars are those of *Cannabis indica* which have shorter inter-nodal spaces between the branches where the flower tops appear and therefore produce higher yields. True skunk is usually sinsemilla but the term is also applied to ordinary leaf-based marijuana and, today, the name is generically applied to any home-grown marijuana.

It has been claimed by British government chemists that some skunk varieties have up to twenty times the THC content of imported marijuana and that this can cause memory loss, increase the risk of heart disease or adversely affect the unborn child during pregnancy. It seems, however, that the reason for this analytical result is that the skunk tested is sinsemilla which is investigated when still very fresh, before any of the THC content has had a chance to deteriorate as it would have had under normal conditions before reaching the street and end user, just as the THC in imported marijuana is already degraded.

Indoor cultivation, apart from the provision of artificial light, varies considerably from ordinary outdoor growing. Most often, hydroponic techniques are used. This means that soil is not the growing medium but sterilized sand, fibre chips, rock wool, gravel, vermiculite, polystyrene pellets or even animal bedding made from industrial hemp core. The medium is saturated with nutrient-rich water permanently circulating past the roots driven by an electric pump or seeped into the medium close to the roots by a controlled wick. Levels of light and nutrient can be controlled to promote maximum growth rates. Apart from the advantage of secrecy, hydroponic cultivation creates faster growth and higher yields. Any location can be adapted from a loft space or cupboard to a garage, barn or warehouse. Most are small, cottage-industry-type ventures but some illicit cannabis factories are engaged in substantial commercial production capable of three or four harvests per annum. As the product is sinsemilla, seeds are not produced and the next generation of plants is usually created from cuttings. A crop of skunk takes about eight weeks to reach maturity and a space the size of a single car garage, properly managed, can produce approximately fifty thousand pounds' worth of sinsemilla a year.

Supplies for the home growing of cannabis are widely obtainable. The first supply companies were Dutch, such as Sensi SeedS in Rotterdam, but now a plethora of companies advertise on the internet, from all over the Western world, offering not only seeds but instruction manuals, hydroponic equipment and even cylinders of carbon dioxide: the plants are known to thrive in a $CO_2$-rich atmosphere. Between August 2001 and April 2002, the sale of hydroponic equipment in Britain trebled. British supply companies stay within the law because it contains so many anomalies. It is not illegal to sell cannabis-using paraphernalia nor is it against the law to sell seeds, even of high-THC-content strains, so long as these are retailed specifically as a food additive. It is, of course, legal to sell hydroponic equipment (most commercially grown tomatoes are raised this way) and nutrients, but it is illegal to supply cannabis plants or cuttings. (As one British police spokesman caustically remarked in the summer of 2002, there appears to be no indication of a sudden explosion of tomato growing in the shires of England.)

The most famous cannabis supplier (of everything but the drug itself) is the mail-order internet firm of WHSpliff.net, which advertises with the somewhat redundant preface, *It remains illegal to grow cannabis without a Home Office Licence*. The company is based in Taunton, Somerset, one of the most conservative-minded towns in Britain.

The British marijuana industry might be growing apace but it has a long way to go to catch up with the Canadian province of British Columbia. Recent RCMP statistics estimate that marijuana is now the province's biggest industry, well in advance even of logging. It is reckoned

150,000 people are involved in cultivation and distribution. At least 80 per cent of the production is overseen by Hell's Angels-type motorcycle gangs and/or Vietnamese Chinese organized-crime gangs who smuggle it into the US. Inevitably, the US authorities are keen to see the RCMP crack down on the cultivators but this would require a massive amount of manpower and it is unofficially believed the eradication of small-time hydroponic growers is impossible.

Just as the cultivators are becoming more determined and sophisticated, so are their opponents.

The DEA operates in a number of countries outside the USA. It has mounted anti-drug operations in Colombia, Bolivia, Panama, Venezuela, Ecuador and a large number of Caribbean states, conducts continuous surveillance of shipping and aircraft, targets and destroys clandestine airstrips, sprays crops with weed killer and monitors all banking transactions conducted by US banks for sums in excess of ten thousand dollars. The scale of activity can be judged from Operation Conquistador, run in March 2000, which involved twenty-six countries. It did not target specifically cannabis but all illicit drugs and resulted in 2,331 arrests, the search of 7,376 buildings, vessels, vehicles and aircraft and the seizure of 4,966 kilos of cocaine, 55 kilos of heroin, 14 kilos of morphine base and 362 metric tons of marijuana. Thirteen boats and 172 vehicles were confiscated along with $2.1 million in assets.

The UNDCP, in collaboration with US and British government scientists, has now developed a fungus that can attack cannabis plants, opium poppies and coca bushes, but it is non-specific and could also wipe out food crops and other vegetation. Attempts to trial it in Colombia have been halted against fears of environmental danger but rumours persist that it has been used in central Asia.

One inescapable fact remains. Cannabis cultivation and distribution will not diminish so long as there is a desire for what it offers and peasant farmers in poor countries – or suburbanites with spare attic space – are willing to grow it.

# 26

# FUDGE, COUNTER-FUDGE
# AND THE FUTURE

ESTIMATES GIVEN BY THE UNITED NATIONS INTERNATIONAL DRUG Control Programme (UNDCP) suggest that 3.5 per cent of the world's adult population (being defined as those over the age of fifteen) was using cannabis in 2000. This is a total of 147 million people. The largest user population, in Asia, accounts for over 25 per cent of world cannabis consumption. Another 50 per cent or so is used in Africa and the Americas, in about equal quantities, with Europe accounting for a further 20 per cent, the remaining 5 per cent used elsewhere.

In some countries, consumption is increasing. In Asia, with the exception of Thailand, most countries have noticed a rise in usage although The People's Republic of China has released no reliable statistics. Those in Africa reporting a rise in cannabis use include Kenya, Malawi, Ghana, the Democratic Republic of the Congo, Morocco, Sierra Leone and the Republic of South Africa whilst, in the Americas, Argentina, Bolivia, Brazil, Chile, Colombia and (to a lesser extent) Venezuela also record increased use. From these calculations UNDCP believes that, globally, cannabis use is still generally increasing, regardless of the international, US- and UN-inspired war on drugs and the fact that, in the vast majority of nations, the cultivation, possession and use of cannabis is illegal.

Throughout the 1990s, the governments of many countries have been persistently and increasingly lobbied to reduce the penalties attached to cannabis, with calls in more than a few for complete decriminalization as regards personal use. If this were done, possession and use would become a civil misdemeanour (such as speeding, jay-walking or littering) addressed with a fine rather than a recorded criminal conviction. Under such a legal regime, possession for medical use, with a doctor's approval, would no longer be a crime. Most governments have ignored or rebuffed all approaches. When, in the middle of the decade, British Members of Parliament requested a royal commission to look into the matter, they went unheeded. The cannabis *status quo* remained and consumption continued to rise, as did arrest statistics for cannabis offences, the police and customs authorities across the western hemisphere diligently concentrating on hitting at traffickers, dealers and users.

In early December 1998, the London Metropolitan Police carried out a bust against the biggest retail cannabis operation of the decade. The target was the premises of the Back Beat Club in Denmark Place, off Charing Cross Road on the eastern fringe of Soho. The club was a major cannabis retailer patronized by a very wide multi-racial clientele that cut across all the social strata, the drug being sold through a small hatch. All the staff were black, some claimed by the police to be members of the Jamaican Yardies criminal fraternity. A substantial number of heavily armed police, said to number in the hundreds, conducted the raid after some months of discreet, twenty-four-hour surveillance from the nearby offices of EMI Music Publishers. When the attack was launched, stun grenades were used. Many of the police officers, acting like a SWAT team, carried automatic weapons. It was hoped to find not only cannabis but also heroin and crack cocaine along with a cache of weapons and armed dealers. No arms or drugs other than cannabis were found. Most of the staff escaped but forty-seven people were arrested with a small number being charged. They were given bail which it was anticipated most prudently would skip. Cannabis with an estimated street value of £250,000 was seized along with £150,000 in cash. Within three months, the club was back in business on another site, prompting the question, had the whole exercise been a waste of police time and money? Had the police even been allowed to keep the cash confiscated (which they were not: all criminal money seized in Britain is appropriated by the central government exchequer), it would not have compensated them for more than a fraction of the cost of the entire operation.

In August 1997, an independent commission, the Independent Inquiry into the Misuse of Drugs Act 1971, was established by the British Police Federation in collaboration with the Prince's Trust, a charity set up by

Prince Charles, Prince of Wales, to help young people fulfil their potential and to address social issues affecting them. Chaired by Viscountess Runciman and consequently unofficially known as the Runciman Report, its findings were published in 2000. It suggested cannabinol, hashish and marijuana be reclassified as Class C substances and be placed in Schedule 2 of the Misuse of Drugs Regulations to permit supply and possession for medical use; possession should not be an arrestable offence; the offence of *knowingly permitting or suffering premises to be used* for cannabis smoking be repealed (although, for some reason, this recommendation also included the smoking of opium); the cultivation of a small number of cannabis plants for personal use should no longer be considered an arrestable offence; and the maximum penalty for trafficking for Class C drugs should be seven years' imprisonment with a discretionary unlimited fine.

Soon after the findings were released, the Police Federation suggested a more tolerant approach be adopted towards cannabis. It was a pragmatic move. Prohibition was a failure. The law was not working to police advantage. Annual statistics published in 1998 showed that, in ten years, cannabis conviction rates had risen tenfold to 96,381. Most arrests were for personal possession. Half of those apprehended were merely cautioned, less than a quarter were fined and only 4 per cent were sent to prison. Of the prison population in 1998, 15 per cent were being held on drug charges, mostly cannabis related. It was reckoned that policing the cannabis laws was costing the country £1.5 billion per annum. By early 2002, it was officially accepted that 30 per cent of all fifteen-year-olds in England had used cannabis, the figure rising to 50 per cent for sixteen- to twenty-four-year-olds and students in higher education. Early in January 2002, Buckingham Palace admitted that Prince Harry, Prince Charles' younger son and third in succession to the throne, had smoked cannabis the previous year. The matter was dealt with discreetly within the royal family.

In June 2001, a new British Home Secretary was appointed to replace Jack Straw, the fervent anti-cannabis minister whose own seventeen-year-old son had been compromised by a tabloid journalist in December 1997, to whom it was alleged he sold a small amount of marijuana. Straw's replacement was David Blunkett, the former minister for education. Within months, he had alienated Keith Halliwell, the one-time Chief Constable of West Yorkshire who had been appointed Britain's first 'drug czar' in 1998, charged with devising a long-term, overall national anti-drugs plan. Halliwell resigned in disgust in 2002 at what he saw as a liberalization of drug policy. Coming into office, Blunkett took personal charge and, with fellow politicians pressing him, stated he was to assess the arguments for decriminalizing certain drugs including cannabis. A Home Affairs Select Committee was ordered to study existing policies.

Experiments in police tolerance began in 2001 with a new attitude towards cannabis being trialled in the London borough of Lambeth, south of the River Thames on the opposite bank to the Houses of Parliament and including the predominantly West Indian area of Brixton. Marijuana being very widely used there, the police knew they could not stamp it out so they tried a different tack. Anyone found in possession had their marijuana confiscated and were given a formal warning on the spot. Otherwise, no arrest was made, with a saving of up to ten police man hours in paperwork per person apprehended. The trial lasted a year. During this time, the police concentrated manpower on violent crime and drug dealers, most of them peddling crack cocaine and heroin as well as cannabis. Although, officially, the trial was deemed a success, predominantly black or Asian local community leaders claimed it encouraged dealers into the area, giving them a greater presence than they had previously held, and encouraged teenagers to take cannabis because they knew they would not be arrested for it. Certainly, police statistics showed a marked increase in drug offences during the trial period, with more dealers moving into the borough selling a wide range of substances (some of them declaiming their wares like street traders) including crack cocaine, amphetamines and ecstasy. Those selling cannabis were mostly offering the more potent skunk and selling it to children as young as twelve. This development considerably alarmed police and other observers.

One of the primary faults of the trial was that it gave the impression that cannabis had been legalized − which it had not − and was totally harmless. This perceived innocuousness was received by the young as tantamount to permission to indulge, which many did. A local doctor reported children smoking skunk before going to school in the morning. They continued at school and, during breaks in classes, in the playground or local park. By afternoon, some were well and truly intoxicated, a good percentage of them playing truant. At the end of the trial period, an opinion poll of mostly ethnic-minority local residents voted it a resounding failure.

Almost simultaneous to the start of the Lambeth experiment, the Labour Party Member of Parliament for Cardiff Central, Jon Owen Jones, introduced a private member's bill to *legalize and regulate the sale, supply and use of cannabis for recreational and therapeutic purposes.* That it would be strongly resisted by the Government and never make it onto the statute books was inevitable. Legalization, as opposed to decriminalization, is a big step for any administration to take, for legalizing cannabis would put it on a par with alcohol, permitting any adult over the age of eighteen to use it. Nevertheless, it passed its first reading in the House of Commons unopposed.

Those in favour of legalization claim that it is up to the individual to decide what they do, want or need, but this is little more than a civil-rights issue and, at least in Britain, there is no constitution or bill of rights under which to argue the point as, for example, exists in the USA. More pertinently, supporters of legalization argue that legalizing cannabis would remove it from the criminal sphere, allowing distribution to be regulated and even taxed. Permitting personal cultivation would also remove the criminal element. Regulation would ensure the quality of cannabis and remove the criminal risk of adulteration with hard drugs in order to ensnare and addict new customers. The benefits of taxation are obvious although one aspect would have to be assessed. The value of the tax revenues would need to be balanced against the cost to society of cannabis use. What would have to be avoided would be the debacle caused by tobacco where the revenue raised does not meet the public-health cost of treating the resultant illnesses.

Opponents of legalization debate the veracity of these assumptions. However, overriding all these arguments is one salient consideration. Can a modern society function effectively if the population is not prevented from acquiring a means of uninhibited hedonism? It is also their opinion that legalization and regulation would not break the criminal link. Street dealers would still operate to undercut licensed traders and smuggle contraband to evade taxation. Home growers would be virtually im-possible to regulate because of their numbers, thereby permitting illicit cannabis to undermine and avoid regulation. They also claim, as did Anslinger, that marijuana is a gateway drug leading to heroin, cocaine or other more dangerous drug use. That cannabis does not create a chemical need in the body nor fuel physical dependency and does not physio-logically act as a gateway, is certain. Yet it may socially do so in that, being prohibited, users have to obtain their supplies from dealers who also sell more dangerous drugs. Legalizing cannabis, say supporters, would sever the link. This same point was made by the Wootton Report, published – and officially ignored – thirty-two years before the Lambeth experiment.

In July 2001, the British pro-legalization lobby received a boost. Peter

Lilley, a former government minister for Social Security and one-time deputy leader of the Conservative Party, called for legalization on the grounds that existing laws on cannabis were, in his judgement, *unenforceable and indefensible* in a country where tobacco and alcohol were sanctioned. He envisaged cannabis being sold through licensed outlets to anyone over eighteen years of age, just as tobacco and alcohol already are. Consumption in public would be banned and supplies restricted at the point of sale to moderate use but cultivation for personal consumption would be allowed. A tax levy would be applied with a tobacco-style health warning. In support of his argument, which he made known in a publication released by The Social Market Foundation, Lilley referred to an article in *The Lancet* which declared that *moderate indulgence in cannabis has little ill effect on health, and decisions to ban or to legalize cannabis should be based on other considerations.*

Lilley's comments as regards tobacco and alcohol re-ignited a long-running accusation levelled against prohibitionists, highlighting the hypocrisy of legislating in favour of known potentially dangerous substances but not cannabis. Pro-cannabis supporters were also quick to remind that all the old shibboleths of cannabis promoting violent crime and sexual libidinousness were unfounded but that alcohol-related violence was well proven and rampant in society. They also drew attention to government statistics that stated 1,200 premature deaths occurred in Britain annually which could be blamed upon drug use, some to prescribed medicines but most to heroin and the like, whilst 35,000 premature deaths were ascribed to alcohol, the number of tobacco-smoking-related fatalities being far higher. The hypocritical government attitude, common throughout the Western world, was further highlighted by pointing out that, whilst tobacco carried a health warning alcohol did not, suggesting that prohibition had little to do with health issues. What might address the situation and remove some of the hypocrisy, it was mooted, was to follow a concept put forward by a New Zealand drug policy unit which believed a Tobacco, Alcohol and Cannabis Authority should be set up to control all three of the most common social drugs.

Some accused Lilley of trying to be a trendsetter whilst the *Daily Telegraph* drew attention to the fact that it had argued for experimental legalization as part of its campaign for a Free Country in the spring of 2000. Two years before, the lively editor of the *Independent on Sunday*, Rosie Boycott, had written to cabinet ministers in Tony Blair's first Labour government asking them if they had ever smoked cannabis. Most ignored her. Then, in 2000, eight members of the Conservative Party shadow cabinet outed themselves from the cannabis closet including Lord Strathclyde (formerly the Conservative Party leader in the House of Lords), Francis Maude (a former Financial Secretary to the Treasury and Minister of State at the Foreign Office) and David Willetts (once Paymaster General) but not Peter Lilley. Others, from the Labour Party, followed, including Yvette Cooper, the minister for Public Health, and Mo Mowlam, the Secretary of State for Northern Ireland, who both said they had smoked cannabis as university students.

Not only Peter Lilley voiced proposals for cannabis legislation in 2001. Lord Jenkins, the Home Secretary who had instigated the Wootton Report, and Lord Baker (another former Home Secretary) suggested the decriminalization of possession. Charles Kennedy, the leader of the Liberal Democrats, echoed them and called for a royal commission to assess policy. His annual party conference endorsed a motion for the legalization of cannabis for personal use.

Three months after Lilley's declaration, David Blunkett announced that cannabis possession should no longer be an arrestable offence and said he proposed to reclassify cannabis a Class C substance, following the recommendation of the Runciman Report and freeing up the police to concentrate on fighting heroin, crack cocaine and other hard drugs. A public opinion poll showed that 65 per cent of the British population favoured legalization with 91 per cent supporting medical cannabis prescription by doctors.

Matters started to move quickly. Early in 2002, the Advisory Council on the Misuse of Drugs recommended cannabis should be reclassified from Class B to Class C, the Home Affairs Select Committee agreeing shortly afterwards. Within ten weeks, Blunkett confirmed he would reclassify. The intention to extend the Lambeth confiscate-and-caution experiment across London and elsewhere was publicized.

Campaigners both for and against cannabis expressed misgivings. It was, to many, a compromise, a fudge. Whilst it might allow the war on hard drugs to start to bite, some claimed it would also lead to a massive expansion in the cannabis market to, it was estimated, an annual turnover in excess of one billion pounds. Furthermore, lowering the classification also significantly lowered the prison sentences for trafficking from fourteen to five years. To counteract this, a proposal was tabled to double cannabis trafficking sentences. Yet HM Customs had, at the same time, ceased to target specifically commercial cannabis smugglers in favour of heroin or cocaine syndicates, under recommendation from the little-known Cabinet Office Concerted Inter-Agency Drugs Action (CIDA) group, established late in 1999, which comprised senior representatives of the secret services, HM Customs and Excise, the National Criminal Intelligence Service (NCIS), the Association of Chief Police Officers and the permanent under-secretaries of state to the relevant government ministries. If any major seizures of cannabis are made in the future it will be primarily as a result of operations against Class A substance smugglers.

This might seem a retrograde step and yet, in recent years, organized-crime syndicates have tended not to be involved in the cannabis business. It is all a matter of profit margins. Cannabis is regarded by organized crime as no longer a high-profit earner and as too risky, especially when seen alongside tobacco smuggling which can be more lucrative and carries lower penalties for those caught. The demand for imported marijuana in Britain has also dropped due to the home-cultivation boom.

With the new tolerant attitude of some police forces and the forthcoming possibility of the relaxation of the laws on cannabis, a number of attempts have been made to open Dutch-style cannabis cafés. The first serious effort was made in September 2001 by Colin Davies in Manchester. Along with a business partner, a Dutch cannabis café owner called Nol van Schaik, he expressed the intent to supply free medicinal cannabis from the premises. The café, to be called The Dutch Experience, was not a covert operation. Davies informed the police of its opening and his intentions. Only minutes before it was due to start to trade, the Greater Manchester Police raided it. Davies was arrested and promptly released on unconditional bail. Over the next few months, he was again apprehended and variously charged with possession, importation, possession with intent to distribute and distribution of marijuana. His café was also raided and, eventually, he was imprisoned. The premises, however, were not shut down and continued to be a rendezvous not only for those with a need for medicinal marijuana but for tourists. It was even featured by the local tourist board.

Davies is not Britain's only high-profile pro-cannabis campaigner. Another is Rob Christopher, a resident of the Somerset town of Glastonbury, who once won the town competition for a summer floral display by exhibiting a stand of cannabis plants which the judges failed to identify. In 1994, he changed his name by deed poll to Free Rob Cannabis and, the subsequent year, founded the Cannabis Information Club to promote public knowledge of all aspects of hemp. He then opened Britain's first cannabis museum and in 1996, in the company of Howard Marks, gave out free cannabis cookies to the public at Speakers' Corner in London's Hyde Park. They afterwards offered themselves up to the police for arrest. The offer was declined. The following year Mr Cannabis, as he was now known, opened a cannabis shop and information centre at 1a, Market Place, Glastonbury, and set up the Free Medical Marijuana Foundation. His first act was to hand out free supplies in front of the offices of the Department of Health. On this occasion, the police decided to act and Mr Cannabis was arrested for possession of 1.57 grams of marijuana. He refused legal representation and to pay the fine levied against him. This signalled the beginning of a number of court appearances for cannabis cultivation (harking back to the floral display), possession and intent to distribute. He was eventually fined one thousand pounds in court costs plus 180 hours of community service. The latter he performed, the former he refused and was jailed for fourteen days in a minimum-security facility. A year on, he was arrested for raffling bags of marijuana to finance medicinal supplies.

Mr Cannabis' main aim was to demystify marijuana and promote it as a medicine. Others see cannabis as an exciting entrepreneurial opportunity, if it were to be legally possible to exploit it. Some businessmen, such as Simon Woodroffe, the founder of the Yo! Sushi chain of sushi bars, consider cannabis cafés could become establishments like cocktail lounges, catering to a young professional clientele and serving not just cannabis but also fine foods and quality wines. In other words, marijuana could become chic. It is estimated that if Britain were to have as many cannabis cafés as the Netherlands, 45,000 jobs would be created, and if the cannabis sold in them were to be consumed at present levels but taxed at source on the same tariff as tobacco or alcohol, the exchequer would reap an annual revenue of approximately £1.6 billion.

The economic advantages of legalization go beyond providing service-sector employment and tax revenue. Regulated cultivation in Britain could bring a new impetus to small farmers who have suffered greatly in recent years due to the BSE scare and the economically devastating foot-and-mouth outbreak of 2001. As the majority of farmers run smallholdings of under 250 acres and are the primary guardians of the countryside, their farming methods maintaining its traditional topo-graphical and land use patterns, to allow them to raise cannabis would be of positive environmental advantage.

Britain is not alone in seeking to decriminalize or legalize cannabis. Regardless of the strictures of the UN Single Convention, many other countries are moving in the same general direction. In western Europe, where it is reckoned at least a third of the adult population has used cannabis, Belgium, Italy, Luxembourg, Spain and Switzerland have all to some extent decriminalized it with certain basic and mostly public-order provisos unique to each. Portugal has acted likewise on all illicit drugs.

Switzerland in particular stands out. Here, the cultivation of cannabis with a high THC content is legal so long as it is not sold as an intoxicant. Nevertheless, hemp farms have appeared all over the country supplying what are in essence head shops selling cannabis and avoiding prosecution by labelling the products as herbal tea, dried flowers or pot pourri sachets. The Government has estimated that 7.25 per cent of the adult population, mostly in the middle social strata, uses cannabis at least monthly.

In neighbouring Germany, the situation seems to be just as equivocal. Cannabis was illegal until 1994 when the federal government declared prohibition for personal use to be unconstitutional. Since then, different areas have applied different criteria. Some areas tolerate it and some have decriminalized it. Schleswig-Holstein, for example, has legalized cannabis for recreational use and sale to those over sixteen.

Elsewhere in Europe, Ireland does not act against users but fines those found in possession; Denmark issues a police caution for possession of small amounts; Greece – which until recently had very harsh cannabis laws – acts likewise but insists apprehended smokers submit to counselling; Austria permits personal consumption and France carries out few prosecutions.

It stands to reason that, where cannabis has been decriminalized, the supply of medical marijuana has become possible yet still with penalties attached to it. This development has been welcomed in many quarters, especially by associations representing victims of specific illnesses, but the overall situation remains ambiguous and confusing for all concerned. Cannabis is caught in a bizarrely convoluted legal maze of Catch-22 proportions. It is – depending on the country – quasi-legal to own it and quasi-legal to buy it, but illegal to sell it. Or it is quasi-legal to grow it and use it but not share it. Or it is legal to grow it and legal to sell it if the retailer does not advertise the fact (universally understood) that it is cannabis. Or it is illegal to buy it and illegal to use it but if you purchase it and use it in a designated place, the law ignores you even though you are technically breaking it. Or it is illegal to possess it, illegal to grow it, illegal to use it and illegal to sell it but, if you get caught, you are not arrested and may or may not be fined or cautioned. In the case of cannabis, the dictum 'the law is an ass' was never more proven.

Not all European countries, however, have such a confusingly vague approach to cannabis. In Sweden, where the decriminalization of amphetamines in the 1960s created a huge upsurge in use, a zero-tolerance regime operates. Possession of even a tiny amount of cannabis demands a minimum sentence of six months' imprisonment rising to ten years and the abuse of any prohibited drug is a criminal offence. The police are even empowered to demand urine or blood testing merely on suspicion of an offence. Drug use has not declined as a result but its rise has slowed. There is an obstacle, however, to government policy. Swedish farmers are seeking the right to grow hemp which is classed as a narcotic regardless of its THC content. The prohibition, they argue, contravenes European free-trade legislation.

Even in the Netherlands, the homeland of cannabis liberalism, stricter rules are gradually being enforced partly at the behest of neighbouring countries eager to prevent their citizens taking too much advantage of Dutch laxity. The number of cannabis cafés has been reduced by half, the minimum age of patrons has been raised from sixteen to eighteen and the maximum single purchase restricted to 5 grams with the permitted personal possession amount similarly reduced. Political moves have been afoot since 2002 to eventually close down all the cafés, partly because some are believed to be forging links with organized-crime groups. This is hardly surprising, considering that the law forces the cannabis supply chain to depend upon criminal smuggling for its sourcing.

The considered efficacy of these various national policies varies according to the commentator or assessor. As far as the Netherlands is concerned, the liberal approach seems not to have given rise to a sharp increase in cannabis use, yet the rate has risen over the twenty years since the laws became flexible. There again, the rate has similarly risen across the Western world during the same period in nations with prohibitive legislation. Amongst teenagers, cannabis use in the Netherlands stands at 31 per cent and is, according to a survey in 2000, actually in very gradual decline. This is favourable compared, for example, with Britain where the figure is 37.5 per cent.

Whatever harm or good the Dutch liberal atmosphere has caused, it has cast a light upon one major concern: the gateway theory so beloved of Anslinger. The premise that cannabis actually 'drove' its users on to other drugs had always been regarded with some scepticism, but there was never any proof one way or the other for all the subjects had been studied retrospectively. Heroin addicts, for example, frequently admitted having first taken cannabis but that was not to say it had forced them on to their deeper addiction. No study existed of cannabis users and how their drug use developed. In the Netherlands, however, such a study was possible. It found that most cannabis users would not even consider graduating to harder drugs, any more than those who, for example, drank alcohol would. Surveys carried out in Amsterdam between 1987 and 1997 corroborated previous evidence that suggested that hard-drug abuse was not dependent upon preliminary soft-drug taking but the character of the individual and their preparedness to experiment. The wide availability of cannabis has not led to any greater increase in the use of harder drugs than that experienced in any other European country.

Nevertheless, there have been adverse effects to cannabis liberalism. The Netherlands is now internationally regarded as a 'druggy' country, attracting 'druggy' tourists in the same way that Thailand attracts sex tourists. Furthermore, they come not only for the cannabis cafés but also events and venues specifically provided for the tourist industry. An annual gathering, the Cannabis Cup, attracts visitors from all over the world to test and judge the year's best marijuana and hashish. Attached to this are an international cannabis trade fair, symposia and, since 1997, a Hall of Fame into which Bob Marley was the first inductee. There is also the Global Hemp Museum in Haarlem (founded by van Schaik), the Hemp Hotel at Frederiksplein 15 in Amsterdam (including the Hemple Temple Bar where hemp drinks and THC-free ice cream are served) and the Cannabis College on the Oudezijdes Achterburgwal in Amsterdam's famous red-light district, where living exhibits of cannabis plants may be seen growing.

The decriminalization issue is not unique to Europe. In 1987 in South Australia and, later, elsewhere in the country, an expiation notice scheme was introduced by which anyone apprehended committing a minor cannabis offence was given what amounted to an immediate but insignificant fine, non-payment of which within a certain period resulted in a court summons. Only if a summons was issued would a conviction be recorded. In 1994, a report by the Australian National Task Force on Cannabis stated, *Any social policy should be reviewed when there is reason to believe that the cost of administering it outweighs the harms reduced*, adding that Australia suffered more social harm from maintaining cannabis prohibition than from the drug itself. However, more recently, in 1999, South Australia amended the expiation notice scheme, bringing in swingeing penalties of up to ten years' imprisonment and A$250,000 fines for anyone growing more than three cannabis plants. Other Australian states have written their own laws but none is in favour of legitimization or complete decriminalization.

More lenient attitudes have been expressed in Canada. Huge public support for complete or partial decriminalization has led to relaxed policing, the decision to charge an offender being left very much up to the discretion of the individual officer. In British Columbia, where marijuana use is higher than elsewhere in the country, the police are more concerned with apprehending marijuana-intoxicated motorists than ordinary users. Traffic patrols are trained in recognizing the signs of recent marijuana use and may administer roadside tests much as they might for drunk drivers. This practice has spread to other parts of Canada, but the main aim is not necessarily to clamp down on cannabis use, rather to ensure road safety.

Few oppose this course of action but there have been challenges to the law on cannabis in other respects.

In 1995, Christopher Clay, owner of a store called the Hemp Nation Shop in London, Ontario, confessed to selling a cannabis plant to an undercover police officer. He was charged with marijuana possession, trafficking and possession with intent to traffic. When his case came to court two years later, he was sentenced to three years' probation, had a fine of C$750 levied against him and was forced to surrender the stock of his shop which was valued at approximately C$65,000. In court, Clay's lawyer argued that the law violated his client's rights under the Canadian Charter of Rights and Freedoms. Clay himself declared he had deliberately sold the plant to challenge the law and went on to express the desire to *get buyers away from the black market, where there're no quality controls and no age restrictions*, adding, *I'm also concerned about the thousands of Canadians who have criminal records just from marijuana possession.*

The Canadian Association of Chiefs of Police called for the decriminalization of marijuana in 1999 but they were anticipating the mood of the country. Judges were loath to prosecute recreational or medicinal users and many police officers were already turning a blind eye to the compassionate cannabis clubs that had been appearing across the country in imitation of the California buyers' clubs, providing medicinal marijuana. Canada, however, faced an obstacle to decriminalization. It shared a border with the USA which was exceedingly hostile to any such legislation.

Public attitude in America might have been softening towards marijuana, but the federal law and its proponents were not. Complete prohibition was considered there the only effective way to tackle drug abuse, whatever the substance. There were two main policy lynchpins. The first, user accountability, forced those using drugs to accept that, no matter what they were taking, someone somewhere was suffering as a result, be it an addict dying from an overdose or a Third World peasant being exploited. The second was zero tolerance by which any drug offence, no matter how slight, was deemed as bad as the next, regardless of the substance involved or the culpability of the perpetrator. In the Anslinger tradition, a drug was a drug was a drug and, even if it was pharmaceutically manufactured by a multi-national drugs company and medicinally valid in other countries, it was still prohibited if it was in any way related to an illegal substance. A case in point was the confiscation of codeine painkillers from European tourists who assumed that, because the drug was a prescription medicine in any pharmacy back home, it would be legal. Yet codeine is manufactured from opium. There have been instances recorded of tourists suffering from severely painful conditions being arrested by US Customs at ports of entry and charged with drug trafficking, although few of these have proceeded to court.

This rigour manifests itself in far more scrupulous ways. Law-enforcement agencies can − and frequently do − demand that any drug offender be remanded in custody prior to trial, with no leave to apply for bail. Substantial mandatory sentences are available to judges in addition to very heavy fines and the sequestration of assets. The DEA is also permitted to search a person or private property without warrant or probable cause, entrap suspects with undercover agents or sting operations, apprehend (also without probable cause) and rely upon paid informers. This has led to serious travesties of justice, especially where the informer, a member of the criminal drug underworld, has used this framework as an opportunity to remove a competing criminal from the business. Under the civil forfeiture legislation, charges need not be filed for property to be seized. The opportunities for corruption this affords are considerable and defence attorneys are known to refer to the forfeiture laws as a charter for police theft. Some even refer to it as the CCTF − the Cops' Colour Television Fund − or a similar acronym.

In the fight against drugs, the federal authorities have deliberately created an atmosphere of fear. Whilst there are those who accept this as valid, it has still undermined the basic civil and human rights of tens of thousands of American citizens. The Bill of Rights has, in effect, been systematically abused with no opportunity for redress.

The legal system aside, this climate of suspicion has permeated society. Employers can and frequently do conduct drug tests on job applicants and employees, even those not in positions where intoxication might be a safety issue. Schools likewise test students for marijuana. A positive result can mean the loss of a job or expulsion from education. In some states, a positive test result leading to a conviction automatically negates health insurance and denies the right to social welfare benefits: these same rights are not withdrawn on conviction from a murderer or rapist. That the marijuana was not used in the place of work or study is considered immaterial. Against this, one must consider that no such random tests are made for alcohol even when safety is an issue.

In 1997, Speaker of the House Newt Gingrich introduced into the US Congress the Drug Importer Death Penalty Act, which was finally ratified in 2001. Under this, anyone importing what the US Attorney General considered to be one hundred usual doses of a controlled substance is to be sentenced to life imprisonment without any possibility of parole. If the defendant has a previous similar drug conviction, the death penalty can be imposed.

When the Act was passed, marijuana activists were not slow in reminding the public that Newt Gingrich had admitted some years before that he had smoked marijuana in his university days. So, too, had President Bill Clinton as well as Vice President Al Gore and, it was even alleged, US Court of Appeals judge Douglas Ginsburg and the US Supreme Court Justice, Clarence Thomas.

When Gingrich admitted his marijuana experience, he tried to justify his action. *When I smoked pot*, he was quoted as having said, *it was illegal, but not immoral. Now it is illegal and immoral. The law didn't change, only the morality. That's why you get to go to jail and I don't.* Quite how the morality of marijuana had changed Gingrich did not care to elucidate.

This moral distinction must have been lost on William Foster in Tulsa, serving out his sentence of ninety-three years in prison.

Federal law may be draconian but some individual state legislatures are occasionally less stringent and a number have actually decriminalized private marijuana use, a federal study showing that *decriminalization has had virtually no effect either on marijuana use or on related attitudes and beliefs about marijuana use among American young people.* Regardless of criminal or civil law, marijuana use has steadily increased over the past fifteen years with the medicinal marijuana lobby furthering the public opinion that the drug is comparatively innocuous. DEA statistics in 2000 estimated thirty million Americans regularly used marijuana. More than half the population viewed cannabis taking as an accepted social ill but believe it should be addressed with preventative rather than punitive measures.

According to observers such as the Washington DC-based Marijuana Policy Project, a non-profit-making organization founded in 1995 to lobby for marijuana law reform at federal level, with the ultimate goal of having marijuana regulated as is alcohol and permitted for medical use, the laws have led to some startling statistics. The number of marijuana arrests across the USA in 2000 stood at 734,498, 88 per cent of these for possession only; this figure was only slightly less than the combined total for murder, armed robbery, rape and assault; the fiscal national cost of policing specifically marijuana prohibition (as opposed to all controlled substances) was nine billion dollars annually; an estimated seventy million Americans, 24 per cent of the entire population, have tried cannabis; 12.9 per cent of all drug convicted prisoners in state prisons and 18.9 per cent in federal facilities (a total of approximately 38,300) were being held for cannabis related crimes, mostly only for possession; the average cost of housing marijuana convicts in prison was approximately $1.2 billion per annum.

The US government has not restricted its harsh approach to marijuana just to within its national boundaries. For many years, it has applied considerable pressure on other nations to abide by its own principles. Since the attack on New York's World Trade Center in September 2001, the US has seized the opportunity to increase this pressure, with the international community becoming more aware of the relationship between international organized crime, drug trafficking and global terrorism.

The drugs trade and warfare have long been related. Apart from the Lebanese civil war, drugs have played an important financial and political role in the Middle East, Chechnya, Afghanistan, Kosovo, Serbia, Northern Ireland, Uzbekistan and Vietnam. In the latter, the US government supported opium war lords in South-East Asia in order to keep them as allies against the Vietcong, going so far as to fly their opium and heroin out of the region in military or CIA aircraft. Even as far back as the Sino-Japanese and Second World Wars, Japan used heroin to try to demoralize the army of its traditional enemy, China.

Now, the drug–war relationship is seen by some as being simplified. The fewer drugs there are around, the less income there is available for terrorist factions. The war on terrorism becomes synonymous with the war on drugs. Yet this is not necessarily what will happen, nor is it an accurate portrait of the situation. Asa Hutchinson, the director of the DEA, stated a month after the New York atrocities of September 2001, that the US government's close focusing on terrorism was permitting more Colombian cocaine to reach US shores, due to the diversion of DEA and US Customs personnel to anti-terrorist duties. In July 2002, the director of the FBI, Robert S. Mueller III, voiced a similar concern, declaring that his agents would only concentrate on narcotics enforcement when this coincided with counter-terrorist activity.

There is also a degree of hypocrisy involved. Although it is internationally condemned for unofficially condoning the drugs trade, less diplomatic pressure is being applied to the Pakistan government which Western administrations hope to keep 'on side', being a front-line state in the war against terrorism and Muslim fundamentalism. This, in turn, affords the terrorists the opportunity to fund themselves from hashish and other drugs, and it is no coincidence that those Al-Qaeda forces that escaped military confrontation in Afghanistan have chosen to settle in northern Pakistan amongst fellow tribesmen and their cannabis fields.

Whatever the US government might want to do internationally, it has to accept that, in many countries, cannabis continues to be used, despite being officially banned, because it is traditional and to hope to stamp out its use is an arrogant assumption. It is akin to a teetotal Muslim country demanding America ban bourbon whiskey. In at least a dozen countries, cannabis occupies a cultural position as a religious sacrament. In India, it features in *puja*, the Hindu act of worship expressing devotion to the gods, and in major religious festivals such as Kumbh Mela, one of the greatest religious gatherings on earth. When the annual festival was held in the holy city of Varanasi for the first time after the Indian government made cannabis illegal, it was feared that there would be major rioting because there was no hashish available. With over ten million pilgrims present, the police grew so worried they sent a truck to New Delhi where they were able to obtain over a ton of the drug from Afghan merchants. However, the hashish was impressed with Islamic markings so the police had to scrape each slab smooth before it was distributed.

It is now some decades since the hippy trail reverberated to the sound of the sandalled feet of those seeking enlightenment and the ultimate high, but the way is still trod by large numbers of backpack-burdened Westerners. Today, however, they have to be not only hardy but also extremely cautious. The days of Love and Peace are over and their destinations in the valleys of the high Himalayas are now very dangerous places indeed. In the 1990s, at least fourteen latter-day hippies or backpackers went missing, Indian police claiming the number could be as great as forty. Well over one hundred were arrested, primarily on hashish-trafficking and immigration violations. It is thought many more would have been arrested were the police not thoroughly corrupt and readily bribed. Westerners with money make good targets for corrupt officials.

One place in particular where foreigners have to be on their guard is the former Portuguese enclave of Goa on the west coast of India. Once a transit point on the hippy trail to Kathmandu, it is now a major holiday destination for the twenty-something generation. Marijuana and hashish are both there for the buying at very cheap prices. However, despite appearances, they are illegal, no distinction is made between cannabis and opiates, some police officers are known to be dishonest and the law is exactingly applied to foreigners. A ten-year mandatory prison sentence is enforced for possession and, under Indian law, the accused is considered guilty until proven innocent. Not only do the police encourage the offer of bribes but they have also been known to plant drugs on the un-suspecting, therefore obliging them to buy their way out of trouble. One such frame-up occurred in 1990 when a British tourist, Nicholas Brown, was arrested and given the mandatory sentence. He stated his only crime was one of omission in not offering a bribe. He served eighteen months in prison prior to trial and two years of his sentence, his mother finally obtaining his release on a hard-fought appeal.

Cannabis may provide corrupt law-enforcement officers with a means to supplement their salary but, in some Third World countries, it presents other opportunities, especially to a morally pliable administration.

In Nigeria in the 1960s, the west of the country fell into anarchy and local politicians established their own private army, recruiting from the ill-educated and, at the time, starving rural population. The recruits, known as party stalwarts, were paid in meat, maize flour, money and marijuana. Their loyalty purchased and bolstered by cannabis, they went on an ethno-centric political killing spree that lasted until the summer of 1966 when, after the reformist Major General Johnson Aguiyi-Ironsi was murdered, General Yakubu Gowon took over the country and imposed martial law. Almost immediately, as a reaction to the misdeeds of the party stalwarts, he instituted a summarily issued death penalty for cannabis cultivation with long periods of imprisonment for possession. The use of cannabis to incite civil unrest and purchase political muscle has more recently been used in Zimbabwe by the regime of President Robert Mugabe. His thuggish National Youth Brigade, which intimidates electors and political opponents, is militarily trained and given cannabis. This was particularly prevalent before the March 2002 presidential election when brigade members, stoked up on local beer and marijuana, were dispatched on what was termed community service patrols to attack opposition sup-porters and politicians. A similar tactic has been used with the so-called War Veterans, who have been driving white farmers from their proper-ties, thereby bringing the country to the brink of starvation and economic collapse from which, some observers believe, officially ignored or unofficially sanctioned cannabis cultivation may prove to be a new foreign currency earning cash crop.

There are countries in which penalties for cannabis are exceedingly harsh. The best known of these is Malaysia where the possession of 200 grams of cannabis attracts a mandatory death sentence. According to Amnesty International, at least 150 people have been hanged since the law was passed, including foreigners, but this figure is only a guess as the country will not release the actual statistics. In March 2000, Mohamed Naziff Ahmad, aged eighteen, was found guilty by a court in Johore of growing one cannabis plant. He was sentenced to be lashed with a *rotan* (a rattan cane) and life imprisonment. He was told he was fortunate to have escaped the gallows. A similar regime exists in Singapore. On 19 March 1999, a Malaysian Chinese called Fok Chia-siong was executed for attempting to import about 1.5 kilograms of marijuana two years before. In 2001, Vietnam executed fifty-five people although these sentences were mostly for opiate possessing and trafficking. Thailand and China execute drug traffickers by firing squad, in the latter country in public.

The UN Single Convention remains in force and, although signatory countries could break the treaty, they do not for there is not the political will to open this Pandora's box, even though the restrictions it poses are anachronistic, scientifically dubious and often counter-productive, especially in the case of medical marijuana. Most UN member countries also admit that a complete prohibition of cannabis is impossible – and perhaps not entirely desirable – but they are not prepared to address the matter for fear of incurring American displeasure.

From time to time, the INCB criticizes member countries for their stance on cannabis. A recent report has chided Western nations for their permissive attitudes, stating that while *developing countries struggle to eradicate cannabis and fight illicit trafficking of the substance, certain developed countries have chosen to tolerate the cultivation, trade and abuse of cannabis on their territory . . .* and asking *How can we require Morocco to prevent cannabis coming to European markets if . . . demand is tolerated, decriminalized or even de facto legalized?* No action will be considered by the UN to alter the Single Convention until member countries provide the World Health Organization (WHO) with incontrovertible proof that cannabis is benign. This is hardly likely to happen as, in recent years, WHO has suppressed any submitted scientific analysis that has not supported the Single Convention and US government viewpoint. As far as the UN is concerned, Anslinger's basic premise that cannabis is inherently evil prevails.

Yet there have been significant advances made in the study and understanding of cannabis. Many of the myths about it have been totally dispelled. It does not have a propensity to induce criminality or immoral behaviour and does not cause insanity, aberrant sexual behaviour, psychosis, amotivational syndrome or other personality disorder, sterility or any noteworthy clinical physiological or psychological damage. It is not physiologically addictive and does not progress the user on to more dangerous narcotics. Occasional use appears not to be harmful but prolonged extensive use, as of any substance, can be detrimental. It exhibits considerable potential as a medicine and the plant as a whole offers a valuable and highly versatile commercial crop. Whilst, as Grinspoon allows, the extensive use of psycho-active substances may be harmful to a society as a whole, in the case of cannabis this seems to be less of a threat than that already posed by alcohol, tobacco and other prohibited drugs.

Despite the many dozens of independent and government commissions, scientific investigations, sociological, pharmacological, criminological and medical studies, legislative assessments and political evaluations conducted throughout the world over the last hundred years, there is still no consensus of opinion. Either cannabis is regarded as an innocuous social drug or as a serious danger to society. As soon as it is mentioned, argument – whether between individuals or governments – tends to become instantly polarized. That it can offer relief from some of the worst illnesses that afflict mankind is ignored. That it could provide a versatile and environmentally friendly new industrial material is dismissed. Instead, it is condemned and prohibited as being a problem not because it is harmful but because arbitrary moral decisions have decreed it to be so.

The war on cannabis is being fought from a concern not for public health or order (as might be said of the war on heroin or crack cocaine) but for public morality. If health were the issue, tobacco and strong liquor would have been banned long ago. To accept cannabis into society is a cultural decision not a political one. Western countries might decry its presence but it must be remembered that, in Islamic countries, cannabis is as accepted as coffee, tobacco or tea but alcohol is banned as decadent and debauched. At different periods of history, when 'newly discovered' substances have appeared on the merchant's table, they have not infrequently incurred the wrath of governments and those in power. In the sixteenth century, when tobacco was first imported into Europe from the New World, it was prohibited in Bavaria, Saxony, and parts of Switzerland. Smokers were jailed. In Russia and the Ottoman Empire, tobacco smokers and traders were executed whilst in Japan, after the introduction of tobacco by Dutch and Portuguese merchants in the seventeenth century, the ruling Tokugawa shogunate tried to ban it, but in vain.

Louis Lewin wrote in his book *Phantastica, From the beginning of our knowledge of man, we find him consuming substances of no nutritive value, but taken for the sole purpose of producing for a certain time a feeling of contentment, ease and comfort.* We are attracted to these substances, which we now call drugs, because they stimulate us, relax us, take us out of ourselves, bring experiences to us that might otherwise be unattainable. Some do irreparable physical or mental damage. Some do not. Yet, as a society, we seem unable to accept that one drug and plant beyond all the others is essentially benign and offers so much.

It may be that, in time, perceptions will shift and we will take the beneficence the cannabis plant has to give. Meanwhile, we must learn to admit it into our lives and our society, where it has had a presence, like it or not, for generations. And, perhaps, it is now time we stopped blinding ourselves with our narrow-minded bigotry and started, as the hippy jargon of the Swinging Sixties would have put it, to 'get real'.

# BIBLIOGRAPHY

Abel, Ernest L., *Marihuana – The First Twelve Thousand Years*, Plenum Press, New York, 1980

Albutt, R.C., *A System of Medicine*, MacMillan, New York, 1900

Alexander, Bruce K., *Peaceful Measures – Canada's Way Out of the 'War on Drugs'*, University of Toronto Press, Toronto, 1990

Anderson, Patrick, *High in America*, The Viking Press, New York, 1981

Andrews, George and Vinkenoog, Simon (eds), *The Book of Grass: An Anthology of Indian Hemp*, Peter Owen, London, 1980

Anslinger, Harry J. and Oursler, Will, *'The Murderers' – The Story of the Narcotics Gangs*, Farrar, Straus and Co., New York, 1961

Auld, John, *Marijuana Use and Social Control*, Academic Press, London, 1981

Baum, Dan, *Smoke and Mirrors – The War on Drugs and The Politics of Failure*, Little, Brown, Boston, 1996

Boire, Richard Glen, *Marijuana Law*, Ronin Publishing, Berkeley, 1996

Bonnie, Richard J. and Whitebread II, Charles H., *The Marihuana Conviction*, The Lindesmith Center, New York, 1999

Booth, Martin, *Opium: A History*, Simon & Schuster, London, 1996

Booth, Martin, *A Magick Life – A Biography of Aleister Crowley*, Hodder & Stoughton, London, 2000

Bowles, Paul, *Without Stopping*, Peter Owen, London, 1972

Boyd, Neil, *High Society – Legal and Illegal Drugs in Canada*, Key Porter Books, Toronto, 1991

Brotteaux, Pascal, *Hachich: Herbe de folie et de rêve,* Les éditions Véga, Paris, 1934

Bryant, A.T., *The Zulu People,* Shuter & Shooter, Pietermaritzburg, 1967

Burman, Edward, *The Inquisition*, The Aquarian Press, Wellingborough, 1984

Burman, Edward, *The Assassins*, Crucible, Wellingborough, 1987

Charters, Ann, *Kerouac*, André Deutsch, London, 1973

Clarke, Robert Connell, *Hashish!*, Red Eye Press, Los Angeles, 1998

Culpeper, Nicholas, *Culpeper's Colour Herbal* (ed. David Potterton), W.Foulsham & Co., London, 1983

Davis, Stephen, *Bob Marley*, Plexus, London, 1983

De Montfreid, Henry, *Hashish*, Penguin Books, Harmondsworth, 1985

De Quincey, Thomas, *The Confessions of an English Opium Eater*, Bodley Head, London, 1930

De Ropp, Robert S., *Drugs and the Mind*, Victor Gollancz, London, 1958

Driberg, Tom, *Ruling Passions*, Jonathan Cape, London, 1977

Dulchinos, Donald P., *Pioneer of Inner Space: The Life of Fitz Hugh Ludlow, Hasheesh Eater*, Autonomedia, New York, 1998

Ebin, David (ed.), *The Drug Experience*, Grove Press, New York, 1965

Fabian, Robert, *London After Dark*, The Naldrett Press, London, 1954

Finlayson, Iain, *Tangier – City of the Dream*, Harper Collins, London, 1992

Fordham, John, *Let's Join Hands and Contact the Living – Ronnie Scott and His Club*, Elm Tree Books, London, 1986

Frank, Mel, *Marijuana Grower's Guide*, Red Eye Press, Los Angeles, 1997

Gardner, Paul, *The Drug-Smugglers*, Robert Hale, London, 1989

Grattan, J.H.G. and Singer, Charles, *Anglo-Saxon Magic and Medicine*, Oxford University Press, London, 1952

Gray, Michael, *The Art of Bob Dylan*, Hamlyn, London, 1981

Green, Timothy, *The Smugglers*, Michael Joseph, London, 1969

Grinspoon, Lester, *Marihuana Reconsidered*, Harvard University Press, Cambridge, MA, 1971

Grinspoon, Lester and Bakalar, James B., *Marihuana, the Forbidden Medicine*, Yale University Press, New Haven, 1993

Haining, Peter (ed.), *The Hashish Club – An Anthology of Drug Literature [Volume One: The Founding of the Modern Tradition]*, Peter Owen, London, 1975

Haining, Peter (ed.), *The Hashish Club – An Anthology of Drug Literature [Volume Two: The Psychedelic Era]*, Peter Owen, London, 1975

Harris, Lee and Render, Chris (eds.), *Best of Home Grown 1977–1981* Red Shift Books, London, 1994

Hayter, Alethea, *Opium and the Romantic Imagination*, Faber and Faber, London, 1968

Herer, Jack, *The Emperor Wears No Clothes*, AH HA Publishing Co., Austin, Texas, 2000

Himmelstein, Jerome L., *The Strange Career of Marihuana*, Greenwood Press, Westport, Connecticut, 1983

Hollingshead, Michael, *The Man Who Turned On the World*, Blond and Briggs, London, 1973

Hopkins, James F., *A History of the Hemp Industry in Kentucky*, University of Kentucky Press, Lexington, 1951

Inglis, Brian, *The Forbidden Game – A Social History of Drugs*, Hodder and Stoughton, London, 1975

Jeffares, A. Norman, *W. B. Yeats*, Hutchinson, London, 1988

Jones, Max and Chilton, John, *Louis – The Louis Armstrong Story 1900–1971*, Studio Vista, London, 1971

Jonnes, Jill, *Hep-Cats, Narcs, and Pipe Dreams*, Scribner, New York, 1996

Kamstra, Jerry, *Weed: Adventures of a Dope Smuggler*, Harper & Row, New York, 1974

Kaplan, John, *Marijuana – The New Prohibition*, World Publishing Company, Cleveland, 1970

Kimmens, Andrew C. (ed.), *Tales of Hashish*, William Morrow, New York, 1977

Kohn, Marek, *Narcomania*, Faber and Faber, London, 1987

Kohn, Marek, *Dope Girls – The Birth of the British Drug Underground*, Laurence & Wishart, London, 1994

La Barre, Weston, *Culture in Context; Selected Writings of Weston La Barre*, Duke University Press, Durham, 1980

Laurie, Peter, *Drugs – Medical, Psychological and Social Facts*, Penguin Books, Harmondsworth, 1967

Lefebure, Molly, *Samuel Taylor Coleridge: A Bondage of Opium*, Quartet Books, London, 1977

Levenson, Samuel, *Maud Gonne*, Cassell, London, 1976

Lewis, Bernard, *The Assassins*, Weidenfeld and Nicolson, London, 1967

Lewin, Louis, *Phantastica*, Park Street Press, Rochester, Vermont, 1998

Marchbank, Pearce (ed.), *Bob Dylan In His Own Words*, Omnibus Press, London, 1978

Marks, Howard, *Mr Nice*, Minerva, London, 1997

Marks, Howard (ed.), *The Howard Marks Book of Dope Stories*, Vintage, London, 2001

Marwick, Arthur, *The Sixties*, Oxford University Press, Oxford, 1998

Matthews, Patrick, *Cannabis Culture*, Bloomsbury, London, 1999

McNally, Dennis, *Desolate Angel – Jack Kerouac, the Beat Generation, and America*, McGraw-Hill Book Company, New York, 1979

Merlin, Mark David, *Man and Marijuana*, Fairleigh Dickinson University Press, Rutherford, 1972

Mezzrow, Milton and Wolfe, Bernard, *Really the Blues*, Secker & Warburg, London, 1957

Michaux, Henri, *Light Through Darkness – Explorations Among Drugs*, Bodley Head, London, 1964

Mikuriya, Tod H., *Marijuana: Medical Papers (1839–1972)*, Medi-Comp Press, Oakland, 1973

Miles, Barry, *Ginsberg*, Simon and Schuster, New York, 1989

Muggeridge, Malcolm, *Chronicles of Wasted Time – 1. The Green Stick*, Collins, London, 1972

Musto, David F., *The American Disease – Origins of Narcotic Control*, Oxford University Press, New York, 1987

Novak, William, *High Culture – Marijuana in the Lives of Americans*, Alfred A. Knopf, New York, 1980

O'Day, Anita with Eells, George, *High Times Hard Times*, Limelight Editions, New York, 1993

Oman, John Campbell, *Mystics, Ascetics and Saints of India*, T. Fisher Unwin, London, 1905

Polsky, Ned, *Hustlers, Beats, and Others*, Aldine Publishing Company, Chicago, 1967

Rätsch, Christian, *Marijuana Medicine*, Healing Arts Press, Rochester, Vermont, 2001

Robinson, Rowan, *The Great Book of Hemp*, Park Street Press, Rochester, Vermont, 1996

Rosenthal, Franz, *The Herb: Hashish versus Medieval Muslim Society*, E.J. Brill, Leiden, 1971

Rosevear, John, *Pot: A Handbook of Marihuana*, University Books, New York, 1967

Rubin, Vera (ed.), *Cannabis and Culture*, Mouton, The Hague, 1975

Russell, Thomas, *Egyptian Service 1902–1946*, John Murray, London, 1949

Sabbag, Robert, *Smoke Screen*, Canongate, Edinburgh, 2002

Sander, Ellen, *Trips – Rock Life in the Sixties*, Scribner, New York, 1973

Schofield, Michael, *The Strange Case of Pot*, Penguin, London, 1971

Schultes, Richard Evans and Hofman, Albert, *Plants Of the Gods,* Healing Arts Press, Rochester, Vermont, 1992

Shapiro, Harry, *Waiting for the Man – The Story of Drugs and Popular Music,* Quartet Books, London, 1988

Sherman, Carol and Smith, Andrew with Tanner, Eric, *Highlights – An Illustrated History of Cannabis,* Ten Speed Press, Berkley/Toronto, 1999

Soloman, Larry, *Reefer Madness,* St. Martin's Griffin, New York, 1998

Solomon, David (ed.), *The Marijuana Papers,* Panther Books, London, 1969

Sounes, Howard, *Down the Highway: The Life of Bob Dylan,* Black Swan, London, 2002

Stockley, David, *Drug Warning,* Optima, London, 1992

Sumach, Alexander, *A Treasury of Hashish,* Stoneworks Publishing Company, Toronto, 1976

Szasz, Thomas, *Ceremonial Chemistry – The Ritual Persecution of Drug Addicts and Pushers,* Routledge & Kegan Paul, London, 1975

Tendler, Stewart and May, David, *The Brotherhood of Eternal Love,* Panther Books, London, 1984

Tietjen, Arthur, *Soho: London's Vicious Circle,* Allan Wingate, London, 1956

Thorp, Raymond, *Viper: The Confessions of a Drug Addict,* Robert Hale, London, 1956

Walton, Robert P., *Marihuana – America's New Drug Problem,* J. B. Lippincott, Philadelphia, 1938

Weintraub, Stanley, *Beardsley,* Penguin Books, Harmondsworth, 1972

Wild, Antony, *The East India Company,* Harper Collins, London, 1999

X, Malcolm with Haley, Alex, *The Autobiography of Malcolm X,* Hutchinson, London, 1966

Zimmer, Lynn and Morgan, John P., *Marijuana Myths, Marijuana Facts,* The Lindesmith Center, New York and San Francisco, 1997

Zimmerman, Bill with Bayer, Rick and Crumpacker, Nancy, *Is Marijuana the Right Medicine For You?,* Keats Publishing, New Canaan, 1998


Miscellaneous sources: *Daily Telegraph, Sunday Telegraph, Guardian, The Times, The Sunday Times, Observer, Express, Express on Sunday, Independent, Independent on Sunday, The Financial Times, Scotsman, Scotland on Sunday, The Irish Times.*

*The New York Times, The Washington Post, Juneau Empire, Honolulu Advertiser, Honolulu Star, Salt Lake Tribune, Denver Rocky Mountain News, Sacramento Bee, San Jose Mercury, Seattle Times, Los Angeles Times, San Luis Obispo County Tribune, Inquirer, Time Magazine.*

*Vancouver Sun, Edmonton Sun, Edmonton Journal, Western Producer, Calgary Herald, Ottawa Citizen, Globe and Mail, Halifax Daily News, Toronto Star.*

*Sydney Morning Herald, Herald Sun, Advertiser, Canberra Times, The Australian, The West Australian, The Age, New Zealand Herald, Northern News, Otago Daily Times, The Dominion.*

*Le Monde, De Standaard, Copenhagen Post, Helsingin Sanomat International Edition, Aftenposten. The Star* (Malaysia), *Kathmandu Post, Sri Lanka Sunday Observer, The Japan Times.*

In addition to the above sources, all individual government, United Nations and similar reports and conventions are available either on the relevant official websites or from the governmental or NGO authorities.

Of the more than two thousand websites concerning cannabis, the following were found to be particularly accurate and/or of especial value and interest:

The Drug Policy Alliance: www.lindesmith.org

The Fitz Hugh Ludlow Hypertext Library: www.nepenthes.lycaeum.org

US Dept. of Justice: www. usdoj.gov

Federal Bureau of Investigation: www.fbi.gov
Central Intelligence Agency: www.cia.gov
HM Customs & Excise: www.hmce.gov.uk
The United Nations: www.un.org
NORML: www.norml.org
Marijuana Policy Project: www.mpp.org
The Marijuana News: www.marijuananews.com
Medical Marijuana Research: www.maps.org
Cannabis.com: www.cannabis.com
International Association for Cannabis as Medicine: www.acmed.org
Drug Reform Coordination Network: www.drcnet.org

# INDEX